THE NEW DYNAMIC

Volume

Edited by Alan Walker

P

First published in Great Britain in 2018 by

Policy Press
University of Bristol
1-9 Old Park Hill
Bristol
BS2 8BB
UK
t: +44 (0)117 954 5940
pp-info@bristol.ac.uk
www.policypress.co.uk

North America office:
Policy Press
c/o The University of Chicago Press
1427 East 60th Street
Chicago, IL 60637, USA
t: +1 773 702 7700
f: +1 773-702-9756
sales@press.uchicago.edu
www.press.uchicago.edu

© Policy Press 2018

British Library Cataloguing in Publication Data
A catalogue record for this book is available from the British Library

Library of Congress Cataloging-in-Publication Data
A catalog record for this book has been requested

ISBN 978-1-4473-1473-8 paperback
ISBN 978-1-4473-1472-1 hardcover
ISBN 978-1-4473-1477-6 ePub
ISBN 978-1-4473-1476-9 Mobi
ISBN 978-1-4473-1475-2 ePdf

The right of Alan Walker to be identified as editor of this work has been asserted by him in accordance with the Copyright, Designs and Patents Act 1988.

Cover design by Policy Press
Front cover image: istock
Printed and bound in Great Britain by CPI Group (UK) Ltd, Croydon, CR0 4YY
Policy Press uses environmentally responsible print partners

Contents

List of figures and tables

Figures

Tables

Preface

This volume and its companion stem from the New Dynamics of Ageing (NDA) programme 2005-15, which was funded by no less than five UK research councils: the Arts and Humanities Research Council, the Biotechnology and Biological Sciences Research Council, the Engineering and Physical Sciences Research Council, the Economic and Social Research Council (ESRC) and the Medical Research Council. In breaking the mould of previous inter-council collaborations to create this single programme the research councils are to be congratulated and thanked, not only for the pooled funding, but also for the enormous effort involved to fashion a single commissioning process from five different systems. The Cross-Council Committee on Ageing did the bulk of the heavy lifting and is duly thanked most warmly. Special thanks are due to the ESRC, which led for the other research councils, and especially to Joy Todd for both her initial hard work and constant support over the life of the programme.

Thanks also to the numerous researchers who took part in commissioning panels and in the extensive peer review processes. The NDA Advisory Committee, chaired by Sally Greengross, was a tremendous source of support. Other members were Alan Beazley, Alan Blackwell, Chris Carey, Mark Gorman, Tessa Harding, David Leon, Angela McCullagh, Bronagh Miskelly, Naina Patel, Chris Phillipson, Jim Soulsby and Anthea Tinker. Previous members included Keith Bright, Paul Cann, Steve Cook, Rachel Kyrs, Janet Lord and Tony Martin. Special praise must be given to Anthea Tinker, whose wise advice, clear judgement, enthusiasm and warm friendship could always be relied on.

The Older Persons Reference Group, while rightly challenging at times, was also an essential ingredient in this programme's success. Led by Mary Sinfield, its members included John Barry, Mary Brown, Cynthia Conrad, Jim Harding, Anthony Hill, John Jeffrey, Savita Katbamna, Teresa Lefort, Irene Richards, Elsie Richardson, Elizabeth Sclater, Harbhajan Singh and Brian Todd. Previous members included Diane Andrews, John Appleyard, Bob Bell, Brian Booker, Tony Carter, John Christie, Janet Cullup, Iris Dodds, Christine Hamilton, David Hart, Shirley Heselton, Pauline Richards, Norman Richards, Barbara Shillabeer, Diane Smeeton, Steve Thornett, Stephen Townsend and Urmilla Tanna.

Lastly, sincere thanks to those most closely engaged in the final production process: Sarah Howson, Adele Blinston and Vanessa

Rodgers at Sheffield; and Laura Vickers, Isobel Bainton and Rebecca Tomlinson at Policy Press, together with the anonymous reader who provided helpful comments.

Alan Walker

List of contributors

Vasilios Baltzopoulos is Head of the Research Institute for Sport and Exercise Sciences (RISES), School of Sport and Exercise Sciences at John Moores University, UK.

Armando Barrientos is Professor of Poverty and Social Justice at the Global Development Institute at the University of Manchester, UK.

Yoav Ben-Shlomo is Professor of Clinical Epidemiology at the University of Bristol, UK.

Ann Bowling is a Visiting Professor in the Faculty of Health Sciences at the University of Southampton, UK.

Stacy Clemes is a Reader in Active Living and Public Health at Loughborough University, UK.

Adelina Comas-Herrera is Assistant Professorial Research Fellow at the Personal Social Services Research Unit, London School of Economics and Political Science, UK.

Rachel Cooper is a Programme Leader Track and Senior Lecturer at the MRC Unit for Lifelong Health and Ageing at University College London, UK.

Andrea Creech is Professor in Instrumental Didactics, and Canada Research Chair in Music in the Community, in the Faculty of Music at Université Laval, Canada.

Amanda Crummett is a community worker in Liverpool, UK.

Leela Damodaran is Emeritus Professor of Digital Inclusion and Participation at Loughborough University, UK.

Irene Di Giulio is a Lecturer in Human Anatomy and Biomechanics at King's College London, UK.

Myanna Duncan is a Lecturer in Psychology at King's College London, UK.

Jane Elliott is Professor of Sociology at the University of Exeter, UK.

Alistair Ewen is a Researcher in the Orthopaedic Department at the Golden Jubilee National Hospital, Glasgow, Scotland, UK.

Catharine Gale is Professor of Cognitive Epidemiology at the University of Southampton, UK.

James Gavin is a Lecturer in Sport at Bournemouth University, UK.

Arul George is a lawyer in India.

Alistair Gibb is ECI Royal Academy of Engineering Professor at Loughborough University, UK.

Elaine Yolande Gosling is Research Associate, Design School at Loughborough University, UK.

Diane Gyi is a Reader in Health Ergonomics and Design at Loughborough University, UK.

Catherine Hagan Hennessy is a Visiting Professor in the Faculty of Health and Social Sciences, Bournemouth University, UK.

Susan Hallam is Emeritus Professor of Education and Music Psychology at University College London, UK.

Ruth Hancock is Professor in Economics of Health and Welfare at the Norwich Medical School, University of East Anglia, UK.

Rebecca Hardy is a Programme Leader at the MRC Unit for Lifelong Health and Ageing at University College London (UCL) and Professor in Epidemiology and Medical Statistics at UCL

Barbara Harriss-White is a Senior Research Fellow at the University of Oxford, UK.

Cheryl Haslam is Professor of Health Psychology and Director of the Work and Health Research Centre at Loughborough University, UK.

Roger Haslam is Professor of Ergonomics at Loughborough University, UK.

Joe Henry is a farmer developing sustainable farming and forestry in India.

Bo Hu is a Research Officer at the Personal Social Services Research Unit, London School of Economics and Political Science, UK.

Marlia Hussain is a homemaker in India.

David Jones is Emeritus Professor of Muscle Physiology at Manchester Metropolitan University, UK.

Aadil Kazi is Research Programmes Manager, NIHR Imperial Biomedical Research Centre (BRC), Faculty of Medicine, Imperial College London & Imperial College Healthcare NHS Trust, London, UK.

Leonie Kellaher is Emeritus Professor at the Cities Institute, London Metropolitan University.

Lois Kerr, Research Assistant, Loughborough University, UK.

Stephanie King is a Lecturer in Biomechanics in theDepartment of Sport, Health and Exercise Science at the University of Hull, UK.

Diana Kuh is Professor of Life Course Epidemiology at University College London, UK. Director of the MRC Unit for Lifelong Health and Ageing 2007-17.

Clare Lawton is a former Research Associate at the Design School, Loughborough University, UK

Peter Lloyd-Sherlock is Professor of Social Policy and International Development in the School of International Development at the University of East Anglia, UK.

Jane McCann is a design and research consultant based in County Down, Northern Ireland, UK.

Hilary McDermott is a Senior Lecturer in Psychology at Loughborough University, UK.

Alastair S. Macdonald is a Senior Researcher in the School of Design at the Glasgow School of Art, Scotland, UK.

Constantinos Maganaris is Professor of Musculoskeletal Biomechnics at the Research Institute for Sport and Exercise Sciences, School of Sport and Exercise Sciences, John Moores University, UK.

Martin Maguire is a Lecturer and Research Fellow in User-Centred Design at the Design School, Loughborough University, UK.

Becky Mallaband is a Lecturer in Product Design at Aston University, UK.

Russ Marshall is a Reader at the Design School, Loughborough University, UK.

Julia Mase is a Researcher at the Global Development Institute, University of Manchester, UK.

Robin Means is Emeritus Professor of Health and Social Care in the Faculty of Health and Life Sciences, University of the West of England, UK.

Valerie Møller is Emeritus Professor of Quality of Life Studies at Rhodes University, Grahamstown, South Africa.

Marcello Morciano is a Research Fellow at the Health Economics Group, University of East Anglia, UK.

Kevin Morgan is Professor of Psychology at Loughborough University, UK.

Michael Murphy is Professor of Demography at the London School of Economics and Political Science, UK.

Michael Murray is Professor of Social and Health Psychology at Keele University, UK.

Colette Nicolle is a former Senior Lecturer and Research Fellow at the Design School, Loughborough University, UK.

Wendy Olphert is Horizon Digital Economy Researcher at the University of Nottingham, UK.

Sheila Peace is Emeritus Professor of Social Gerontology at the Open University, UK.

John Percival is a social worker, independent consultant and Researcher at the Centre for Innovative Ageing, Swansea University, UK.

Neil Reeves is Professor of Musculoskeletal Biomechanics at Manchester Metropolitan University, UK.

Mike Roys is a consultant in health, safety and wellbeing in buildings.

João Saboia is Professor of Economics at the Institute of Economics, Federal University of Rio de Janeiro, Brazil.

Jatinder Sandhu is a Research Associate in the School of Social Sciences at Nottingham Trent University, UK.

Rachael Scicluna is a Lecturer in Social Anthropology at the University of Kent, UK.

Ruth Sims is a Senior Lecturer in Psychology and Ergonomics at the College of Life and Natural Sciences, University of Derby, UK.

Rachel Talbot is a Research Associate at the Design School, Loughborough University, UK.

Ricardo Twumasi is Lecturer in the Alliance Manchester Business School, University of Manchester, UK.

Eleanor van den Heuvel is a Research Fellow at the Institute of Environment, Health and Societies, Brunel University London, UK.

Suresh Veeraraghavan is Director of the Centre for Law, Policy and Human Rights Studies, Chennai, India.

Penny Vera-Sanso is a Senior Lecturer in Development Studies and Social Anthropology at Birkbeck, University of London, UK.

Alan Walker is Professor of Social Policy and Social Gerontology at The University of Sheffield, UK, and a Fellow of the British Academy. He directed the New Dynamics of Ageing Programme 2005–15.

Tracey Williamson is a Reader in Public Involvement, Engagement and Experience at the University of Salford, UK.

Raphael Wittenberg is an Associate Professorial Research Fellow at the Personal Social Services Research Unit, London School of Economics and Political Science, and Deputy Director of the Centre for Health Service Economics and Organisation at the University of Oxford, UK.

ONE

Introduction

Alan Walker

This book is the first of two volumes of work arising from the New Dynamics of Ageing (NDA) programme. The necessity for two volumes arises from the sheer scale and scope of the programme: 10 years, £22 million, 200-plus researchers, funding from five UK research councils covering the arts and humanities, biological sciences, engineering, the social sciences and medical research. In short, the NDA was the largest single multidisciplinary research programme ever mounted in the UK and probably the largest in Europe. The programme generated hundreds of scientific papers, several books and a comprehensive series of lay findings documents (www.newdynamics. group.shef.ac.uk). The purpose of these two volumes is to bring together all of that work in an accessible form, as an aid to students and researchers. Here and in the twin volume you will find the very rich variety and depth of analyses of ageing carried out by most of the 35 research teams involved. While it cannot be claimed that every facet of ageing is covered, it is the case that most of the major issues are dealt with. Each chapter has been specially prepared for these volumes and follows an agreed standard format, which locates the particular problem in the wider literature, describes the methods used, reports the key findings and discusses their implications.

The first volume in the Policy Press NDA series, *The new science of ageing*, gives a full account of the significant changes that have taken place in the broad field of gerontology. These include the rise of multidisciplinarity, user engagement and knowledge exchange as initial elements of research. That background will not be repeated here. It is essential though to outline the NDA programme from which the following chapters are derived.

The New Dynamics of Ageing research programme

The NDA programme was the first of its kind: a multidisciplinary collaboration between five UK research councils. At the beginning, in April 2005, there were four research councils behind the programme:

the Biotechnology and Biological Sciences Research Council, the Engineering and Physical Sciences Research Council, the Economic and Social Research Council (ESRC) and the Medical Research Council (MRC). A year later, the Arts and Humanities Research Council (AHRC) joined in as a co-funder of the programme. Later, in 2008, the Canadian Institute of Ageing (part of the Canadian Institutes of Health Research) also became a co-funding partner in the programme as 10 new projects were linked to existing UK ones.

The NDA programme was established with the aim of understanding the new dynamics of ageing, the various influences shaping them and their implications for individuals and society. It had five specific objectives:

- to explore the ways in which individual ageing is subject to different influences over the life course;
- to understand the dynamic ways in which the meaning and experience of ageing are currently changing and becoming more diverse;
- to encourage and support the development of innovative interdisciplinary research groups and methods;
- to provide a sound evidence base for policy and practice (including the development of prototype systems, procedures and devices) so that research contributes to wellbeing and quality of life; and
- to promote new opportunities for UK science to link with researchers in the EU and beyond.

The NDA programme consisted of two substantive research themes – ageing well across the life course and ageing and its environments – with eight sub-themes:

- active ageing
- autonomy and independence
- later life transitions
- the oldest old
- resources for ageing
- locality, place and participation
- the built and technological environment
- the global dynamics of ageing.

The multifaceted and lengthy commissioning process produced a total of 35 projects, (excluding the Canadian ones), each of which lasted anywhere between 18 months and four years, with the majority spanning two to three years. These projects fell into two broad groups. On the one hand, there were 11 large collaborative research projects. Those multidisciplinary and multi-work package collaborations (involving disciplines under at least two of the participatory research councils) could be said to represent the essence of the NDA programme. On the other hand, there were 24 smaller-scale programme projects that included a few that were not multidisciplinary. Box 1.1 contains a list of these projects with the names and affiliations of the principal investigators. (The projects from which this volume's chapters are drawn are marked by an asterisk.)

Introducing the book

The collection starts with a strongly policy-oriented discussion of the future public spending costs of an ageing population in Chapter Two, which is based on the MAP2030 project (Modelling Needs and Resources of Older People to 2030). The project team concentrates on one important element of its research and one that is at the forefront of policy interests: the projected costs of long-term care. The analysis is contextualised by a discussion of the policies of the 2010-15 UK coalition government in comparison with those of the Dilnot Commission on the Funding of Care and Support (2011). Using microsimulation models, Mike Murphy and his colleagues quantify the likely future cost implications of the plans announced by the government: an extra £1.3 billion in 2020, rising to £2 billion by 2030. They also project that, under the government plans, there would be around 115,000 more care service users receiving some public funding in 2030 than if the current system continued. Whether or not these spending increases are too much or too little is, of course, a matter for political decision making. It is worth noting in this context that Britain is a relatively low spender on long-term care in European terms: one half and one third of the Netherlands and Sweden respectively (as a proportion of gross domestic product). The final part of the analysis considers the distributional effects of the proposed changes in both care home residents and home care recipients. In absolute (monetary) terms, there is a substantial bias towards the better off, although as a proportion of income the benefits are spread more evenly. As well as providing valuable data on the likely effects of a major policy change, in both financial and human terms, this chapter reveals how changes to key parameters in a complex system may affect the costs to public funds and the benefits to older people.

The active and healthy ageing section of the book opens with a major challenge accompanying population ageing but one that is rarely connected to it, workforce ageing. Based on the Working Late project, Chapter Three reports a continuation of age discrimination in the labour market, despite previous research with similar findings, many examples of good practices in combating age barriers and, most importantly of all, legislation outlawing age discrimination in the workplace. A major aspect of the project consisted of specific interventions aimed at overcoming barriers to continued employment among older workers. For example the Walking Works Wonders intervention aimed to encourage physical activity and reduce body mass. The Organiser for Working Late is a substantial output from the project and NDA. It includes design tools, personal stories, and audio and video clips of design ideas to aid discussion of health needs with employees. Chapter Three emphasises the need for organisations to provide flexible working practices to support longer working lives. The promotion of an age-positive organisational culture is a central requirement. Widespread adoption of the resources from the Working Late project would go a long way towards enabling society to respond adequately to the challenge of workforce ageing.

Chapter Four discusses the Healthy Ageing across the Life Course (HALCyon) project. This major investigation harnessed the power of nine UK cohort studies to try to understand functional ageing and wellbeing. The central focus of HALCyon was the life course and the project produced very rich data on the lifetime determinants and consequences of healthy ageing. As well as systematic literature reviews, the project undertook in-depth analyses of data within single cohorts and new cross-cohort research using harmonised data. There were also qualitative biographical interviews with 60 cohort members.

There is such depth in the HALCyon project that it is impossible to do justice to it in one chapter; however, Diana Kuh and her colleagues do convey much of importance in the findings. Particularly notable are the close associations between physical and mental capacity and wellbeing, with higher levels of physical capacity being associated with higher levels of mental wellbeing. Variations in wellbeing are significantly related to changes in cognition, and high levels of physical activity moderate this relationship by protecting cognition against the adverse impact of low wellbeing. Of similar note is the robust connection demonstrated between disadvantaged socioeconomic circumstances in childhood and lower capabilities in later life (such as poor walking speed and chair rise times). Moreover, lifetime area-level, as well as individual-level, socioeconomic characteristics influence physical capacity. Childhood cognitive ability and other aspects of early life were also found to be associated with adult cognitive capacity and wellbeing. Finally, the evidence from HALCyon is that genetic effects on physical and cognitive capabilities are limited. By any standards, the findings reported in this chapter are of major importance in terms of both science and public policy.

In Chapter Five, Ann Bowling summarises her important body of research on quality of life under both the ESRC Growing Older programme (1999-2005) and the multidisciplinary NDA programme. This research is important not only in the creation of a purpose-built tool for assessing the quality of older people's lives – the Older People's Quality of Life Questionnaire – which is available to both researchers and practitioners, but also in demonstrating the prognostic value of quality of life measures with regard to older people. Thus the tool and its subcomponents were independent predictors of several adverse health outcomes such as falls, nursing home placement and death. The chapter also reports on the perspectives of older people themselves concerning what brings quality to their lives. As indicated previously, these expressed preferences emphasise active participation and engagement.

Chapter Six focuses on a very specific activity: music making. Susan Hallam and Andrea Creech report key findings from their Music for Life NDA project, which explored the ways in which participating in creative music making could enhance the lives of older people. Most importantly, the project found that musical activities can be positive contributors to health and wellbeing in later life. More specifically, measures of wellbeing were consistently higher among those participating in musical activities compared with those undertaking other group activities and, moreover, the social, cognitive, emotional and health benefits of participation in music appeared to span the fourth as well as the third age. The research identified several barriers to participation, including physical, financial, psychological and logistical barriers, and demonstrated the influential role of facilitators in overcoming some of them.

Chapter Seven highlights the potential of activities based in community projects with older people living in disadvantaged urban areas to combat social exclusion and promote participation. Call-Me was an action research project consisting of close engagement with older people in a series of community arts activities. The benefits identified by participants covered both self-actualisation and social participation. The former included a personal sense of achievement, while the latter, more frequently mentioned, benefits meant increased opportunities for social interaction and forming new friendships. At the end of the project, the older participants were very enthusiastic about continuing and, in fact, established a community arts group that they called Young at Heart. In their concluding comments, Michael Murray and Amanda Crummett point to the long-term commitment required to work in disadvantaged neighbourhoods where initial enthusiasm can be dulled by frequent frustration. The central involvement of older residents in the development and ongoing planning of community activities is crucial.

Catherine Hagan Hennessy and Robin Means, in Chapter Eight, report some of the findings from the multidimensional Grey and Pleasant Land project, which researched older people's participation in rural community life. This path-breaking study was conducted in six separate locations in south-west England and Wales. Seven broad types of connectivities were identified and elaborated in the research: civic engagement; social participation; intergenerational relations; connections to the landscape; connectivity and group identity; virtual connectivity; and imaginative connectivity. The project also identified five main barriers to connectivity: limited material resources, limited mobility, digital exclusion, declining health and social barriers. Hennessy and Means emphasise both the ageing of rural areas and the severe public expenditure cuts being imposed by the coalition government. They suggest that an important leverage point exists, despite the adverse economic context, in the manifold contributions being made by older people that may be used to challenge negative perceptions of them as a burden on the younger generations. They do caution, however, about unequal ageing in rural areas: low income rural elders in deprived areas face far more barriers to connectivity than those that are living in better-off communities.

Chapter Nine, by Leela Damodaran, Wendy Olphert and Jatinder Sandhu, opens the design section of the book and addresses the pressing issue of the 'digital divide' – the big gap between older and younger people in the use of digital technologies and the internet. Their major NDA project SUS-IT went beyond cataloguing this under-usage by older people to try to find ways of both raising and then, crucially, sustaining internet engagement. The SUS-IT team employed an innovative combination of methods, including a survey of digital use, an interactive forum theatre, co-design 'sandpits', problem-solving sessions and workshops, and testing and evaluation of the software and product concepts developed by the project. As well as describing the challenges confronting older people in the use of ICTs, Damodaran and her colleagues propose a range of practical steps that can be taken to overcome them, focusing especially on appropriate design and good support. Without support, the challenges may become overwhelming, especially for those who are living alone or with limited or unreliable sources of assistance. The UK government has a national digital inclusion agenda and a key aspect of this chapter is a list of proposals to help to reduce the digital divide. The authors emphasise the importance of gaining 'buy-in' from target users; making access cheap and easy; inclusive design for all potential user groups; and measuring success from user feedback. The chapter also gives details of the various resources developed by the project to promote awareness among ICT innovators and developers about the digital needs of older people – a DVD, a design catalogue of innovative product concepts and a toolkit, which are available free from the NDA and SUS-IT websites.

Chapter Ten continues the section theme of design for an older population by focusing on smart clothing. Jane McCann, one of the pioneers of both design and research in this field, and Tracey Williamson discuss the clothing needs of active older people, especially those who engage in walking on a regular basis, a rapidly growing but market-neglected group. The Design for Ageing Well project employed a novel co-design approach, involving different academic disciplines, industry stakeholders and older people to understand the latter's clothing and wearable technology design requirements in order to guide the design and development of technology-enabled functional clothing, with the potential to facilitate outdoor healthy exercise and social engagement, and to enhance wellbeing. This new co-design methodology, new in the clothing industry, represented a major output for the project. It provides the basis for the clothing industry to address the current gap in the market for the active older consumer. Key issues for industry designers and product developers include age-appropriate size, shape and fit; less transient styling; colour and texture; branding – no logos; and price – higher prices must be justified by superior quality.

In Chapter Eleven, Eleanor van den Heuvel tackles the taboo topic of continence. Urinary incontinence affects 55% of women over 65 and 20% of men, but is rarely discussed or researched. The NDA TACT3 project set out to overcome this relative neglect by finding ways to challenge the environmental barriers to continence, improving continence services, and developing assistive devices for people who use continence pads. The overall aim of the project was to try to reduce the impact of continence difficulties in later life. As well as uncovering the key issues facing those with incontinence and their design priorities, this breakthrough project led to major innovations such as the Great British Public Toilet Map, a prototype odour detector and smart underwear.

Chapter Twelve focuses on a virtual aspect of design: the innovative visualisation of dynamic biomechanical data for healthcare purposes. Biomechanics is the study of mechanical laws relating to movement or the structure of living organisms and it has been successfully applied to assess movement problems in individuals, such as impaired mobility. Instead of replicating expensive clinical analyses, Alastair Macdonald evaluated a prototype software tool that visualised dynamic biomechanical data captured from older adults undertaking activities of daily living. From motion-capture data and muscle-strength measurements a 3D animated 'stick figure' is generated, on which the biomechanical demands of activities were represented visually at the hip and knee joints as a percentage of the person's maximum capability. This innovation not only saves time and money, but also enables other health professionals and non-experts to understand the physical processes at work. The project's evaluation showed how valuable this visual tool can be in both diagnosis and patient understanding.

Sheila Peace and her colleagues focus on kitchen living and design in Chapter Thirteen. This unique project examined the kitchen as the key domestic setting of everyday life. The research comprised comprehensive mixed methods: oral history informed by a housing history record and life topic event guide; self-completion records; semi-structured interviews; photographic recording; and sketches, measurements and the recording of light levels. The project's data therefore ranged over past and present, with a future perspective as well. There are important recommendations in the chapter about kitchen design, but, for me, the key challenge identified for designers, manufacturers, retailers and installers is the crucial importance of the kitchen as the place that enables people in later life to remain in their own home as their physical and cognitive capacities change.

Chapter Fourteen concludes the design section of the book by focusing on a hugely important, but unexplored topic: stair negotiation. As Costas Maganaris and his colleagues point out, it is stair descent rather than ascent that is the most risky for frail older people, and the majority of falls in old age occur during the former. By examining both stair design and muscular strength and joint mobility training, this NDA project aimed to find ways of improving the confidence and competence of older people in stair and step descent. They found, among other things, that step-rise (the height of each stair) is the most critical factor influencing the muscular strength demands of older people as well as for younger people. However, surprisingly, balance was not a major factor in stair descent. In practical terms, this research emphasises the importance, on the one hand, of optimising step-rise and, on the other, of resistance training that concentrates on the muscles around the ankle and knee joints. As the authors point out, many older residences throughout Europe have staircases that would no longer be permitted in modern residential buildings, and it is primarily of these staircases that training interventions are most urgent.

The third section of the book, on global ageing, opens with a comparative study of Brazil and South Africa. Armando Barrientos and his colleagues examined the impact of individual ageing on the wellbeing of older people and their households in low-income areas of the two countries using a longitudinal and comparative survey of around 1,000 people. The comparison of older people's wellbeing levels in 2002 and 2008 found improvement over time. This was true for a range of wellbeing indicators: per capita household income and expenditure; multidimensional measures; and life satisfaction. For low income households, pension income, especially non-contributory pensions, are essential to wellbeing, livelihoods and social inclusion. The major policy transfer lesson for other developing countries is the critical role of social pensions in sustaining wellbeing and social inclusion in later life.

The final main chapter, by Penny Vera-Sanso and her colleagues, concerns the smallest of the NDA projects, but the one that packed the biggest punch in terms of impact on older people's lives. The research on which the chapter is based took place in India's fourth largest city, Chennai. By situating older people at the centre of this study of urban poverty and focusing on what they do rather than on what they need, Vera-Sanso uncovered older people's contribution to the economy, social reproduction and to care. In fact, older people's work links the rural economy, where 50% of India's working population reside, to the urban economy. By making up shortfalls in government social and physical infrastructure, older people have released women into the workforce and have themselves provided low-cost inputs to industry and low-cost services to the urban population, thereby buttressing the city's role in the global economy. The pressing need was for an increase in the minimal social pension, which, by a planned strategy of engagement, the project succeeded in achieving.

The concluding chapter provides summaries of the key findings from each of the NDA projects included in this volume.

As is obvious by now, the precise complexion of the final NDA programme could not be manipulated or predicted because, although specific topics of interest were highlighted in the calls for proposals, the commissioning processes were rightly subject to rigorous peer review. Although the programme director was able to have some influence over the final shape of most of the large collaborative projects (see Box 1.1), their topic areas and central foci were already determined and validated by peer review. While the formal approach to project commissioning built a scientifically robust and varied programme, it also bequeaths the challenge of how to most coherently arrange the projects represented in this and its companion volume. Unlike the usual editorial process of filling the desired topic or thematic slots by commissioning tailor-made chapters, these two volumes started with a predetermined topic list. Thus, although the chapters were written specifically, their primary subject matter consisted of a particular research project. The option of dropping some projects to create one more finely focused volume was rejected in favour of the comprehensive representation of this unique programme. The result is that the sections in each volume are uneven. Nonetheless, taken together, the two books provide a comprehensive and in-depth analysis of many of the issues that are key to understanding the changing dynamics of ageing.

Box 1.1: The NDA projects
Collaborative research projects

- SomnIA – Optimising Sleep among Older People in the Community and Care Homes: An Integrated Approach – Sara Arber, Surrey University (May 2011).
- NANA: Novel Assessment of Nutrition in Ageing – Arlene Astell, St Andrews University (March 2013).
- SUS-IT: Sustaining IT Use by Older People to Promote Autonomy and Independence – Leela Damodaran, Loughborough University (September 2012).*
- Working Late: Strategies to Enhance Productive and Healthy Environments for Older Workers – Cheryl Haslam, Loughborough University (March 2013).*
- Grey and Pleasant Land? An Inter-disciplinary Exploration of the Connectivity of Older People in Rural Civic Society – Catherine Hennessy, Plymouth University (March 2012).*
- Healthy Ageing across the Life Course (HALCyon project) – Diana Kuh, University College London (December 2013).*
- Design for Ageing Well: Improving the Quality of Life for the Ageing Population using a Technology Enabled Garment System – Jane McCann, Newport School of Art, Media and Design (April 2012).*

- Mappmal: Multi-disciplinary Approach to Develop a Prototype for the Prevention of Malnutrition in Older People: Products, People, Places and Procedures – Paula Moynihan, Newcastle University (April 2012).
- Modelling Needs and Resources of Older People to 2030 (MAP2030) – Michael Murphy, London School of Economics (June 2010).*
- Migration, Nutrition and Ageing across the Lifecourse in Bangladeshi Families: A Transnational Perspective – Janice Thompson, Bristol University (November 2011).
- Tackling Ageing Continence through Theory Tools and Technology TACT3 – Eleanor van den Heuvel, Brunel University (April 2012).*

Programme projects
- A Combined Genetic and Small Molecule Approach to Studying the Role of the p38/MK2 Stress Signaling Pathway in a Human Premature Ageing Syndrome – Mark C. Bagley, Cardiff University (December 2012).
- Ageing, Well-being and Development: A Comparative Study of Brazil and South Africa – Armando Barrientos, University of Manchester (June 2011).*
- Ages and Stages: The Place of Theatre in Representations and Recollections of Ageing – Miriam Bernard, Keele University (July 2012; follow-on funding August 2012 to July 2013).
- Transitions, Choices and Health at Older Ages: Life Course Analyses of Longitudinal Data – David Blane, Imperial College London (December 2009).
- Psychometric Testing of the Multidimensional Older People's Quality of Life (OPQoL) Questionnaire and the Causal Model of QoL Under-pinning it – Ann Bowling, University College London (March 2009; follow-on funding October 2010 to September 2011).*
- Towards Understanding the Biological Drivers of Cellular Ageing – Lynne Cox, University of Oxford (September 2012).
- Detecting and Preventing Financial Abuse of Older Adults: An Examination of Decision-making by Managers and Professionals – Mary Gilhooly, Brunel University (March 2011; follow-on Knowledge Transfer Grant September 2011 to August 2012).
- Promoting Social Engagement and Well-being in Older People through Community Supported Participation in Musical Activities – Susan Hallam, Institute of Education (January 2011; follow-on funding September 2011 to December 2012).*
- Maintaining Dignity in Later Life: A Longitudinal Qualitative Study of Older People's Experiences of Supportive Care – Liz Lloyd, Bristol University (June 2011).
- Synergistic Effects of Physical and Psychological Stress Upon Immunesenescence – Janet Lord, Birmingham University (December 2012).

- Innovation in Envisioning Dynamic Biomechanical Data to Inform Healthcare and Design Practice – Alastair Macdonald, Glasgow School of Art and Design (January 2009).*
- Biomechanical and Sensory Constraints of Step and Stair Negotiation in Old Age – Constantinos Maganaris, Manchester Metropolitan University (February 2013).*
- New Metrics for Exploring the Relationship between Mobility and Successful Ageing – Lynn McInnes, Northumbria University (December 2009).
- Promoting Independence and Social Engagement among Older People in Disadvantaged Communities – Michael Murray, Keele University (February 2011).*
- Contemporary Visual Art and Identity Construction – Well-being Amongst Older People – Andrew Newman, Newcastle University (October 2011; follow-on funding January 2012 to January 2013).
- Transitions in Kitchen Living – Sheila Peace, Open University (November 2011).*
- Older People's Use of Unfamiliar Space – Judith Phillips, University of Wales (April 2010).
- Dynamics of Cardiovascular Ageing – Aneta Stefanovska, Lancaster University (March 2012).
- Trajectories of Senescence through Markov Models – David Steinsaltz, Oxford University (June 2012).
- Fiction and the Cultural Mediation of Ageing – Phillip Tew, Brunel University (May 2012; follow-on funding September 2012 to July 2013).
- Ageing, Poverty and Neoliberalism in Urban South India – Penny Vera-Sanso, Birkbeck College (April 2010).*
- Families and Caring in South Asian Communities – Christina Victor, University of Reading (June 2011).
- Representing Self – Representing Ageing – Lorna Warren, University of Sheffield (November 2011).
- Landscapes of Cross-generational Engagement – Peter Wright, Sheffield Hallam University (December 2010).

The Canadian NDA
Partnership was formed with the Canadian Institutes of Health Research, which enabled Canadian researchers to bid for funds to link themselves to NDA research teams. Two commissioning rounds were carried out, in 2008 and 2009, which produced the following 10 linked projects.

- Health and Creative Ageing: Theatre as a Pathway to Health Ageing – Janet Fast, University of Alberta.

  This project is linked to the NDA project Ages and Stages: The Place of Theatre in Representations and Recollections of Ageing, led by Miriam Bernard, Keele University (2012).
- How do Catastrophic Events by Modulating the Immune Response Lead to Frailty? – Tamos Fulop, Université de Sherbrooke.

  This project is linked to the NDA project Synergistic Effects of Physical and Psychological Stress Upon Immunesenescence, led by Janet Lord, Birmingham University (2012).
- Working Late: Strategies to Enhance Productive and Healthy Environments for the Older Workforce – the Canadian Context – Lan Gien, Memorial University of Newfoundland.

  This project is linked to the NDA project Working Late: Strategies to Enhance Productive and Healthy Environments for Older Workers, led by Cheryl Haslam, Loughborough University (2013).*
- Interactive Analysis of Functional and Cognitive Change Across the IALSA (Canada) and HALCyon (UK) Longitudinal Research Networks – Scot Hofer, University of Victoria.

  This project is linked to the NDA project Healthy Ageing across the Life Course (HALCyon project), led by Diana Kuh, University College London (2013).*
- Developing and Validation of a Questionnaire to Measure the Psychological Impact of Assistive Technologies for Continence in Elderly Individuals – Jeffrey Jutai, University of Ottawa.

  This project is linked to the NDA project Tackling Ageing Continence through Theory Tools and Technology TACT3, led by Eleanor van den Heuvel, Brunel University (2012).*
- Connectivity of Older Adults in Rural Communities: Health in Context – Norah Keating, University of Alberta.

  This project is linked to the NDA project Grey and Pleasant Land? An Inter-disciplinary Exploration of the Connectivity of Older People in Rural Civic Society, led by Catherine Hennessy, Plymouth University (2012).*
- Effects of Normal and Impaired Cognitive Function on Stair Descent Mobility for Older Adults – Bradford McFadyen, Université Laval.

  This project is linked to the NDA project Biomechanical and Sensory Constraints of Step and Stair Negotiation in Old Age, led by Costantinos Maganaris, Manchester Metropolitan University (2013).*
- The Extension of the COACH Prompting System to Nutrition-related Activities Among Older Adults – Alex Mihailidis, University of Toronto.

  This project is linked to the NDA project NANA: Novel Assessment of Nutrition in Ageing, led by Arlene Astell, St Andrews University (2013).

• Sustaining Information Technology Use by Older Adults to Promote Autonomy and Independence: Newfoundland and Labrador Cohort – Wendy Young, Memorial University.

> This project is linked to the NDA project SUS-IT: Sustaining IT Use by Older People to Promote Autonomy and Independence, led by Leela Damodaran, Loughborough University (2012).*

• Improving Continence Across Continents, an RCT of Continence Promotion Intervention for Older Women in the Community – Cara Tannenbaum, University of Montreal.

> This project is linked to the NDA project Tackling Ageing Continence through Theory Tools and Technology TACT3, led by Eleanor van den Heuvel, Brunel University (2012).*

Note: * denotes those projects in this volume.

TWO

Modelling ageing populations to 2030: financing long-term care in England

Michael Murphy, Ruth Hancock,
Raphael Wittenberg, Bo Hu, Marcello Morciano and
Adelina Comas-Herrera

Introduction

Countries across the developed world are recognising the need to reconsider and reform their policies for older people, driven in large part by concerns over their future affordability and sustainability in the face of rising demand and decreasing potential support ratios (the number of people in a conventional working age range such as 20 to 64 for each person in a conventional retirement age of 65 and over). In Europe, the number of people aged 65 and over is projected to increase from 107 million in 2000 to 194 million in 2050, while the number of those aged 20 to 64 will decline from 442 million to 370 million over the same period (United Nations, 2015). Trends in countries such as Japan are more startling; there, the proportion of people aged 65 and over is projected to increase from 17% in 2000 to 36% by 2050. Potential support ratios will decline across developed countries. While this fall is likely to be more pronounced in some countries such as Japan than in the UK, even here the ratio is likely to fall by 42% from 3.7 to 2.2 in the period 2000 to 2050, having been essentially constant in earlier decades (Figure 2.1). The next two decades are likely to experience particularly rapid population ageing as the large birth cohorts from the babyboomer generation are making the transition from work to retirement.

Much discussion centres on the need for resources to meet increased pensions, healthcare and social care costs across developed societies and, increasingly, across developing ones as well. A number of solutions to these problems have been advanced. These include some or a combination of the following measures:

- increasing the age of retirement;
- increasing immigration;
- increasing fertility among the native population;
- raising taxes.

Figure 2.1: Potential support ratio: United Kingdom and Japan, 1980-2050

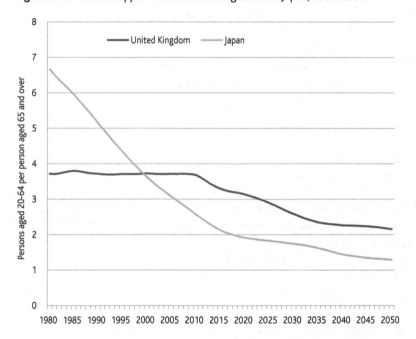

Note: Potential support ratio: number of persons aged 20-64 for one person aged 65 and over.
Source: United Nations (2015).

The difficulties in ensuring financial stability in the face of these major demographic trends were highlighted in the long-term fiscal sustainability report of the Office for Budget Responsibility (OBR) (OBR, 2012), which pointed out that costs associated with population ageing were likely to be the main factors that would put substantial pressures on public finances in decades to come. The OBR estimated that in the period between 2017-18 and 2062-63, the share of gross domestic product (GDP) allocated to state-funded health costs would increase from 7% to 8.8%; state pension costs from 5.8% to 8.4%; and long-term social care costs from 1.3% to 2.4%. The largest proportionate increase is likely to be in social care, 85%, compared with 44% for pensions and 25% for healthcare. The latest OBR report (2017) estimates suggest that health and social care costs are likely to grow at similar rates over this period.

In England (and the UK more generally), considerable debate has focused on the reform of the pensions and long-term care systems. Both are crucial to the wellbeing of older people as well as to financial sustainability. The research project Modelling Needs and Resources of Older People to 2030 (MAP2030) developed a set of projection models to estimate not only future numbers of older people, but also their family circumstances, income, pensions, savings, disability, and formal and informal care needs. These projections included estimates of public and private expenditure on pensions, disability benefits and care services under different scenarios for reform of pensions and long-term care funding under a range of alternative population futures. The programme was undertaken as part of the New Dynamics of Ageing (NDA) programme in the period 2007 to mid-2010. The devolved nature of social care (but not state pensions) means that most attention is given to England, where there has been both the greatest debate about policy options and availability of data to undertake detailed modelling. However, in some cases, such as with data produced by international organisations, coverage may extend beyond England, especially to the UK.

This modelling covered a range of issues, showing how future public expenditure on pensions depends on trends in mortality and how long-term care is affected in addition by morbidity and disability rate trends. It also provided new evidence on the costs and distributional effects of changes in the funding system for long-term care. The principal method was simulation using a range of models including those concerned with mortality projections; development of chronic disease and years lived with and without disability in good and poor health; demand for and supply of long-term care; and pensions needs. Particular emphasis was given to the analysis of which groups would benefit most from possible policy changes.

The MAP2030 project still provides the most comprehensive detailed analysis of the joint impact of key drivers to date. The wide range of factors that influence the changing need for social care and social care expenditure will mean that our projections will turn out to be incorrect, as all projections inevitably are, unanticipated events such as Brexit – the UK's intended withdrawal from the European Union – being an obvious example of such problems. Additional factors include changes in both the drivers of need for social care and the way in which those needs are met, the former of which are likely to be more predictable and will continue to underpin any decisions that are made. For example, people aged 80 in 2031 who have no living children will lack a major source of informal care. We know the proportion of that cohort childless in 2016 when they were aged 65 and their children were aged about 35 on average. The chance of a child dying in the next 15 years is about one in 20, and as most people have at least two children, the additional proportion likely to become childless in the next 15 years is tiny. Other key variables are subject to more uncertainty. The number of older people, for example those aged 85 and over in England and Wales in 2031, was projected to be 1.59 million in the 1994-based official projections published in 1994: 10 years later, that figure had increased by 0.68 million to 2.14 million (ONS, 1996, 2006). Revisions recently have been less substantial, but it must be recognised that the number of older people requiring social care may be larger – or possibly smaller – than anticipated. Recently, mortality, which is the key driver numbers of older people in years to come, has been improving at a greater rate than future values assumed in current official projections. Analyses of the sensitivity of future pensions expenditure to alternative trends formed one part of the MAP2030 project (Malley at al, 2011).

A second key factor determining social care costs is the health status of the older population. There is evidence that some health trends show improvement, whereas others show deterioration, so identifying both the most probable trends and how they translate into care needs as well as assessing the likely degree of uncertainty associated with these trends is not straightforward. The projections discussed here are based on assumptions about need for care produced as part of the research project by Carol Jagger and others. These were based on the implications for the number of disabled people requiring care by projecting a number of the key diseases associated with disability – arthritis, stroke, coronary heart disease, dementia and cognitive impairment – and the way that these changes translated into numbers of older disabled people requiring social care. While the results shown below are based on one central scenario, the outturn could be more pessimistic or more optimistic than assumed here. The projected number of people aged 65 and over in the United Kingdom who are disabled in 2030 with a central health scenario was 1.9 million; with an improved population health scenario, this figure would be reduced to 1.74 million, but with a continuation of current trends the figure would actually be rather greater with 2.06 million disabled people in 2030 (Jagger et al, 2011). We are now about one third of the way through the 2010-30 projection period and these projections, which are concerned with the demand for care, appear to be in line with observed trends to date. However, the supply of state-funded care has been different from what was anticipated in 2010, a point we address later.

The analysis presented here concentrates on costs to the public purse. However, a substantial fraction of formal care is met from resources of individuals themselves, rather than from state provision. The balance between self and public funding is at the heart of the debate about funding of social care systems. However, the greatest volume of personal care is provided not through formal mechanisms but through informal help, often from close relatives. The availability and willingness of such people to provide often intense levels of personal care is a factor that needs to be recognised even when the discussion is centred on the somewhat dry issue of who should pay. Work as part of the MAP2030 project by Linda Pickard (Pickard, 2015) showed that the supply of informal care will be put under intense pressure in decades to come. Changing demographic patterns in the latter part of the 20th century, with low fertility, reduced levels of partnership formation and higher rates of partnership breakdown, mean that the advantaged position of today's older population in terms of potential informal carers will change substantially as those who were partnering and childbearing in the 1980s start to enter the age groups where need increases sharply. This period was identified as a 'tipping point' when the ability of relatives to provide the volume of informal care needed will come under severe pressure.

While these are important factors that need to be considered in making comprehensive assessments of future needs, the number of alternative combinations quickly becomes overwhelming. Therefore we concentrate on one topic that includes insights from these various work packages, but has become of particular relevance since it is the area most directly subject to policy, namely the financing of the social care system. The projections associated with long-term care were conducted using three linked models – the University of East Anglia CARESIM microsimulation model, the Personal Social Services Research Unit (PSSRU) cell-based long-term care finance model, and Newcastle University's SIMPOP macrosimulation model linking disease and disability – all of which were improved and expanded under this project. The PSSRU model makes projections of demand for long-term care and associated expenditure, under clearly specified assumptions. It makes projections of future numbers of disabled older people; future levels of long-term care services and disability benefits; future public and private expenditure on long-term care; and the future social care workforce. One input to the PSSRU model is the disability rates conditional on various health scenarios produced from SIMPOP. CARESIM simulates the incomes and assets of future cohorts of older people and their ability to contribute towards care home fees or the costs of home-based care, should such care be needed. It uses data from several years of the British Family Resources Survey to perform simulations for single people currently aged 65 and over, and for the older partner in couples where at least one partner is aged 65 years or more. The simulations are performed for a base year and for future years. As part of this project, an informal care extension to the PSSRU model was built, in order to make projections of receipt of informal care contingent on the availability of living children.

The purpose of these projections was to inform the development of policies on pensions and long-term care, since the appropriate way of financing social care for older people has been under discussion for many years. There have been substantial developments on the policy on and funding of adult social care under successive governments, including a number of official enquiries, and it was clear that the existing system in the early 2000s was unsustainable and that major reforms were required. The MAP2030 project contributed to the evidence base, in particular, by assessing the impacts and robustness of alternative policy proposals to a range of different mortality and morbidity scenarios. The topic became of major political interest during the 2010 UK general election, especially since the Scottish Parliament had made personal care free for Scottish residents. A number of options have been put forward although the full implications of these were often unclear. The former Labour government published a White Paper in spring 2010, the new Conservative/Liberal Democrat coalition government published a *Vision for social care* in late 2010 (DH, 2010a), and it also established in summer 2010 a Commission on Funding of Care and Support (CFCS), the Dilnot Commission, which reported in July 2011 (Commission on Funding of Care and Support, 2011). Members of the MAP2030 project team including Ruth Hancock and Raphael Wittenberg contributed to the development of this report, continuing earlier work in this area. Its main recommendation was for a lifetime cap on individual liability to meet care costs. Some of these recommendations were included in a *Caring for our future* White Paper in July 2012 (Her Majesty's Government, 2012a) and the 2014 Care Act (DH, 2014), which provided for a cap on liability to meet social care costs that was intended to come into force in April 2016. However, the incoming Conservative government announced in July 2015 that this measure would be delayed until April 2020 and there were no undertakings about the level at which the cap would be set (Jarrett, 2015). More recently, the government announced in its Budget of March 2017 that it plans to publish a Green Paper on the funding of social care later in the year.

Since key questions about state funding of long-term social care remain for decision, it is therefore opportune to review developments in the seven years since the project finished, drawing on insights obtained from the programme and using models developed at this time. Some of the proposals that were put forward in earlier years have been rejected. Clearly, these were suggested as competing alternatives and they needed to be assessed in detail, which was one of the objectives of the project. Given that social care has moved substantially up the social and political agenda, especially as a major factor placing strains on the National Health Service, it seems appropriate to take a fresh look at recent developments in long-term care policy, the analysis of which was a prime focus of the project, but before doing so, we briefly review developments in the intervening period.

Background to the analysis

Under the current system, people with savings above an upper threshold of £23,250 are not generally eligible for publicly funded care and support. There is also a lower threshold of £14,250 below which savings are completely disregarded in the means test for social care. If the individual has capital above the upper threshold, the individual pays the full cost of their care. For residential care, the value of the home is usually included in capital after the first 12 weeks. Much of the debate over the past 20 years has been about these provisions, and in particular the balance between public and private responsibilities for funding care.

In February 2013, the UK government issued a policy statement on care and support funding (DH, 2013). The key features of its planned reforms were:

- a lifetime cap on the costs an individual will need to pay towards eligible care and support needs , expected to have been £72,000 if it had been introduced in 2016 (£61,000 in 2010 prices);
- an increase, for residential care when the value of the home is taken into account, in the upper capital threshold above which there is no state help towards care home fees; the threshold was expected to have been £118,000 in 2016 (£100,000 in 2010 prices) compared with £23,250 now;
- for residential care, an expectation that eligible care costs that count towards the cap comprise the difference between the publicly funded rate for care home fees and so-called 'hotel costs', with hotel costs

set at around £12,000 in 2016 (£10,000 in 2010 prices). Public help with hotel costs will remain means tested.

The coalition government said that it intended to introduce these changes in 2016, with a cap of around £72,000 and an upper capital threshold in residential care of £118,000 in 2016 prices (Chancellor of the Exchequer, 2013). The lifetime cap is higher than the £35,000 (2010 prices) recommended by the Dilnot Commission (Commission on Funding of Care and Support, 2011). The increase in the capital threshold and the level of hotel costs match the CFCS central recommendation.

The following analyses were designed to permit a comprehensive assessment of the viability and consequences of both current policy and some policy options under consideration at that time, which informed the content of the 2014 Care Act. Access to publicly funded social care in England is currently subject to an assessment of needs and a financial assessment of savings and income. Local authorities are responsible for setting local eligibility criteria for adult social care within the framework of the central *Fair access to care services* guidance (DH, 2010b). Under the 2014 Care Act, local authorities are charged to ensure that people's wellbeing is at the centre of all it does, and to operate national minimum eligibility criteria for social care. They conduct assessments of people seeking access to publicly funded care and determine whether they meet the local eligibility criteria and, if so, how much (if anything) they need to contribute to the costs of their care through user charges.

Financing schemes examined

We analysed the CFCS recommendations (Wittenberg et al, 2011) and we subsequently prepared updated analysis to take account of the government's February 2013 policy statement, examining also two variations on the government's planned reform (Hancock et al, 2013). These variations illustrate the effect of providing a little more state help to those with capital below the new higher threshold. For comparison, we compare our results with a cap of £35,000 (2010 prices) recommended by the CFCS, which would be around £43,000 in 2017 prices.

Under the existing means test for public support, as previously indicated, individuals with capital above the upper threshold, currently £23,250, have to meet their care home fees in full without any state help. For residential care, the value of the individual's home is usually included in capital. Those with capital below the upper limit may be entitled to state help depending on their income. The first £14,250 of capital is disregarded completely, but capital between this lower threshold and the upper threshold is assumed to generate a 'tariff' income of £1 per week for every £250 of capital. This tariff income is added to other sources of income when applying the means test.

The proposed increase in the upper threshold will extend the range of capital on which this tariff income will be calculated. The effect of the tariff will offset the effect of the increase in the upper threshold – partially for those with capital well below the new upper threshold but potentially fully for those with capital near the new upper threshold. We therefore examine two ways in which the effect of this offset could be reduced:

- A reduction in the tariff rate to £1 for every £500 of capital, which is the rate used in means–tested social security benefits.
- An increase in the lower capital threshold in residential care, thereby increasing the amount of capital that is disregarded completely and hence entirely protected. We examine an increase in the lower capital threshold to £41,600 in 2017 prices (the CFCS had recommended a lifetime cap of £35,000 in 2010 prices, or about £43,000 in expected 2017 prices) since the cost to the public purse would be close to the cost of reducing the tariff rate to £1 in £500.

The current means test and these reform options are described in more detail in Box 2.1.

Box 2.1: Details of the current (2010-17) means test for long-term care and reforms

An individual's entitlement to state help with the costs of long-term care depends on an assessment of their care needs and on a means test.

The current capital means test

• If the individual has capital above an '**upper capital threshold**', currently £23,250, the individual pays the full cost of their care. For residential care, the value of the home is usually included in capital after the first 12 weeks.

• When capital is below £23,250, the state meets some of the cost depending on the individual's assessable income.

• Assessable income includes a notional weekly income, known as '**tariff income**' on capital between a '**lower capital threshold**', currently £14,250, and the upper capital threshold. The current rate of tariff income is £1 for each £250 between the lower and upper capital thresholds. Capital up to the lower capital threshold, and any income from it, is ignored completely in the means test.

The government's announced reforms in 2014
- Once an individual has received '**eligible care**' to the value of the lifetime cap, the state will meet their '**eligible care costs**'. Eligible care is the package of care that the individual has been assessed as needing; eligible care costs are the costs of that care calculated at the prices that the local authority pays. In residential care, eligible care excludes the general living costs element of care home fees sometimes known as '**hotel costs**' – board, food, heating and so on. The lifetime cap was expected to be £72,000 in 2016.
- The upper capital threshold in residential care when the value of the person's home is taken into account will be increased and was expected to be £118,000 in 2016.
- In residential care, hotel costs will remain means tested and were expected to be £12,000 in 2016.

Two variants on the government's announced reforms
We examine two variations on the government's announced reforms. In addition to changes outlined earlier, these would:

- halve the rate of tariff income from £1 per £250 to £1 per £500; or, at a similar cost
- increase the lower capital threshold to £41,600 in 2017 prices.

The central recommendation of the Dilnot Commission on Funding Care and Support
- This is similar to the government's plans except that the recommended lifetime cap was £35,000 in 2010 prices, or about £43,000 in 2017 prices.

Methods and assumptions

We use two linked simulation models: the PSSRU's aggregate long-term care projections model and the University of East Anglia's CARESIM dynamic microsimulation. The former is a cell-based model that makes projections of future numbers of disabled older people, numbers of service users and recipients of unpaid care, public and private expenditure and social care workforce. The latter is a dynamic microsimulation model, which makes projections of how much individuals need to pay toward the costs of their care should they receive residential or community-based care. Our projections are produced through linkages between these two models: for example, CARESIM estimates of the proportion of older people who would meet the means test criteria for public support if they needed care are fed into the PSSRU model.

The models had a base year of 2010 and incorporated the 2010-based official population projections (ONS, 2011) and projections of GDP made by the OBR (2012). These models allowed us to make projections of the public costs of the current funding system for long-term care for older people in England (the base case), and of potential reforms to it, along with the distribution of gains from reforms according to care recipients' income levels. More details on the models' methods, data sources and assumptions are given in Wittenberg et al (2011).

Key points to note are as follows:

- The results relate to England: since social care services are a devolved function the government's plans relate specifically to England only.
- Our analysis relates to people aged 65+ only: since fewer younger people needing care are likely to have substantial capital, the costs will relate mainly to older people.
- The base year for the projections is 2010 and all results are given in 2010 prices.
- Public expenditure on long-term care is defined to include not only expenditure on social care services provided via local authorities but also expenditure on disability benefits that are used by their recipients to fund social care.
- Patterns of care, such as the balance between formal and informal care and residential and home-based care, are held constant.
- Future unit costs of care are assumed to rise in line with real earnings growth.
- Real earnings growth is assumed to be zero until 2015 and 2% per annum thereafter.
- The lifetime cap and hotel costs are assumed to rise over time at the rate of real earnings growth.
- All capital thresholds are assumed to stay constant in real terms under the current funding system. Under the potential funding reforms, they are assumed to rise at the rate of real earnings growth until 2017 and to remain constant in real terms thereafter. In a sensitivity test we assume that, under the potential reforms, capital thresholds and hotel costs rise by real earnings indefinitely.

Results

Projections of public expenditure on long-term care

To set the scene, Figure 2.2 shows projected public expenditure on social care for older people in England, under the original funding system from 2010. The chart shows projected public expenditure in absolute terms and as a percentage of GDP. In 2010, the base year for the projections, public expenditure is estimated at just over £12 billion and projected to rise to £16.3 billion in 2020 and £25.5 billion in 2030 (in constant 2010 prices). Expressed as a percentage of GDP, these correspond to just under 1%, rising to 1.1% by 2020 and 1.3% by 2030.

Our modelling suggests that the government's announced plans would have added an extra £1.3 billion to public expenditure in 2020, rising to an extra £2 billion by 2030 at 2010 prices (Figure 2.3). These public expenditure costs were likely to have been overestimates to the extent that the cap would not have been applied in respect of care received prior to 2016. It is not possible to compare this estimate directly with the government's estimates of costs, in part because of differences in the time periods to which the respective estimates relate and in price bases; but subject to that caveat, the estimates appear to be reasonably compatible with those published in the government's 2012 progress report on funding reform (Her Majesty's Government, 2012b).[1]

Figure 2.2: Projected public expenditure on social care for older people in England, original scheme

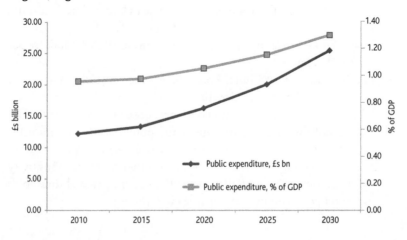

Source: Authors' analysis.

If the rate of tariff income on capital assumed for residential care was halved, in addition to the measures proposed by the government, the cost compared with the current funding system would have been an extra £1.4 billion in 2020, rising to £2.1 billion in 2030, increases of about 8%. As an alternative to cutting tariff income, raising the lower capital threshold in residential care to £41,600 in 2017 would have cost a similar amount. In contrast the central recommendation of the Dilnot Commission would have cost an extra £2.1 billion in 2020, increasing to £3.3 billion by 2030.

Our projections suggest that under the government plans, there would be some 115,000 more care service users receiving some public funding in 2030 than if the current system continued. This is in contrast to around 185,000 more publicly funded users in 2030 that we project under the central Dilnot recommendation. Supplementing the government plans with a halving of the rate of tariff income on capital between the upper and lower thresholds or increasing the lower threshold to £40,000 would mean a very small increase of around 1,500 more publicly funded users than under the government plan alone.

If capital thresholds were linked to real earnings indefinitely, the public expenditure cost of the government's plans would be £2.23 billion in 2030 compared with £1.96 billion if they were held constant in real prices terms after 2017. This is an additional cost of just under

Figure 2.3: Projected extra public expenditure from 2013 reform options, post-reform capital thresholds linked to earnings up to 2017, prices thereafter

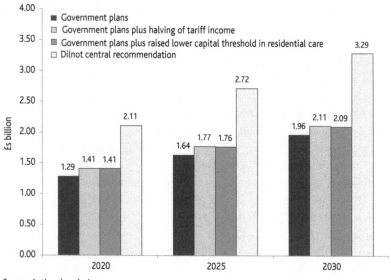

Source: Authors' analysis.

£0.3 billion in 2030 or 14% of the cost when capital thresholds are held constant after 2017. The additional costs of indefinite earnings linking of capital thresholds for the two variants on the government's plans (halving the rate of tariff income or raising the lower capital threshold in residential care) are £0.4 billion in 2030 or an additional 18% of the cost when capital thresholds are linked to earnings only until 2017. The additional costs of indefinite earnings linking of capital thresholds for the central Dilnot recommendation would be £0.3 billion in 2030 or 8% of the costs when capital thresholds are held constant in real terms after 2017.

Distributional effects of funding reforms

Figure 2.4 shows how the projected average gain from the funding reforms varies across quintiles (fifths) of the income distribution, for recipients of care aged 85+ in 2030, by which time reforms introduced in 2016 would be close to being mature. Figure 2.4a shows the average gains in absolute terms, that is, in pounds per week at 2010 prices. Figure 2.4b shows average gains expressed as a percentage of income. In absolute terms, all reforms favour those in highest income quintile most and those in the lowest income quintile the least:[2] average gains in the highest income quintile are around 2.5 times those in the lowest income quintile for all reforms examined. As a percentage of income, the average gains are more uniformly distributed across income quintiles, although with a tendency to be highest in the top and bottom quintiles. This is particularly noticeable for the Dilnot central recommendations.

Since some aspects of the reforms – changes to the upper capital and, in the variants, changes to the lower capital threshold or reduction in tariff income – affect only those in care homes, Figure 2.5 shows the distributional results for care home residents only. From these it can be seen that the difference in absolute average gains between the government's plans and the two variants that we have modelled is proportionately greater in the lower income quintiles than in the higher income quintiles. For example, in the lowest income quintile, the average gain when a reduction in tariff income is combined with the government plans is £41 per week, which is 17% higher than the average gain (£35) if the rate of tariff income is unchanged. Corresponding comparisons for quintiles 2 and 3 are of similar size. However, the comparison for the highest quintile is between £83 if tariff income is reduced and £78 if it is not, a difference of just 6%. The distributional effects of the variant in which the lower capital threshold

Figure 2.4a: Distribution of gains by income: care home residents and home care recipients aged 85+, 2030, post-reform capital thresholds linked to earnings up to 2017, prices thereafter (mean gains £s per week)

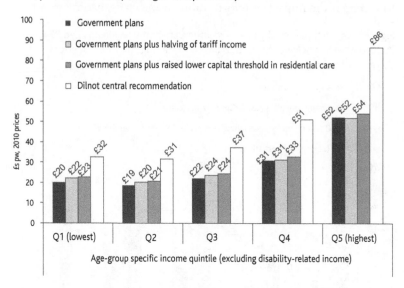

Figure 2.4b: Distribution of gains by income: care home residents and home care recipients aged 85+, 2030, post-reform capital thresholds linked to earnings up to 2017, prices thereafter (mean gains as % of income)

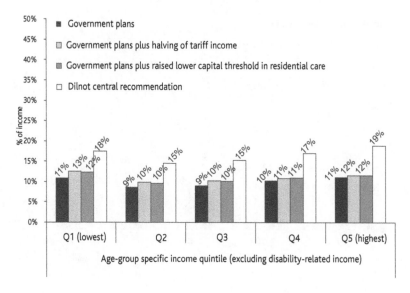

is raised to £41,600 are remarkably similar to the variant in which tariff income is halved. The adoption of one of the variants would thus render the impact of reform more even across income groups.

Figure 2.5a: Distribution of gains by income: care home residents aged 85+, 2030, post-reform capital thresholds linked to earnings up to 2017, prices thereafter (mean gains £s per week)

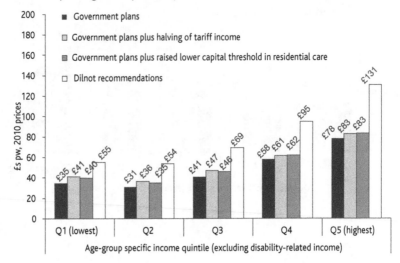

Figure 2.5b: Distribution of gains by income: care home residents aged 85+, 2030, post-reform capital thresholds linked to earnings up to 2017, prices thereafter (mean gains as % of income)

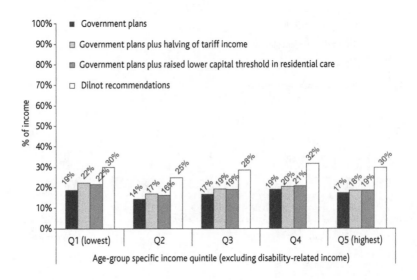

Conclusion

We have assessed in the research discussed in this chapter the public expenditure costs and the distributional effects of plans to reform the funding system for long-term care for older people in England in the early years of this decade. We have contrasted the effects of the coalition government's planned reforms with the central recommendations of the Dilnot Commission and with two variants on the then government's plans that would give additional help to care home residents with capital below the proposed higher capital threshold (£123,000 in 2017). While it is unclear how far these plans will be implemented, they form the basis of the 2014 Care Act.

Our projections are that the then government's plans would have added just under £2 billion to public expenditure on long-term care for older people by 2030 (at 2010 prices), compared with an extra £3.3 billion for the central Dilnot recommendations. Combining the government's plans with a halving of the rate of tariff income on capital between the lower threshold and the new higher upper threshold would have a public expenditure cost of £2.1 billion by 2030. An alternative approach with a similar cost would be to raise the lower capital threshold to around £40,000 in 2010 prices (£41,600 in 2017 prices).

We project that under the then government's plans there would have been some 115,000 more care service users receiving some public funding in 2030 than if the current system continued. This is in contrast to around 185,000 more publicly funded users in 2030 that we project under the central Dilnot recommendation. Supplementing the government plans with a halving of the rate of tariff income on capital between the upper and lower thresholds or increasing the lower threshold to £40,000 would mean around 1,500 more publicly funded users than under the government plan alone.

The estimated weekly gains in absolute terms from all the reform options are greatest among care recipients in the highest quintile (fifth) of the income distribution for older people. For example, in 2030, the then government's plans would be worth £52 per week (2010 prices) on average to care recipients aged 85 and over in the highest quintile compared with £20 for those in the lowest quintile. Expressed as percentages of income, the gains vary much less across the income distribution.

Focusing on care home residents, both of the two variants on the government's plans would be particularly advantageous, compared with the then government's planned reform, to care home recipients in the lowest three quintiles of the income distribution. In 2030, the average gains of care home residents aged 85+ would be about 16% higher under these variants than under the proposed reforms compared with around 6% higher for the upper two quintiles.

These projections assume that the level of the cap is linked to real earnings growth indefinitely but that capital thresholds are linked to real earnings growth only until 2017 and are held constant in real terms thereafter. If capital thresholds were linked to real earnings indefinitely, the public expenditure cost of the government plans would be £2.23 billion in 2030 compared with £1.96 billion if they were held constant after 2017.

The system of financing long-term care in England is complex and it is likely to remain so. This makes it hard to assess the effects of reforms without analysis such as we have prepared. Our analyses have shown how altering different parameters in this complex system affect the costs to public funds and the financial benefits for older people in different parts of the income distribution.

The ways in which the funding regime for social care will evolve remains unclear pending the forthcoming Green Paper. The reluctance of successive governments to take decisive action has started to have increasingly serious impacts beyond the funding of care by individuals and the state, including impacts on the effectiveness of the National Health Service and the viability of the residential care and home care sectors. The danger is that when action is taken it will be in response to a perceived emergency or political crisis without the detailed analysis such as presented here.

Acknowledgements

We are grateful to the UK research councils for funding the MAP2030 project, under grant number RES-339-25-0002. We are also grateful for funding from various other sources for the more recent research on which this chapter draws: AXA Research Fund; the Economic and Social Research Council (ESRC) through the ESRC Research Centre on Micro-social Change; and the Department of Health, which funded our research for the Commission on Funding Care and Support.

The chapter also draws substantially on a discussion paper by Hancock and colleagues (2013).

Notes

[1] Figure 4 on page 34 of that report gives estimates of the cost for older people of a £75,000 cap and a £100,000 upper capital threshold introduced in 2015/16 of £1.3 billion by 2025/26 in 2012/13 prices, allowing for savings on disability

benefits. Note that estimates are also given of the assessment costs associated with the cap. Our cost estimates do not include assessment costs.

[2] The government's policy statement also contained an analysis of the distributional effects of its planned reforms. Although that analysis takes a slightly different approach from ours, the general picture that emerges is very similar.

References

Chancellor of the Exchequer (2013) 'Budget 2013 statement'. Available at www.gov.uk/government/speeches/budget-2013-chancellors-statement.

Commission on Funding of Care and Support (2011) *Fairer care funding. The report of the Commission on Funding of Care and Support.* Available at http://webarchive.nationalarchives.gov.uk/20130221130239/http://dilnotcommission.dh.gov.uk/files/2011/07/Fairer-Care-Funding-Report.pdf.

DH (Department of Health) (2010a) *A vision for adult social care: Capable communities and active citizens.* Available at http://webarchive.nationalarchives.gov.uk/20130107105354/http://www.dh.gov.uk/prod_consum_dh/groups/dh_digitalassets/@dh/@en/@ps/documents/digitalasset/dh_121971.pdf.

DH (2010b) *Prioritising need in the context of Putting People First: A whole system approach to eligibility for social care. Guidance on eligibility criteria for adult social care, England 2010.* Available at http://webarchive.nationalarchives.gov.uk/20130107105354/http:/www.dh.gov.uk/prod_consum_dh/groups/dh_digitalassets/@dh/@en/@ps/documents/digitalasset/dh_113155.pdf.

DH (2013) *Policy statement on care and support funding reform and legislative requirements*, London: Department of Health. Available at

DH (2014) *The Care Act.* Available at www.gov.uk/government/uploads/system/uploads/attachment_data/file/365345/Making_Sure_the_Care_Act_Works_EASY_READ.pdf.

Hancock, R., Wittenberg, R., Hu, B., Morciano, M. and Comas-Herrera, A. (2013) *Long-term care funding in England: An analysis of the costs and distributional effects of potential reforms*, HEG Working Paper 13-01. Available at www.uea.ac.uk/documents/2363053/0/Hancock+-+13-01.pdf/5cf20514-c8ae-49a3-8bd2-7b091fc0edd3.

Her Majesty's Government (2012a) *Caring for our future: reforming care and support*, Cm 8378, London: The Stationery Office. Available at www.gov.uk/government/uploads/system/uploads/attachment_data/file/136422/White-Paper-Caring-for-our-future-reforming-care-and-support-PDF-1580K.pdf.

Her Majesty's Government (2012b) *Caring for our future: Progress report on funding reform*, Cm 8381, London: The Stationery Office. Available at www.gov.uk/government/uploads/system/uploads/attachment_data/file/236050/8381.pdf.

Jagger, C., Matthews, R., Lindesay, J. and Brayne, C. (2011) 'The impact of changing patterns of disease on disability and the need for long-term care', *Eurohealth*, vol 17, no 2-3, pp 7-10. Available at www.lse.ac.uk/LSEHealthAndSocialCare/pdf/eurohealth/VOL17No2-3/Jagger_Matthews_Lindesay_Brayne.pdf.

Jarrett, T. (2015) 'Social care: announcement delaying introduction of funding reform (including the cap) and other changes until April 2020 (England)', Commons Briefing Paper CBPO-7265, 6 August. Available at http://researchbriefings.parliament.uk/ResearchBriefing/Summary/CBP-7265.

Malley, J., Hancock, R., Murphy, M., Adams, J., Wittenberg, R., Comas-Herrera, A., Curry, C., King, D., James, S., Morciano, M. and Pickard, L. (2011) 'The effect of lengthening life expectancy on future pension and long-term care expenditure in England, 2007 to 2032', *Health Statistics Quarterly*, vol 52, no 1, pp 33-61.

OBR (Office for Budget Responsibility) (2012) *Fiscal sustainability report, July 2012*, London: The Stationery Office. Available at http://budgetresponsibility.org.uk/fsr/fiscal-sustainability-report-july-2012.

OBR (2017) *Fiscal sustainability report, January 2017*, London: The Stationery Office. Available at http://budgetresponsibility.org.uk/fsr/fiscal-sustainability-report-january-2017.

ONS (Office for National Statistics) (1996) *National population projections, 1994-based*, Series PP2 No. 20, London: The Stationery Office.

ONS (2006) *National population projections, 2004-based*, Series PP2 No. 25, Basingstoke: Palgrave Macmillan.

ONS (2011) *National population projections, 2010-based projections*. Available at http://webarchive.nationalarchives.gov.uk/20160105160709/http://ons.gov.uk/ons/rel/npp/national-population-projections/2010-based-projections/index.html.

Pickard, L. (2015) 'A growing care gap? The supply of unpaid care for older people by their adult children in England to 2032', *Ageing and Society*, vol 35, no 1, pp 96-123.

United Nations (2015) *World Population Prospects: The 2015 Revision*, New York, NY: United Nations Department of Economic and Social Affairs/Population Division. Available at https://esa.un.org/unpd/wpp.

Wittenberg, R., Hu, B., Hancock, R., Morciano, M., Comas-Herrera, A., Malley, J. and King, D. (2011) *Projections of demand for and costs of social care for older people in England, 2010 to 2030, under current and alternative funding systems: Report to the Commission on Funding of Care and Support*, PSSRU Discussion Paper 2811, London: Personal Social Services Research Unit. Available at http://eprints.lse.ac.uk/40720/1/2811-2.pdf.

Part One
Active and healthy

THREE

Working Late: strategies to enhance productive and healthy environments for an older workforce

Cheryl Haslam
Working Late team: Cheryl Haslam, Myanna Duncan,
Aadil Kazi, Ricardo Twumasi, Stacy Clemes, Diane Gyi,
Roger Haslam, Alistair Gibb, Elaine Yolande Gosling,
Lois Kerr, Colette Nicolle, Martin Maguire, Rachel Talbot,
Becky Mallaband, Kevin Morgan, Hilary McDermott

Introduction

Demographic changes, including increased life expectancy and falling birth rates, are reflected in the increasing age of the workforce. Current estimates suggest that by 2020, over a third of the workforce will be aged 50 years or over (DWP, 2013). The increasing age of the workforce presents new opportunities and challenges for government and other agencies, employers and occupational health services, as well as for individual employees and their families. It is now essential to facilitate extended working lives by promoting health in the workplace. The Working Late project investigated the policy issues associated with later life working and developed interventions and design solutions to promote health, productivity and quality of working life of older people. Working Late was conducted between 2008 and 2013 and was uniquely placed to explore the impact of major legislative changes such as increasing the pension age and removing the default retirement age on older workers' employment opportunities and experiences.

New policies are needed to achieve the change in culture necessary to encourage and enable people to work longer (Walker and Maltby, 2012). Improved older worker integration and enhanced employment outcomes among older workers will be key means for enabling economies to adjust to the pressures of population ageing (Banks, 2006). A number of barriers to later life working have been identified, including health conditions or disabilities, caring responsibilities, lack of relevant work experience and vocational skills, transport difficulties and age discrimination (Crawford et al, 2010). Research has shown that age discrimination is still prevalent. Using a matched job application methodology, Riach and Rich (2007) and Tinsley (2012) found significant age discrimination in the job application process regardless of legislation (2006 Employment Equality [Age] Regulations and 2010 Equality Act) against age discrimination in employment.

Previous studies have indicated that age-related decline in health is a major contributor to early exit from the workplace (Strijk et al, 2012). The ageing workforce creates a demand for research to support evidence-based policy and practice promoting and maintaining the health, quality of life and employability of older workers. The workplace is an ideal arena for delivering health education and intervening to promote healthy lifestyle change. It is widely recognised that most adults do not perform sufficient levels of physical activity (Troiano et al, 2008; Conn et al, 2009), yet there is there is compelling evidence to indicate that individuals who are physically active live longer and have lower morbidity that those who are inactive (Allender et al, 2007). Economic advances and industrial innovation have resulted in large numbers of people employed within sedentary occupations (Stamatakis et al, 2007), and data suggests that most adults now spend half their waking hours in the workplace (Church et al, 2011). Recent research has demonstrated that workers spend more time sitting at work than they do sleeping at night (Kazi et al, 2014). Worksite interventions have the potential to reach large numbers of individuals (Pratt et al, 2007) and overcome one of the most widely cited barriers to increasing physical activity: lack of time (Abraham and Graham-Rowe, 2009).

There is growing recognition of the role of occupational health (OH) services in promoting the health of workers across the life course (Ilmarinen, 2006, 2010; Crawford et al, 2010). OH providers are already facing important challenges, including the prevention of work-related diseases; reductions in work performance due to chronic diseases; and the promotion of health and workability (Ilmarinen, 2006). OH services are likely to play a key role in 'healthy ageing management' in the workplace, offering considerable scope for improving employee health outcomes and improving the quality of working life.

Workplace and work systems design are also important in supporting the ageing workforce, with these needing to adapt to accommodate changing physical and cognitive abilities across the life course (Moyers and Coleman, 2004). While such an approach has intuitive appeal, little work to date has focused on the needs of older workers. Stubbs

(2000) recommended a multidisciplinary approach to workplace design incorporating ergonomics and occupational medicine, using participatory design techniques to allow users to communicate their needs and aspirations. Workplace design can have a substantial influence on working practices and an individual's ability to undertake certain aspects of work. Loch and colleagues (2010) reported the adaptations made by car manufacturer BMW, which developed a pilot line of production workers with a mean age of 47, the mean age projected for BMW plant workers by 2017. Seventy changes were made, such as managing healthcare, enhancing workers' skills and the workplace environment, and instituting part-time policies and change management processes. These changes resulted in a 7% increase of productivity in one year. With demographic changes transforming the structure of today's workforce, there has never been a more pressing need to develop new tools and resources supporting the inclusion and wellbeing of older workers.

Aims and methods of the research

Working Late explored the practice and policy issues associated with later life working. The research investigated later life working across three main contextual themes: employment context, occupational health context and the work environment. The project developed and evaluated interventions and design solutions to promote health and quality of working life across the life course.

The project aims were:

- to adopt continuous and active engagement with agencies, employers and older workers to guide the research process and deliver effective and wide-ranging dissemination of the findings and outputs;
- to identify barriers and facilitators to working late, including examination of work participation and organisational policies, the impact of age discrimination legislation and the logistics of the journey to work;
- to identify optimal, evidence-based occupational health provision and collate current best practice in occupational health services accommodating the older worker;
- to develop, implement and evaluate workplace interventions to promote the health and workability of workers across the life course, and produce evidence-based interventions and innovative health education materials to promote health at work;

- to focus on work environment design to develop the Organiser for Working Late (OWL), a web-based resource to facilitate the design of work systems, equipment, tools, technologies, facilities and the built environment to achieve inclusive, productive workplaces.

The Working Late research comprised a series of interlinked projects. The research involved a mixed-methods approach, comprising focus groups, interviews, surveys and interventions. The project was underpinned by extensive user engagement to inform the research process. Users were defined as those individuals ultimately affected by the research, as well as individuals who use the findings. User engagement involved a bottom-up approach to the research process, ensuring the research incorporated input from older workers rather than being just 'about' older workers. Throughout the research, user engagement forums were held with older workers, representatives from industry and trade unions and members of the New Dynamics of Ageing programme's Older People's Reference Group (OPRG). Involving users in the research process provided a wide range of benefits, including added perspectives and expertise of user groups, new contacts and organisational links, and help with recruitment and dissemination.

To ensure wide distribution of the research outputs, a mixed-media dissemination strategy was employed whereby findings were shared with the scientific community, organisations and policymakers through journal articles, conference papers, press releases and news reports, videos, the Working Late website (www.workinglate.org) and social media promotion. A Working Late newsletter was produced on a six-monthly basis. The final research outputs were presented and the project resources launched at the Working Late showcase event held at the BT Auditorium in London in March 2013.

Dynamics of later life working

Many legislative changes have occurred in recent years in response to the ageing population. These include age discrimination legislation, removal of the default retirement age and equalisation of men's and women's state pension ages. Given the widespread impact of these changes, the Working Late research sought to identify the practice and policy implications of later life working. A comprehensive literature review was conducted to inform the development of the interview schedules used in the research. To further inform the development of the interview schedule, user engagement panels were conducted with representatives from trade unions, Age UK and the OPRG.

A total of 110 interviews were conducted, comprising 51 employees aged over 50 years, 20 employers, 27 jobseekers over the age of 50, and 12 recently retired individuals. Following data transcription and analysis, the findings were presented and discussed at a series of four expert panels with human resources (HR) professionals, OH experts, line managers, employment lawyers, trade union representatives, civil servants and academics. The aim of the expert panels was to explore the practice and policy implications of the findings.

The journey to work

Issues with the journey to work may be a factor influencing workers' decisions about whether to continue working in later life. This aspect of the Working Late project examined the journey to work from the perspective of older workers and explored the problems that older workers may experience with their commute to work and the strategies they adopt to mitigate travel issues.

The first stage of the research involved identifying the main issues associated with the journey to work and their influence on employment. This was achieved by holding user engagement discussions with experts, employer representatives and older workers. The discussions served to inform the development of a questionnaire that aimed to examine the extent to which the journey to work may prove a barrier to older workers. A total of 1,215 completed questionnaires were returned, which provided insight into travel difficulties encountered as well as potential future travel difficulties anticipated. In order to gather more detailed information on problems with the journey to work and strategies that employees may use to overcome them, 36 interviews were conducted with employees over the age of 45. Finally, 12 employers were interviewed to assess the ways in which employers may assist employees with their journey to work. The findings were presented to an expert panel to explore the practical implications.

Occupational health provision

The research also aimed to evaluate the strategies used by OH services to promote health and wellbeing at work. This was initially guided by a literature review that suggested that there is a need for occupational health provision and intervention that takes account of the older workforce (McDermott et al, 2010). Fifty-one preliminary interviews were conducted with OH experts and stakeholders in order to identify current workplace health promotion initiatives. These interviews helped inform the development of a survey targeted at employees that aimed to explore access to, and experiences of, OH services. The survey, completed by 1,141 employees, also provided detailed information on employees' physical activity levels, sitting time, work ability, general health and job attitudes. Finally, six focus groups were conducted (four with employees and two with OH representatives) to assess the barriers and facilitators to delivering health interventions, and to explore opportunities for future workplace health promotion activities. This phase of the research served to inform the development of the workplace intervention.

Walking Works Wonders intervention

The findings from the OH provision research were used to guide the development of a 12-month multidimensional physical activity health intervention that promoted incidental walking, active commuting, exercise at work and pedometer-based initiatives. The intervention was targeted at employees of all ages.

A total of 1,120 employees took part in the intervention. Participants were recruited from 10 different worksites across the UK: Dundee, Edinburgh, Glasgow, Leeds, Liverpool, London, Newcastle and Ipswich (three sites) and were drawn from two different organisations (one medium-sized public sector and one large private sector organisation). The 10 worksites were each assigned one of three conditions: staged intervention, standard intervention or control group. In the staged intervention group, the health information received was tailored according to recipients' readiness for change. Those thinking about increasing their levels of physical activity were given practical advice about changing behaviour, whereas those not thinking about increasing their physical activity levels were targeted with awareness-raising information about the risks of sedentary behaviour and the benefits of physical activity. In the standard condition, participants received generic physical activity promotion material already available via health promotion organisations. All participants, including the control group, received Working Late pedometers to record daily step counts.

Participants received one-to-one physiological health assessments at six-monthly intervals. Assessments included measures of blood pressure, resting heart rate, waist-to-hip ratio, height and body composition analysis. Participants also completed psychological health measures in the form of a questionnaire at each assessment period. Following the one-year intervention period, a further two health assessments were conducted at 18 and 24 months to evaluate the long-term impact of the intervention. To supplement the quantitative data collected from the health screenings, 56 interviews were conducted with participants. These interviews provided real-life examples of the ways in which participating in the health intervention affected individuals' lives both inside and outside of the workplace.

The Working Late team partnered with the Royal Society for the encouragement of Arts, Manufactures and Commerce to launch a national competition for designers to develop innovative ways of encouraging people to be more active at work. The competition was judged by a panel chaired by Professor Jeremy Myerson, Director of the Helen Hamlyn Centre of Design at the Royal College of Art. The winners of the competition were graduates from Kingston University, Jenny Rice and Rachael Ball Risk, who designed the Walking Lunch initiative.

Walking Lunch involves placing a large map (one metre in diameter) in a communal area of a worksite (see photographs overleaf). The map covers a radius of 1.5 km and displays the surrounding areas of the workplace. The aim is to encourage employees to use their lunchtime breaks for a local walk. When employees arrive at an area on the map, they are encouraged to take a photo on their mobile phone or digital camera; they then return to the office, print out the photo and pin it to the map using tags. The tags have space for employees to record the number of steps taken to get to the location in the image and any other useful information. This encourages other employees to visit these areas. Participants in the Walking Works Wonders intervention were also provided with an individual (smaller) paper version of the map to track their journey and make any notes.

Organiser for Working Late

Through close collaboration with industry, this component of the research aimed to encourage managers and workers to think about healthy ageing at work. This led to the co-development of the OWL resource, which aims to facilitate communication in relation to design in the workplace. Underpinning the research was a belief that industry can learn from older and experienced workers about good design, in terms of encouraging healthy behaviour and healthy ageing.

A total of 21 industrial collaborators participated in a questionnaire survey (n = 719) that explored the design of work tasks, tools, environments and the effect of these on workers, both physically and

mentally. Ergonomic observations and interviews were conducted with employees (n = 32) in four collaborating organisations in the areas of construction, office work, manufacturing and animal care. In order to explore employee interactions within the workplace and the influence of design issues, ergonomic observations were conducted using an ergonomics toolkit incorporating the Nordic Musculoskeletal Questionnaire, anthropometry and discomfort ratings, and the Rapid Entire Body Assessment. The aim was to gain an in-depth understanding of how employees interact with the design in their workplace. This resulted in 130 hours of observations. Images, audio and video recordings were captured to highlight individual working conditions.

Following the observations, a series of focus groups were conducted where employees were encouraged to reflect on their work, to consider how health and ageing affected their ability to work and discuss design ideas and solutions to specific problems. These findings contributed to the production of the OWL resource, iteratively co-developed by the research team and participating organisations. The resource further included evaluation by 15 programme testers, managers and associated stakeholders who focused on checking the accuracy and quality of the content during implementation and evaluation.

Findings

Dynamics of later life working

Employers reported that older workers were essential in maintaining knowledge, skills and experience in their organisations. Recruiting and retaining older workers was seen as a benefit in responding to the changing demographics and needs of customers and clients. However, a minority of line managers, with little experience of age-diverse workforces, reported selection of candidates on the basis of age, irrespective of organisational policy or discrimination legislation. An insight into age bias in recruitment was shared by a 26-year-old manager who was in the process of recruiting a replacement for his role in the marketing and communications sector:

> We're actually looking for someone between the ages of 25 and 35. That's not being ageist but that's just ensuring they've got the energy, the drive and the passion to learn. It is a development role as such so you wouldn't necessarily want an expert to just come in because they would find it too easy and it wouldn't be demanding enough for them.

In line with this, older jobseekers often felt that age is taken into account in recruitment. Some older jobseekers reported that they sometimes concealed details that could be used to work out their age from their CV, or they specifically targeted age-friendly employers rather than make complaints about applications that they feel may have been rejected on the grounds of their age. The majority of jobseekers over 50 reported that the advice they received from job centres and other employment agencies was inadequate and that they needed support more tailored to older jobseekers.

Flexible working policies such as flexi-time, part-time working, jobsharing, working from home, and workplace accommodations were considered most beneficial in helping employees continue working into later life. However, it was interesting to note that older workers would like these policies to be available to all age groups and are typically against specific 'older worker policies'. Although these policies are most sought after by employees with health concerns or caring responsibilities, they offer benefits to employees of all age groups. A senior manager at a large UK organisation reinforced this point:

> The carers' and flexible working policies are not just aimed at older people, it's actually for everybody so that it's a fair policy.

Offering policies that aim to extend healthy working lives across the workforce is an important step in taking a life-span approach to promoting later life working. An age-positive organisational culture is also essential in responding to the demographic changes of the workforce. Examples of best practice, and, in particular, promotion of best practice initiatives, may help organisations, particularly those without HR departments, to effectively manage age diversity.

In many interviews with older workers, the term 'career development' was deemed inappropriate in reference to an older individual's working life. The majority of interviewees aimed to keep the same role, or secure long-term contracts in a particular role, rather than progress their career. With an increasing number of individuals on short, fixed-term contracts, the securing of a long-term contract was a commonly stated goal. Additionally, many interviewees aimed to achieve a satisfactory work–life balance. In the context of discussing possible career moves, the following quote from a 53-year-old employee captures this outlook:

> I'm not intending to look for promotion but to maintain the grade that I'm on and just maybe a sideways move really.

These perceptions formed a theme defined by the authors as 'homeostasis of career', which refers to stability or balance of career. Older workers regarded this balance of work in relation to other commitments as a positive career position in later-life working.

A series of representative video case studies have been filmed using quotes from this research and, in some cases, the participants from the interviews. These video case studies are accompanied by a series of videoed interview responses from a range of experts (www.youtube.com/user/workinglateproject).

The journey to work

Issues with the journey to work may be a factor influencing older workers' choices about whether to continue working. This aspect of the Working Late project therefore examined the journey to work from the perspective of older workers and explored the issues that older workers may experience with their commute to work and the strategies adopted to alleviate travel problems.

Around a quarter of the survey sample reported problems with their journey to work (involving cost, stress, health, fatigue and time), although the likelihood of an employee reporting problems with their journey to work did not necessarily increase with age. However, the implications of travel difficulties did change as individuals became older. Specifically, a younger person having problems may be more likely to change jobs, while an older person experiencing difficulties may be more likely to consider giving up work.

A wide range of strategies were identified that could help alleviate issues with the journey to work. These strategies included downsizing to a smaller or more efficient car; changing travel route; car sharing; flexible working; and working from home. The research also explored initiatives employers had used to assist their employees with their journey to work. For the majority of employers, no specific schemes were adopted except for general working practices, such as working from home and/or other flexible working patterns.

The research results guided the development of the Improving the Journey to Work resource pack, which was designed and evaluated by employee and employer representatives with the aim of feeding into practical policy initiatives to support older workers. The resource is available online and in paper form to ensure ease of accessibility in the workplace (www.workinglate.org/research/journey).

Occupational health provision

Contact with OH services and participation in health initiatives was not commonly reported by participants in this survey. Over two thirds had never had contact with OH services, and for those that did, the main reasons were sickness absence monitoring and musculoskeletal disorders. Where OH initiatives had been promoted within organisations, 62.3% of respondents stated that they did not participate because they felt such schemes were not suitable or were poorly executed, with limited information and/or communication to employees.

The research also obtained data on employees' physical activity levels, indicating that only 22% of the sample met recommended guidelines for physical activity, namely 30 minutes of moderately intensive activity five times a week. Data was also obtained on sitting time in a range of different contexts, for example, at work, in transport, at home, and sleeping. The data indicated that sitting time at work accounted for more than half of the total daily sitting time and that individuals spend more time sitting at work than they do sleeping at night (Kazi et al, 2014). When body mass index (BMI) was examined in relation to sitting time, individuals in the obese BMI category (30+) reported significantly higher sitting times compared with individuals in the normal (18.5-24.9) and overweight (25-29.9) BMI categories.

Walking Works Wonders intervention

Individuals provided with staged intervention information demonstrated the biggest reduction in BMI. Walking for staged and standard intervention groups increased, whereas the control group showed a reduction.

Figure 3.1: Walking activity reported for the standard intervention, tailored intervention and control groups

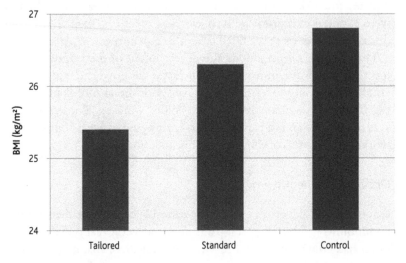

There were significant reductions in self-reported sickness absence for employees participating in the study: this averaged 1.16 days per person per year. Employees also reported their work performance increasing by 10% over the previous year. Exploration of age revealed no differences between the results for employees aged over or under 50 years, indicating that the intervention was effective for workers of all ages. Finally, an economic evaluation calculated that the return on investment for the intervention was strongly positive. Specifically, for

Figure 3.2: BMI for the tailored intervention, standard intervention and control groups at 12 months

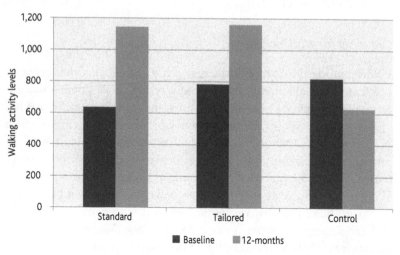

every £1 the organisation invested, savings of £26–£32 could be made in terms of reduced absence and increased performance.

The Walking Lunch concept was very well received, and the Walking Lunch map was viewed by participants as an innovative means of promoting physical activity and reducing sedentary time. Participants were keen to share the photographs they had taken during their explorations of the areas surrounding their worksites, and readily pinned them to the Walking Lunch map. One of the worksites in particular embraced the Walking Lunch initiative and created a number of supplementary leaflets, including details of local walks provided for all staff. Allied to this, the Walking Works Wonders website was exceptionally popular, with participants logging over 60,000 step counts, demonstrating their commitment and engagement to the initiative. Further evidence for this was provided during our interviews, where participants were very keen to share with us the ways in which engaging in the Walking Works Wonders initiative had had an impact on their lives. Many individuals commented how the project had made them realise how sedentary they were, and they discovered how making small, sustainable changes could have a big impact on overall activity levels. Participants also discussed the wider, positive influence on family life, dietary behaviour and health attitudes.

An online film was produced showcasing the impact of the intervention on the employees and organisations that took part in the research. It contains very positive testimonials from employee participants and strong endorsements from chief medical officers and OH advisers of participating organisations (www.youtube.com/watch?v=9ZKm9OsclNI).

Organiser for Working Late

Underpinning this aspect of the research was the belief that industry can learn from older and experienced workers about good design, in terms of encouraging healthy behaviours, and therefore healthy ageing.

The findings indicated that many workers from a cross-section of different industries and job types experienced a high level of musculoskeletal symptoms. The prevalence was high for both older workers (aged 50 and over) and younger workers (aged 49 or less). Workers aged 50 years and over expressed concerns about being able to remain fit and healthy for work, their ability to complete job tasks and keeping up work performance as they age. Workers recognised that their workplaces could be better designed to promote their health but they perceived they were not empowered to make changes. The concept of a 'workplace good design champion' was suggested to facilitate the identification and implementation of good practice.

More than 200 design ideas relating to healthy working and reducing physical and mental stress on the body were captured from the research, with over half deemed as low- or no-cost ideas. The outputs from the research led to the co-development of the OWL resource, which aims to facilitate communication in relation to design in the workplace. OWL includes design tools, personal stories, and audio and video clips of design ideas to assist discussion of health needs with employees. The tool is based around two themes, namely **the body at work**, which includes a suite of image and word cards based around the body, the work environment, equipment and actions, and **healthy ageing through design**, which demonstrates the diversity of the ideas and personal stories that workers had in relation to their health and age at work. OWL is available online through a variety of platforms, including PC, tablet and smart phone (www.workinglate-owl.org).

Implications of the research

The findings and outputs from the Working Late project have wide-ranging implications, not only in terms of organisational policy and practice, but also at an individual and societal level.

The research findings from the dynamics of later life working component have highlighted the importance of organisations providing flexible working policies to support employees continuing their jobs into later life. It is evident that if age discrimination is left unchallenged, this will present a significant barrier to the opportunities of older workers, in turn contributing to a loss of skills and experience in the workforce. Promoting an age-positive organisational culture is therefore of key importance, and examples of best practice may be particularly beneficial in helping smaller organisations effectively manage issues surrounding age diversity. The video case studies and expert responses from this research have generated significant interest, with organisations and academic institutions requesting to use these videos in their training and educational materials. There is significant scope to extend this further, and the aim is to develop these videos into an interactive training resource for HR staff and managers to facilitate best practice in responding to the changes of an ageing workforce within their organisations.

The tangible suggestions provided in the Improving the Journey to Work resource pack offer many and varied solutions for both employers and employees when considering issues surrounding transportation to and from the workplace. While the likelihood of an employee having problems with their journey to work does not necessarily increase with age, the implications may differ. In particular, younger employees may consider changing jobs to address travel problems, while older employees may consider retiring earlier. Consequently, the research has highlighted that the provision of flexible working policies may assist older employees considering retirement as a result of journey difficulties to consider other options. The Improving the Journey to Work resource may also serve to stimulate discussions between employees and employers regarding travel problems.

The Working Late research has further provided insights into the barriers and facilitators of engaging employees in OH programmes and has subsequently developed tailored programmes based on this feedback. It is evident that considerable scope exists for the promotion of workplace health interventions across a range of organisational contexts. This has the potential to provide opportunities for sharing best practice in occupational health provision to the benefit of individuals and organisations alike. Furthermore, the research was particularly fruitful in identifying that while future workplace physical activity interventions may target physical activity, it is also important to consider addressing the amounts of time employees spend sitting at work, given that this is increasingly recognised as a major public health issue.

The implications of the OWL initiative stem from the support provided for both workers and managers when considering workplace design. The OWL encourages employers to understand, engage with and respond positively to diversity in the workplace. The portfolio of tools incorporated into the OWL, including audio and video clips of design ideas, personal stories and design tools, facilitate discussion of health needs with employees. Consequently, OWL may facilitate communication within and between organisations for creating inclusive workplaces. OWL has applications across a range of industries and offers design solutions for promoting a healthy work environment, including consideration of layout and equipment issues.

Finally, and importantly, one of the key features of the Working Late project has been the active and continuous engagement with agencies, employers and older workers to guide the research process and deliver effective and wide-ranging dissemination of the findings and outputs. This has implications for the way in which research is conducted and provides an exemplar for future user engagement.

Working Late has generated worldwide media interest. The next steps for dissemination and extension of the research include wider distribution of the resources to industry, further collaboration with industry partners and further publication of research outputs at the academic, policy and practice level. Following the success of the Walking Works Wonders research, the intervention has now been developed into a commercial service for organisations and is being offered to businesses in the public and private sector (www.walkingworkswonders.com).

Recommendations

There are five key recommendations from the research:

- The ageing workforce presents challenges and opportunities, and to benefit from an increasingly age-diverse workforce, organisations need to promote the integration of younger and older workers.
- For older jobseekers, the perception of age discrimination represents an important barrier to confidence, motivation and opportunities during the employment search. If age discrimination is left unchallenged, it may lead to a significant loss of skills and experience in the workplace. Age-positive organisational culture is essential to respond to demographic changes of the workforce.
- Problems with the journey to work may be a factor influencing workers' decisions about whether to continue working in later life. A range of strategies is available to alleviate travel difficulties, and organisations should facilitate discussion of such issues among

employees and managers and develop practical policy initiatives to support older workers in this respect.

- With the shift from manufacturing to service industries, combined with technological advances, work has become increasingly sedentary. Sedentary behaviour is an important risk factor for a wide range of chronic diseases. To support later-life working, organisations must manage this health risk and consider implementing interventions to encourage physical activity and reduce sedentary behaviour.
- To support later–life working, workplace design needs to adapt to the changing needs of workers as they age in a way that is sensitive, socially acceptable and inclusive.
- Older and experienced workers are a valuable source of knowledge; such knowledge can inform good design aimed at encouraging healthy behaviour and healthy ageing in the workplace.

Key findings

- An age-diverse workforce maintains knowledge, skills and experience within organisations. Promoting an age-positive culture is key, and examples of best practice can help organisations manage age diversity.
- Flexible working practices such as flexi-time, part-time working and working from home can prove beneficial in helping employees continue working into later life.
- Work is becoming increasingly sedentary and this is a major public health issue, given that sedentary behaviour is an independent risk factor for a wide range of chronic diseases.
- The research developed tailored workplace interventions to promote physical activity and reduce sedentary behaviour in workers of all ages. The Walking Works Wonders intervention improved productivity and quality of working life, and reduced sickness absence, thus providing economic benefits to organisations.
- Issues with the journey to work may influence employees' choices about whether to continue working into later life. The Improving the Journey to Work resource was developed to help explore different methods of travelling to work and to facilitate discussion among employees and employers.
- Older workers have concerns about being fit for work and their ability to do their job in the future. Workers can provide useful input to design when thinking about reducing physical stress on the body. More than 200 design ideas relating to healthy working and reducing physical and mental stress on the body were captured from participants in the research. Over half were deemed to be low- or no-cost ideas.

Conclusion

The increasing age of the working population presents opportunities and challenges for individuals and employers alike. The Working Late project endeavoured to provide evidence-based resources to facilitate active ageing and later life working. Working Late has raised the profile of the ageing workforce and produced new knowledge of how organisational policy and practice affects the employment experiences of older workers. Investigating experiences of older jobseekers has highlighted some of the ways employers may discriminate on the basis of age. The journey to work and the options, enablers and barriers workers may face were investigated and a travel resource was generated to help identify and manage commuting problems. The research evaluated employees' experiences of previous workplace health promotion initiatives and used the results to inform the development of a new and innovative physical activity intervention. The Walking Works Wonders intervention was designed, implemented and successfully evaluated in worksites across the UK. Finally the web resource OWL was developed to support workers and managers using tools that aid communication in relation to good design and ergonomics, promoting an inclusive workplace. Widespread adoption of the Working Late resources will contribute to improved working practices, support services and working environment, allowing freedom of access to work and improved quality of working life for older people.

References

Abraham, C., and Graham-Rowe, E. (2009) 'Are worksite interventions effective in increasing physical activity? A systematic review and meta-analysis', *Health Psychology Review*, vol 3, no 1, pp 108-44.

Allender, S., Foster, C., Scarborough, P. and Rayner, M. (2007) 'The burden of physical activity-related ill health in the UK', *Journal of Epidemiology and Community Health*, vol 61, no 4, pp 344-48.

Banks, J. (2006) 'Economic capabilities, choices and outcomes at older ages', *Fiscal Studies*, vol 27, no 1, pp 281-311.

Church, T.S., Thomas, D.M., Tudor-Locke, C., Katzmarzyk, P.T., Earnest, C.P., Rodarte, R.Q., Martin, C.K. et al (2011) 'Trends over 5 decades in U.S. occupation-related physical activity and their associations with obesity', *PLOS ONE*, vol 6, no 5, E19657.

Conn, V.S., Hafdahl, A.R., Cooper, P.S., Brown, L.M. and Lusk, S.L. (2009) 'Meta-analysis of workplace physical activity interventions', *American Journal of Preventive Medicine*, vol 37, no 4, pp 330-9.

Crawford, J.O., Graveling, R.A., Cowie, H.A., Dixon, K. and MacCalman, L. (2010) 'The health safety and health promotion needs of older workers', *Occupational Medicine*, vol 60, no 3, pp 184-92.

DWP (Department for Work and Pensions) (2013) *Employing older workers: An employer's guide to today's multi-generational workforce*, London: DWP.

Ilmarinen, J. (2006) 'The ageing workforce – challenges for occupational health', *Occupational Medicine*, vol 56, no 6, pp 362-4.

Ilmarinen, J. (2010) '30 years of work ability and 20 years of age management in Finland', Paper presented at the 4th Symposium on Work Ability, Tampere, Finland, June.

Kazi, A., Duncan, M., Clemes, S. and Haslam, C. (2014) 'A survey of sitting time among UK employees', *Occupational Medicine*, vol 64, no 7, pp 497-502.

Loch C.H., Sting F.J., Bauer, N. and Mauermann, H. (2010) 'How BMW is defusing the demographic time bomb', *Harvard Business Review*, vol 88, no 3, pp 99-104.

McDermott, H., Kazi, A., Munir, F. and Haslam, C. (2010) Developing occupational health services for active age management', *Occupational Medicine*, vol 60, no 3, pp 193-204.

Moyers, P.A. and Coleman, S.D. (2004) 'Adaptation of the older worker to occupational challenges', *Work*, vol 22, no 2, pp 71-8.

Pratt, C.A., Lemon, I.D.F., Goetzel, R., Stevens, V.J., Vogt, T.M. and Webber, L.S. (2007) 'Design characteristics of worksite environmental interventions for obesity prevention', *Obesity*, vol 15, no 9, pp 2171-80.

Riach, P.A. and Rich, J. (2007) *An experimental investigation of age discrimination in the English labor market*, Bonn: Institute for the Study of Labor.

Stamatakis, E., Ekelund, U. and Wareham, N.J. (2007) 'Temporal trends in physical activity in England: the Health Survey for England 1991 to 2004', *Preventive Medicine*, vol 45 no 6, pp 416-23.

Strijk, J.E., Proper, K.I., Van Der Beek, A.J. and Van Mechelen, W. (2012) 'A worksite vitality intervention to improve older workers' lifestyle and vitality-related outcomes: results of a randomised controlled trial', *Journal of Epidemiology & Community Health*, vol 66, no 11, pp 1071-8.

Stubbs, D.A. (2000) 'Ergonomics and occupational medicine: future challenges', *Occupational Medicine*, vol 50, no 4, pp 277-82.

Tinsley, M. (2012) *Too much to lose: Understanding and supporting Britain's older workers*, London: Policy Exchange.

Troiano, R.P., Berrigan, D., Dodd, K.W., Masse, L.C., Tilert, T. and McDowell, M. (2008) 'Physical activity in the United States measured by accelerometer', *Medicine & Science in Sports & Exercise*, vol 40, no 1, pp 181-8.

Walker, A. and Maltby, T. (2012) 'Active ageing: a strategic policy solution to demographic ageing in the European Union', *International Journal of Social Welfare*, vol 21, no s1, pp S117-S130.

FOUR

Healthy ageing across the life course

Diana Kuh, Rebecca Hardy, Catharine Gale, Jane Elliott,
Yoav Ben-Shlomo, Rachel Cooper and the HALCyon team

Introduction

The New Dynamics of Ageing (NDA) project Healthy Ageing across
the Life Course (HALCyon) responded to a growing consensus from
scientists, research funders and policymakers that ageing needs to
be studied from an interdisciplinary and life course perspective to
inform strategies for maintaining a population that remains healthy
and independent for longer.

Healthy ageing is a term that is used by many and is either undefined
or has multiple meanings; this inhibits both the research and policy
agendas. In HALCyon, we use the term **biological ageing** to capture
the progressive generalised impairment of function ('senescence') that
occurs post-maturity, caused by multiple factors, such as the growing
dysregulation of homeostatic equilibrium, inflammation, oxidative
stress and loss of immune function. There is a growing consensus that
molecular and cellular damage that underlies biological ageing starts
in utero and accumulates across life. We defined healthy biological
ageing as including three components: first, survival to old age; second,
delay in the onset of chronic diseases or disorders (the compression of
morbidity); and third, optimal functioning for the maximal period of
time, both at the individual level (measured by self-reports or objective
tests of capacity to undertake the physical and mental tasks of daily
living), and at the molecular, cellular and body system levels (Kuh et
al, 2014b; Ferrucci et al, 2015; Ben-Shlomo et al, 2016).

HALCyon research focused on the third component of healthy
biological ageing: optimal functioning. We used the terms physical
and cognitive capability to describe functioning at the individual level
as these terms emphasise the positive, and are distinguished from the
functioning of each of the many different body systems on which
capability depends (Cooper et al, 2014b; Richards et al, 2014).

Healthy ageing is also viewed, especially by older people themselves, as maintaining psychological and social wellbeing, namely how one feels and functions socially, with increasing age. Unlike physical and cognitive capability, there is little evidence for a decline in psychological and social wellbeing with age, except perhaps at the oldest ages. As evidence grows that most people age with some form of chronic disease or disorder, (Pierce et al, 2012), finding ways to support individuals or adapt the environment to maintain wellbeing gains importance.

A life course approach to healthy ageing

There is growing evidence from life course research in the population sciences that the ability to respond adaptively, either biologically, mentally or socially, is governed not only by current environmental challenges and genetic factors, but also by the response to earlier life challenges, especially at times of developmental plasticity (Kuh and Ben-Shlomo, 2004; Gluckman et al, 2009). Evidence was initially drawn from single cohort studies and the research generally focused on chronic diseases and their foetal and infant origins (Barker, 1992). Increasingly, systematic reviews are bringing together all of the available evidence, with meta-analyses being carried out where possible, and the research is now focused on functional ageing as well as chronic disease outcomes, and on social and biological risk factors across life and not just *in utero* and infancy (Kuh et al, 2014a). What remains missing is any life course perspective on healthy ageing; until recently studies of healthy ageing have been cross-sectional or limited to the study of factors from midlife at the earliest, with little attempt at cross cohort research (Ben-Shlomo et al, 2016).

HALCyon harnessed the power of using data from a number of UK cohort studies to investigate functional ageing and wellbeing, and their lifetime determinants and consequences. The UK has an enviable wealth of birth cohort studies as well as longitudinal studies starting later in life with regular repeated waves of data collection. The birth cohort studies are maturing into studies of ageing. Combining information from several cohorts maximises their value, by increasing power to detect associations, and testing whether these associations are robust and generalisable across cohorts, or differ in response to changing societal conditions. This requires comparable harmonised data across studies, as well as the application of longitudinal methods to model ageing and risk factor trajectories, and the development of additional methods to combine data across cohorts.

Aims and methods of the research

HALCyon brought together investigators on nine cohort studies covering 30,000 participants born between 1921 and 1958, to investigate how healthy ageing is affected by factors operating across the whole of life. The cohorts included were the two oldest British birth cohort studies, the Medical Research Council (MRC) National Survey of Health and Development (NSHD) and the National Child Development Study (NCDS), which have followed large nationally representative samples of the British population since their birth in March 1946 and March 1958 respectively; five historical cohorts (the Lothian Birth Cohort 1921, Aberdeen Birth Cohort 1936, Hertfordshire Cohort Study [HCS], Hertfordshire Ageing Study and Boyd Orr Cohort Study) where some data (for example, birth and infant health records, childhood cognitive test results) were collected in childhood and participants were retraced and followed up in adulthood; and two cohorts (the English Longitudinal Study of Ageing [ELSA] and the Caerphilly Prospective Study [CaPS]) that started in adult life but have repeat measures of functional ageing. A description of the HALCyon cohort studies and information on 28 investigators is given on the website (www.halcyon.ac.uk).

HALCyon investigated three domains of healthy ageing: physical and cognitive capability; psychological and social wellbeing; and aspects of underlying biology at the cellular and physiological system levels. For capability, we focused on objective measures such as grip strength, gait speed, chair rise and standing balance times, verbal memory and processing speed. For wellbeing, we initially used measures of anxiety and depression, until comparable measures of positive wellbeing, namely the Warwick Edinburgh Mental Wellbeing Scale (WEMWBS) (Tennant et al, 2007), a neighbourhood cohesion scale (Buckner, 1988) and the Diener Life Satisfaction Scale (Diener et al, 1985) had been collected across a number of the HALCyon cohorts. For the biological measures, we concentrated on telomere length, measured twice in four of the cohorts, the stress hormone cortisol (measured in four of the cohorts), and a range of genetic variants (single nucleotide polymorphisms) where there was growing evidence of their link with age-related diseases and functional measures.

As well as looking at the interrelationships between the three different domains, other factors chosen for investigation in association with these three domains included lifetime socioeconomic position; childhood cognitive ability and education; and diet and body size. This choice partly was based on scientific evidence, at least from single studies, that these life course factors are important for healthy ageing; the aim of HALCyon therefore was to supply more robust cross-cohort evidence. The choice was also pragmatic as these factors had each been assessed in several of the cohorts.

HALCyon's analytical strategy was threefold: to undertake systematic reviews of the literature and, where appropriate, meta-analyses of all available studies; new cross-cohort research with harmonised data, consistent analysis, and investigation of confounding variables; and in-depth analysis of data from single cohorts that exploited their special features. Data harmonisation is widely and regularly discussed but less often undertaken, especially in ageing research (Cooper et al, 2011a). The experience gained by the HALCyon core team in data harmonisation of both outcomes and explanatory variables is being shared with the wider scientific community, and being applied to other cross-cohort collaborations under the auspices of research networks such as Cohort & Longitudinal Studies Enhancement Resources (CLOSER; www.closer.ac.uk) and Integrative Analysis of Longitudinal Studies of Aging and Dementia (IALSA; https://www.maelstrom-research.org/mica/network/ialsa). Supplementary funding from the Canadian Institutes of Health Research facilitated joint research between IALSA and HALCyon.

To complement this quantitative approach, we also undertook qualitative biographical interviews with 60 study members from two of the cohort studies (NSHD and HCS), in addition to a sample of 220 already undertaken for the 1958 cohort. This qualitative study used narrative methods to understand the meanings for individuals of life events and experiences; this was a powerful tool to understand healthy ageing from an individual's perspective, particularly when also combined with a quantitative approach (Elliott et al, 2014; Parsons et al, 2014).

So far, 56 papers and a book reviewing the evidence for life course influences on healthy ageing (Kuh et al, 2014b) have been published from the HALCyon project. The next section summarises the key findings.

Findings

Two systematic reviews from the HALCyon team showed that weaker grip strength, slower walking and chair rise speeds and poorer standing balance performance were consistently associated with higher rates of mortality and subsequent morbidity risk in older community-dwelling populations (Cooper et al, 2010, 2011b), providing support for these objective indicators of physical capability as summary measures of ageing (Lara et al, 2015). We have subsequently addressed some of the research gaps identified in these reviews by investigating the associations of physical capability with all-cause mortality in the NSHD, which measured physical capability at a younger age than many previous studies (Cooper et al, 2014b). These additional analyses highlighted the value of assessing physical capability in midlife and the potential of these measures to identify at relatively young ages those people who are less likely to achieve a long and healthy life.

With harmonised HALCyon datasets we showed that older study participants have lower levels of performance in all of these tests than younger participants, and that men generally perform better in these tests than women, although gender differences in grip strength diminish with increasing age (Cooper et al, 2011a). In contrast, Gale and colleagues showed no evidence of difference in the mean wellbeing score by age across the HALCyon cohorts using WEMWBS (Gale et al, 2012b). We subsequently added data from other available studies to provide normative data on grip strength at different ages (Dodds et al, 2014) and to show its global variation (Dodds et al, 2016).

Does it all go together when it goes?

One question commonly asked is whether 'it all goes together when it goes'. While cross-sectional evidence is consistent in showing that physical and cognitive capability are strongly correlated, far fewer longitudinal studies exist. A HALCyon and IALSA systematic review of the dynamic relationship between physical capability and cognition in longitudinal ageing cohorts (Clouston et al, 2013) identified 36 studies of interest, but only seven had investigated *change* in fluid cognition with *change* in physical capability. Overall, findings were not sufficiently strong or consistent to support evidence of a common process of decline. Measurement challenges limited comparability, identifying the need for common protocols and approaches.

The HALCyon team also looked at the bidirectional links between capability and wellbeing. Our review of the literature provided reasonable evidence that wellbeing may be protective of physical and cognitive capability, as well as being affected by functional decline (Gale et al, 2014). Using five of the HALCyon cohorts, the team showed that higher levels of physical capability were associated with higher levels of subsequent mental wellbeing (as measured by WEMWBS). However, these associations were modest, and adjustment for potential confounders including age, gender, socioeconomic position, living alone, health status and levels of neuroticism explained a large part of these associations (Cooper et al, 2014a). The next step is to identify key factors that may modify the relationship between physical and cognitive capability and wellbeing. Using data from ELSA, we showed that variation in wellbeing between individuals had a small, but significant, effect on change in cognition over time, after adjustment for covariates. This effect was moderated by physical activity, such that being more physically active protected cognition against the adverse impact of low wellbeing (Allerhand et al, 2014).

Narratives of healthy and unhealthy ageing

Qualitative biographical interviews, carried out with a small subsample of members of NSHD and HCS (n = 60), allowed for development of an understanding of individuals' own perceptions of the experience of ageing. For example, it was possible to explore how perceived advantages and disadvantages of being in the 'third age' differ by respondents' self-reported physical capability. Cohort members associated ageing far more readily with aspects of physical decline than with the enhanced freedom and opportunities outlined by the 'positive ageing' literature (Laslett, 1989). However, as many as two thirds of all respondents did see some advantages to their age, with men and women in their seventies as likely to see advantages as the babyboomers in their mid-sixties. Indeed, those with relatively 'poor' physical capability were as likely to see some advantage to being the age they were as those with 'average' or 'good' capability. There were some differences in what was perceived as an advantage or disadvantage by respondents' level of physical capability – more respondents with good physical capability cited being wiser, lucky, enjoying more leisure time and good health as advantages and anxiety about future health problems as a disadvantage. Those with poor capability were more likely to talk of not working, having grandchildren and a bus pass as advantages, with problems with joints and arthritis and being closer to dying as disadvantages (Parsons et al, 2014).

The collection of biographical qualitative material from cohort members has allowed the development of case studies to illustrate the lived experiences of individuals with very different experiences of ageing (Carpentieri et al, 2014). Case studies can provide an insight into the difficulties of daily life and help the researcher to understand the challenges faced by the respondent. In turn, this can lead to an understanding of some of the mechanisms by which poor health and reduced capability may have an impact on wellbeing and quality of life. A further key message of these case studies is that healthy ageing cannot be looked at only at the individual level. The health of one's partner can significantly affect the quality of one's ageing.

The opportunity to analyse qualitative biographical material alongside quantitative data within HALCyon also allowed for some innovative mixed-methods research. For example, cross-cohort analysis demonstrated that there was a stronger association between wellbeing and perceived neighbourhood cohesion for participants from HCS and NSHD than from NCDS, and that this association was robust to adjustment for a wide range of covariates. In tandem with this work, analysis of the biographical interviews demonstrated the salience of social participation, that is, participation in local groups and organisations, as key to the perception of neighbourhood belonging among older adults (Elliott et al, 2014).

Lifetime influences on healthy ageing

Childhood socioeconomic circumstances and early experience

The team provided robust evidence that socioeconomic circumstances in childhood as well adulthood need to be taken into account when trying to improve capability at older ages. A HALCyon systematic review and meta-analysis showed that across all available studies worldwide, there were modest associations between disadvantaged childhood socioeconomic position (SEP) and slower walking and chair rise speeds that remained after adjustment for adult risk factors (including adult SEP) (Birnie et al, 2011). By taking the estimated difference in mean levels of walking speed by childhood SEP alongside our meta-analysis findings on the associations of walking speed with mortality, we were able to calculate that the differences in physical capability by childhood SEP translate into 11% higher rates of mortality for those who were most deprived in childhood compared with those who were least deprived. In an in-depth NSHD study, Murray and colleagues (2013) showed that lifetime area-level socioeconomic characteristics, as well as individual-level socioeconomic characteristics, are associated with physical capability.

In an attempt to understand the associations between childhood socioeconomic circumstances and adult physical capability, an in-depth study of NSHD indicated that part of the associations in this cohort were explained either by childhood growth and home environment or by neurodevelopmental indicators, such as childhood cognitive ability and motor milestones (Strand et al, 2011a). This builds on other evidence from the NSHD that neurodevelopment as well as neurodegeneration influences midlife physical capability (Kuh et al, 2009) and possibly its subsequent decline (Cooper et al, 2017). Maternal health when the study member was a child is another early life factor that may be important for adult physical capability; again the evidence is from the NSHD; but this time measured using the self-reported physical functioning component of the Short Form (SF) 36 scale (an overall measure of health status) at 60-64 years as the outcome (Mishra et al, 2014a).

Childhood cognitive ability and other aspects of early experience were also found to be associated with adult cognitive capability and wellbeing. A joint HALCyon and IALSA study across three cohorts showed that midlife fluid cognition was associated with childhood cognition and level of educational qualifications (Clouston et al, 2012). Gale and colleagues have also shown that across the HALCyon cohorts there are links between childhood cognitive ability and other earlier life factors and adult anxiety and depression (Gale et al, 2012a), building on an established field of research usually based on single cohort studies. They have since shown similar and more novel findings in relation to adult wellbeing (Gale et al, 2012b), although in this case the relation with childhood cognition was weak.

Adult health behaviours

Modifiable factors, such as diet, are thought to be important for physical and cognitive capability at all stages of life, but our review of the literature showed that evidence from cross-cohort studies has been inconsistent and limited, and not supported by trial evidence (Mishra et al, 2014b). The lack of harmonised measures across cohorts limited the comparisons that the HALCyon team could make. For example, creating harmonised dietary measures from food frequency questionnaires and dietary diaries in the HALCyon cohorts was very challenging, so studies in single cohorts were undertaken. For example, Mulla and colleagues showed small associations between energy intake and grip strength in the NSHD (Mulla et al, 2013).

There is more robust evidence from observational studies, randomised controlled trials and experimental studies of the importance of physical activity (Cooper et al, 2014b; Ekelund, 2014). Various HALCyon cohorts have contributed to this evidence (for example, Cooper et al, 2011c), but cross-cohort comparisons were not possible within the HALCyon cohorts as methods used to measure physical activity in different cohorts made it difficult to harmonise data. This remains a future challenge.

Analyses using data from a range of studies including HALCyon cohorts have also demonstrated that other health behaviours, including smoking, are associated with physical capability (Cooper et al, 2014b; North et al, 2015).

Birth weight and childhood growth

HALCyon research has shown that growth in early life is associated with later life capability, most likely through its influence on the maximum level of function achieved at maturity. For example, a systematic review provided robust evidence that birth weight is positively related to subsequent grip strength in children, young adults and in those at older ages (Dodds et al, 2012), suggesting that factors *in utero* or early postnatal life may leave long-term biological imprints on later life function. There is earlier evidence from single cohorts (for example, NSHD, HCS), cited elsewhere (Cooper et al, 2014b), that good growth in the prepubertal period is associated with better adult chair rise and standing balance performance, while good growth in the pubertal period is associated with better grip strength.

Adult adiposity

There was evidence from a meta-analysis of eight of the HALCyon cohorts (Hardy et al, 2013), consistent with findings from single cohort studies, that adult adiposity was negatively associated with chair rise and walking speeds and standing balance performance. The large sample size allowed us to assess the shape of the relationship, and we found that the detrimental impact of higher adiposity on these measures of physical performance was greatest in the highest two fifths of body mass index (BMI), and tended to be slightly stronger in women than men. Low grip strength was also associated with poorer performance; again, associations were generally stronger in women than men, and particularly poor performance was seen in those in the lowest fifth of grip strength. Those with the lowest grip strength and the highest BMI had the poorest performance through an additive effect.

Underlying biology

Despite high estimates of heritability, the evidence of genetic effects on physical and cognitive capability is limited. Across the HALCyon cohorts and other relevant studies identified, we showed no consistent evidence of associations between physical capability and common polymorphisms of *TERT*, a telomere maintenance gene (Alfred et al, 2011a); *ACTN3*, a genotype related to athletic status (Alfred et al, 2011b); genetic variants on the growth hormone and IGF-1 axis (Alfred et al, 2012); and genetic markers of bone and joint health (Alfred et al, 2013). However, we did find that carriers of a classic respiratory disease gene have enhanced respiratory capacity and greater height and size; this has potential relevance to physical capability as well as to drug development (North et al, 2016). As part of our review, Davies and colleagues (2014) provided a plethora of genetic insights into ageing.

HALCyon findings on associations between change in telomere length and physical capability were also weak and inconsistent (Gardner et al, 2013b). Here we have also contributed through the technical and methodological work undertaken. Measurement of telomere length in four of the HALCyon cohorts has resulted in the creation of one of the largest telomere datasets in the world (n = 6,200), including repeat measures in a significant proportion (n = 2,100). Work so far includes inter-lab comparisons of telomere measurements (Martin-Ruiz et al, 2015), and a systematic review of gender differences in telomere length (Gardner et al, 2014). Telomere length is now thought unlikely to be a robust marker of biological ageing; a biomarker index may be more fruitful, but the strongest contenders are biomarkers of physiological systems (such as lung function and grip strength) rather than markers at the molecular or cellular levels (Martin-Ruiz et al, 2014).

Somewhat more positive were the results of the relationships between markers of the HPA axis and physical and cognitive capability. There is growing evidence that ageing is associated with dysregulation of the HPA axis, which is most easily captured by examining the diurnal drop in cortisol. Older people, on average, show evidence of dysregulation with a less marked diurnal decline and hence greater levels of cortisol over the whole day. However, there is marked variability between individuals. Across the four HALCyon cohorts, and with the addition of two other studies that collaborated with HALCyon, we found that slower walking and chair rise speeds in cross-sectional analyses (Gardner et al, 2013a) were associated with less diurnal variability; however, there was little evidence of associations with grip strength or standing balance. In a single cohort study (CaPS), higher fasting morning cortisol levels measured 20 years earlier were associated with walking speed, in ways that suggested that the ability to mount a good stress-induced response may be a marker of a more reactive and healthier HPA axis (Gardner et al, 2011; Ben-Shlomo et al, 2014). In addition, the HALCyon group have also examined HPA patterns in relation to cognitive function. Again, those individuals with less marked decline across the day scored worse on fluid cognitive abilities such as logical thinking (Ben-Shlomo et al, 2014). Though HALCyon focused on one neuroendocrine axis, it is likely that a more integrated approach linking the HPA axis to other endocrine systems (growth, sex, thyroid hormones) will be more powerful to detecting influences on biological ageing.

Policy and practice implications

An important aspect of HALCyon was the establishment of a knowledge transfer group at the beginning of the project, chaired by the head of research at Age UK. This group, consisting of members of the NDA's Older People's Reference Group, representatives from relevant third sector organisations and government departments, and experts in ageing research followed the progress of the work packages at their six-monthly meetings, and reviewed the findings as they emerged. Based on the World Health Organization framework for knowledge translation on ageing and health (WHO, 2012), they worked with members of the HALCyon team to affect some of the key elements of knowledge exchange: the climate and context for research; linkage and exchange efforts that build relationships between researchers and users; 'push' efforts from the research team; and 'pull' efforts to facilitate policymakers identifying this research.

As well as disseminating the HALCyon findings through published articles and 70 presentations, the Knowledge Transfer Steering Group agreed that a major component of HALCyon's strategy should be the publication of an edited book, *A life course approach to healthy ageing.* This book discussed HALCyon findings within the context of the wider scientific literature (Kuh et al, 2014b), and was accompanied by a brochure, downloadable from the HALCyon website, summarising the book's key points. The book provides an integrated life course model of ageing, and discusses how aspects of healthy ageing are conceptualised, defined and measured; how they relate to each other; how they change across life; and how they are influenced by biological, psychological and social factors operating from early life onwards. In the last chapter, we identify research gaps and policy implications, and suggest how evidence from observational studies can be strengthened through improved study design and longitudinal analysis, increasing the research contribution to practice or policy change.

Recommendations

There are three key messages from the HALCyon project:

- There is good evidence that the promotion of healthy ageing needs to start early in life and continue across life, in order to maximise the level of peak function achieved at maturity as well as modifying the age at onset and rate of functional decline.
- Given that biological ageing is affected by lifetime social inequalities, patterns of growth, and prior changes in weight, function, health and health behaviours, we need to develop opportunities to monitor risk and functional ageing longitudinally, to know when to intervene to try to slow down the rate of ageing, by promoting physiological resilience. The clinical utility of the tests of physical capability for longitudinal monitoring is receiving much interest from researchers and health professionals.
- Social and psychological wellbeing in older people have bi-directional relationships with biological ageing, and are affected by factors such as parental care in early life, the presence and quality of lifelong relationships, personality and socioeconomic factors. We need to identify ways of maintaining wellbeing and promoting social and psychological resilience in the face of accelerated biological ageing.

There are five main implications for policy and practice:

- It is never too late to improve the chance of healthy ageing.
- More appropriate, timely and anticipatory care will be provided if we listen to people's life stories because they give important clues to the future as well as to the present and the past.
- Investing in early life lays down foundations for lifelong health, and requires action at the individual and societal levels.
- Care from others, and of oneself, is required to maintain health throughout life. We all need to take a long hard look at our lifestyle, and aim to maintain physical activity, eat healthily, refrain from smoking, enjoy the company of others, and stay engaged.
- Most importantly, tackling social inequalities is essential; the differences in healthy ageing by socioeconomic circumstances in the 21st century are unacceptably large, and seemingly small steps could have important impacts on these differentials.

For further discussion of the implications for a life course perspective on health policy and practice change, we refer readers to other recent publications (Kuh et al, 2014a, 2014c).

Key findings

- Objective measures of physical capability are useful markers of healthy ageing; older community-dwelling adults who have stronger grip strength, faster walking speed and better performance on chair rising and standing balance tests live longer, have fewer health problems and have higher levels of positive mental wellbeing than people who perform less well in these tests.
- There is robust evidence that those in better socioeconomic circumstances in childhood as well as adulthood have better capability at older ages. Not only an individual's own socioeconomic circumstances but also those of the area in which they live matter; living in a wealthier neighbourhood in childhood or adulthood is linked with better capability later in life.
- Childhood cognitive ability and other aspects of early experience are associated with adult cognitive capability and wellbeing. There are modest associations between cognitive capability and subsequent levels of positive wellbeing.
- Despite high estimates of heritability, the evidence of genetic effects on physical and cognitive capability is limited, highlighting the importance of the lifetime environment.
- Associations between telomere length and its change with age and with physical capability are weak and inconsistent.
- Dysregulation of the HPA axis is associated with lower levels of physical capability.

Conclusion

HALCyon is recognised as one of the first UK projects to integrate data from a number of cohort studies (Pell et al, 2014), and to use this to investigate factors that influence healthy ageing. HALCyon and IALSA have now joined forces with the help of five-year funding from NIH to foster further cross cohort research on ageing, and develop and apply life course methodology to make the best use of these valuable cohort resources (MRC, 2014). Encouraged by projects like HALCyon, funding calls on healthy ageing such as EU Horizon2020, and guidance on standardised protocols for healthy ageing indicators from the US National Institutes of Health toolbox (www.nihtoolbox.org) and from the MRC (described in Kuh et al, 2014d and Lara et al, 2015), a growing number of studies are including and repeating measures of capability and wellbeing according to standardised protocols. Along with the conceptual life course framework on ageing developed by the HALCyon team, this will provide opportunities to fill the various research gaps that the project identified (Kuh et al, 2014c).

References

Alfred, T., Ben-Shlomo, Y., Cooper, R., Hardy, R., Cooper, C., Deary, I.J., Elliott, J., Gunnell, D., Harris, S.E., Kivimaki, M., Kumari, M., Martin, R.M., Power, C., Sayer, A.A., Starr, J.M., Kuh, D. and Day, I.N. (2001a) 'Absence of association of a single-nucleotide polymorphism in the TERT-CLPTM1L locus with age-related phenotypes in a large multicohort study: the HALCyon programme', *Aging Cell*, vol 10, no 3, pp 520-32.

Alfred, T., Ben-Shlomo, Y., Cooper, R., Hardy, R., Cooper, C., Deary, I.J., Gaunt, T.R., Gunnell, D., Harris, S.E., Kumari, M., Martin, R.M., Sayer, A.A., Starr, J.M., Kuh, D. and Day, I.N. (2012) 'A multi-cohort study of polymorphisms in the GH/IGF axis and physical capability: the HALCyon programme', *PLoS ONE*, vol 7, no 1, e29883.

Alfred, T., Ben-Shlomo, Y., Cooper, R., Hardy, R., Cooper, C., Deary, I.J., Gunnell, D., Harris, S.E., Kumari, M., Martin, R.M., Moran, C.N., Pitsiladis, Y.P., Ring, S.M., Sayer, A.A., Smith, G.D., Starr, J.M., Kuh, D. and Day, I. N. (2011b) 'ACTN3 genotype, athletic status, and life course physical capability: meta-analysis of the published literature and findings from nine studies', *Human Mutation*, vol 32, no 9, pp 1008-18.

Alfred, T., Ben-Shlomo, Y., Cooper, R., Hardy, R., Cooper, C., Deary, I.J., Gunnell, D., Harris, S.E., Kumari, M., Martin, R.M., Sayer, A.A., Starr, J.M., Kuh, D. and Day, I.N. (2013) 'Genetic markers of bone and joint health and physical capability in older adults: the HALCyon programme', *Bone*, vol 52, no 1, pp 278-85.

Allerhand, M., Gale C.R. and Deary I.J. (2014) 'The dynamic relationship between cognitive function and positive wellbeing in older people: a prospective study using the English Longitudinal Study of Ageing, *Psychological Medicine*, vol 29, no 2, pp 306-18.

Barker, D.J.P. (ed) (1992) 'Fetal and infant origins of adult disease', *British Medical Journal*, London: BMJ Publishing Group.

Ben-Shlomo, Y., Cooper, R. and Kuh, D. (2016) 'Life course epidemiology: the last two decades and future directions', *International Journal of Epidemiology*, vol 45, no 4, pp 973-87.

Ben-Shlomo, Y., Gardner, M. and Lightman, S. (2014) 'A life course approach to neuroendocrine systems: the example of the HPA axis', in D. Kuh, R. Cooper, R. Hardy, M. Richards and Y. Ben-Shlomo (eds) *A life course approach to healthy ageing* (1st edn), Oxford, Oxford University Press, pp 133-45.

Birnie, K., Cooper, R., Martin, R.M., Kuh, D., Sayer, A.A., Alvarado, B.E., Bayer, A., Christensen, K., Cho, S.I., Cooper, C., Corley, J., Craig, L., Deary, I.J., Demakakos, P., Ebrahim, S., Gallacher, J., Gow, A.J., Gunnell, D., Haas, S., Hemmingsson, T., Inskip, H., Jang, S.N., Noronha, K., Osler, M., Palloni, A., Rasmussen, F., Santos-Eggimann, B., Spagnoli, J., Starr, J., Steptoe, A., Syddall, H., Tynelius, P., Weir, D., Whalley, L.J., Zunzunegui, M.V., Ben-Shlomo, Y. and Hardy, R. (2011) 'Childhood socioeconomic position and objectively measured physical capability levels in adulthood: a systematic review and meta-analysis', *PLoS ONE*, vol 6, no 1, e15564.

Buckner, J.C. (1988) 'The development of an instrument to measure neighbourhood cohesion', *American Journal of Community Psychology*, vol 16, no 6, pp 771-91.

Carpentieri, J.D. and Elliott, J. (2014) 'Understanding healthy ageing using a qualitative approach: the value of narratives and individual biographies', in D. Kuh, R. Cooper, R. Hardy, M. Richards and Y. Ben-Shlomo (eds) *A life course approach to healthy ageing* (1st edn), Oxford: Oxford University Press, pp 118-29.

Clouston, S.A.P., Brewster, P., Kuh, D., Richards, M., Cooper, R., Hardy, R., Rubin, M.S. and Hofer, S.M. (2013) 'The dynamic relationship between physical function and cognition in longitudinal aging cohorts', *Epidemiologic Reviews*, vol 35, no 1, pp 33-50.

Clouston, S.A.P., Kuh, D., Herd, P., Elliott, J., Richards, M. and Hofer, S.M. (2012) 'Benefits of educational attainment on adult fluid cognition: international evidence from three birth cohorts', *International Journal of Epidemiology*, vol 41, no 6, pp 1729-36.

Cooper, R., Hardy, R., Aihie Sayer, A., Birnie, K., Cooper, C., Craig, L., Deary, I.J., Demakakos, P., Gallacher, J., McNeill, G., Martin, R.M., Starr, J.M., Steptoe, A. and Kuh, D. (2011a) 'Age and gender differences in physical capability levels from mid-life onwards: the harmonisation and meta-analysis of data from eight UK cohort studies', *PLoS ONE*, vol 6, no 11, e27899.

Cooper, R., Hardy, R., Sayers, A. and Kuh, D. (2014a) 'A life course approach to physical capability', in D. Kuh, R. Cooper, R. Hardy, M. Richards and Y. Ben-Shlomo (eds) *A life course approach to healthy ageing* (1st edn), Oxford: Oxford University Press, pp 16-31.

Cooper, R., Kuh, D., Cooper, C., Gale, C.R., Lawlor, D.A., Matthews, F. and Hardy, R. (2011b) 'Objective measures of physical capability and subsequent health: a systematic review', *Age and Ageing*, vol 40, no 1, pp 14-23.

Cooper, R., Kuh, D. and Hardy, R. (2010) 'Objectively measured physical capability levels and mortality: systematic review and meta-analysis', *British Medical Journal*, 341, c4467.

Cooper, R., Mishra, G.D. and Kuh, D. (2011c) 'Physical activity across adulthood and physical performance in midlife: findings from a British birth cohort', *American Journal of Preventive Medicine*, vol 41, no 4, pp 376-84.

Cooper, R., Richards, M. and Kuh, D. (2017) 'Childhood cognitive ability and age-related changes in physical capability from midlife', *Psychosomatic Medicine*, 79(7): 785-91.

Cooper, R., Stafford, M., Hardy, R., Aihie Sayer, A., Ben-Shlomo, Y., Cooper, C., Craig, L., Deary, I.J., Gallacher, J., McNeill, G., Starr, J.M., Kuh, D. and Gale, C.R. (2014a) 'Physical capability and subsequent positive mental wellbeing in older people: findings from five HALCyon cohorts', *Age*, vol 36, no 1, pp 445-56.

Cooper, R., Strand, B.H., Hardy R., Patel, K.V. and Kuh, D. (2014b) 'Physical capability in mid-life and survival over 13 years of follow-up: British birth cohort study', *British Medical Journal*, 348, g2219.

Davies, T., Alfred, T. and Day, I. N. (2014) 'Genetic aspects of ageing', in D. Kuh, R. Cooper, R. Hardy, M. Richards and Y. Ben-Shlomo (eds) *A life course approach to healthy ageing* (1st edn), Oxford: Oxford University Press, pp 187-97.

Diener, E., Emmons, R.A., Larsen, R.J. and Griffin, S. (1985) 'The Satisfaction With Life Scale', *Journal of Personality Assessment*, vol 49, no 1, pp 71-5.

Dodds, R., Denison, H.J., Ntani, G., Cooper, R., Cooper, C., Aihie Sayer, A. and Baird, J. (2012) 'Birth weight and muscle strength: a systematic review and meta-analysis', *Journal of Nutrition, Health and Aging*, vol 16, no 7, pp 609-15.

Dodds, R.M., Syddall, H.E., Cooper, R., Benzeval, M., Deary, I.J., Dennison, E.M., Der, G., Gale, C.R., Inskip, H.M., Jagger, C., Kirkwood, T.B., Lawlor, D.A., Robinson, S.M., Starr, J.M., Steptoe, A., Tilling, K., Kuh, D., Cooper, C., Aihie Sayer, A. (2014) 'Grip strength across the life course: normative data from twelve British studies', *PLoS ONE*, vol 9, no 12, e113637.

Dodds, R.M., Syddall, H.E., Cooper, R., Kuh, D., Cooper, C. and Aihie Sayer, A. (2016) 'Global variation in grip strength: a systematic review and meta-analysis of normative data', *Age and Ageing*, 45, pp 209-16.

Ekelund, U. (2014) 'Lifetime lifestyles II: physical activity, the life course, and ageing', in D. Kuh, R. Cooper, R. Hardy, M. Richards and Y. Ben-Shlomo (eds) *A life course approach to healthy ageing* (1st edn), Oxford: Oxford University Press, pp 229-45.

Elliott, J., Gale, C.R., Parsons, S. and Kuh, D. (2014) 'Neighbourhood cohesion and mental wellbeing among older adults: a mixed methods approach', *Social Science & Medicine*, vol 107, pp 44-51.

Ferrucci L., Cooper R., Shardell M., Simonsick E.M., Schrack J.A. and Kuh D. (2016) Age-related change in mobility: perspectives from life course epidemiology and geroscience. *J Gerontol A Biol Sci Med Sci*, 71(9): 1184-94.

Gale, C.R., Allerhand, M. and Deary, I J. (2012a) 'Is there a bidirectional relationship between depressive symptoms and cognitive ability in older people? A prospective study using the English Longitudinal Study of Ageing', *Psychological Medicine*, vol 42, no 10, pp 2057-69..

Gale, C.R., Cooper, R., Craig, L., Elliott, J., Kuh, D., Richards, M., Starr, J.M., Whalley, L.J. and Deary, I.J. (2012b) 'Cognitive function in childhood and lifetime cognitive change in relation to mental wellbeing in four cohorts of older people', *PLoS. One*, vol 7, no 9, e44860.

Gale, C.R., Deary, I.J. and Stafford, M. (2014) 'A life course approach to psychological and social wellbeing', in D. Kuh, R. Cooper, R. Hardy, M. Richards and Y. Ben-Shlomo (eds) *A life course approach to healthy ageing* (1st edn), Oxford: Oxford University Press, pp 46-61.

Gardner, M.P., Bann, D., Wiley, L., Cooper, R., Hardy, R., Nitsch, D., Martin-Ruiz, C., Shiels, P., Aihie Sayer, A., Barbieri, M., Bekaert, S., Bischoff, C., Brooks-Wilson, A., Chen, W., Cooper, C., Christensen, K., De Meyer, T., Deary, I., Der, G., Diez Roux, A., Fitzpatrick, A., Hajat, A., Halaschek-Wiener, J., Harris, S., Hunt, S.C., Jagger, C., Jeon, H.S., Kaplan, R., Kimura, M., Lansdorp, P., Li, C., Maeda, T., Mangino, M., Nawrot, T.S., Nilsson, P., Nordfjall, K., Paolisso, G., Ren, F., Riabowol, K., Robertson, T., Roos, G., Staessen, J.A., Spector, T., Tang, N., Unryn, B., van der Harst, P., Woo, J., Xing, C., Yadegarfar, M.E., Park, J.Y., Young, N., Kuh, D., von Zglinicki T. and Ben-Shlomo, Y. (2014) 'Gender and telomere length: systematic review and meta-analysis', *Experimental Gerontology*, 51, pp 15-27.

Gardner, M.P., Lightman, S., Aihie Sayer, A., Cooper, C., Cooper, R., Deeg, D., Ebrahim, S., Gallacher, J., Kivimaki, M., Kumari, M., Kuh, D., Martin, R.M., Peeters, G. and Ben-Shlomo, Y. (2013a) 'Dysregulation of the hypothalamic pituitary adrenal (HPA) axis and physical performance at older ages: an individual participant meta-analysis', *Psychoneuroendocrinology*, vol 38, no 1, pp 40-9.

Gardner, M.P., Lightman, S.L., Gallacher, J., Hardy, R., Kuh, D., Ebrahim, S., Bayer, A. and Ben-Shlomo, Y. (2011) 'Diurnal cortisol patterns are associated with physical performance in the Caerphilly Prospective Study', *International Journal of Epidemiology*, vol 40, no 6, pp 1693-702.

Gardner, M.P., Martin-Ruiz, C., Cooper, R., Hardy, R., Aihie Sayer, A., Cooper, C., Deary, I.J., Gallacher, J., Harris, S.E., Shiels, P.G., Starr, J.M., Kuh, D., von Zglinicki T. and Ben-Shlomo, Y. (2013b) 'Telomere length and physical performance at older ages: an individual participant meta-analysis', *PLoS ONE*, vol 8, no 7, e69526.

Gluckman, P.D., Hanson, M.A., Bateson, P., Beedle, A.S., Law, C.M., Bhutta, Z.A., Anokhin, K.V., Bougneres, P., Chandak, G.R., Dasgupta, P., Smith, G.D., Ellison, P.T., Forrester, T.E., Gilbert, S.F., Jablonka, E., Kaplan, H., Prentice, A.M., Simpson, S.J., Uauy, R. and West-Eberhard, M.J. (2009) 'Towards a new developmental synthesis: adaptive developmental plasticity and human disease', *The Lancet*, vol 373, no 9675, pp 1654-7.

Hardy, R., Cooper, R., Aihie Sayer, A., Ben Shlomo, Y., Cooper, C., Deary, I.J., Demakakos, P., Gallacher, J., Martin, R.M., McNeill, G., Starr, J.M., Steptoe, A., Syddall, H., Kuh, D. and on behalf of the HALCyon study team (2013) 'Body mass index, muscle strength and physical performance in older adults from eight cohort studies: the HALCyon programme', *PLoS ONE*, vol 8, no 2, e56483.

Kuh, D. and Ben-Shlomo, Y (2004) *A life course approach to chronic disease epidemiology* (2nd edn), Oxford: Oxford University Press.

Kuh, D., Ben-Shlomo, Y., Tilling, K. and Hardy, R. (2014a) 'Life course epidemiology and analysis', in R. Detels, M. Gulliford, Q. Abdool Karim and C.C.Tan (eds) *The Oxford textbook of public health* (6th edn), Oxford: Oxford University Press, pp 1-12.

Kuh, D., Cooper, R., Hardy R., Richards M. and Ben Shlomo, Y. (2014b) (eds) *A life course approach to healthy ageing* (1st edn), Oxford: Oxford University Press.

Kuh, D., Cooper, R., Hardy, R., Goodwin, J., Richards, M., and Ben-Shlomo, Y. (2014c) 'What we have learnt for future research and knowledge exchange', in D. Kuh, R. Cooper, R. Hardy, M. Richards and Y. Ben-Shlomo (eds) *A life course approach to healthy ageing* (1st edn), Oxford: Oxford University Press, pp 261-72.

Kuh, D., Cooper, R., Hardy, R., Guralnik, J. and Richards, M. (2009) 'Lifetime cognitive performance is associated with midlife physical performance in a prospective national birth cohort study', *Psychosomatic Medicine*, vol 71, no 1, pp 38-48.

Kuh, D., Karunananthan, S., Bergman, H. and Cooper, R. (2014d) 'A life-course approach to healthy ageing: maintaining physical capability', *Proceedings of the Nutrition Society*, vol 73, no 2, pp 237-48.

Lara, J., Cooper, R., Nissan, J., Ginty, A.T., Khaw, K.T., Deary, I.J., Lord, J.M., Kuh, D., Mathers, J.C. (2015) 'A proposed panel of biomarkers of healthy ageing', *BMC Medicine*, vol 13, no 1, p 222.

Laslett, B.A. (1989) *Fresh map of life: The emergence of the third age*, Cambridge, MA: Harvard University.

Martin-Ruiz, C.M. and von Zglinicki, T. (2014) 'A life course approach to biomarkers of ageing', in D. Kuh, R. Cooper, R. Hardy, M. Richards and Y. Ben-Shlomo (eds) *A life course approach to healthy ageing* (1st edn), Oxford: Oxford University Press, pp 177-86.

Martin-Ruiz, C.M., Baird, D., Roger, L., Boukamp, P., Krunic, D., Cawthon, R., Dokter, M.M., van der Harst, P., Bekaert, S., de Meyer, T., Roos, G., Svenson, U., Codd, V., Samani, N.J., McGlynn, L., Shiels, P.G., Pooley, K., Dunning, A., Cooper, R., Wong, A., Kingston, A. and von Zglinicki, T. (2015) 'Reproducibility of telomere length assessment: an international collaborative study', *International Journal of Epidemiology*, vol 44, no 5, pp 1673-83.

Mishra, G.D., Black, S., Stafford, M., Cooper, R. and Kuh, D. (2014a) 'Childhood and maternal effects on physical health related quality of life five decades later: the British 1946 birth cohort', *PLoS ONE*, vol 9, no 3, e88524.

Mishra, G.D., Richards, M., Mihrshahi, S. and Stephen, A. (2014b) 'Lifetime lifestyles I: diet, the life course, and ageing', in D. Kuh, R. Cooper, R. Hardy, M. Richards and Y. Ben-Shlomo (eds) *A life course approach to healthy ageing* (1st edn), Oxford: Oxford University Press, pp 229-245.

MRC (Medical Research Council) (2014) *Maximising the value of UK population cohorts*, London: MRC.

Mulla, U.Z., Cooper, R., Mishra, G.D., Kuh, D. and Stephen, A.M. (2013) 'Adult macronutrient intake and physical capability in the MRC National Survey of Health and Development', *Age and Ageing*, vol 42, no 1, pp 81-7.

Murray, E.T., Ben-Shlomo, Y., Tilling, K., Southall, H., Aucott, P., Kuh, D. and Hardy, R. (2013) 'Area deprivation across the life course and physical capability in midlife: findings from the 1946 British birth cohort', *American Journal of Epidemiology*, vol 178, no 3, pp 441-50.

North, T., Palmer, T.M., Lewis, S.J., Cooper, R., Power, C., Pattie, A.M., Starr, J.M., Deary, I.J., Martin, R.M., Aihie Sayer, A., Kumari, M., Cooper, C., Kivimaki, M., Kuh, D., Ben-Shlomo, Y. and Day, I.N.M. (2015) 'Effect of smoking on physical and cognitive capability in later life: a multi-cohort study using observational and genetic approaches', *BMJ Open*, vol 5, no 12, e008393.

North, T.L., Ben-Shlomo, Y., Cooper, C., Deary, I.J., Gallacher, J., Kumari, M., Kivimäki, M., Martin, R., Pattie, A., Sayer, A., Starr, J., Wong, A., Kuh, D., Day, I. (2016) 'A study of common Mendelian disease carriers across ageing British cohorts: meta-analyses reveal heterozygosity for alpha-1 antitrypsin deficiency increases respiratory capacity and height', *Journal of Medical Genetics*, vol 53, no 4, pp 280-8.

Parsons, S., Gale, C.R., Kuh, D., Elliott, J. and on behalf of the HALCyon study team (2014) 'Physical capability and the advantages and disadvantages of ageing: perceptions of older age by men and women in two British cohorts', *Ageing & Society*, vol 34, no 3, pp 452-71.

Pell, J., Valentine, J. and Inskip, H. (2014) 'One in 30 people in the UK take part in cohort studies', *The Lancet*, vol 383, no 9922, pp 1015-16.

Pierce, M.B., Silverwood, R.J., Nitsch, D., Adams, J.E., Stephen, A.M., Nip, W., Macfarlane, P., Wong, A., Richards, M., Hardy, R., Kuh, D. and on behalf of the NSHD scientific and data collection teams (2012) 'Clinical disorders in a post war British cohort reaching retirement: evidence from the first National Birth Cohort Study', *PLoS ONE*, vol 7, no 9, e44857.

Richards, M. and Deary, I.J. (2014) 'A life course approach to cognitive capability', in D. Kuh, R. Cooper, R. Hardy, M. Richards and Y. Ben-Shlomo (eds) *A life course approach to healthy ageing* (1st edn), Oxford: Oxford University Press, pp 32-45.

Strand, B.H., Cooper, R., Hardy, R., Kuh, D. and Guralnik, J. (2011a) 'Lifelong socioeconomic position and physical performance in midlife: results from the British 1946 birth cohort', *European Journal of Epidemiology*, vol 26, no 6, pp 475-83.

Strand, B.H., Mishra, G., Kuh, D., Guralnik, J.M. and Patel, K. V. (2011b) 'Smoking history and physical performance in midlife: results from the British 1946 birth cohort', *Journals of Gerontology - Series A Biological Sciences and Medical Sciences*, vol 66, no 1, pp 142-9.

Tennant, R., Hiller, L., Fishwick, R., Platt, S., Joseph, S., Weich, S., Parkinson, J., Secker, J. and Stewart-Brown, S. (2007) 'The Warwick-Edinburgh Mental Wellbeing Scale (WEMWBS): development and UK validation', *Health and Quality of Life Outcomes*, 5, 63. WHO (World Health Organization) (2012) *Knowledge translation on ageing and health: A framework for policy development*, Geneva: WHO.

FIVE

Measuring the quality of later life

Ann Bowling

Introduction

This chapter provides an overview of research funded by the New Dynamics of Ageing (NDA) programme on quality of life (QoL) in older age (Bowling, 2009; Bowling and Stenner, 2011; Bowling et al, 2013). The research built on previously funded research from the Economic and Social Research Council (ESRC) Growing Older programme (Bowling et al, 2003; Bowling and Gabriel, 2004; Gabriel and Bowling, 2004; Bowling, 2005). A focus on QoL in older age was justified by increasing numbers of older people, including people with possibly higher expectations than previous generations (Bowling et al, 2012). These factors have led to international interest in the enhancement, and measurement, of QoL in older age. Public policy is increasingly concerned with enabling older people to maintain their mobility, independence and active contribution to society, and to respond effectively to the physical, psychological and social challenges of older age – in effect, to add quality to years of life. This reflects a shift of emphasis away from a traditional view of structured dependency, in which the focus of research is on ill health, functional decline and poverty in older age. It moves towards a positive view of old age as a natural component of the life span, and development of personal fulfilment, although this can still be restricted by limited resources, ill health or frailty. It also builds on the model of cognitive efficiency proposed by Baltes and Baltes (1990) and Baltes and colleagues (1996), with its emphasis on control over life, role functioning, cognitive competence, and adaptability to the challenges encountered at older ages, consistent with the current focus on reablement in social care (Francis et al, 2011).

Broader quality of life

Quality of life encompasses how an individual perceives the 'goodness' of multiple aspects of their life. The increasing emphasis on evidence-based practice, and inclusion of user-based outcomes in evaluative research, focuses mostly on QoL outcomes. Maintaining people's broader QoL is a potentially important factor in ensuring that they can 'live well' and that their care and support up until death meets their needs. While several measures of broader QoL, embedded within holistic models of functioning, life and needs satisfaction, have been developed for use with people with chronic mental illnesses (Thornicroft and Tansella, 1996), the development of broader models and measures for use with older populations, grounded in older people's own views, has been slower (Bowling et al, 2003; Gabriel and Bowling, 2004; Bowling and Stenner, 2011).

Broader QoL is more than just health; it is more multidimensional than health-related or disease-specific QoL, and is relevant when examining the whole person, and also in evaluating interventions – or conditions – that can affect one's whole life, as in many chronic mental and physical illnesses, particularly in older age. Much conceptual confusion has been created by clinical investigators who erroneously identify QoL with health status, and then incorrectly attempt to measure QoL with a health status instrument. While health may be relevant to one's QoL, a narrow focus is unlikely to capture the full impact of social care on a person's life.

QoL has been defined in macro (societal, objective) and micro (individual, subjective) terms (Bowling and Windsor, 2001). There is increasing recognition of the individual nature of QoL, summed up in the World Health Organization Quality of Life (WHOQOL) Group definition (WHO, 1993; WHOQOL Group, 1995):

> ... an individual's perception of their position in life in the context of the culture and value systems in which they live and in relation to their goals, expectations, and standards and concerns. It is a broad-ranging concept affected in a complex way by the persons' physical health, psychological state, level of independence, social relationships, and their relationships to salient features of their environment.

Each of these areas is relevant to younger and older adults, to those who live in their own homes and those who live in care homes. However, different people, and people in different age groups, with different characteristics, levels of health, and living circumstances, may have different priorities. For example, relationships, finances and opportunity to work may be prioritised more highly by younger adults, and health and relationships more highly prized by people aged 65 and over (Bowling, 1995a, 1995b, 1996). People who have social care needs, particularly those living in care homes, might prioritise the ability to control aspects of their lives and the way they spend their days (Qureshi et al, 1994).

Broader models of QoL were heavily influenced by the early social science literature on wellbeing and satisfaction with life (for example, Andrews and Withey, 1976; Campbell et al, 1976). Some consider life satisfaction to be a major component of QoL in later life, along with psychological components such as self-esteem that may be affected by life challenges (George and Bearon, 1980). A popular model in relation to older adults is Lawton's multidimensional perspective, involving assessment of QoL by the individual, and by social–normative criteria, of four domains: behavioural competence (ability to function in adaptive and socially appropriate ways); objective environment (everything that exists externally to the individual, including physical and interpersonal factors); psychological wellbeing (mental health, emotional state); and one's subjective satisfaction with overall QoL (Lawton, 1991, 1994). Lawton (1997) expanded on his conceptualisation of QoL to include the multiple domains of affect (happiness, agitation, depression, affect state, emotional expression, spirituality); self-esteem (self-esteem, life satisfaction, morale); appraisal of physical functioning (self-care); social relationships (satisfaction with family and friends); social environment (social engagement, meaningful time use, physical safety, presence of amenities, privacy, stimulating quality, aesthetic quality, satisfaction with spare time, housing [institution] and healthcare, freedom from barriers); and health (behavioural symptoms, psychiatric symptoms).

A small proportion of literature on QoL in older age considers older people's own definitions of, and priorities for, their QoL. Grundy and Bowling and Bowling (1999) asked small samples of older people how they perceived a 'good old age'; this formed the basis of a composite model of QoL that discriminated between respondents who said they felt young or old, as opposed to their actual age, and that predicted mortality up to 30 months (Grundy and Bowling, 1999). Fry's (2000) research was based on a combination of survey data and in-depth interviews with older people in Vancouver. She concluded that older adults valued personal control, autonomy and self-sufficiency, their right to pursue a chosen lifestyle and a right to privacy. Farquhar's (1995) in-depth interviews with people aged 65 and over in East

London and Essex reported that family, social activities and social contacts were the three commonly mentioned areas that gave quality to their lives. Browne and colleagues (1994), on the basis of semi-structured interviews using the Schedule for Self-Evaluation of QoL with people aged 65 and over in Ireland, reported that both family and health were nominated as most important to QoL, with almost equal frequency, followed by social and leisure activities. Bowling and Windsor (2001) reported, on the basis of a national survey of adults in Britain, that the highest proportion of adult respondents nominated relationships with family, relatives, friends and others (for example, neighbours) as the most important area. However, among those aged 65+, relationships were ranked second in importance after health (Bowling, 1995b). Population surveys of all adults and people aged 65 and over have reported that people themselves have identified a wider range of life areas as important to them, and to their QoL (Bowling, 1995a, 1996; Bowling et al, 2003; Gabriel and Bowling, 2004). The core components, and the central planks, of QoL, which were consistently emphasised by qualitative and quantitative methods, were self-constructs and cognitive mechanisms (psychological outlook, optimism–pessimism, independence and control over life), health and functional status, personal social networks, support and activities, neighbourhood social capital and financial circumstances (Bowling et al, 2003; Gabriel and Bowling, 2004). There is also a dynamic interplay between people and their surrounding social structures, which influences QoL. Brown and colleagues (2004) reviewed the literature on QoL and developed a taxonomy of QoL comprising the following components: objective indicators; subjective indictors; satisfaction of human needs; psychological characteristics and resources; health and functioning; social health; social cohesion and social capital; environmental context; and ideographic approaches. Brown and colleagues' review concluded that older people's views of QoL overlapped with theoretical models. However, the latter need to be multidimensional in order to encompass people's values and perceptions.

A pragmatic approach to measurement prevails in the literature, and clarification of the concept of quality of life is typically bypassed or justified with reference to its abstract nature, and the selection of measurement scales often appears ad hoc. This has resulted in many investigators adopting a narrow, or discipline-bound, perspective of QoL, and selecting single domain measures such as scales of physical functioning, mental health, broader health status, life satisfaction and so on. Some have used broader measures that aim to assess a person's needs for resources or services, which also overlap with QoL domains. Others have selected combinations of single domain measures, in an attempt to adopt a broader view of QoL, although this often results in lengthy schedules with high respondent and researcher burden.

Moreover, the models of quality of life that have been developed are not consistent. Some have incorporated a needs–based satisfaction model, based on Maslow's (1954, 1968) hierarchy of human needs for maintenance and existence (physiological needs, safety and security, social needs and belonging, ego, status and self-esteem, and self-actualisation). Higgs and colleagues (2003), for example, based their model of QoL in older age on a needs-satisfaction model of self-actualisation and self-esteem. In contrast, traditional US social science models of quality of life have been based primarily on the overlapping, positive concepts of 'the good life', 'life satisfaction', 'social wellbeing', 'morale', 'the social temperature', or 'happiness' (Andrews and Withey, 1976; Andrews, 1986; Lawton, 1996). The focus among psychologists, meanwhile, is on psychological resources (Baltes and Baltes, 1990). The WHOQOL Group adopted a multifaceted approach, while emphasising subjective perceptions, values and cultural context, and from which was developed the WHOQOL assessment instrument (100–item and brief version) (WHO, 1993; Skevington, 1999; Skevington et al, 2004).

Broader measures of QoL for older people

Many investigators have used measures of wellbeing, life satisfaction or morale as proxy measures of the broader QoL of older people. One example is the Medical Research Council trial of assessment and management of older people aged 75 years and over living at home in the community. This involved evaluations of outcomes, over 36 months, of packages of assessments in primary care, including a multidisciplinary geriatric assessment team (Fletcher et al, 2002). Apart from mortality outcomes and use of services, the investigators aimed to measure QoL outcomes. In home interviews, they used the 17-item Philadelphia Geriatric Morale Scale (Powell-Lawton, 1975) and the QoL domain of the Sickness Impact Profile, which is a health status measure (Bergner et al, 1981) (the QoL domain was limited to items on mobility, self-care, home management and social interaction). The CASP-19 was developed with a sample of older people; it has 19 items within the four domains of control, autonomy, pleasure and self-realisation (Hyde et al, 2003), but was developed as a 'top-down' measure, based on a theory of needs satisfaction and self-actualisation.

The WHO quality of life measure for older people (WHOQOL-OLD) contains 24 items within six sub-scales: sensory abilities, autonomy, past present and future activities, social participation, death and dying, and intimacy (Power et al, 2005). This was based on the WHO's multidimensional definition of QoL (quoted earlier), and was tested across countries with convenience samples. The WHOQOL-OLD consists of the pre-existing main WHOQOL questionnaire developed for all adults (Power et al, 1999) with physical functioning added, as suggested by focus groups. None of these instruments was developed truly from the bottom up, based on representative samples of older people's priorities and views.

Baseline research on QoL leading to the NDA QoL study

The ESRC Growing Older (GO) programme funded our baseline QoL interview survey among people aged 65 and over, living at home in Britain (n = 999) (L480254003). The aim was to develop a body of knowledge on QoL, grounded in older people's views. Thus in 1999-2000, 999 of people aged 65+ (77% of those invited) took part in a national survey of quality of life among people aged 65+. Eighty people were also followed up qualitatively. This led to the development of a lay-based, multidimensional model of positive and negative influences on QoL in older age, which substantially overlapped with theoretical models when taken in combination. The indicators of QoL were derived subjectively (qualitatively, using open-ended and in-depth questions) and objectively (quantitatively, using structured scales relating to theoretically relevant variables).

Respondents at baseline emphasised the importance of living in a neighbourly and safe area, and having good local facilities to promote friendly and helpful relationships with other people, including neighbours. This was also seen to be important in preventing loneliness and isolation. Having good local facilities (shops, markets, post office), good health services and good local council services (street lighting, refuse collection, police, repairs), including a good local mobile/library, and having a pleasant landscape/surroundings was said to be important to respondents' quality of life. Creation of local opportunities to meet other people and to maintain a role in society (through work or voluntary work, for example), access to transport and having enough money were said to be important for retaining independence (see Box 5.1).

Box 5.1: Building blocks of quality of life

Elements governing quality of life in older age were as follows:

- people's standards of social comparison and expectations in life;
- having a sense of optimism and a belief that 'all will be well in the end' rather than a tendency to think the worst;
- enjoying good health and physical functioning;
- engaging in a large number of social activities and feeling supported;
- living in a neighbourhood with good community facilities and services, including transport;
- feeling safe in one's neighborhood;
- feeling independent, in control over life, and having enough money.

Consistent with the literature and theories of social networks, social relationships were ranked highest overall by respondents as the key dimension of QoL – even higher than health. Eighty-one per cent of respondents said social relationships gave quality to life, for the following reasons:

- 'for companionship';
- 'to do things with';
- 'to take me out';
- 'to make life bearable';
- 'to know there is someone there willing to help me';
- 'to look after me';
- 'for confidence';
- 'someone to depend on me'.

One respondent added: "Oh, and my little cat. I talk to her a lot, she's just like a little child. She doesn't like being left alone, I love her to bits. Now and again I give her a little kiss."

Box 5.2 gives some further examples of how relationships were important to quality of life.

Box 5.2: Responses to questions about QoL and social and community relationships, from the 1999-2000 survey and in-depth follow-up interviews

"... family ... just [to] ... know I'm not completely alone in the world and knowing there's someone who cares about you ... my brother, his wife, and two daughters and a son, three grandchildren. We are very close, not a big family but a family ... [I] either visit them or they fetch me out."

"My grandchildren. Well I'm noted for activity. I can't keep still. The grandchildren love to come here and go out with me. We like the cinemas, we like the parks, you name it.... At least somebody thinks I'm useful."

"No hand to hold.... Socially I am a person non-gratis, being seen by other wives as a threat ... I am pulling myself up, all I want is mature company to help me."

"I had a very good friend [GM] who ... died now eight or nine years ago, but we used to talk a lot over problems, but ... when I lost him, I lost ... my main supporter from that point of view, 'cause if I wanted to have a chat about something what I wasn't sure about I'd go and see him, and he'd do the same to me, so it was always, it was a mutual thing, but ... that's the trouble, you lose your confidante, you know ... the older you get."

"So we've really got somebody we can knock, you know, if we're in trouble, we've got help ... it's the quality of the neighbours I suppose, you've got to live with ... they're ever so nice round this way ... they're ready to help ... it's the quality of life, as you say – the life, and that, and the people that actually live in your street."

The findings of the GO survey led to the development of the Older People's QoL (OPQOL) questionnaire. The OPQOL questionnaire (Bowling and Stenner, 2011), then, was developed from the GO findings, based on open-ended questions, asked at the outset of the interviews, about what gave participants' lives quality, what took quality away from their lives and their relative importance, and compared with psycho-social theory (Bowling et al, 2003). It is important to identify these dimensions as influencing variables of perceived life quality in order to distinguish between the multiplicity of the causal sources of QoL, and the dimensionality of the concept. In order to attempt to separate predictor from component variables of QoL, this concept should be considered as unidimensional, but with multiple causes (Fayers and Hand, 2002). Thus we included a global QoL rating scale (see Box 5.3 for the QoL questions used).

Box 5.3: Open-ended questions to elicit views of QoL

Thinking about your life as a whole, what is it that makes your life good – that is, the things that give your life quality? You may mention as many things as you like.

What is it that makes your life bad – that is, the things that reduce the quality in your life? You may mention as many things as you like.

Thinking about all these good and bad things you have just mentioned, which one is the most important to you?

Global QoL rating scale: Again, thinking about the good and bad things you have mentioned that make up your quality of life, which of the answers on this card best describes the quality of your life as a whole? [Seven-point QoL self-rating scale, from 'QoL so good, could not be better' to 'QoL so bad, could not be worse'.]

Thinking about all these good and bad things you have just mentioned, which one is the most important to you?'

And what single thing would improve the quality of your life?

And what single thing, in your opinion, would improve the overall quality of life for people of your age?

Source: Bowling et al (2003).

The full version of the OPQOL has 35 items (one version contained 32 of these items) covering: social relationships and participation; independence, control over life and freedom; psychological and emotional wellbeing; perceived financial circumstances; area (home and neighbourhood); life overall; health; and religion and culture. A short version comprising 13 items was also developed with good reliability and validity. The 13-item version was further prioritised in workshops with over 200 people from Older People's Forums in England (Bowling et al, 2013). Enjoyment of life and independence achieved the highest rankings in this exercise.

Boxes 5.4 and 5.5 show the 32-35 and 13-item versions, respectively. Respondents are asked to indicate the extent to which they agree with each statement by selecting one of five possible options ('strongly disagree', 'disagree', 'neither agree nor disagree', 'agree' and 'strongly agree'), each with a score of 1 to 5.

Higher scores indicate a better QoL. The total score ranges from 35 (worst possible QoL) to 175 (best possible QoL). The 35 statements of the full OPQOL questionnaire cover life overall (four items, score range 4-20), health (four items, 4-20), social relationships and participation (eight items, 8-40), independence, control over life and freedom (five items, 5-25), home and neighbourhood (four items, 4-20), psychological and emotional wellbeing (four items, 4-20), financial circumstances (four items, 4-20), and culture and religion (two items, 2-10).

Box 5.4: The 32-35 item versions of OPQOL

The full OPQOL contains 32 items, and a 35 item version was developed which included 3 items requested by people in diverse ethnic minority group.

Please indicate the extent to which you agree or disagree with each of the following statements (five-point Likert response scale: strongly agree to strongly disagree)

Life overall
1. I enjoy my life overall
2. I am happy much of the time
3. I look forward to things
4. Life gets me down

Health
5. I have a lot of physical energy
6. Pain affects my wellbeing
7. My health restricts me looking after myself or my home
8. I am healthy enough to get out and about

Social relationships/leisure and social activities
9. My family, friends or neighbours would help me if needed
10. I would like more companionship or contact with other people
11. I have someone who gives me love and affection
12. I'd like more people to enjoy life with
12a. I have my children around which is important*

29. I have social or leisure activities/hobbies that I enjoy doing
30. I try to stay involved with things
31. I do paid or unpaid work or activities that give me a role in life

Independence, control over life, freedom

13. I am healthy enough to have my independence
14. I can please myself what I do
15. The cost of things compared to my pension/income restricts my life
16. I have a lot of control over the important things in my life
32. I have responsibilities to others that restrict my social or leisure activities

Home and neighbourhood

17. I feel safe where I live
18. The local shops, services and facilities are good overall
19. I get pleasure from my home
20. I find my neighbourhood friendly

Psychological and emotional wellbeing

21. I take life as it comes and make the best of things
22. I feel lucky compared to most people
23. I tend to look on the bright side
24. If my health limits social/leisure activities, then I will compensate and find something else I can do

Financial circumstances

25. I have enough money to pay for household bills
26. I have enough money to pay for household repairs or help needed in the house
27. I can afford to buy what I want to
28. I cannot afford to do things I would enjoy

Religion/culture

33. Religion, belief or philosophy is important to my quality of life*
34 (35). Cultural/religious events/festivals are important to my quality of life*

Box 5.5: The 13 OPQOL items rated as most important by workshop participants (% rating item most important) (n = 236)

• I enjoy my life overall (81%)
• I look forward to things (52%)
• I am healthy enough to get out and about (75%)
• My family, friends or neighbours would help me if needed (71%)

- I have social or leisure activities/hobbies that I enjoy doing (61%)
- I try to stay involved with things (58%)
- I am healthy enough to have my independence (82%)
- I can please myself what I do (59%)
- I feel safe where I live (78%)
- I get pleasure from my home (53%)
- I take life as it comes and make the best of things (60%)
- I feel lucky compared to most people (54%)
- I have enough money to pay for household bills (71%)

Aims and methods of the research

The aim of the study was to assess the performance of the lay-based OPQOL, and to compare it for validation with two existing, widely used, measures of QoL: the CASP-19 (Higgs et al, 2003; Hyde et al, 2003), and the WHOQOL-OLD (Power et al, 1999).

The NDA-funded study was based on three national surveys of people aged 65+, living at home in Britain. Given the ethnic diversity of urban populations in Britain, including those at younger end of the older age continuum, we also aimed to capture this diversity. The 2001 Research Governance Framework for Health and Social Care states that:

> Research and those pursuing it should respect the diversity of human culture and conditions and take full account of ethnicity, gender, disability, age, and sexual orientation in its design, undertaking, and reporting. Researchers should take account of the multicultural nature of society. It is particularly important that the body of research evidence available to policy makers reflects the diversity of the population. (DH, 2001, para 2.2.7)

Two of the three surveys were cross-sectional, and the third was longitudinal:

- Ethnibus survey of people aged 65+ responding to two waves of the national Ethnibus Surveys (www.ethnibus.com) in 2008. This is a rolling face-to-face interview survey with adults aged 16+, living at home, based on focused enumeration, stratified random sampling of postcodes in Britain, and statistically robust sampling of people in common ethnic minority groups in Britain; the response rate was 70% (n = 400).

- Office for National Statistics (ONS) survey of people aged 65+ responding to two waves of the national ONS Omnibus Surveys (www.statistics.gov.uk) in 2008. This is a rolling face-to-face interview survey with adults aged 16+, living at home, based on a stratified random sample of postcodes across Britain; the response rate was 61% (n = 589).
- QoL follow-up survey in 2007-08, of people living at home in Britain, aged 65+ at baseline, who had responded to four national ONS Omnibus Surveys. These were based on stratified random samples of postcodes across Britain during 1999/2000; response was 77% (n = 999) at baseline and 58% among survivors (n = 287) at 2007-08 follow-up. The QoL follow-up survey is included here as the longitudinal design provided the opportunity to test the causal model of the OPQOL, as well as a willing sample for test-retest reliability assessment.

Prior to administration in the surveys reported here, the items in the OPQOL were pre-tested with 179 volunteers from a previous QoL follow-up survey wave (in 2006). Statistical tests of reliability and validity were applied. Following amendments, it was further assessed for face and content validity with three focus groups of older people. Two versions of the OPQOL resulted from these processes, consisting of 32 and 35 items. A 13-item version was also tested (Bowling et al, 2013); this was developed with 236 older people in three Older People's Forums in England, who prioritised the most important OPQOL items to them.

Findings from the research

Just over half of each sample comprised women (52%/207 Ethnibus, 55%/324 ONS, 54%/154 QoL follow-up). While most Ethnibus respondents were aged 65<75 (91%/363), just over half of ONS Omnibus (55%/326), and less than a fifth of QoL follow-up respondents (17%/47), were aged 65<75. Thirty-eight per cent (152) of the Ethnibus sample were Indian, 29% (117) were Pakistani, 22% (86) were Black Caribbean and 11% (45) were Chinese. Most, 94% (555) of the ONS Omnibus sample, were White British; all QoL follow-up respondents were White British. In reflection of their younger age, more of the Ethnibus than other respondents were married or cohabiting (58%/230, 49%/285, 49%/138, respectively). Fewer

Ethnibus than the other respondents were home owners (53%/208, 73%/429, 85%/239 respectively); and fewer lived alone (5%/19, 48%/286, 49%/137 respectively). Few (12%/70) of the ONS Omnibus sample, compared with more (45%/113) of the older QoL follow-up sample and 73%/290 of the Ethnibus sample were in the lowest two OPQOL categories (< 119), indicating worse QoL. (All differences were statistically significant at least at $p < 0.01$.)

The OPQOL performed well in psychometric tests of reliability and validity, and results were better than those for the CASP-19 and WHOQOL-OLD. For example, the criterion validity of all three QoL scales was indicated by their moderate to strong, significant correlations with global self-rated QoL. The Spearman's rho correlations for the OPQOL by self-rated QoL overall in each sample were Ethnibus −0.347; ONS −0.602; QoL follow-up −0.659; for the CASP, in the two cross-sectional samples, they were Ethnibus −0.273; ONS −0.577; and for the WHOQOL-OLD, in the two cross-sectional samples, they were Ethnibus −0.128; ONS: −0.466. All correlations were significant at least at $p < 0.01$, with the exception of WHOQOL-OLD in the Ethnibus sample, which was $p < 0.05$. (Minus signs simply reflect opposite coding directions.) The validity of the OPQOL was further supported by significant correlations between its sub-scales and the independent QoL domain ratings, in theoretically expected, similar directions; for example, OPQOL health and functioning sub-scale correlated with self-rated health − Spearman's rho: Ethnibus −0.122 ($p < 0.05$); ONS Omnibus −0.679 ($p < 0.01$); QoL follow-up −0.713 ($p < 0.01$). There were no significant correlations with dissimilar pairs (for example, health and religion), again as expected. The Cronbach's alpha tests of internal consistency exceeded the 0.70 threshold of acceptability for the OPQOL in each of the three samples (alpha: 0.75, 0.88, 0.90). In contrast, the CASPE-19 achieved alphas of 0.55-0.87, and the WHOQOL-OLD achieved alphas of 0.42-0.85. Table 5.1 shows the distributions between samples for the OPQOL total score only. This shows that QoL total scale scores were significantly worse for the Ethnibus sample, indicating that, overall, they rated their QoL as worse than did the other samples.

Comparisons of QoL item responses and sub-scale scores between samples showed that these were also consistently worse for the Ethnibus sample, compared with the other two samples (see Table 5.2 for some examples).

The detailed psychometric properties of the grouped OPQOL scores and sub-scale scores, by sample, can be found in Bowling and Stenner (2011). Multivariable analyses, to examine independent predictors of

Table 5.1: OPQOL scale and sub-scale distributions

	Ethnibus	ONS Omnibus	QoL follow-up
OPQOL total (Ethnibus, ONS Omnibus 35 items; 5-point scale [1-5], range 35-175; QoL follow-up: 32 items, range 32-160)	% (n)	% (n)	% (n)
≤ 99 QoL as bad as can be	6 (24)	1 (6)	7 (17)*
100-119	67 (266)	11 (64)	38 (96)
120-139	25 (100)	52 (289)	43 (108)
140-159	2 (9)	32 (178)	12 (29)
160-175 QoL as good as can be	– (1)	4 (23)	–
Number of scaled responses	400	560	250

Note: * p < 0.0001

Table 5.2: Comparisons between samples: OPQOL social relationships

% Strongly agree/agree	Ethnibus %	ONS Omnibus %	QoL follow-up %
+ My family, friends or neighbours would help me if needed	37	94	93*
I would like more companionship/ contact with other people	36	20	23*
+ I have someone who gives me love/affection	55	88	80*
I'd like more people to enjoy life with	35	29	26*
+ I have my children around which is important (0 children=SD)	44	68*	Not asked

Note: * p < 0.001

QoL, showed that perceptions of ageing more actively, having optimal self-ratings of health, independence, home and neighbourhood, psychological wellbeing and finances, more social activities and female sex significantly, and independently, predicted optimal OPQOL scores in each sample, explaining 65-77% of the variances in OPQOL scores (adjusted R^2).

Discussion

This body of research provided valuable indications about how QoL can be improved for older people. The baseline research indicated that there are a number of drivers of QoL in old age, including making positive social comparisons with others; having realistic expectations; having good health and mobility; and feeling safe in the community. Survey respondents emphasised the importance of living in a neighbourly and safe area, and having good local facilities to promote friendly and helpful relationship with other people, including neighbours. Respondents mentioned the importance of having someone for 'companionship', 'to take me out' and 'to make life bearable'. Meaningful contact, either face to face or by telephone, with sons and daughters, was important to most respondents for enjoyment, help and security. Contact with grandchildren (and being able to play and go out with them), was frequently mentioned. Many respondents referred to the importance of having social or voluntary activities in the context of the importance of 'keeping busy' – to stop them worrying, feeling alone, or dwelling on the past. Their responses were consistent with social and psychological theories of the building blocks of QoL, and they led directly to the development of the OPQOL questionnaire. The later surveys tested the OPQOL, and reported excellent psychometric properties, which supported its potential use in population research and service evaluation. Bowling and Stenner (2011) also found that far more respondents in the ethnically diverse Ethnibus survey than other respondents reported poor QoL, despite being more likely than other survey members to be at the younger end of the older age spectrum – aged 65<75 rather than 75+. This merits further investigation, particularly as wellbeing (a component of QoL) has been reported to be a U-shaped curve over the lifecycle (Blanchflower and Oswald, 2008) and that it rises in middle to early older age before declining in advanced old age (Mroczek and Spiro, 2005).

This research resulted in a tested QoL measure that can be used in descriptive and evaluation research at no charge. The overall research led to several recommendations, specifically the need for people to stay involved in social activities throughout life, and build up support networks from a young age onwards – to ensure a stock of such social resources in later life; and the need to develop positive thinking techniques, and to learn to find ways to feel more in control of everyday life. Society also needs to work harder, in partnership with local people, to promote neighbourly local communities with good facilities for the enhancement of QoL, including in older age.

Key findings

- Ethnic minority elders had poorer health status than their White British counterparts, despite being younger on average: 18% rated their health as 'poor' compared with 4-5% of the average. They were also more likely to live in large households: only 5% reported that they lived alone, compared with 48-49% of the general population of older people. They had twice as many relatives to help them, but fewer friends.
- Ethnic minority elders were less likely than the general older population to consider themselves as ageing 'very' or 'fairly' actively.

Conclusion

In conclusion, the OPQOL achieved good levels of reliability and validity in British population samples, and in the ethnically diverse sample. The OPQOL was sensitive to differences in responses between White British and ethnically diverse samples (including when controlling for age, sex, socio-economic status). Health and social care interventions can have a multifaceted impact on people's lives. This research supports the use of the OPQOL in older populations in Britain. Its potential use in service evaluation is supported by research in Italy among community-dwelling geriatric outpatients (Bilotta et al, 2011). In this study, poor QoL and health-related QoL, as described by the lowest score-based quartiles of the OPQOL total score and health-related OPQOL sub-score respectively, were independent predictors of several adverse health outcomes: falls and emergency admissions for overall QoL as well as falls, nursing home placement and death for health-related QoL. These findings lend support to the prognostic value of QoL measures in older people and provide insight into the association between QoL and adverse health events. The OPQOL has also been shown to be associated with frailty status among trial participants in the UK, and QoL score changed in expected directions with changes in frailty over time (Kojima et al, 2016).

The NDA study was disseminated to stakeholders, academics and older people's groups by the International Longevity Centre (www.ilcuk.org.uk), and a summary of findings and details of the OPQOL can be found in its archives (www.ilcuk.org.uk/index.php/publications/publication_details/good_neighbours_measuring_quality_of_life_in_old_age, and www.ilcuk.org.uk/images/uploads/publication-pdfs/pdf_pdf_159.pdf).

Acknowledgements

This research was funded by the UK cross-research council New Dynamics of Ageing programme (grant number RES-352-25-0001), and the initial baseline survey of QoL was funded by the ESRC Growing Older programme (grant number L480254003).

References

Andrews, F.M. (ed) (1986) *Research on the QoL*, Ann Arbor, MI: Institute for Social Research, University of Michigan.

Andrews, F.M. and Withey, S.B. (1976) *Social indicators of well-being: Americans' perception of life quality*, New York, NY: Plenum.

Baltes, P.B. and Baltes, M.M. (eds) (1990) *Successful aging. Perspectives from the behavioral sciences*, New York, NY: Cambridge University Press.

Baltes, M.M., Mayer, M., Borchelt, M. et al (1996) 'Everyday competence in old and very old age: an interdisciplinary perspective', *Ageing & Society*, vol 13, pp 657-80.

Bergner, M., Bobbit, R.A., Carter, W.B. and Gilson, B. (1981) 'The Sickness Impact Profile: development and final revision of a health status instrument', *Medical Care*, vol 19, pp 787-805.

Bilotta, C., Bowling, A., Nicolina, P. et al (2011) 'Older People's Quality of Life (OPQOL) scores and adverse health outcomes at a one-year follow-up. A prospective cohort study on older outpatients living in the community in Italy', *Health and Social Care in the Community*, vol 9, p 72.

Blanchflower, D.G. and Oswald, A.J. (2008) 'Is well-being U-shaped over the life cycle?', *Social Science & Medicine*, vol 66, pp 1733-49.

Bowling, A. (1995a) 'What things are important in people's lives? A survey of the public's judgments to inform scales of health related QoL', *Social Science & Medicine*, vol 10, pp 1447-62.

Bowling, A. (1995b) 'The most important things in life. Comparisons between older and younger population age groups by gender', *International Journal of Health Sciences*, vol 6, pp 169-75.

Bowling, A. (1996) 'The effects of illness on QoL', *Journal of Epidemiology and Community Health*, vol 50, pp 149-55.

Bowling, A. (2005) *Ageing well. Quality of life in old age*, Maidenhead: McGraw Hill.

Bowling, A. (2009) 'Psychometric properties of the Older People's Quality of Life questionnaire validity', *Current Gerontology and Geriatrics Research*, Open access 'Volume 2009 (2009), Article ID 298950, 12 pages doi:10.1155/2009/298950. www.hindawi.com/journals/cggr/2009/298950.abs.htm

Bowling, A. and Gabriel, Z. (2004) 'An integrational model of quality of life in older age. A comparison of analytic and lay models of quality of life', *Social Indicators Research*, vol 69, pp 1-36.

Bowling, A. and Stenner, P. (2011) 'Which measure of QoL performs best in older age? A comparison of the OPQOL, CASP-19 and WHOQOL-OLD', *Journal of Epidemiology and Community Health*, vol 65, pp 273-80.

Bowling, A. and Windsor, J. (2001) 'Towards the good life. A population survey of dimensions of QoL', *Journal of Happiness Studies*, vol 2, pp 55-81.

Bowling, A., Gabriel, Z., Dykes, J. et al (2003) 'Let's ask them: a national survey of definitions of QoL and its enhancement among people aged 65 and over', *International Journal of Aging and Human Development*, vol 56, pp 269-306.

Bowling, A., Rowe, G., Lambert, N. et al (2012) 'The measurement of patients' expectations for health care: a review and psychometric testing of a measure of patients' expectations', *Health Technology Assessment*, vol 16, no 30.

Brown, J., Bowling, A. and Flyn, T. (2004) 'Models of quality of life: A taxonomy, overview and systematic review of quality of life', Paper presented at European Forum on Population Aging Research 2004, Department of Sociological Studies, University of Sheffield.

Browne, J.P., O'Boyle, C.A., McGee, H.M. et al (1994) 'Individual QoL in the healthy elderly', *Quality of Life Research*, vol 3, pp 235-44.

Campbell, A., Converse, P.E. and Rogers, W.L. (1976). *QoL in America*, New York, NY: Russell Sage.

DH (Department of Health) (2001) *Research governance framework for health and social care*, London: DH.

Farquhar, M. (1995) 'Elderly people's definitions of QoL', *Social Science & Medicine*, vol 41, pp 1439-46.

Fayers, P.M. and Hand, D.J. (2002) 'Causal variables, indicator variables and measurement scales: an example from quality of life', *Journal of the Royal Statistical Society*, vol 165, pp 1-21.

Fletcher, A.E., Jones, D.A., Bulpitt, C.J. and Tulloch, A.J. (2002) 'The MRC trial of assessment and management of older people in the community: objectives, design and interventions [ISRCTN23494848]', *BMC Health Services Research*, vol 2, p 21.

Francis, J., Fisher, M. and Rutter, D. (2011) 'Reablement: a cost-effective route to better outcomes', *Research Briefing 36*, London: Social Care Institute for Excellence.

Fry, P.S. (2000) 'Whose QoL is it anyway? Why not ask seniors to tell us about it?', *International Journal of Aging and Human Development*, vol 50, pp 361-83.

Gabriel, Z. and Bowling A. (2004) 'Perspectives on quality of life in older age: older people talking', *Ageing & Society*, vol 24, pp 675-91.

George, L.K. and Bearon, L.B. (1980) *QoL in older persons: Meaning and measurement*, New York, NY: Human Sciences Press Inc.

Grundy, E. and Bowling, A. (1999) 'Enhancing the quality of extended life years. Identification of the oldest old with a very good and very poor quality of life', *Aging & Mental Health*, vol 3, pp 199-212.

Higgs, P., Hyde, M., Wiggins R. and Blane, D. (2003) 'Researching quality of life in early old age: the importance of the sociological dimension', *Social Policy & Administration*, vol 37, pp 239-52.

Hyde, M., Wiggins, R.D., Higgs, P. and Blane, D. (2003) 'A measure of quality of life in early old age: the theory, development and properties of a needs satisfaction model (CASP-19)', *Aging & Mental Health*, vol 7, pp 186-94.

Kojima, G., Iliffe, S., Morris, R.W., Skelton, D.A., Kendrick, D., Masud, T., Taniguchi, Y. and Bowling, A. (2016) 'Frailty predicts trajectories of quality of life among community-dwelling older people', *Quality of Life Research*, vol 25, no 7, pp 1743-50.

Lawton, M.P. (1991) 'A multidimensional view of QoL in frail elders', in J.E. Birren, J.E. Lubben, J.C. Rowe and G.E. Deutchman (eds) *The concept and measurement of QoL in the frail elderly*, New York, NY: Academic Press, pp 4-27.

Lawton, M.P. (1994) 'QoL in Alzheimer's disease', *Alzheimer Disease & Associated Disorders*, vol 8, Suppl 3, pp 138-50.

Lawton, M.P. (1996) 'Quality of life and affect in later life', in C. Magai, S.H. McFadden et al (eds) *Handbook of emotion, human development, and aging*, San Diego, CA: Academic Press.

Lawton, M.P. (1997) 'Assessing QoL in Alzheimer's disease research', *Alzheimer Disease & Associated Disorders*, vol 1, pp 91-9.

Maslow, A. (1954) *Motivation and personality*, New York, NY: Harper.

Maslow, A.H. (1968) *Toward a psychology of being* (2nd edn) Princeton, NJ: Van Nostrand.

Mroczek, D.K. and Spiro, A. (2005) 'Change in life satisfaction during adulthood: findings from the Veterans Affairs Normative Aging study', *Journal of Personality and Social Psychology*, vol 88, pp 189-202.

Powell-Lawton, M. (1975) 'The Philadelphia Geriatric Morale Scale. A revision', *Journal of Gerontology*, vol 30, pp 85-9.

Power M, Harper A, Bullinger M, and the WHO Quality of Life Group. (1999) 'The World Health Organisation WHOQOL-100: tests of the universality of quality of life in 15 different cultural groups worldwide', *Health Psychology*,18: 495-505.

Power, M., Quinn, K., Schmidt, S. and WHOQOL-OLD Group (2005) 'Development of WHOQOL-OLD module', *Quality of Life Research*, vol 14, pp 2197-214.

Qureshi, H., Nocon, A. and Thompson, C. (1994) *Measuring outcomes of community care for users and carers: A review*, York: Social Policy Research Unit, University of York.

Skevington, S.M. (1999) 'Measuring quality of life in Britain: introducing the WHOQOL-100', *Journal of Psychosomatic Research*, vol 47, pp 449-59.

Skevington, S.M., O'Connell, K.A. and the WHOQOL Group (2004) 'Can we identify the poorest quality of life? Assessing the importance of quality of life using the WHOQOL-100', *Quality of Life Research*, vol 13, pp 23-4.

Thornicroft, G. and Tansella, M. (eds) (1996) *Mental health outcome measures*, Berlin: Springer.

WHO (World Health Organization) (1993) *Measuring QoL: The development of the World Health Organization QoL Instrument (WHOQOL)*, Geneva: WHO.

WHOQOL Group (1995)'The World Health Organization Quality of Life assessment (WHOQOL): position paper from the World Health Organization', *Social Science & Medicine*, vol 41, no 10, pp 1403-9.

SIX

Engagement in musical activities

Susan Hallam and Andrea Creech

Introduction

Participation in musical activities has been shown to enhance social cohesion, enjoyment, personal development and empowerment (Sixsmith and Gibson, 2007; Hallam et al, 2017). Many benefits have been reported for older people (Creech et al, 2013a), with research on singing demonstrating how it contributes to increased energy; reduction in stress; enhanced self-perceived wellbeing, self-confidence and sense of purpose; stimulation of a range of cognitive capacities (attention, concentration, memory and learning); and improved health (Stacey et al, 2002; Clift et al, 2008, 2010). Lower mortality rates are also evident among those who make music or sing in a choir (Byrgen et al, 1996). In the US, Cohen and colleagues (2006, 2007) carried out non-randomised controlled studies with 166 participants with a mean age of 80 who participated in 30 singing workshops and 10 performances over one year. The participants reported fewer health issues, fewer falls, fewer doctor's visits and less use of medication than control groups. Their morale was higher, there was less reported loneliness and evidence of increased activity. In the UK, Hillman (2002) surveyed 75 retired participants who had, during retirement, participated in a community singing project. Long-term benefits attributed to participation in music included overall improvements to the quality of life and no overall deterioration in physical health.

There is also evidence of the power of music from intergenerational research. Saarikallio (2011) carried out group interviews with 21 Finnish adults aged 21-70, investigating the use of music (listening and active participation) for emotional self-regulation. For the oldest participants, singing or participating in instrumental ensembles offered opportunities for alleviating loneliness and coping with the challenges of ageing, providing opportunities for progression and enjoyment and adding meaning to life. Focusing on instrumental ensembles, Gembris (2008) used questionnaires to explore the function of amateur music making among a group of 308 adults aged 40-97. Participants attributed enjoyment, happiness and community belongingness to their musical engagement. Although many reported age-related constraints, they also identified compensatory strategies and generally maintained a strong musical self-concept.

Aims of the Music for Life project

Between 2009 and 2011, a team from the Institute of Education and the Guildhall School of Music & Drama carried out research investigating whether there were any benefits of community music making among older people. The aims of the project were to explore the ways in which participating in creative music making might enhance the lives of older people; to consider the extent to which active engagement with music making might influence social, emotional and cognitive wellbeing; and to explore the specific processes through which any possible impact might occur. A follow-on project developed a set of resources (videos and a training guide) to support the training of musicians who wished to develop their skills as leaders or facilitators of musical groups for older people.

Three institutions acted as partners in the research: the Sage, Gateshead; Westminster Adult Education Service; and the Connect programme at the Guildhall School of Music. The Sage, Gateshead offered an extensive programme of choirs and instrumental groups facilitated by community musicians. Some groups took place in the Sage, Gateshead, an iconic arts centre/concert hall, while others took place in outreach locations. The Music Department of the Westminster Adult Education Service was a more formal adult learning context, offering choirs, music appreciation classes and keyboard classes. Finally, the Guildhall Connect programme offered creative intergenerational music workshops within sheltered housing centres, delivered by facilitators who had been trained as community music leaders. The musical activities included singing in small and large groups, rock groups, and classes for guitar, ukulele, steel pans, percussion, recorder, music appreciation and keyboard. A control group was made up of individuals attending language classes (four groups); art/craft classes (five groups); yoga; social support (two groups); a book group; and a social club.

The research adopted a quasi-experimental approach using mixed methods including:

- questionnaires for participants, music (n = 398) and non-music (n = 102), at the beginning of the research including the CASP-12 measure of quality of life and the Basic Psychological Needs Scale (Deci and Ryan, 2010);
- questionnaires for music participants at the end of the nine-month period (n = 143);
- individual interviews with music participants (n = 29);
- focus group interviews with music participants (15 focus group interviews);
- videos and observations of music sessions (45 videos, notes made of 25 sessions);
- videos and observations of musical performances (three);
- data relating to drop-outs from musical activities (records of the participating providers);
- questionnaires for music facilitators including two scales (assessment of views of successful leadership, and Basic Needs Satisfaction at Work scale [Deci and Ryan, 2010]); and
- interviews with music facilitators (12).

A needs–satisfaction approach was adopted in relation to the measurement of quality of life. This approach is underpinned by a belief that quality of life, and specifically subjective wellbeing, may be assessed in relation to the extent to which basic universal and innate psychological needs are met. The CASP-12 measure was used (Wiggins et al, 2007). This consists of a four-point Likert scale, comprising 12 individual items organised into four subscales (control, autonomy, self-realisation and pleasure).

Deci and Ryan's (2000, 2008) general Basic Psychological Needs scale was also used. This seven-point Likert scale is conceptually similar to the CASP-12, comprising 21 items organised into sub-scales for control, autonomy and relatedness. Overall, these two scales were adopted to provide a robust measure of quality of life, focusing on cognitive, emotional and social wellbeing.

Findings from the research

Which older people participated in musical activities?

The study made it possible to identify who in the older population was likely to engage in music making (Hallam et al, 2012a). Eighty per cent of the musical group sample was female and the majority was white. It should be noted that although the research team had hoped to recruit a gender-balanced sample that included members of a range of ethnic minority groups, the sample was broadly representative of the participants within musical activities at the case study sites. The nature of the sample was in itself a finding that led to exploration of some of the barriers that potentially made it difficult for some older people to take part in community music activities. The age range was 50-93 with 246 members of the music group in the third age (50-75) and 92 in the fourth age (75+) (60 did not state their age). The majority of those participating in the music groups had been involved in professional occupations. There was no statistically significant difference in this respect between the music participants and those in the other groups.

Seventy-six per cent of those in the musical groups had some kind of prior musical experience. Twenty-nine per cent classed themselves as musical beginners. Only 4% described themselves as 'very good', while the remainder described themselves as either average or good. Seventy-three per cent indicated that they could read music, but for most this was at a basic level. Only 8% reported that they had 'very good' reading skills.

The participants in the control group were asked how important music was in their lives. Eleven per cent reported that music played a central role in their lives; for the remainder, music had 'no importance' or they 'listened to music from time to time'.

The benefits of participation: quantitative measures of wellbeing

There were statistically significant differences with regard to scores on the CASP-12 and psychological needs measures between those participating in the musical and non-musical groups. Consistently, more positive responses were found among the musical groups (Hallam et al, 2011; Creech et al, 2013b; Hallam and Creech, 2016a). Analysis of variance of the four components of the CASP-12 measure (control, autonomy, self-realisation and pleasure) comparing those participating in the music groups and those participating in other activities showed statistically significant differences in relation to control and pleasure but not autonomy or self-realisation (Table 6.1).

Analysis of variance was undertaken in relation to the sub-components of the Basic Needs Satisfaction Scale (Deci and Ryan, 2000) (control, autonomy and relatedness) and comparisons made between those participating in the music and non-music groups. There were no statistically significant differences between music and non-music participants on measures of autonomy or competence. However,

Table 6.1: Total scale and sub-scales of CASP-12

	Music Mean*	Standard Deviation	Non-music Mean*	Standard Deviation	
Control	9.43 (332)	1.89	8.28 (85)	1.90	F = 25.3 (1,415) p = .0001
Autonomy	9.92 (338)	1.83	9.67 (86)	1.83	F = 1.2 (1,422) Not statistically significant
Pleasure	11.32 (335)	1.5	10.59 (87)	1.61	F = 15.73 (1,420) p = .0001
Self-realisation	10.38 (138)	1.8	10.00 (31)	1.82	F = 3.59 (1,167) Not statistically significant
Total	40.98 (138)	5.13	39.67 (18)	4.95	F = .97 (1, 101) Not statistically significant

Notes: * Maximum score for sub-scales = 12; maximum score for total scale = 48. Figures in brackets indicate the sample size for that measure.

there were differences in relation to relatedness and in relation to the total score representing all three of the sub-scales combined (Table 6.2).

It was clear from these analyses that although the constructs proposed were similar, the two measures utilised in the research were assessing slightly different elements. To establish the nature of any underlying conceptual constructs, a principal component analysis (PCA) with

Table 6.2: Comparison between music participants and non-participants on the sub-components of the Basic Needs Satisfaction Scale

Scale	Music groups Mean*	Standard Deviation	Non-music group Mean*	Standard Deviation	
Autonomy	40.3 (319)	5.78	39.17 (72)	9.6	F = 1.74 (1,389) Not statistically significant
Competence	30.19 (308)	5.47	29.7 (70)	6.05	F = .442 (1,376) Not statistically significant
Relatedness	48.17 (319)	5.79	45.73 (71)	6.52	F = 9.82 (1,388) p = .002
Total	119.29	13.61	113.98	18.32	F = 6.79 (1,361) p = .01

Notes: * Autonomy and relatedness: minimum score = 7, maximum score = 49; competence: minimum score = 6, maximum score = 42; total scale: minimum score = 21, maximum score = 147. Figures in brackets indicate the sample size for that measure.

orthogonal rotation (varimax) was undertaken using the items from the CASP-12 and the Basic Psychological Needs Scale. The Kaiser-Meyer-Olkin measure verified the sampling adequacy for the analysis, KMO = .849) and all KMO values for individual items were well above the acceptable limit of 0.5 (Field, 2009). Bartlett's test of sphericity (X^2 (528) = 4040.336, p = .0001) indicated that the correlations between items were sufficiently large for PCA. Analysis of the scree plot suggested that the most appropriate solution was a three-factor solution. Factor 1 had an eigenvalue of 7.5 and related to having a positive outlook on life (purpose), factor 2 had an eigenvalue of 2.9 and related to lack of autonomy and control (autonomy/control), and factor 3 had an eigenvalue of 2.2 and related to positive social relationships, competence and a sense of recognised accomplishment (social affirmation). Together these accounted for 38.3% of the variance. This analysis suggested a need for a re-evaluation of the use of these measures in research focusing on the wellbeing of older people.

Comparisons of those engaged in music making with those participating in other activities revealed statistically significant differences on all three factors with the music groups having more positive responses (Table 6.3).

Table 6.3: Comparison of factor scores between music and non-music groups

	Music (280)	Non-music (62)	
Factor 1: purpose	0.088	−0.398	F = 12.39 (1,340) p = .0001
Factor 2: autonomy/control	−0.068	0.310	F = 7.423 (1,340) p = .007
Factor 3: social affirmation	0.052	−0.234	F = 4.19 (1,340) p = .041

As shown in Table 6.4, comparisons of those in the third and fourth age in the music groups revealed no differences in relation to the factors relating to autonomy/control or social affirmation, although there was a deterioration in relation to sense of purpose (Hallam et al, 2014).

These findings suggest that engagement in musical activities can support sustained autonomy/control and social affirmation into the fourth age. A multiple regression analysis revealed that for those involved in musical activities (but not for those involved in other activities), high scores for the third wellbeing factor – social affirmation – were predicted by strong agreement that participation in their groups provided opportunities to remain involved with the community,

Table 6.4: Differences in factor scores for third- and fourth-age participants in the music groups

	Third age (209)	Fourth age (64)	
Factor 1: purpose	0.157	−0.179	$F = 5.819$ (1,271) $p = .017$
Factor 2: autonomy/control	−0.107	0.032	$F = .943$ (1,271) Not statistically significant
Factor 3: social affirmation	0.060	0.056	$F = .001$ (1,271) Not statistically significant

was intellectually stimulating, helped to manage stress, and provided opportunities for performance (Hallam et al, 2011).

Perceived benefits of group participation: quantitative measures

Participants were asked to respond to a series of statements relating to the perceived benefits of group activity using a four-point rating scale. High ratings were given by those participating in music and non-music groups to a series of statements relating to:

• sustaining wellbeing, quality of life and reducing stress;
• acquiring new skills;
• providing opportunities for mental activity and intellectual stimulation;
• promoting social activity and involvement in the community;
• providing opportunities for demonstrating skills and helping others; and
• maintaining physical health.

There were no statistically significant differences in response to these elements between the music and non-music groups, with one exception: the means for those participating in the music groups were higher in relation to their level of enjoyment of the group activity, with a mean of 3.73 compared with a mean of 3.43 for the control groups.

Benefits attributed to engagement with music: qualitative data

The data from the individual and focus group interviews was analysed using NVivo. The participants and facilitators revealed a range of perceived benefits of active musical engagement including those related to social activity, cognition, emotional and mental health and physical health (Hallam et al, 2012b; Varvarigou et al, 2012a). In the following sections, examples from the analysis of the individual interviews with participants are set out. The themes emerging from the focus group interviews reflected those from the individual interviews. The boxes set out the number of participants referring to a particular theme (sources) and the number of times a particular theme was referred to (references).

Social benefits

Participants noted that music activities gave a structure to their life after retirement, providing an activity to look forward to every week. They were motivated to make the effort to attend the groups, which were described as fun and enjoyable, and represented places where participants felt a sense of community. Participants also expressed an interest in mixing with younger people and children in joint musical activities. Through participation in musical groups, some individuals fulfilled a need to socialise with like-minded people, to work together as a team and to belong to a group that supported their musical aspirations. For some participants, participation in musical groups offered the opportunity to give something back to their communities, by sharing their skills and helping to create enjoyable experiences for others (Box 6.1).

Box 6.1: Participants' social relationships and interactions through musical groups

Activities give structure to my life
16 sources; 20 references

> "I have only been with the Silver Singers two weeks but love every minute of it. Cannot wait for each Wednesday morning. Thank you."

> "My activities at the Sage help to keep me motivated, otherwise I think I'd become a television addict. I have to get up at a reasonable hour to allow for travelling time from home, and plan other appointments round Breves, Divas and Pans. Even holiday breaks come second!"

> "It has also taught me to arrange my other activities in such a way that I can fit in time for practice and consolidating my skills."

Intergenerational activities
14 sources; 23 references

"I love the activities but do feel I have entered an older age group. Might be nice to join forces with younger people occasionally." [One friend wouldn't join for this reason.]

"... different generation they want a different kind of music. They like their rap, they have their own kind of music what they like, so they want the modern music for the 18-year-old. You know you can't get an 18-year-old to learn about Frank Sinatra, they say who is he? But they might know Michael Jackson, everybody know [sic] Michael Jackson."

Fun – laugh a lot
11 sources; 11 references

"It is such fun and I love being surrounded by like-minded people."

"It got us together to sing and play and we have a good laugh. It has been good for us and we say how much we enjoy it."

"Takes me to another world. Some discipline but a lot of fun and laughter, coming together as a group."

"Can be or is fun and have a laugh while still taking the music seriously."

Belonging
48 sources; 69 references

"It's a positive experience for me because it gets you out of the house and into the company of others, rehearsing the music and singing the songs together."

"I recently retired from full-time work and being involved in music making has made me feel part of an important new community."

"I feel that the group that I'm in is – people more or less my age, we're old age pensioners, and it seems that when we're up there as a group, whether we do a single on our own or we all sing together as a group, it's got some meaning to it."

Opportunities to socialise
47 sources; 59 references

"Meeting other people, which is a great help when living on one's own."

"Helped me to socialise with others."

"Opportunities are also there to meet other people who often are in similar circumstances to one's own. Music being one of the common denominations."

"Has helped me to stay open-minded, take risks and form new friendships ... which continue to be important in older age."

Giving back to the community
12 sources; 22 references

"It's just that, as in performing, you are allowing people to hear you; you want to give a rendition of yourself, you want everybody to give a rendition of everything. You want to feel that what you've learnt is going to be enjoyed by someone else."

"I have made new friends, I am able to support people less experienced in their music making and enjoy teaching beginner recorder to adults."

"First we sing as a choir, then on our own. It gives me, at my age [tearful], I'm 85, it gives me a great feeling inside me that I can sing and it makes other people happy."

Cognitive benefits

Participants attributed enhanced cognitive wellbeing to their participation in musical activities. For example, singing in parts, memorising music and the concentration required for listening to new music and taking part in ensemble playing were perceived as stimulating cognitive challenges that contributed to feeling active and alert. Progression and a sense of accomplishment when goals had been attained were important in supporting motivation and commitment (Box 6.2).

Box 6.2: Cognitive benefits reported by participants

Challenge
24 sources; 37 references

"I found that [singing in parts] more difficult, but I found it good because it is a challenge. It did, you know, make us think."

"Music is proving to be an amazing enjoyable opportunity for me in retirement. It is both mentally challenging and socially involving."

"It's good for memory and concentration and is relaxing, except when some phrases are difficult to master, then it becomes a challenge."

Sense of achievement – acquiring new skills
48 sources; 60 references

"Learning something new at an older age can be enjoyable, successful and stimulating.

That you've done something and somebody else has appreciated it. And you feel 'Oh, yes we have accomplished something.'"

"They give us a chance to ... socialise as well as learning new skills which give us a sense of achievement."

"I want to get something out of it. I don't see the point in coming back for another three terms because I'm not moving forward. I do want to progress a bit."

Helps with concentration and memory
16 sources; 17 references

"I feel samba and drum-kit are particularly good for the grey cells! – have to concentrate and remember. I enjoy it all – it's *fun*."

"I definitely feel that my concentration and memory have improved since joining."

"It's good for memory and concentration and is relaxing, except when some phrases are difficult to master, then it becomes a challenge."

Keeps me active, alert and young
38 sources; 52 references

> "It keeps me active, alert and organised. It allows me to use and build on previous experience."

> "It keeps my mind active and I have felt better emotionally after singing sessions."

> "I do think that being involved in music definitely keeps you young.... Because, like I am saying, you are using this mental ability all the time and that's got to be good, hasn't it?"

Appreciation of music
47 sources; 65 references

> "The music class has encouraged me to listen to classical music and go to BBC recordings. All the classes I attend have encouraged and kept me from feeling bored."

> "It introduces me to new ideas and extends my appreciation of different musical genres."

Physical health benefits

The participants talked about health constraints such as hearing, arthritis and other mobility problems that sometimes made participation in and enjoyment of music difficult. However, improvements to physical health were attributed to participation in music. These physical benefits included respiratory benefits, physical exercise and increased use of joints. During the focus group discussions, the idea was floated that musical activities should be available on prescription from the National Health Service (Box 6.3).

Box 6.3: Physical health benefits reported by participants

Individual interview responses
Health – good for asthma and breathing
18 sources; 19 references

"Always feel better after singing. Asthma has almost disappeared."

"Helps in my control of breathing."

"Singing in choirs has helped me relax and feel more healthy – those breathing exercises really *are* good for you!"

"It has improved my breathing and helps me to relax and feel less anxious. I can sing with my grandchildren (which I couldn't have done prior to the Silver Singers)."

General positive physical health
38 sources; 52 references

"Would like to see 'singing as prescription' being offered by GPs. Newcastle has 'exercise as prescription' – singing could be offered, too. Maybe with a friend to link the referred person.

Playing the ukulele is good exercise for my finger joints."

"Exercise, walking down to the Sage two to three times a week."

Focus group responses
Music as a physical workout
3 sources; 4 references

"It is quite a hard work, too. When I come away bits are aching."

"It is a workout."

Music as a therapy
2 sources; 2 references

"I think as regards funding it must save the health service and the social services an enormous amount if they put these in place everywhere because just the coming out, the having an ending view, you know, you've got to be want to learn this thing and you don't want to let the rest of the band down.... So it must be good for our health to get us out of the house so that we have to walk about and all the things that we are supposed to do."

"I think music is therapy, you know. I think it can really pick you right up."

Emotional benefits and mental health

Participants made many references linking music participation and positive mental health. Individuals described how participation in music had helped them to cope effectively with stress, depression and bereavement. The participants attributed many positive feelings such as a sense of rejuvenation, an emotional 'lift' and spirituality to singing and playing musical instruments. Participation in music offered opportunities for creative expression and in some cases provided a sense of purpose in life (Box 6.4).

Box 6.4: Emotional benefits and positive mental health reported in individual interviews

Protection against depression
10 sources; 11 references

"I have been suffering from depression. Singing has had a really good effect on me. I feel more positive."

"For many years I have suffered periodic bouts of depression. Since being welcomed into the Silver Programme at the Sage Gateshead, I am happy to report that I have been 'depression-free'. Unless you have had this condition you cannot imagine what a blessed relief it is to be without it for almost a whole year!"

"Well, I have to say that because I was already ... I had had a bit of a breakdown but I was still, sort of, climbing out of it when I joined. And so now that I am sort of out of it life is just definitely for living myself as much as I can. So, it was more part and parcel of the general recovery from that."

Protection against stress
19 sources; 19 references

"It gives pleasure and as you become involved you forget the stresses in your life."

"Participating in music has enriched my life by relieving stress, and my experience of this wonderful class has been a very positive one. I hope it will continue next term."

"Participating at events and activities at the Sage, Gateshead, has added a new dimension to my life! As prime carer for parents with Alzheimer's disease, I am sometimes stressed. All stress leaves me when participating in musical activities and I leave with a spring in my step. This rubs off on my parents as I often sing to them or play my ukulele for them when visiting or having them to my house!"

Music and positive feelings
72 sources; 83 references

"It has helped me come to terms with retirement following a long and fulfilling career."

"When I participate in music making the rest of my life gets left behind and I become totally involved. It lifts the spirits and facilitates connection with other people."

"I can go to Divas feeling really fed up with myself as I do have several health problems. But spending time with the Divas and E. gives me a good boost and simply makes me feel good.

"Benefits – singing gives me a real 'lift'. Makes me feel great!"

"Music brings joy into my life and particularly singing in choirs lifts me up and takes my mind off any problems."

Support after bereavement
6 sources; 7 references

"Following the death of my husband, our close and loving relationship over almost 50 years, has left me with some very negative feelings. My answers would have been quite different before my bereavement." [she claimed that attending the music activities had supported her through this period].

"After the loss of a daughter – 12 months ago.... Singing is the best anti-depressive in the world!"

"I joined the Sage Silver programme about four years ago. My husband died suddenly over two years ago and I found the participation in the singing and an instrumental group was one of the greatest supports in my life. Singing is always uplifting and it is difficult to be sad while playing the ukulele!"

Creative expression
7 sources; 7 references

"Enjoy the opportunity to sing, express myself and be creative. Now retired and can get back to participating in music. Before my professional career took over my life."

Sense of purpose
8 sources; 8 references

"It has given more purpose to my life and given me reasons to meet each day as it comes."

"Given me one morning per week that is *me* time."

Confidence growth
34 sources; 48 references

"It has encouraged me to have higher expectations of myself and greater confidence socially."

"My experiences with music have given me strength and confidence in myself, the laughter, the fun and also when I can associate certain pieces of music with things or people in my life."

"People grow in confidence as they are able to have a go at a wide variety of activities and learn new skills."

Feeling rejuvenated
3 sources; 3 references

> "Because they encouraged us, you know, to dress like rock in leathers and other stuff and you should see the pictures ... I am 72, you know and we are all at that age and you should see the way we come from the start. Very nice [laughter]."

> "Whoops – I don't consider myself old."

> "When I play the tambourine the backing singers are all ... [laughter] and you think we are about 16!"

Creativity and expression

Overall, when questioned about what was special about music as opposed to other activities, participants attributed positive benefits to its creative and expressive qualities. One participant, who had had no previous musical training, wrote a song. Initially, he was afraid to acknowledge it as his own, but once it was well received by the group he was very proud of his achievement and planned to continue his creative activities (Varvarigou et al, 2013).

Musical identity

For some, music was a vehicle for redefining their identity or rediscovering a lost 'possible self' (Creech et al, 2014a). Through music making, participants developed, or in some cases rekindled, a strong musical identity. After a period of participation, some older people identified themselves as musicians.

Developing musical self-concepts were supported by a sense of being part of a community of musicians, by having performed with the professional musician facilitators and having spent many hours making music and practising. Participants also referred to how they thought others perceived them; being a 'musician' was a new role, bringing with it interest, importance and enjoyment to others.

Performance

Having opportunities for performance played a major role in the perceived benefits, constituting a means of receiving position affirmation from others. For many participants, performances offered an important opportunity to 'be a musician', sharing the results of their hard work with friends and relatives. Performances were opportunities for positive feedback and contributed significantly to a strong musical self-concept. Performances seemed to be a significant part of the participants' individual and collective musical journeys.

Intergenerational activities

Some of the older people engaged in intergenerational activities with children from local primary schools (Varvarigou et al, 2012a; Varvarigou et al, 2015). For them, the presence of children in their sheltered accommodation gave them energy, made them feel happy and gave them an opportunity to relate to the younger generation. The children reported enjoying the activities, and their teachers and the music facilitator also commented on the mutual benefits. The intergenerational activity was an opportunity for different generations to socialise, show respect for each other and enjoy each other's company. The children, their teachers and the music leader all commented on the social relationships and interpersonal interactions that were fostered among young and old. In particular, teachers observed the sense of enjoyment and respect among the children, while the children described the experience as exciting, interesting and fun.

The characteristics of the facilitators

Facilitators played a wide range of instruments (most more than one), worked in a range of different genres, and had a wide range of qualifications at different levels. Some had participated in community music training courses, while others had learnt on the job. They indicated that there were a number of benefits to themselves of working with older people. These included opportunities for professional development and to increase their knowledge of different genres and repertoire; personal satisfaction and fulfilment; warm and mutually respectful interactions; appreciation by others of their expertise; and a sense of belonging (Hallam et al, 2016a).

Teaching and learning

The role of the facilitator was seen as crucial in ensuring the widest possible benefits to the older people (Hallam et al, 2013). Facilitators attempted to balance having fun with challenge, although the emphasis varied. They referred to adopting humanistic and progressive principles in their teaching (McQueen et al, 2013). Activities were designed to provide interest, but also to offer support. Choice of repertoire was important. Participants preferred music that was relevant to their life histories. They rejected materials or practices that they felt were childish. Facilitators stressed the need to adopt inclusive teaching practices, creating a welcoming atmosphere and having an open door policy.

The facilitators adopted varying approaches to their groups, with some functioning informally as fellow musicians and others taking a more traditional leadership role. This depended on the nature of the activity, the size of the group and available space. In all of the different types of group, positive peer interactions were noted, with some groups offering each other emotional support while others engaged in peer learning (most obviously in the instrumental groups) and celebrated their musical achievements as a group. However, there was also evidence of some negative peer interactions. For example, some participants were critical of others who did not integrate with the group.

Analysis of the data from the recorded musical sessions showed that, overall, the greatest amount of time for facilitators was spent in 'scaffolding' and 'music making and practical work' for participants. Scaffolding included conducting, accompanying, and singing or playing along with participants. Facilitators used modelling on average approximately 15% of the time, in comparison with approximately 48% of time spent conducting, 10% on organisational activities, 6% diagnosing performance issues, and explaining or answering questions, 5% asking questions, and 4% in directing activities. Feedback to participants was positive and expressed in general terms, such as 'good', 'well done'. Participants spent 30% of their time listening passively, 10% in vocal or physical warm-ups, and the remainder on questioning, discussing, or offering opinions (Creech et al, 2014c).

All of the groups worked towards a musical outcome (Creech et al, 2014b; Creech and Hallam, 2015; Hallam and Creech, 2016b). Facilitators reported that they had learned:

- the need for repetition and revisiting repertoire;
- to manage resistance to unfamiliar music, different genres and styles;

- the need to adapt activities for differing physical abilities;
- that games can work with older people;
- that older people can present challenging behaviour in relation to others in the group or the facilitator in relation to, for example, seating or choice of repertoire, and that this has to be managed;
- that sessions cannot be too long or participants tire;
- the need to adjust to individual and cultural expectations in terms of musical genres;
- not to use too many foreign language songs;
- the richness of the participants' social, professional and personal histories;
- the importance of making sessions fun, yet purposeful;
- increased patience;
- to adopt a slower pace, and speak slowly and clearly;
- to maintain a positive, uncritical atmosphere (to avoid encouraging criticism among participants);
- to keep the content relatively simple;
- the need to deal with poor punctuality to avoid disrupting the functioning of the group, particularly where key players were late; and
- to reflect on their usual teaching style (for example, content-driven) in relation to older learners.

The facilitators themselves, participants, and other stakeholders were asked about the qualities of good music leaders. They described a good leader as knowledgeable; patient but in charge; positive, enthusiastic and enhancing motivation; having a sense of humour; responding to needs; and keeping a good pace and focus (Hallam et al, 2013; Hallam et al, 2016a).

Supporting participation and overcoming barriers

Although there were very few drop-outs among the music participants, a number of potential barriers to participation were identified. Structural barriers were those that related to physical access to facilities, perceptions of the location as being too elitist, financial constraints and time of day (daytime was preferable). Information barriers were also identified. It was apparent that many participants had come across information about music sessions purely by chance. There did not seem to be any systematic knowledge or place where older people could access reliable information about what was available in their area. Some personal and social barriers were also identified, including caring responsibilities, social orientations and personal interest, willingness to socialise, confidence and motivation (Hallam et al, 2011; Creech et al, 2012).

Several suggestions were made with regard to how the barriers might be overcome. First and foremost, it was emphasised that music sessions needed to be welcoming and inclusive, led by facilitators who established mutually respectful communication and set challenging tasks that took account of the prior experience their adult participants brought to the group. It was also thought that care had to be taken over ensuring that the physical context was accessible, for example, making use of outreach locations. Finally, pastoral support (for example, 'buddy' systems, time for socialising) was thought to be vitally important in helping individuals to develop confidence and motivation to attend group sessions (Hallam et al, 2011; Creech et al, 2012).

Implications for policy and practice

The interviews with those responsible for arranging and managing musical activities for older people indicated difficulty in recruiting musicians. The follow-on to the Music for Life project was able to contribute to addressing this issue by offering training sessions to musicians at venues in each of the nine geographical regions in England drawing on the findings from the research. A facilitators' handbook was also devised (Creech et al, 2012). This is now freely available on the Soundsense website (the professional body for community musicians: www.soundsense.org). The training sessions and the manual offered general guidance about working with older people, pedagogical issues and, importantly, how to advocate at a local level for provision to be set up and how to overcome the barriers that older people may experience in engaging with musical activities. A key issue remains: the extent to which information is readily available about such activities, within local communities.

Overall, the implications are that:

- opportunities need to be made available for older people to engage in active music making in the community;
- information about music-making activities needs to be widely available in communities, and those offering such opportunities need to be proactive in encouraging engagement;
- musicians need to be trained to work in the community with older people.

Key findings
- Measures of wellbeing were consistently higher among the music participants (n = 398) than among the comparison group (n = 102).
- There was some positive change over time on quality of life measures, for those involved in musical activities.
- Participants reported social, cognitive, emotional and health benefits from participation in music.

Conclusion

The findings of the Music for Life project showed that:

- measures of wellbeing were consistently higher among those participating in musical rather than other group activities;
- the benefits of participating in musical activities seemed to continue from the third age into the fourth age;
- there were social, cognitive, emotional and health benefits to participation in music;
- facilitators played a key role in fostering positive outcomes;
- there were barriers to participation relating to access to information, and to structural, dispositional and social issues.

The research indicated that engagement with musical activities can act to promote and maintain health and wellbeing in older people, although any benefits depend on the quality of the provision. Policymakers should therefore turn their attention to provision that can act to prevent social isolation and depression and provide older people with opportunities for challenge, learning and social interaction, thus enhancing their confidence and self-esteem. While there is evidence that musical activities can have benefits for those recovering from illness or those who already are experiencing severe cognitive decline, it may be more beneficial, and cheaper, to set in place provision that will have a preventative effect.

Ageing research, by its very nature, tends to emphasise what older people are unable to do; there is a need to demonstrate what they are *able* do and to ensure that they are enabled to participate in activities that will promote their health and wellbeing. There were also benefits from intergenerational activities for all participants. Schools, arts organisations and those public and charitable bodies supporting older people should work together to exploit this.

Overall, the findings from the measures of wellbeing and the various interviews suggested that musical activity has a role to play in promoting wellbeing in older people and that the effects are greater for those participating in musical rather than the other groups. The power of music to influence moods and emotions is likely to be the crucial factor here (see Mitchell and McDonald, 2012).

Acknowledgements

This research was part of the New Dynamics of Aging programme which was funded across the five UK research councils: Arts and Humanities Research Council, Biotechnology and Biological Sciences Research Council, Engineering and Physical Sciences Research Council, Economic and Social Research Council and Medical Research Council.

References

Byrgen, L.A., Konlaan, B.B. and Johansson, W.E. (1996) 'Attendance at cultural events, reading books or periodicals, and making music or singing in a choir as determinants for survival: Swedish interview survey of living conditions', *British Medical Journal*, *313*, pp 1577-80.

Clift, S., Hancox, G., Staricoff, R. and Whitmore, C. (2008) *Singing and health: Summary of a systematic mapping; a review of non-clinical research*, Canterbury: Canterbury Christ Church University.

Clift, S., Nicol, J., Raisbeck, M., Whitmore, C. and Morrison, I. (2010) *Group singing, well-being and health: A systematic mapping of research evidence*, Folkestone: Sidney De Haan Research Centre for Arts and Health, Canterbury Christ Church University.

Cohen, G.D., Perlstein, S., Chapline, J., Kelly, J., Firth, K.M. and Simmens, S. (2006) 'The impact of professionally conducted cultural programs on the physical health, mental health, and social functioning of older adults', *The Gerontologist*, vol 46, no 6, pp 726-34.

Cohen, G.D., Perlstein, S., Chapline, J., Kelly, J., Firth, K.M. and Simmens, S. (2007) 'The impact of professionally conducted cultural programs on the physical health, mental health and social functioning of older adults – 2-year results', *Journal of Ageing, Humanities and the Arts*, vol 1, pp 5-22.

Creech, A. and Hallam, S. (2015) 'Critical geragogy: a framework for facilitating older learners in community music', *London Review of Education*, vol 13, no 1, pp 43-57.

Creech, A., Hallam, S. and Varvarigou, M. (2012) *Facilitating music-making for older people: Facilitator's handbook*, London: Institute of Education.

Creech, A., Hallam, S., Gaunt, H., Pincas, A., McQueen, H. and Varvarigou, M. (2013a) 'The power of music in the lives of older adults', *Research Studies in Music Education*, vol 15, no 1, pp 87-102.

Creech, A., Hallam, S., McQueen, H. and Varvarigou, M. (2014b) *Active ageing with music: Supporting well being in the third and fourth ages*, London: IOE Press.

Creech, A., Hallam, S., Varvarigou, M. and Gaunt, H. (2013a) 'Active music making: a route to enhanced subjective well-being amongst older people', *Perspectives in Public Health (Special Edition)*, vol 133, no 1, pp 36-43.

Creech, A., Hallam, S., Varvarigou, M., Gaunt, H., McQueen, H. and Pincas, A. (2014a) 'The role of musical possible selves in supporting subjective well-being in later life', *Music Education Research*, vol 16, no 1, pp 32-49.

Creech, A., Varvarigou, M., Hallam, S., McQueen, H. and Gaunt, H. (2014c) 'Scaffolding, organisational structure and interpersonal interaction in musical activities with older people', *Psychology of Music*, vol 42, no 3, pp 430-47.

Deci, E.L. and Ryan, R.M. (2000) 'The "what" and "why" of goal pursuits: human needs and the self-determination of behavior', *Psychological Inquiry*, vol 11, no 4, pp 227-68.

Deci, E. and Ryan, R. (2008) 'Facilitating optimal motivation and psychological well-being across life's domains', *Canadian Psychology*, vol 49, no 1, pp 14-23.

Gembris, H. (2008) 'Musical activities in the third age: An empirical study with amateur musicians', Paper presented at the Second European Conference on Developmental Psychology of Music, Roehampton University, England.

Hallam, S. and Creech, A. (2016a) 'Can active music making promote health and well-being in older citizens? Findings of the Music for Life Project', *London Journal of Primary Care*, vol 8, no 2, pp 21-5.

Hallam, S. and Creech, A. (2016b) 'Promoting well-being in older citizens through musical engagement: implications for teaching', in J. Bugos (ed) *Contemporary research in music learning across the lifespan*, New York, NY: Routledge, pp 259–67.

Hallam, S., Creech, A. and Varvarigou, M. (2017) 'Well-being and music leisure activity through the lifespan: a psychological perspective', in R. Mantie and G.D. Smith (eds) *Oxford handbook of music making and leisure*, Oxford: Oxford University Press, pp 31-60.

Hallam, S., Creech, A., Gaunt, H., McQueen, H. and Varvarigou, M. (2011) *Music for Life Project: Promoting social engagement and well-being through community supported participation in musical activities. Final report*, London: Institute of Education and Guildhall School of Music & Drama.

Hallam, S., Creech, A., McQueen, H. and Varvarigou, M. (2013) 'Perceptions of effective leadership in music facilitators working with older people', *Journal of Arts and Communities*, vol 3, no 3, pp 229-48.

Hallam, S., Creech, A., McQueen, H. and Varvarigou, M. (2016b) 'The role of the facilitator in community music making with older learners', *International Journal of Music Education*, vol 34, no 1, pp 19-31.

Hallam, S., Creech, A., McQueen, H., Varvarigou, M. and Gaunt, H. (2016a) 'The facilitator of community music-making with older learners: characteristics, motivations and challenges', *International Journal of Music Education*, vol 34, no 1, pp 19-31.

Hallam, S., Creech, A., Varvarigou, M. and McQueen, H. (2012a) 'What are the characteristics of the older people who engage in community music making, their reasons for participation and the barriers that they face?', *Journal of Adult and Continuing Education*, vol 18, no 2, pp 21-43.

Hallam, S., Creech, A., Varvarigou, M., McQueen, H. and Gaunt, H. (2012b) 'Perceived benefits of active engagement with making music in community settings', *International Journal of Community Music*, vol 5, no 2, pp 155-74.

Hallam, S., Creech, A., Varvarigou, M., McQueen, H. and Gaunt, H. (2014) 'Does active engagement in community music support quality of life in older people?', *Arts and Health*, vol 6, no 2, pp 101-16.

Hillman, S. (2002) 'Participatory singing for older people: a perception of benefit', *Health Education*, vol 102, no 4, pp 163-71.

McQueen, H., Hallam, S., Creech, A. and Varvarigou, M. (2013) 'A philosophical perspective on leading music activities for the over 50s', *International Journal of Lifelong Education*, vol 32, no 3, pp 353-77.

Mitchell, L. and McDonald, R. (eds) (2012) *Music, health and wellbeing*, Oxford: Oxford University Press.

Saarikallio, S. (2011) 'Music as emotional self-regulation throughout adulthood', *Psychology of Music*, vol 39, no 3, pp 307-27.

Sixsmith, A. and Gibson, G. (2007) 'Music and the well-being of people with dementia', *Ageing & Society*, vol 27, no 1, pp 127-45.

Stacey, R., Brittain, K. and Kerr, S. (2002) 'Singing for health: an exploration of the issues, *Health Education*, vol 102, no 4, pp 156-62.

Varvarigou, M., Creech, A., Hallam, S. and McQueen, H. (2012) 'Bringing different generations together in music-making – an intergenerational music project in East London', *International Journal of Community Music*, vol 4, no 3, pp 207-20.

Varvarigou, M., Creech, A., Hallam, S. and McQueen, H. (2013) 'Different ways of experiencing music-making in later life: creative music sessions for older learners in East London', *Research Studies in Music Education*, vol 15, no 1, pp 103–18.

Varvarigou, M., Hallam, S., Creech, A. and McQueen, H. (2012) 'Benefits experienced by older people who participated in group music-making activities', *Journal of Applied Arts and Health*, vol 3, no 2, pp 183-98.

Varvarigou, M., Hallam, S., Creech, A. and McQueen, H. (2015) 'Intergenerational music-making: a vehicle for active ageing for children and older people', in S. Clift and P. Camic (eds) *Oxford textbook of arts, health, and well-being: International perspectives on practice, policy, and research*, Oxford: Oxford University Press, p 259–67.

Wiggins, R.D., Netuveli, G., Hyde, E.M., Higgs, E.P. and BLane, E.D. (2007) 'The development and assessment of a quality of life measure (CASP-19) in the context of research on ageing', available at www.crm.umontreal.ca/Latent05/pdf/wiggins.pdf.

SEVEN

Combating social exclusion through community arts

Michael Murray and Amanda Crummett

Introduction

Older people frequently report social exclusion from a range of activities, decreased levels of social engagement and high levels of loneliness. This is particularly the case among older residents of disadvantaged neighbourhoods where there are fewer resources and facilities than in better-off neighbourhoods. Despite these challenges older people also report a high degree of attachment to their neighbourhood and the presence of informal social support. The aim of this chapter is to explore the potential value of community arts activities as a means of building social solidarity in disadvantaged neighbourhoods and of challenging social exclusion. This does not imply a neglect of structural inequalities and the promotion of a reactionary community-blaming approach. Rather, as we shall see, to be successful local initiatives require an active commitment of resources to provide ongoing support to ensure their sustainability.

Social exclusion is broadly defined as the process whereby certain groups are excluded from full participation in society. There is increasing evidence that many older people, particularly those who are resident in disadvantaged neighbourhoods, experience many forms of physical, social and emotional exclusion. In a study of older residents of six inner-cities, Scharf and colleagues (2002) found that many participants reported feeling excluded from organisations and institutions in their own neighbourhoods and not having the opportunity to become involved in social and civic activities. In addition, a significant minority had limited social contact with others and reported feelings of loneliness and social isolation.

There is continuing debate in the social policy arena about the meaning of the concept social exclusion (Kneale, 2012). There is an apprehension that by focusing on the social and cultural aspects of everyday living researchers are ignoring the structural and political issues that exclude people from active participation in society. Any action to combat social exclusion needs to address both dimensions. As Kneale emphasises, 'social exclusion among older people often occurs as a result of loss of independence – including pension wealth, public transport and housing, prompting the need for state intervention' (2012, p 7).

Much research has demonstrated that social connectedness promotes health and wellbeing, and conversely, social isolation and loneliness contributes to a deterioration in health. For example, a longitudinal study of older people by Mendes de Leon and colleagues (1999) found that greater social involvement predicted subsequent ability to carry out everyday activities of daily living. In a later study (Mendes de Leon et al, 2003), the researchers found that those older people who participated in more social and productive activities reported less subsequent disability. Similarly, in a longitudinal study of later-life engagement in social and leisure activities (Wang et al, 2001), it was found that frequent engagement in social, mental and productive activities was inversely related to dementia incidence. It was suggested that participation in social activities sustains the person's social concept of competence. Access to sources of social support also predicts more rapid recovery from illness. For example, Glass and colleagues (1993) found that older patients who had greater perceived sources of social support resumed activities of daily living more quickly than those with fewer sources of support after hospitalisation for a stroke. Conversely, Newall and colleagues (2012) found that self-reports of loneliness predicted subsequent mortality. A comprehensive meta-analysis of studies exploring the linkages between social connections and health (Holt-Lunstead et al, 2010) found that people with strong social relationships had a 50% increased likelihood of survival. Such evidence contributes to the argument that not only does social exclusion restrict people's access to resources, but it also contributes to social isolation and ill health.

Despite reporting the many challenges of living in disadvantaged inner-city districts, residents also often report a strong attachment to their neighbourhood. A recent study by Batty and colleagues (2011) of six low-income neighbourhoods across Britain found that although many of the residents reported many social problems in their districts, this was not coupled with a desire to leave. Rather, the residents reported a desire to support their families and contribute to the betterment of society. Batty and colleagues (2011, p 5) described this as evidence of how the residents' sense of self was strongly rooted in place, 'giving many of them a basis for some security in a context of growing economic uncertainty'. The authors go further to argue that 'neighbourhood often mattered most to people where both the economic legacy of and future prospects for their community were least favourable' (Batty et al, p 6). Thus in times of increasing economic uncertainty, the residents express greater connections to their community. It becomes in many ways a refuge from wider social and political uncertainty.

These comments are particularly apposite for the older residents of disadvantaged neighbourhoods. In their study, Scharf and colleagues (2002) also found that three out of four of their older study participants reported positive features of their neighbourhood, including its friendliness, having good neighbours and access to family and friends. Many older residents had lived in their neighbourhoods for a large part of their lives and developed various social relationships with their neighbours.

However, this attraction to neighbourhood has been challenged by the absence or loss of facilities and by the dispersal of family members. It is also often hampered by the stigmatisation of the residents by officialdom, which contributes to the residents' reluctance to engage in social activities outside their immediate neighbourhood, further enhancing their social exclusion. These social relationships could be enhanced if there were facilities and opportunities in their neighbourhoods. Richard and colleagues (2009) found that older people who reported greater access to such facilities as corner shops, pubs, libraries and parks also reported higher levels of social and cultural participation. However, in many neighbourhoods there are few such facilities and thus reduced opportunity for connecting with other local people.

Buffel and colleagues (2012) refer to the 'paradox of neighbourhood participation', whereby although older people spend more time than most in the neighbourhood, they are given less opportunity to participate in local decision making. Further, whereas younger people can get involved in activities and decision making outside the neighbourhood through both work and leisure, this is less of an option for older people.

There is a need to explore ways of promoting greater social inclusion among older residents of disadvantaged neighbourhoods. It is these residents who despite reporting attachment to their district often also report loneliness and social isolation. While developing new facilities in the physical regeneration of such neighbourhoods is an important component of such a strategy, there is still the need to explore strategies of actively engaging such residents both in the use of these and other facilities but also in promoting their greater involvement in decision making about their communities.

Forms of intervention

In a review of the impact of community health interventions for older people Cattan and colleagues (2005) identified certain factors that predicted greater success. They found little evidence of the benefit of one-to-one interventions, but some evidence of success for group-based interventions. A central feature of successful interventions was the active involvement of older people in the planning and implementation of the intervention. In concluding, the authors noted the need for more qualitative evaluations to explore the inner workings of interventions. They also indicated the need for a wider socio-political and environmental-ecological approach that could go beyond both the individual and the group. Such an approach could begin the movement from promoting social engagement to challenging social exclusion.

Another important feature of success identified by Findlay (2003) was the extent to which the intervention took account of existing community resources and contributed to building community capacity. Thus, rather than imposing an intervention on older people, effective interventions worked with older people by involving them in the project as well as building their confidence and sense of ownership.

Community arts have been historically used as a means of promoting social solidarity and challenging social exclusion. They are not restricted to one art form, but rather aim to develop multiple creative activities in community settings through the active participation of the residents. This approach is mindful of the broader social and political determinants of health and wellbeing. It locates its activities within this broader context as a means of developing change and resistance. It is designed not only to promote greater social interaction, but also to strengthen social bonds and to draw attention to local manifestations of social injustice and social exclusion. While on their own community arts can build participants' self-confidence and sense of wellbeing, they also provide an opportunity for the participants to come together and to begin share their experiences. Community arts can thus be both personally and socially transformative. Underlying them is the philosophy of cultural democracy, which was defined by Webster and Buglass (2005, p 21) as a way to:

> ... promote the Arts in a way that is accessible, where
> all communities are valued, and where everyone has an

opportunity to take a part. [This] would be a democracy in the real sense of the word, full of discussion, action and vibrancy. A culture made up of many voices, defined and representing all cultures and communities.

In this sense, community arts can be both inwardly satisfying and outwardly challenging. They represent a challenge to social exclusion and a call for an active form of social inclusion – not simply a passive assimilation. Webster and Buglass (2005, p 9) continue:

[A] participatory arts activity would not only give people the understanding and knowledge to undertake arts activities, but [...] this process would give them insight into the nature of the oppressive ways in which society functions and give them the tools to do something about it.

Community arts are thus informed by a Freirean social philosophy (see Dworakowska, 2012; Murray, 2012) designed to build understanding and forms of social critique and action. In this way, they also connect with the more materialist approach to participatory practice recently advocated by Blencowe and colleagues (2015). They emphasised that participatory practice should be more concerned with 'overcoming alienation' rather than 'attaining freedom from power'. In our case, such overcoming of alienation is part of the process of developing forms of social action and transformation.

Call-Me

The Call-Me study consisted of the participatory development and evaluation of a series of community projects with older residents living in disadvantaged areas of a large metropolis. A range of different community activities – including arts, gardening and physical activities (see Middling et al, 2011) – were developed with groups of older residents in four different neighbourhoods. These neighbourhoods had been identified by the city council as scoring high on multiple indices of disadvantage. The focus here is on a community arts project that was developed in one neighbourhood (Murray and Crummett, 2010). This took place over a period of 18 months, during which a series of smaller art projects was organised with a group of older residents with the guidance of a number of community arts workers.

Perceptions of neighbourhoods

Our interviews with the older people who participated in the project confirmed that they identified very closely with their immediate neighbourhood. They talked about the area in terms of its residents and physical characteristics, and particularly as a community of which they were members. Physically, the community was considered in terms of a small number of streets where the older people spent most of their time. They were able to define the physical boundaries of their community.

The older people we interviewed clearly separated themselves from others who lived only a short distance away in similar social housing. This sense of separateness included their unwillingness to access resources in nearby districts, which were instead cited as evidence of the official neglect of their own neighbourhood:

> "I know they have things going on in other centres, further down but we don't belong to them, really those things are for them that live there." (Female, 64 years)

This sense of community was expanded in the stories the participants told about their neighbourhood. Most had lived in the area since it had been built over 40 years ago and recalled memories of their lives there in those early days. The stories they told of their neighbourhood since then were ones of steady physical deterioration and social decline. They recalled the extensive local and wider social relationships they had enjoyed when they first moved into the area. People had jobs then, which gave them resources for accessing facilities and often took them outside the area. In addition, they recalled that local shopkeepers were very proactive in offering services. They also commented on the role of the local clergy who had previously been central to organising various social activities. There were several churches near the district but these had since been demolished or converted for alternative use as their congregations declined.

Conversely, the neighbourhood today was described in terms of limited social opportunities, little social interaction with newer residents, and no local facilities for social activities. Some explicitly referred to a loss of a sense of community. One women referred to the way the local shops used to welcome residents and how the local clergy had organised events:

"When we first moved we had cards from most of the shops welcoming us and we had the minister up from the church to see us. He asked me and my husband if we would help set up a club for the pensioners, brew up and help out like, so that's what we did. We used to go down and we would have raffles, potato pie supper. We would go out on outings to different places.... See, everybody helped out. If you were asked to help out and you could, well you did ... not just us; lots of people helped each other. They don't seem to bother nowadays." (Female, 83 years)

Now they had to travel outside the area to the large supermarket for shopping. Whereas previously they visited the local shops on an almost daily basis and enjoyed the frequent social interaction, now they only visited the supermarket once a week and there were fewer familiar faces with whom they could talk.

The men referred to the local pub as having been the centre of their local social lives until it had closed:

"I mean in the good old days you had the local pub, everybody had their own little local – the pub was the hub of the community. That's where all the socialising, arguing, etc, was done. I mean, don't forget there was a fire in every pub and when the lads got in, the cards started. And then the televisions went in and I think that changed it – the conversation, arguments, joking. And then we had slum clearance, that's when communities were lost. And then we got the drugs, don't get me wrong, we always had drugs but in my day hard drugs were a rich man's habit. The working class couldn't afford drugs, now they're on every street corner. Yes, it was the loss of the local pub and the drugs destroyed the traditional working-class communities." (Male, 71 years)

This social representation (see Moscovici, 2000) of a distinct and under-resourced community was further strengthened by the negative social representation that respondents felt others had of their neighbourhood. This added to respondents' sense of social exclusion. While they accepted that there were a few antisocial individuals living in their neighbourhood, the older people felt that outsiders focused on those individuals to the detriment of the whole neighbourhood. As one man said:

"There's some good people on this estate, but you see over the years we've been stigmatised – 'Them up there, they're this and that' – but it's a minority that cause the trouble and people seem to forget that." (Male, 60+ years)

Thus, while they accepted that their neighbourhood may have certain negative aspects, it was still their home. This was evident in the rejection of the term 'deprived'. For example, one woman recalled her reaction to a council worker who had been collecting information on housing quality in the area:

"They came here with one of these tick-box sheets, and when he'd finished, I said, 'Well, what's the verdict?' And do you know what he said, he said I was deprived. Have you ever heard such rubbish, all of this [indicating her garden] and he said I was deprived." (Female, 64 years)

While there were reports of crime in the area, this did not negate the basic integrity of the residents. Even those who engaged in criminal behaviour had a certain level of goodness that was evident in this account by an older woman:

"It's alright round here. I mean it's not bad at the moment; in fact it's pretty quiet. We get the usual gangs, antisocial behaviour, but it's been quiet as far as robberies and that sort of thing. I mean we had the shooting, a young girl. She's on life support at the moment but I've heard she's going to be OK. It was a young lad. He turned himself in." (Female, 60+ years)

Combining their narrative accounts of social and physical decline in the neighbourhood with the perceived outsider negative social representation of their community led to a range of reactions. On the one hand, there was the limited acceptance that the outsider representation had some legitimacy. This negative representation was only applicable to a minority within the neighbourhood.

On the other hand, there was the rejection of this outsider representation and a resistance to the wider social exclusion. One man expressed considerable anger and frustration at what he saw as their exclusion from civic participation:

"We're a forgotten area and always have been. When you get the newsletter it's all about that end, there's never anything about us. I think it's happened because they give us nothing, well that's how it seems to me ... we have nothing as far as activities or opportunities for older people on this estate ... we're very much a forgotten area, what you might call the poor relation in comparison to other areas in the ward." (Male, 54 years)

The contrast was with the neighbouring district which was perceived as advantaged. Another man added:

"Well you've been round, you've seen what we've got, bugger all [laughter]. This area, and it's been the same since I moved in, has been forgotten by the powers that be. Ask the others when you go round, they built the estate and then forgot about it." (Male, 67 years)

This sense of exclusion was also accompanied with anger and hostility towards council officials and public representatives. As one man said:

"You only see the councillors at election time; they come banging on your door wanting your vote. Never see hide nor hair of them in between. Don't ask me what they do in between because they have done nothing for this estate from what I can tell you." (Male, 67 years)

This perception of the neglect of the community was heightened by the city plans to demolish many of the houses and to build new ones. One woman commented: "The houses have only been here 40 years". Although the housing agency promised a substantial improvement in their living conditions, the residents were very sceptical and referred to previous broken promises:

"When we first moved here in 1969 they were still building the estate, and we got plans for what they were going to build and it all looked smashing, green patches with forms for older people to sit on, 10 shops lower down ... then they took them [sic] plans and come back with some more and we were getting nothing. We never got the green patch with the forms and them [sic] 10 shops. That was the first time they did the work, 40 years ago and now they're at it again. It's ridiculous really, because they never give you what they promise and I don't think we will be any better off when they finish." (Female, 64 years)

Activity

The Call-Me project adopted the standard cyclical process of action research – plan, act, observe, reflect and then repeat the cycle (Brydon Miller, 2014). At the outset, the two key researchers spent considerable time in the community getting to meet the residents on an informal basis and exploring with them their interest in working with us on an arts project. Over several weeks, we identified a group of older people who were keen to participate and agreed to meet to discuss it further. A number of reasons were offered for their participation. These centred largely on the lack of local opportunity for social interaction. As one woman said:

> "I just sit in this flat staring at the television or the walls. You get to a point where you think I can't cope. I mean, you think what's the point being stuck in this flat day in, day out." (Female, 51 years)

Another woman described living in a flat as being imprisoned:

> "They're [flats] like prisons. You shut the door of that flat – you see no one. If it weren't for my carer I could go days without seeing a living soul." (Female, 66 years)

Although participants were frustrated and lonely sitting at home, a frequent complaint was that there was nothing to do in the neighbourhood. For example, one 83-year-old woman said: "I would like to go out more but there's nothing going on. I couldn't tell of any club around here for the old people."

While the opportunity for social interaction seemed to be the main attraction of participating in the project, for some of the residents it was the prospect of participating in an arts project. These individuals reported previous experience of artwork, often when they were much younger. Some recalled negative comments from their teachers about their drawing or singing ability that had stayed with them throughout their lives. Others had pursued some interest in art, but it was a very solitary activity. As one 53-year-old woman said:

"I've always liked arts and crafts. I like writing poems and making cards but you don't seem to, see, do it on your own ... if we got something going, a group of us, I'd really enjoy it, a couple of hours each week to do something, something a bit different from sitting, cleaning, cooking."

Over the 18 months of the project, a series of arts activities was conducted with the group. The initial one was an exploration of different art forms – drawing, painting, glass etching, pottery and tie dying. This sequence was suggested by the community arts worker, who facilitated the activities as a means of building the participants' confidence about completing an art product. The sessions lasted roughly two hours each week and were very informal, providing an opportunity for the participants to share stories about their families and life on the estate. The community arts worker emphasised the importance of the participants taking ownership of the activities rather than foisting an agenda on them. At the end of the initial three-month series of sessions, it was decided to hold an exhibition. This became a very important part of the project, as it provided an opportunity for the participants to display their work to the broader community. This was a very successful event, attracting a large number of local residents and promoting broader awareness of the arts activities.

At the end of this initial project, the older people were very enthusiastic and wanted to continue with the project and to formally establish a community arts group that they called 'Young at Heart'. In conversation with the researchers, they identified various personal benefits of participating in the project, including a sense of achievement. As one 61-year-old woman said: "I have achieved something that I didn't know I could do. Other people would enjoy this as well. It should be for everybody, every week. This sort of activity will go far with people."

However, it was the social benefits of the arts project that the participants most frequently mentioned. They talked about the increased opportunity for social interaction and forming new friendships, with one participant being "very pleased with everything that's happened and everyone's so friendly". Some of the participants referred back to earlier days on the estate and felt that the project was contributing to community building, with one participant observing: "It seems to be getting people together."

Several of the older participants referred to the wider impact of the project. They were beginning to challenge the outsider negative social representation of their neighbourhood and their sense of social exclusion. As one woman said:

> "Everybody's talking about what we've been doing. Even the councillors when they come to the meetings. See, I don't think they knew we could do these sorts of things but then we've never had it before, people coming and showing us and giving us a chance." (Female, 64 years)

The success of this trial project and accompanying exhibition encouraged the older residents to continue their participation. After discussion with the community arts worker, it was decided to develop a new community mapping project, which started by drawing a map of the neighbourhood and then inserting pictures and other images that the participants brought to the meetings and that reflected the changes in the neighbourhood. Participants decided on the community map after discussing the changes in their community:

> Mary: "Well it came about because we talked about making a time capsule – it would be about us and the estate for the 40 years that it has been here."

> Ann: "Yes, because all this will be gone. It's all going to look different. So we wanted to save bits of it, our stories and memories, if you like."

At the end of the project, the community map was mounted on the wall of the community rooms and a subsequent open community forum drew in more local residents. This project provided a further opportunity not only to build the participants' confidence, but also to enable them to reflect on their strengths and how to access more resources. Over the following year other projects were developed, including a silk-screen printing project that involved the production of a series of prints about the neighbourhood that were proudly displayed on the walls of the rooms, and a shared arts competition with the local school.

As the group grew in confidence, it began to explore other activities, including trips to the seaside and a Christmas dinner in a nearby pub. All of these activities required considerable coordination by the group members. Some of the group members began to take on more leadership roles – initially tentatively.

Key findings

- Older people, especially those who live in disadvantaged areas, can experience multiple forms of exclusion, including social isolation. Such social exclusion can contribute to detriments in health and quality of life. There is a need to explore ways of promoting greater opportunities for social engagement by older people.
- A range of different community activities – including arts, gardening and physical exercise – were developed as part of the Call-Me project. Interviews and questionnaires were used to assess the views of older residents and relevant community stakeholders.
- In addition, the researchers documented the processes involved in developing the activities. Participants reported evidence of social isolation and were enthusiastic about the activities. While they emphasised the benefits of participation, they also articulated some concerns about continuing financial and human support for the activities.

Conclusion

Although this was a small community arts project with older people, it showed its potential to engage the older people and to challenge social exclusion. While the community arts worker provided direction to the arts activities, a key role was played by one of the authors, Amanda Crummett (AC), who was trained as a community worker. She was actively involved on the ground at every meeting of the group. In addition, she sometimes visited the participants in their homes and discussed with them their problems and worries. She kept a diary of all her meetings and a review of some of its entries highlights the processes involved in building the project. Early on she noted in her diary an interaction with one of the older people:

> The art session is due to start at 11:30–12:00. It is 10:45. I called at Ann's house. She was pleased to see me and in a very good mood. 'Oh come in, you're early. Oh, look, look at these.' Ann had framed the silk paintings she had made at the arts class last week. They really do look nice. She has put one at the bottom of the stairs on the wall and one in the kitchen. Ann makes me a cup of tea. She says she will take her framed pictures along to the community rooms to show the others what they look like framed. I took a photograph of Ann with the paintings – she is very pleased.

This short extract shows the active involvement of AC not only in the project but in the lives of the participants. She listened to their problems as well as boosted their confidence about their arts ability. In doing so, she was combining what Sools (2012) has described as small and big stories. In discussing everyday problems, AC was sharing the small stories, which strengthened her bonds with the older people. It also gave her legitimacy when she encouraged their participation in the arts project, which can be described as the big story. It was this combination of small and big stories that helped to galvanise the project, to take it forward.

Looking through the diary, another feature was the frequent reference to health complaints. For example, AC notes in one entry:

> Jane arrives with her son's girlfriend. She is limping and using her stick. 'I can't stay today. I'm in terrible pain with my back and have a chest infection.' Jane sits down and I make her a cup of tea. Her son's girlfriend says she is looking after her and is sleeping over to make sure she is OK. She explains: 'I have to keep an eye on her and help her now after the heart attack she had last October – she died on the table at the hospital, we thought we had lost her.'

Such detailed accounts of the participants' health problems and the mutual support provided by family and friends were not uncommon. Despite residents reporting incidences of social exclusion and loneliness, they also provided lots of examples of local social support and determination to overcome obstacles.

While older residents had lots of lifetime experience of engaging in social relationships with family and neighbours, they had less experience in taking responsibility for organising group activities. They were enthusiastic about the opportunity provided by locally organised activities, but they were apprehensive about taking on any leadership or organisational responsibilities. Certain local leaders may accentuate this challenge by informally excluding some residents from activities.

Nationally, a series of policy initiatives around urban regeneration have promoted the need for community engagement (Jarvis et al, 2011). This has been followed by the establishment of a range of community-based workers who are employed by local councils, regeneration agencies, housing associations and so on. The remit of these workers generally centres on promoting residents' involvement. However, this remit is often difficult to achieve. In some cases, community workers have not been formally trained and experience varying levels of support from their employers. Working in disadvantaged neighbourhoods requires commitment and perseverance. The initial enthusiasm can be dulled by frequent frustrations. Workers often have to work alone at unsocial hours. They may have targets imposed by their employers that are difficult to meet (Murray and Zeigler, 2015). Neighbourhoods may also have a range of local groups, voluntary organisations and professional agencies working within them but with little contact with the residents outside agents' immediate case load. It seems that there are opportunities for such groups to work together to address some of the social needs of the older and other residents.

While projects can be established with considerable enthusiasm, there is a need to plan carefully how they can be sustained and resourced. Older residents need to be centrally involved in the development and ongoing planning of community activities along with the various stakeholders and community workers. Community arts activities are not a panacea to the problems of social isolation experienced by many older residents of disadvantaged neighbourhoods. They can, however, be part of a broader programme of social rejuvenation of neighbourhoods that have experienced sustained poverty and neglect. In her memoir of life as a community activist, Cathy McCormack (2009) stressed the need to connect community action with broader action for societal change. This small project has shown the role of the arts in inspiring older people who have often felt excluded.

References

Batty, E., Cole, I. and Green, S. (2011) *Low-income neighbourhoods in Britain. The gap between policy ideas and residents' realities*, York: Joseph Rowntree Foundation.

Blencowe, C., Brigstocke, J. and Noorami, T. (2015) 'Theorising participatory practice and alienation in health research: a materialist approach', *Social Theory & Health*, vol 13, no 3-4, pp 397-417.

Buffel, T., Phillipson, C. and Scharf, C. (2012) 'Ageing in urban environments: developing "age-friendly" cities', *Critical Social Policy*, vol 32, no 4, pp 597-617.

Brydon-Miller, M. (2015) 'Using action research methodologies to address community health issues', in M. Murray (ed) *Critical health psychology* (2nd edn) London: Palgrave Macmillan, pp 217-32.

Cattan, M., White, M., Bond, J. and Learmouth, A. (2005) 'Preventing social isolation among older people: a systematic review of health promotion', *Ageing & Society*, vol 25, no 1, pp 41-67.

Dworakowska, Z. (ed) (2012) *Creative communities: Field notes*, Warsaw: Sntytut Kultury Polkiej.

Findlay, R.A. (2003) 'Interventions to reduce social isolation amongst older people: where is the evidence?', *Ageing & Society*, vol 23, no 5, pp 647–58.

Glass, T.A., Matchar, D.B., Belyea, M. and Feussner, J.R. (1993) 'Impact of social support on outcome in first stroke', *Stroke*, vol 24, no 1, pp 64–70.

Holt-Lunstead, J., Smith, T. and Layton, J.B. (2010) 'Social relationships and mortality risk: a meta-analytic review', *PLoS Medicine*, vol 7, no 7, e1000316.

Jarvis, D., Berkeley, N. and Broughton, K. (2011) 'Evidencing the impact of community engagement in neighbourhood regeneration: the case of Canley, Coventry', *Community Development Journal*, vol 47, no 2, pp 232–47.

Kneale, D. (2012) *Is social exclusion still important for older people?*, London: AgeUK/ILC.

McCormack, C. (2009) *The wee yellow butterfly*, Glasgow: Argyll Publishing.

Mendes de Leon, C.F., Glass, T.A. and Berkman, L.F. (2003) 'Social engagement and disability in a community population of older adults: the New Haven EPSES', *American Journal of Epidemiology*, vol 157, no 7, pp 633–42.

Mendes de Leon, C.F., Glass, T.A., Beckett, L.A., Seeman, T.E., Evans, D.A. and Berkman, L.E. (1999) 'Social networks and disability transitions across eight intervals of yearly data in the New Haven EPSES', *Journal of Gerontology: Psychological Sciences and Social Sciences, Series*, 54B, no 3, S162–S172.

Middling, S., Bailey, J., Maslin-Prothero, S. and Scharf, T. (2011) 'Gardening and the social engagement of older people', *Working with Older People*, vol 15, no 3, pp 112–22.

Moscovici, S. (2000) *Explorations on social psychology*, Cambridge: Polity Press.

Murray, M. (2012) 'Critical health psychology and the scholar-activist tradition', in C. Horrocks and S. Johnson (eds) *Advances in health psychology: Critical approaches*, London: Palgrave, .

Murray, M. and Crummett, A. (2010) '"I don't think they knew we could do these sorts of things": social representations of community and participation in community arts by older people', *Journal of Health Psychology*, vol 15, no 5, pp 777–85.

Murray, M., Ziegler, F. and Sools, A. (2015) 'The narrative psychology of community workers', *Journal of Health Psychology*, vol 20, no 3, pp 338-49.

Newall, N.E.G., Chipperfield, J.G., Bailis, D.S. and Sewart, T.L. (2012) 'Consequences of loneliness on physical activity and mortality in older adults and the power of positive emotions', *Health Psychology*, vol 32, no 8, pp 921-4.

Richard, L., Gauvin, L., Gosselin, C., and Laforest, S. (2009) 'Staying connected: Neighbourhood correlates of social participation among older adults living in an urban environment in Montréal, Québec', *Health Promotion International*, vol 24, no 1, pp 46-57.

Scharf, T.S., Phillipson, C., Smith, A. and Kingston, P. (2002) *Growing older in socially deprived areas: Social exclusion in later life*, London: Help the Aged.

Sools, A. (2012) 'Narrative health research: exploring big and small stories as analytical tools', *Health*, vol 17, no 1, pp 93-110.

Wang, H.-X., Karp, A., Winblad, B. and Fraiglioni, L. (2001) 'Late-life engagement in social and leisure activities is associated with a decreased risk of dementia: a longitudinal study from the Kungsholmen project', *American Journal of Epidemiology*, vol 155, no 12, pp 1081-7.

Webster, M. and Buglass, G. (2005) *Making choices: Creativity for social change*, Nottingham: Educational Heretics Press.

EIGHT

Connectivity of older people in rural areas

Catherine Hagan Hennessy and Robin Means

Introduction

Reflecting global demographic trends, the older population in rural areas of the UK is growing faster than its urban counterpart and has a higher median age – a phenomenon that is projected to continue and intensify over the next 25 years (Champion and Shepherd, 2006). Despite this situation, to date the circumstances and experiences of older people in the countryside have received significantly less attention by researchers compared with those of urban elders. As with urban areas, the impact of population ageing in rural locations has been predominantly framed in terms of the envisaged burden of increasing numbers of older adults on service systems. Previous studies of rural ageing in the UK have therefore tended to adopt a problem-focused approach emphasising the disadvantages that affect older rural residents' wellbeing and participation in community life. Less is known about the ways in which older people are connected to rural society through their voluntary and other civic and social activities, and how the positive contributions they make to the social fabric of these communities can be maintained and promoted (Le Mesurier, 2006). This information is crucial to both enhancing older rural residents' quality of life and the sustainability of rural communities through a better understanding of the experiences of, and conditions and needed supports for, societal engagement in later life (Brooks, 2011).

The interdependence of older people and their communities in creating a sustainable countryside has been highlighted by gerontologists worldwide for more than a decade (see for example, Joseph and Chalmers, 1998). One of the key issues underlined in the expert group report that informed the First International Conference on Rural Aging in 2000 (West Virginia University Center on Aging, 1999, p i) was stated as follows: '*Rural elders can contribute*. With effective planning and policy development allowing communities to tap the resources of older citizens, rural elders will be perceived as contributors to society and not simply consumers of services' (emphasis in original). As Wiersma and Koster (2013) point out, however, although civic participation is often seen as central to active ageing, rural communities' ability to encourage and support the contributions of their older members is dependent on economic, social and other structural conditions, many of which are in flux in contemporary rural settings.

This chapter reports on the Grey and Pleasant Land project (GaPL),[1] a three-year (2009-12) interdisciplinary investigation into the participation of older people in rural community life, focusing in particular on their involvement in civic society. The project comprised six interlinked sub-studies ('work packages') that examined participation as part of and enabled by different aspects of older people's connections to rural community and place.[2] In doing so, this research sought to shed light on important aspects of rural contexts that facilitate and foster these connections. The research was carried out in south-west England and Wales, in rural areas experiencing similar trends in population ageing (National Assembly for Wales, 2002; Brown et al, 2005; Hartwell et al, 2007).

Project aims

The overall aim of this project was to explore older people's connections to rural community life, in particular the role they play in civic society in rural areas and the factors that support or act as barriers to their participation. A range of key issues around these connections was investigated, in particular, civic engagement; leisure participation; transport and mobility; digital inclusion; and the lived experience of rural ageing, including among rural minorities and older people in low-income households. These issues reflect a number of longstanding and emerging topics in gerontology and include domains and mediators of community inclusion that have been examined in other recent studies of older rural populations (for example, Dwyer and Hardill, 2010; Walsh et al, 2012). The principal research questions addressed in the GaPL project were as follows:

- How and in what ways are older people connected to civic society in rural settings in England and Wales?
- What is the impact of this connectivity on older people's quality of life in rural areas?

- How is later life experienced across diverse rural contexts and within subgroups of older people?

The focus on older rural residents' 'connectivity' to community and place in our research developed as a conceptual vehicle for integrating the perspectives of the different disciplines involved in the GaPL project (Hennessy and Means, 2015). The project employed what Thompson Klein (2010) has referred to as 'broad' or 'wide' interdisciplinarity, incorporating perspectives from across disciplines with significantly different paradigms and methods. In our study, these encompassed several empirically based disciplines (social, behavioural and geographical sciences, transport studies and informatics) as well as arts and humanities disciplines (visual arts and museum and heritage studies). In seeking to embed and synthesise the various approaches of these disciplines, we identified 'connectivity' as a construct that was common to the participating disciplines (for example, White and Harary, 2001; Narayanan et al, 2005; Brierly et al, 2006) and could be employed as what Klamor and Leonard (1994) have termed a 'heuristic metaphor'. This is the use of a shared concept in a flexible and non-discipline bound manner that accommodates epistemological and methodological differences and facilitates interdisciplinary exchange. In this way we used 'connectivity' as a joint conceptual focus for investigating the social, cultural, spatial, digital and other aspects of older people's connections to rural community (Hennessy et al, 2014b). The broader interdisciplinary conceptual framework through which we addressed the research questions was principally based in social science theory around human capitals (Bourdieu, 1985; Putnam, 2000) that was expanded to include an environmental dimension through human critical ecology applied to rural ageing (Keating and Phillips, 2008).

Methods and location of the research

In order to examine older people's connections to rural civic society, including individuals' circumstances, understandings and experiences of rural community and place, a mixed-methods approach was employed across the research. The range of methods included quantitative, qualitative and arts-based techniques intended to capture and represent objective and subjective aspects of connectivity in later life in rural areas. The research was conducted in six sites in south-west England and Wales representing a continuum of rural locations. In view of the plurality of existing definitions of 'rural', we employed a combination of conceptual and policy-driven definitions (including the Department

149

of Environment, Food and Rural Affairs' 2004 'new' definition of rural [Defra, 2006]) to formulate a typology for differentiating rural locales. This comprised three categories of rural places – 'remote and deprived', 'less remote and deprived' and 'relatively affluent and accessible' – and one of each of these rural place types was selected in both countries.

In these six locations, a quantitative survey of the types, levels and influences on older people's connections to and participation in rural community life was carried out with 920 respondents aged 60 and over. The survey covered individuals' views of their local community; the kinds, extent and context of their participation in activities within and beyond the community; their social networks and availability of support; transport and access to services; and their use of media and telecommunications. The survey data was used as a platform for the overall project from which the particular aspects of older people's connectivities in rural areas were investigated in greater depth using additional methods in the other work packages. The foci of the research of each project work package (WP) and the methods employed in each are shown in Table 8.1.

Findings from the research

This section describes selected key findings of the GaPL project that are organised here in terms of the types of connectivities outlined across the work packages. Seven broad types of connectivities were identified and elaborated in the research: civic engagement; social participation; intergenerational relations; connections to the landscape; connectivity and group identity; virtual connectivity; and imaginative connectivity. Findings illustrating these forms of older people's connections in the rural areas studied are presented with reference to the specific work packages.

Civic engagement

Older people's connections to rural community through civic engagement were found at substantial levels in the six study areas surveyed (WP1): 31% of respondents reported that they did some form of voluntary or charity work in their community, and nearly half (47%) claimed to have undertaken activities that actively 'assisted others' in the 12 months prior to the survey. Of these 47% overall, participation was significantly higher among those who had greater levels of personal resources and support, including having a spouse/ partner, better health, and higher income, former occupational status

Table 8.1: Principal foci of the research and methods employed by project work package

Research foci	Methods
WP1 The types and extent of older people's connectivities (social, cultural, spatial and technological) to their rural communities	Primary survey, secondary analysis of existing survey datasets
WP2 Life course patterns and determinants of leisure participation among rural older people Older people's contributions to community capital through their leisure activities The comparative experience of later-life leisure among rural older people in the majority population and in an ethnic minority group (Gypsy Travellers)	WP1 survey, oral histories, focus group
WP3 Older rural residents' experiences and perceptions of mobility needs and preferences How transport options facilitate or restrict community engagement Meaning of physical aspects of living in the countryside and everyday experiences of getting around in rural places	WP1 survey, semi-structured qualitative interviews, phenomenological interviews
WP4 (project 1) Gay and lesbian older people's experiences of rural ageing and community inclusion	Biographic narrative interpretive method, visual ethnography, focus group
WP4 (project 2) Older rural adults' links with the physical, social and cultural landscapes in which they locate themselves, evoking 'place' as the basis of these connections and the subject of their arts-based representations of this experience	Deep mapping, ethnography
WP5 The nature and extent of material deprivations experienced by older people on state pension only The relations between these deprivations and rural social inclusion in later life	WP1 survey, semi-structured interviews, diaries, participant observation
WP6 The feasibility of connecting stakeholders in rural ageing through internet-based methods Older participants' preferences, experiences and patterns of use of these various online methods and their effect on levels of participation	WP1 survey, discourse analysis of online discussion forum

and levels of qualification (Curry et al, 2014; Doheny and Milbourne, 2014). The reasons most frequently given for non-participation in community activities were lack of interest (27%), limitations in health (11%) and lack of time (9%). Older rural residents' involvement in activities organised by community organisations and associations was typically through their place of worship (41%), formal voluntary or charity groups (31%) or community groups (27%). The level of voluntary or charity work was found to be lowest in the most remote study areas (30% of respondents in England and 19% in Wales), suggesting a lack of opportunities for such activities in these locales where fewer community and voluntary services were found (Curry et al, 2014; Doheny and Milbourne, 2014). Further qualitative research into the forms of older residents' civic participation in the study areas (WP4, project 2) found many individuals playing key roles in community life: organising and running community events, caring for the physical landscape, conserving local history (and so a certain sense of identity), promoting community engagement and planning for the future (Bailey et al, 2014).

Social participation

Social participation through involvement in leisure activities was another identified aspect of connectivity in later life in these rural areas. Survey respondents reported engaging in a wide variety of leisure pursuits and hobbies both individually and within the wider community (WP1). While the survey results demonstrated a significant overall decline with age in leisure participation, particularly in more physically demanding activities (Hennessy et al, 2014c), from qualitative interviews (WP2) we found that even at the oldest ages individuals actively sought opportunities to pursue personal interests, meaning and enjoyment through leisure. Moreover, individuals' leisure engagement could and did also function as a means of generating connections to rural community and beyond. This is highlighted in one man's account of the hobby that he and his wife took up at the time of his retirement:

> "We started making these miniature [dolls'] houses ... we went mad, we went to exhibitions everywhere.... After a few years we joined the Cornwall dolls' house group ... I became chairman for eight years. We decided one year to hold an exhibition for the public. There were about 40 odd exhibits there, all of which they had made themselves."

Significant barriers to older people's social participation described by interviewees in these rural areas included lack of appropriate leisure opportunities and access to transport (WP2). The availability of local venues for social interaction like village halls and libraries and the means to get to them were identified as facilitators of participation in community activities. While the majority of older people surveyed did not regard transport as a barrier to participation in local community activities (WP3), important minorities found transport to be a severe limitation (5%) or in fact prevented involvement (7%). Nearly half of those respondents aged 80 and over reported some degree of difficulty participating due to transport and 15% said they were prevented from being involved for this reason (Parkhurst et al, 2014).

Intergenerational relations

As in urban areas, increased personal and social mobility meant that many older rural residents in the GaPL research were living geographically distant from their children and grandchildren. However, our work also revealed evidence of high levels of intergenerational propinquity and interaction in many of the more remote rural locations in which this research was conducted. For example, school children participating in a community oral history project in a village of 1,000 inhabitants (WP2) were all familiar with the vast majority of their community's older residents, and findings from participant observation at events such as community festivals in these areas (WP 4, project 2) showed the considerable extent of intergenerational engagement that these activities could attract.

Connecting to the landscape

A significant aspect of older people's connectivities in rural places revealed in the GaPL research was their sense of connectedness to the landscape. The importance of this dimension of connectivity was highlighted by the survey findings (WP1) that the characteristics of their communities rated by respondents as 'very important' to their sense of belonging mainly related to the place (for example, "being surrounded by beautiful physical landscape") rather than to the people (such as "having people in my community recognise me and talk to me"). Indeed, attachment to place through an appreciation of beautiful scenery and tranquillity was one of the principal ways in which older rural residents felt connected to the countryside (Burholt, 2012). This is reflected, for example, in the finding that 28% of GaPL survey respondents reported walking in the countryside for leisure on a daily basis. Older people in low-income households (WP5), moreover, felt that the attributes of rural landscape and place compensated to some extent for the restrictions imposed by their material deprivation (Doheny and Milbourne, 2014). Qualitative findings on older residents' experiences and understandings of their rural locales (WP4, project 2) illuminated the contrast between those whose perspective was rooted in the land as a 'taskscape' (and site of past work), and those who viewed it solely for its aesthetic qualities (Bailey and Biggs, 2012). The deep attachment to the rural landscape held by some older people in our research is highlighted by the comment of a Gypsy Traveller who had given up his nomadic way of life:

> "This ain't our way of life. We love to roam. Some days we feel like we're cornered. Now you can't even stop in a layby. We're here, but our hearts want to be in the pine woods somewhere." (WP2)

Connectivity and group identity

The strongest sense of connection for significant numbers of older people in the GaPL project seemed to be based on a group identity that was unrelated to the local rural community. In the case of older gay men and lesbian citizens (WP4, project 1), for example, biographic narratives commonly included accounts of experiences of prejudice, particularly in small rural communities:

> "My most rural experience was at a smallholding in a little tiny hamlet in Cornwall…. I remember my next door neighbour came up to us … the day my friend and I moved in, bought this derelict farm …and he took one look at us and fainted dead away, because we were obviously gay girls, and he just removed his cow from our field." (Cited in Jones et al, 2013)

Thus social participation and pursuing wider connections within their rural locale often involved an abundance of caution for these elders, even if they were long-time or native residents. Similarly, among older Gypsy Travellers (WP2), cultural expectations that socialising should be confined to their ethnic community as well as lifetime experiences of discrimination from the majority community were cited as reasons for their reluctance to engage with the local rural population or access mainstream services. Other evidence suggested that older people's identification with communities of interest outside of these rural areas (for example, through online leisure pursuits as described in the next section) is growing and that their sense of connectivity is becoming less dependent on place.

Virtual connectivity

The GaPL project findings highlighted the extent to which getting around and staying connected in rural areas is increasingly occurring 'virtually' through the internet, especially among younger old persons. Sixty per cent of households in the GaPL survey were internet-enabled, and in qualitative interviews (WP3) many older rural residents reported their growing use of the internet for utilitarian purposes such as shopping and banking, as well as for maintaining social connections:

> "Yes, I use the Internet. Buying things and especially emails
> ... it's a godsend. I've got lots of friends all over the place so
> it's a wonderful way of keeping in touch with them. I look
> at it every day and use it quite often." (Cited in Parkhurst
> et al, 2014, p 133)

About a third (32%) of respondents surveyed reported that they used a computer for leisure activities on a daily basis, and a number of interviewees (WP2) described their increasing participation in hobbies and leisure pursuits online. For example, one man in his sixties who was an avid bridge player explained: "I go on the computer and link into Bridge Base Online ... because I've got a computer internet facility ... I don't need to leave here now. Broadband has changed everything." Thus, despite geographic distance or declining health and fitness, older people in rural areas who had online access could remain connected to important services and valued communities of interest. The potential for connecting older people online as stakeholders around issues of rural ageing was also successfully demonstrated in the GaPL project (WP6) (Evans et al, 2014; Jones et al, 2014).

Imaginative connectivity

A potent aspect of older people's connectivities to rural places was through remembering or reimagining past experiences such as family holidays and school days, or being evacuated to the countryside as children during the Second World War. This form of connectivity was elicited, for example, through the intergenerational community oral history project and exhibitions on older people's leisure memories (WP2), and arts-based activities that brought together older rural residents with other members of the community to share and collate their recollections in a jointly produced multimedia 'deep map' of their rural locale (WP4, project 2). Used in these ways, imaginative connectivity was demonstrated to be a form of community cultural capital with significant potential for bonding and bridging members of rural communities (Hennessy et al, 2014c).

Implications of the research

This section draws out the main implications and issues of the GaPL findings. The final chapter of *Countryside connections: Community and place in rural Britain* (Hennessy et al, 2014a) is called 'Towards connectivity in a Grey and Pleasant Land' (Means et al, 2014) and outlines the detailed policy and practice implications of this complex and multifaceted study. This section does not seek to replicate that work, but explores to what extent are our findings 'rural' in that they are strikingly different to what we would have discovered if we had been studying six diverse neighbourhoods in large cities. This is a critical issue to resolve if we are to meet the central challenge of how best to foster connectivity in rural communities so as to maximise social and civic engagement and hence health and wellbeing.

The previous section on project findings profiled the wide range of different types of connectivity uncovered through the GaPL research as well as some significant barriers. We now need to explore the extent to which they are genuinely 'rural' in nature so that, in other words, they would not be found in most major towns or cities or at the least would 'play out' very differently.

From the outset, it needs to be acknowledged that defining 'the rural' is far from straightforward, as mentioned earlier in this chapter when explaining the rationale behind the choice of case study sites. Menec and colleagues (2011) illustrate this point by explaining how du Plessis and colleagues (2002) were able to identify six different definitions of what is a rural area in a Canadian context, leading to estimates of its rural population ranging from 22% to 38% according to the definition adopted. This is before factoring in the complication of the different economic, social and cultural contexts of rural populations in different nation states. Phillipson and Scharf (2005, p 69) illustrate this point by explaining how:

> [w]hat is rural in a nation such as the Netherlands, with its highly urbanised population, consequently differs from that of rural Poland, where a significant proportion of the population continues to live in the countryside and agriculture is still an important sector for local rural income.

It needs to be acknowledged that macro forces such as industrialisation, globalisation and urbanisation have huge impacts on rural as well as urban communities. For example, the drawing of migrant workers into mega-cities and other urban areas has the effect of undermining previous systems of intergenerational support and connectivity (Harper, 2006) in rural communities. An example closer to the focus of the GaPL study would be how some of our rural case study sites provided a commuter option from the market town or rural village into the city while other rural communities had become highly attractive to older people wishing to move away from the city in retirement or pre-retirement (Stockdale and MacLeod, 2013).

Neal (2013) has recently pointed out how these macro forces have served to undermine the urban–rural binary divide. This has seen a ruralisation of urban spaces and practices through such diverse examples as migrants to the city bringing rural practices with them to the promotion of certain neighbourhoods as villages and the growth of interest in urban nature and organic food. Neal argues that there has been an equivalent 'unfixing of rurality' (2013, p 60) as the urban and industrial encroaches through the growing importance of such factors as agri-business, middle-class retirees from cities and the development of large areas of countryside as a leisure playground.

How do these complexities relate to the specific forms of connectivity explored through the GaPL research? In terms of **civic engagement** and **social participation**, it would be hard to argue that our findings identified a spread and approach that was in some way uniquely rural rather than urban in nature. However, some differences do begin to emerge when the nuances of activity are explored. For example, urban and village dwellers might both like countryside walks, but they are more readily 'on tap' for our rural elders, with some having had a history of what Bailey and colleagues (2014) call a 'taskscape' rather than a leisure relationship with the countryside as a result of a lifetime of working on the land. However, it is important to take care not to assume that rural elders are by definition more **connected to their landscapes** than those of urban elders, even though these landscapes will tend to be strikingly different.

With regard to **intergenerational relations**, the GaPL case study areas did show that many rural areas in England and Wales retain a high level of intergenerational propinquity, although this would have been more the case with established residents than incomers. It also needs to be remembered that rural societies undergoing a major out-migration of those of working age will be seeing a fracturing of such relationships (Harper, 2006). In a similar way, urban areas will show enormous variations in terms of the physical closeness of the generations, with some retaining quite high levels of geographic proximity and others seeing intergenerational relations being maintained at much more of a distance (Phillipson et al, 2001).

In terms of **connectivity and group identity**, **virtual connectivity** and **imaginative connectivity**, a similar pattern emerges. All of these important forms of connectivity are to be found in the city as well as the countryside, but the detail of how they play out will be different in different communities. Group identity issues will vary, and hence the issue of acceptance of gay and lesbian elders is likely to be more widespread in urban communities and Gypsy and Traveller issues are likely to be less high profile, though there will be examples where this is not the case. Overall, internet and social media use is growing rapidly in elderly populations, but this will hide significant variations between communities.

The GaPL findings identified five main barriers to connectivity, namely **limited material resources**, **limited motility capital**, **digital exclusion**, **declining health** and **social barriers**. In a similar vein to our discussion of forms of connectivity, all of these barriers would be likely to emerge in an equivalent study of connectivity and urban elders even if the detail of how these barriers played out in practice showed extensive variation to the GaPL study. Place and location have a huge impact on individual ageing experiences but the meta and macro conclusions in terms of policy and practice need to avoid simplistic references to rural– urban differences. Variation within and between rural communities is at least as important as variation and difference within urban communities.

Where does this leave us in terms of understanding how best to foster connectivity for older people in rural areas? First, it further emphasises why the World Health Organisation (WHO) needs to switch from a focus on the age-friendly city to a focus on age-friendly communities if the rural is not to be marginalised. A series of domains are offered in *Global age-friendly cities: A guide* (WHO, 2007), such as outdoor spaces and buildings, housing, transportation, social participation and civic engagement. However, all of these are as relevant to social connectivity in rural areas as they are in urban ones. Menec and colleagues (2011) have further criticised the classic WHO approach as not only being too city-centric but also too static, with a failure to draw out how the different domains interact with each other to either foster or undermine connectivity. This leads them to re-present the domains, as shown in Figure 8.1.

Figure 8.1: A critical human ecology approach to the social connectivity of older people

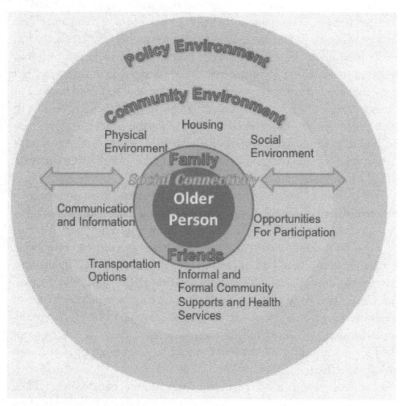

As with Hennessy and colleagues (2014a), they argue for a critical human ecology approach which they see as being based on five principles:

- Factors in the environment are interrelated and interact with each other to influence social connectivity.
- Environmental influences can be described in terms of their immediacy to individuals or groups (close versus distal).
- The fit between the person and the environment is critical in determining social connectivity.
- Personal characteristics and environmental conditions change over time and their relationship to social connectivity is dynamic.
- There are certain 'leverage points' (within the person or the environment) that are particularly key in determining social connectivity.

This framework is extremely helpful in terms of drawing out the implications of the GaPL findings and this will now be illustrated by three examples. First, in terms of how factors interact, two rural elders may participate in the same leisure activity such as an arts club, but the consequence of declining health may be very different for each in terms of maintaining involvement. One may need to travel by car, but the other may live much closer. One may be able to afford a taxi, but the other may not be in such a fortunate position. One may be able to seek a lift from an adult son or daughter, but the other not. One may be able to compensate for not being able to attend by maintaining his network of art enthusiasts through social media, but the other may be much more vulnerable to social exclusion.

The second example concerns the close versus distal issue, which can be illustrated using the example of public facilities such as libraries. A feature of the GaPL research was the growing difference in terms of national policy context for the Welsh as opposed to south-west England case studies. This underlined the power of distal influences to have profound local effects such on whether public libraries do or do not close, with rural elders in Wales standing a much better chance of retaining access to such resources. However, where libraries do close, more immediate factors may come into play, such as whether or not the local community has the social capital to keep them open through voluntary effort.

The final example concerns the importance of identifying key leverage points for facilitating older people's social connectivity in rural places. All urban and rural communities in the UK are facing significant service cutbacks and all are concerned to promote civic engagement by older people. In terms of rural elders, the GaPL study suggests that this can be turned into a leverage point to the advantage of older people by developing mechanisms for auditing their contribution in a way that challenges negative perceptions about older people being a burden on the younger generations. The danger of this approach is that social capital and assets are not evenly distributed across rural communities, and that as a result low-income rural elders in more deprived neighbourhoods face far more barriers to connectivity than those who are living in communities that have significant assets. An emphasis on their overall contribution needs to be balanced by cogent arguments as to why investment must be retained to support the retention of community infrastructures in poorer communities.

Key findings

- The most important aspect of attachment to community for older rural residents was feeling that one's community was safe and secure. The characteristics of respondents' communities rated as 'very important' to a sense of belonging mainly related to the place (for example, "being surrounded by beautiful physical landscape") rather than to the people (for example, "having people in my community recognise me and talk to me").

- Later life was described as a period of continuing or renewed interests in leisure pursuits that involved adaptations to individuals' circumstances and abilities in older age – including living in a rural place. Survey results showed an overall decline with age in leisure participation, particularly in more physically demanding activities, and activity patterns became increasingly centred on the home. Despite this reduction in levels of leisure participation, many individuals, including those in advanced old age, reported taking up new hobbies and leisure pastimes.

- The majority of older people surveyed did not regard transport as a barrier to participation in local community activities. However, important minorities found transport to be a severe limitation (5%) or in fact to prevent involvement (7%). Nearly half of those respondents aged 80 and over reported some degree of difficulty participating due to transport issues and 15% said they were prevented from being involved for this reason.

- Some people are enmeshed within the rural landscape, through lives spent working and living in it, and hence are not accustomed to seeing and discussing it as a separate 'thing out there'. Remembering and sharing deep knowledge of the landscape, gained, for example, through having worked on it, can generate emotions in the present and enrich the listener's sense of place.

- Many of the participants in the survey experienced significant financial difficulties and material hardship: seven out of 10 older people did not receive any interest from their savings, half were unable to make regular savings of £10 per week and more than one third were unable to afford an annual holiday away from home.

- There was a 'normalisation' of poverty, with persons in state pension only households reluctant to mention problems with their standards of living. Older old and more established residents were the least inclined to mention financial difficulties. For example, 16% of the older poor who had lived in the local area for more than 30 years reported financial difficulties compared with 30% of those who had moved to their place of residence in the preceding five years.

Conclusion

The GaPL project has characterised the variety of older people's connections to and levels of participation in their local communities in rural areas of the UK with growing ageing populations. As described in the preceding section, these aspects of older people's connectivity were shown to be conditioned by both personal and environmental factors at a number of levels that interact to determine their opportunities for engagement in rural community life. The current climate of fiscal austerity and reduction in government funding for rural infrastructure and services, in particular, heighten vulnerable older residents' risk of social exclusion in these areas through eroding important supports for connectivity identified in this research. Against this backdrop, however, a number of promising approaches to maintaining and promoting older people's community engagement in rural settings are emerging. These include, for example, rural social enterprise schemes financed through public funds but operating in partnership with voluntary and statutory agencies and featuring older people's direct participation (Le Mesurier, 2011). Such creative solutions could use findings from the GaPL research about the nature and forms of older people's connections in the countryside as a basis for facilitating and safeguarding their social inclusion. In turn, we suggest that supporting these 'connectivities' and, through them, older people's civic contributions, can offer important directions towards the sustainability of ageing rural areas.

Acknowledgements

This research was funded by the UK cross-research council New Dynamics of Ageing programme (grant number RES-353-25-0011 to Catherine Hennessy [principal investigator]). We gratefully acknowledge our Grey and Pleasant Land project team members whose research formed the basis of this chapter.

Notes

[1] The full title of the project was Grey and Pleasant Land? An Interdisciplinary Exploration of the Connectivity of Older People in Rural Civic Society.

[2] A seventh methodological work package examined the effectiveness of the interdisciplinary approach used to conduct this research and promote public engagement with the project findings. The findings of this work package are described elsewhere (Smithson et al, 2012; Means et al, 2014; Hennessy and Means, 2015).

References

Bailey, J., Biggs, I. and Buzzo, D. (2014) 'Deep mapping and rural connectivities', in C.H. Hennessy, R. Means and V. Burholt (eds) *Countryside connections: Older people, community and place in rural Britain*, Bristol: Policy Press, pp 159-92.

Bourdieu, P. (1985) 'The forms of capital', in J. Richardson (ed) *Handbook of theory and research for the sociology of education*, New York, NY: Greenwood, pp 241-58.

Brierly, G., Fryiers, K. and Jain, V. (2006) 'Landscape connectivity: the geographic basis of geomorphic applications', *Area*, vol 38, no 2, pp 165-74.

Brooks, E. (2011) 'Are country towns and villages sustainable environments for older people?', Unpublished doctoral dissertation submitted to the School of Architecture, Planning and Landscape, Newcastle University.

Brown, P., McCann, S., Shaw, M. and Verne, J. (2005) *Second blooming: Towards achieving a healthy and active mature population in the South West*, Bristol: South West Public Health Observatory.

Burholt, V. (2012) 'The dimensionality of "place attachment" for older people in rural areas of South West England and Wales', *Environment and Planning A*, vol 44, no 12, pp 2901-21.

Champion, T. and Shepherd, J. (2006) 'Demographic change in rural England', in L. Speakman and P. Lowe (eds) *The ageing countryside: The growing older population in rural England*, London: Age Concern, pp 29-50.

Curry, N., Burholt, V. and Hennessy, C.H. (2014) 'Conceptualising rural connectivities in later life', in C.H. Hennessy, R. Means and V. Burholt (eds) *Countryside connections: Older people, community and place in rural Britain*, Bristol: Policy Press, pp 31-62.

Defra (Department for the Environment, Food and Rural Affairs) (2006) 'Rural definition and local authority classification'. Available at www.defra.gov.uk/rural/ruralstats/rural-definition.htm.

Doheny, S. and Milbourne, P. (2014) 'Older people, low income and place: making connections in rural Britain', in C.H. Hennessy, R. Means and V. Burholt (eds) *Countryside connections: Older people, community and place in rural Britain*, Bristol: Policy Press, pp 193-219.

du Plessis, V., Beshiri, R., Bollman, R.D. and Clemenson, H. (2002) *Definitions of rural*, Agriculture and Rural Working Paper No 61, Catalogue no 21-601-MIE, Ottawa: Statistics Canada.

Dwyer, P. and Hardill, I. (2010) 'Promoting social inclusion? The impact of village services on the lives of older people living in rural England', *Ageing & Society*, vol 31, no 2, pp 243-64.

Evans, S., Jones, R. and Smithson, J. (2014) 'Connecting with older people as project stakeholders: lessons for public participation and engagement in rural research', in C.H. Hennessy, R. Means and V. Burholt (eds) *Countryside connections: Older people, community and place in rural Britain*, Bristol: Policy Press, pp 221-44.

Harper, S. (2006) *Ageing societies: Myths, challenges and opportunities*, London: Hodder Education.

Hartwell, S., Kitchen, L., Milbourne, P. and Morgan, S. (2007) *Population change in rural Wales: Social and cultural impacts*, Research Report No 14, Cardiff: Wales Rural Observatory.

Hennessy, C.H. and Means, R. (2015) 'Meeting the challenge of interdisciplinarity: lessons and issues from the Grey and Pleasant Land project on rural ageing', *Journal of Geography in Higher Education*, vol 39, no 2, pp 195-205.

Hennessy, C.H., Means, R. and Burholt, V. (eds) (2014a) *Countryside connections: Older people, community and place in rural Britain*, Bristol: Policy Press.

Hennessy, C.H., Means, R. and Burholt, V. (2014b) 'Countryside connections in later life: setting the scene', in C.H. Hennessy, R. Means and V. Burholt (eds) *Countryside connections: Older people, community and place in rural Britain*, Bristol: Policy Press, pp 1-30.

Hennessy, C.H., Staelens, Y., Lankshear, G., Phippen, A., Silk, A. and Zahra, D. (2014c) 'Rural connectivity and older people's leisure participation', in C.H. Hennessy, R. Means and V. Burholt (eds) *Countryside connections: Older people, community and place in rural Britain*, Bristol: Policy Press, pp 63-94.

Jones, K., Fenge, L.-A., Read, R. and Cash, M. (2013) 'Collecting older lesbians' and gay men's stories of rural life in south west England and Wales: "We were obviously gay girls…(so) he removed his cow from our field"', *Forum: Qualitative Social Research*, vol 14, no 2, article 7.

Jones, R., Smithson, J. and Hennessy, C. (2014) 'Failures and success in using webcasts, discussion forums, Twitter, and email to engage older people and other stakeholders in rural ageing', *Journal of Community Informatics*, vol 10, no 1, article 7.

Joseph, A.E. and Chalmers, A.I. (1998) 'Coping with rural change: finding a place for the elderly in sustainable communities', *New Zealand Geographer*, vol 54, no 2, pp 28-36.

Keating, N. and Phillips, J. (2008) 'A critical human ecology perspective on rural aging', in N. Keating (ed) *Rural aging: A good place to grow old?*, Bristol: Policy Press, pp 1-10.

Klamor, A. and Leonard, T.C. (1994) 'So what's an economic metaphor?', in P. Mirowski (ed) *Natural images in economic thought: Markets red in tooth and claw*, Cambridge: Cambridge University Press, pp 20-51.

Le Mesurier, N. (2006) 'The contributions of older people to rural community and citizenship', in P. Lowe and L. Speakman (eds) *The ageing countryside*, London: Age Concern, pp 133-46.

Le Mesurier, N. (2011) *Growing older in the countryside*, Cirencester: Action with Rural Communities.

Means, R., Burholt, V. and Hennessy, C.H. (2014) 'Towards connectivity in a Grey and Pleasant Land?', in C.H. Hennessy, R. Means and V. Burholt (eds) *Countryside connections: Older people, community and place in rural Britain*, Bristol: Policy Press, pp 245-76.

Menec, V., Means, R., Keating, N., Parkhurst, G. and Eales, J. (2011) 'Conceptualising age-friendly communities', *Canadian Journal on Aging*, vol 30, no 3, pp 479-93.

Narayanan, A., Jain, A. and Boonder, B. (2005) 'Providing rural connectivity infrastructure: ICT diffusion through private sector participation', *International Journal of Services Technology and Management*, vol 6, nos 3-5, pp 415-36.

National Assembly for Wales (2002) *A statistical focus on rural Wales*, Cardiff: National Assembly for Wales.

Neal, S. (2013) 'Transition culture: politics, localities and ruralities', *Journal of Rural Studies*, vol 32, October, pp 60-9.

Parkhurst, G., Galvin, K., Musselwhite, C., Phillips, J., Shergold, I. and Todres, L. (2014) 'Beyond transport: understanding the role of mobilities in connecting elders in civic society', in C.H. Hennessy, R. Means and V. Burholt (eds) *Countryside connections: Older people, community and place in rural Britain*, Bristol: Policy Press, pp 125-57.

Phillipson, C., Bernard, M., Phillips, J. and Ogg, J. (2001) *The family and community life of older people: Social support and social networks in three urban areas*, London: Routledge.

Putnam, R.D. (2000) *Bowling alone. The collapse and revival of American community*, New York, NY: Simon & Schuster.

Smithson, J., Hennessy, C. and Means, R. (2012) 'Online interaction and "real information flow": contrasts in talking about interdisciplinarity and achieving interdisciplinary collaboration', *Journal of Research Practice*, vol 8, no 1, article P1. Available at http://jrp.icaap.org/index.php/jrp/article/view/322/260.

Stockdale, A. and MacLeod, M. (2013) 'Pre-retirement age migration to remote areas', *Journal of Rural Studies*, vol 32, October, pp 80-92.

Thompson Klein, J. (2010) 'A taxonomy of interdisciplinarity', in R. Frodman, J. Thompson Klein and C. Mitcham (eds) *The Oxford handbook of interdisciplinarity*, Oxford: Oxford University Press, pp 15–30.

Walsh, K., O'Shea, E. and Scharf, T. (2012) *Social exclusion and ageing in diverse rural communities: Findings of a cross-border study in Ireland and Northern Ireland*, Galway: Irish Centre for Social Gerontology, National University of Ireland.

West Virginia University Center on Aging (1999) *Shepherdstown report on rural aging: The result of the expert group meeting, May 22-25, 1999, Shepherdstown, WV, USA*, Morgantown, WV: West Virginia University Center on Aging.

White, D.R. and Harary, F. (2001) 'The cohesiveness of blocks of social networks: node connectivity and conditional density', *Sociological Methodology*, vol 31, no 1, pp 305–59.

Wiersma, E.C. and Koster, R. (2013) 'Vulnerability, volunteerism, and age-friendly communities: placing rural northern communities into context', *Journal of Rural and Community Development*, vol 8, no 1, pp 62–76.

World Health Organization (WHO) (2007) *Global age-friendly cities: A guide*, Geneva: WHO.

Part Two
Designing for an older population

NINE

Fit for purpose

Leela Damodaran, Wendy Olphert and Jatinder Sandhu

Introduction

Digital technologies are becoming increasingly pervasive and integrated within society. Primarily through the medium of the internet, an ever-expanding range of information, goods, services, entertainment/ leisure, educational and social networking opportunities are available. For those who choose and are able to access them, it has long been recognised that such opportunities can deliver a range of social and economic benefits and contribute to improved quality of life (Bradshaw, 2011). For providers, the internet is increasingly regarded as the most cost-effective way to market and deliver services to customers. In the context of global financial pressures, this applies to government as well as commercial service providers. For example, in the UK, the government's digital transformation policy has for some years included a 'digital by default' strategy for the delivery of benefits such as Universal Credit (Cabinet Office, 2012). There are far-reaching consequences of this accelerating progression towards online delivery of products and services. Although it offers significant potential for considerable cost savings in the public and the private sector and is delivering growth in profits and opportunities for businesses, for those people who face barriers to the internet, the consequences tend to be negative. The multiple barriers are proving difficult for many older people to overcome successfully. Thus much of this large and growing population is being significantly disadvantaged by the growing dominance of online delivery over traditional forms.

Demographic factors relevant to the ability to make use of digital technologies, including age, education and income, are trends that apply worldwide; the UK divisions are comparable to those of similarly developed nations. Older people represent a growing proportion of the world's population. By 2050, it is projected that a fifth (21%) of the worldwide population) will be over 60 (UN, 2006). The divide between those who are digitally connected and those who are not 'is real and pervasive' (Pew Research Centre, 2016, p 11). In 2016, 53.9% of the global population was not connected to the internet (Internet Live Stats, 2016), and in the UK 10.2% (5.3 million adults) had never used the internet (ONS, 2016).

The demographic change over recent decades and the number of people who are still not connected to the internet presents significant challenges for governments and society. Digital technologies and internet-based services are being seen as having a significant role to play in reducing the so-called 'burden of care' associated with an ageing population. In addition to specific telecare and telehealth initiatives (see Turner, 2012), access to the opportunities afforded by the internet in general is also important for older people. Studies suggest that, for older people, computers and the internet can become powerful assistive technologies, helping them to maintain their independence, social connectedness and sense of worth in the face of declining health or limited capabilities, as well as also offering new opportunities to improve their quality of life (Wangberg et al, 2007). Conversely, older people, who are already a group at greater risk of exclusion in society through factors such as poverty, isolation and ill health, face the possibility of new forms of social exclusion if they are unable to access the opportunities and services that are increasingly being delivered through the internet.

Digital engagement and digital divides

To benefit from the opportunities offered through the internet requires older people to be 'digitally engaged'. However, statistics show that access to the internet is currently unevenly distributed among the global population, and older people in most countries are less likely to be internet users than younger people. Recent surveys in the UK (ONS, 2017) show that while around 90% of the total population regularly use the internet, these figures decline to 78% for the 64–75 age group and to less than 40% for those over 75. In some countries, the percentage of older users is much smaller; for example, in Spain, where 73% of the total population are internet users, users over the age of 65 represent less than 10% (BBVA Research, 2016), and in China only around 4% of older people are users, compared with around 50% of the population as a whole (Statista, 2017). Significantly, in the UK, adults aged 75 years and over had the highest rate of lapsed internet usage in 2016 at 4.8%, (compared with only 0.2% of adults aged 16 to 24 years) (ONS, 2016). These statistics reveal the considerable 'digital divide' that leaves many older, disabled and other disadvantaged groups unconnected – and therefore living without the benefits of the e-society.

The term 'digital divide'[1] refers to the gap between those who do and do not enjoy the benefits of access to the internet. Many studies have sought to explore the factors that underlie this phenomenon. These have demonstrated that the digital divide is not a simple binary division between the 'haves' and 'have-nots' (Norris, 2001), but that digital divides arise from three main sources of inequality that occur both between nations and within them. In simple terms, these differences can be categorised as those of connectivity, capability and content (Cabinet Office, 2004). Thus, digital divides are likely to exist where people do not have either access to appropriate equipment (**connectivity**), appropriate **skills and capabilities**, or motivation from the 'pull' of compelling functionality and perceived relevance of **content**.

The large divide between older and younger people in terms of internet usage is explained partly because older people may not have the financial means to pay for equipment and services, partly because they may not have acquired the necessary skills either through education or in the workplace and partly because they often do not perceive the relevance or advantages to their lives of using these new technologies. Chronological age, however, is clearly not a factor in itself, since many older people do use, and enjoy using, computers and the internet (Olphert et al, 2005).

Numerous studies have confirmed these barriers to uptake of the internet (Olphert and Damodaran, 2013; Damodaran et al, 2014). This evidence has led many stakeholders to the conclusion that non–users (the 'digitally unengaged') can be transformed into users (the 'digitally engaged') by an additive model that addresses each of the three types of barrier. Consequently, governments and other bodies in many countries are investing significant resources into providing technical infrastructure, awareness and training initiatives, and the development of digital content and digitally delivered services, with the aim of increasing access to the internet and promoting digital engagement.

In the UK, for example, the Government Digital Strategy (launched 1 March 2017) states that it seeks to simultaneously implement strategies intended to address connectivity issues (with the aim of completing the roll-out of 4G and superfast broadband by 2020) and capability issues (such as creating a Digital Training and Support Framework). The overriding concern to ensure the UK does not fall behind and lose its leading position in Europe on technology appears to have resulted in a digital strategy that gives only very specific and limited consideration to the needs of older people who are no longer in the workplace: 'The framework will focus on basic digital skills training and assistance for citizens who have insufficient digital skills, confidence or access) to use an online government service' (DCMS, 2017). This narrow, instrumental, focus will not foster the wider participation of older people in the digital world that is essential to their social inclusion and connectedness in wider society and therefore to their quality of life in the 21st century. Further, it does not take account of the growing evidence of a greater challenge to be addressed – that of sustaining digital engagement and participation beyond getting online for the first time. The content of the digital strategy suggests there will be little or no government–inspired progress towards filling the major void in the availability of information and communications technology (ICT) learning support that exists outside work organisations. This means that retired or unemployed older people must increasingly rely on friends and family for such support. Without this, many face growing digital, and therefore social, exclusion as the ICT skills gained while they were in the workplace become increasingly outdated.

Data from various surveys indicates that between 3% and 39% of users may give up using their computers/ICTs at some point and for some period of time, and suggest that older and disabled people are more likely to give up than other categories of user. Some reasons for the wide divergence in the statistics are discussed by Olphert and Damodaran (2013), but primarily relate to differences in the length of time used as an indicator of disuse, which ranges from one month since last use to one year. The study with both the largest sample size (25,169,820) and longest interval since last use (one year) shows that while around 3% of the population as a whole may give up using their computers, this rises to almost 10% of older and disabled users (Olphert and Damodaran, 2013). Such an attrition rate raises concerns: achieving the benefits of digital engagement requires not only that people join the 'bandwagon' of digital engagement, but also that they sustain that engagement on an ongoing basis. Yet, to date, most studies of older adults' computer use have focused on understanding the factors that prevent or promote initial adoption (Selwyn, 2004; Gatto and Tak, 2008), and there has been little research to understand the challenges associated with sustaining use of computers and the internet by older people that can lead to disengagement.

This gap in knowledge has had important implications at both policy and practical levels. Knowledge of the risk factors that could lead to disengagement is essential to inform the development of social and technical solutions to reduce or prevent such an outcome. Better understanding of the scale and nature of disengagement, on the other hand, could help to inform the development of facilities and services that support and do not exclude those who are unable to access them online. The overall aim of the New Dynamics of Ageing (NDA) Sus-IT research project was to address this gap in knowledge [Sus-IT: Sustaining ICT Use by Older People to Promote Autonomy and Independence].

Research context

The Sus-IT project was a three-year, multidisciplinary collaborative research project involving a team of academics from eight universities across the UK. The overarching aim of the research was to develop an understanding of the nature of older peoples' digital engagement and the risk factors that could lead to a reduction in use or abandonment of the technology. In particular, it investigated the nature of digital engagement and the actual and potential barriers to sustained and effective use of ICTs by older people. It also explored a range of potential sociotechnical solutions to these barriers to meet the following objectives:

- to create an engaged community of older people who actively participate in exploring problems and solutions related to sustaining and enhancing ICT use;
- to identify and investigate the implications for ICT use of age-related change in a longitudinal study of a diverse sample of older people;
- to develop and pilot a method for automatically detecting and responding to changes in user capability;
- to identify the learning and support needs associated with sustained and effective use of ICTs and to pilot innovative mechanisms for meeting these needs;
- to generate outputs to inform policy, practice, design and research, and in turn enable older people to access, creatively shape, use and adapt ICTs to maintain and enrich their autonomy, independence and quality of life.

In addition, the project sought through its approach to build capacity for multidisciplinary, participatory research with older people.

Approach and methodology

Addressing these complex sociotechnical research questions required knowledge and expertise from a range of disciplines and perspectives.

The Sus-IT team therefore comprised leading researchers and practitioners in the fields of participatory and user-centred design, psychology, gerontology, sociology, computer and information science, human–computer interaction, and learning technologies. Older people themselves have been central to the research. To reach older adults in all their diversity, the researchers worked collaboratively with over 1,000 individuals drawn from 33 existing groups/panels of older people in communities across the UK. Key research users (for example, organisations representing older people and those providing services and products to be used by older people) were also collaborators in the research.

To achieve the project objectives, Sus-IT researchers applied an innovative combination of methods, tools and techniques. These included a survey of digital engagement, interactive forum theatre, co-design 'sandpits', problem-solving sessions and workshops, and testing and evaluation of software and product concepts developed on the project, as outlined below.

The digital engagement questionnaire survey tool was informed by an in-depth review of the literature. It was interactively administered by members of the research team with approximately 750 research participants. It collected demographic data, quantitative data on aspects such as extent, frequency and scope of use of digital technologies, and qualitative data relating to attitudes and experiences with technology. Additionally, quantitative data on cognitive ability and wellbeing was collected from a small sub-set of participants.

This survey data was complemented by data from other activities within the project, including the use of the grounded theory approach to generate an understanding of older peoples' digital identities by a PhD research student on the project. A range of innovative methods were applied to elicit and capture older peoples' requirements and these informed the exploration and co-design of innovative technological solutions to the challenges faced by older users. For example, in forum theatre, enactments of the use of new and emerging technologies in the lives of older people were presented and then feedback on the technologies and their implications was elicited from the audience of older research participants. Similarly, in four 'sandpit' activities, groups of older people were presented with a set of product design concepts related to specific themes (such as memory and identity) and were then given an opportunity to review, revise and to co-design alternative concepts. Some of these concepts are documented in the design catalogue (Fröhlich et al, 2012).

Design solutions to mitigate the impact of reducing capability were also investigated. This work led to development of a framework to match problems experienced by people with mild to moderate impairments to appropriate adaptations (available from the wealth of pre-existing but under-utilised assistive technology in operating systems and software applications) – see the following section.

The ICT learning and support needs of older people were investigated first by a review of the literature and then through the digital engagement survey. In addition, a study of existing provision in a sample of UK towns and cities was conducted (Ramondt et al, 2013). Further, a case study of ICT learning opportunities in an ICT club for 'adventurous use of ICTs' in Saltburn (Smith, 2012) and a case study of outreach provision in the homes of housebound individuals (Damodaran et al, 2012a) were undertaken. The generic findings were presented and validated in workshops jointly hosted with KT Equal[2] with older people who then co-produced a user requirements specification for ICT learning and support that became the basis for a detailed proposition for community-based ICT learning and support.

Findings

This section presents key findings from the research and their implications for sustained digital engagement by older people.

Diversity

Diversity in characteristics, capabilities and needs of older ICT users exceeded expectations, with important implications for design and delivery of ICT-based systems, services and products (Keith, 2010; Fröhlich et al, 2012).

Extent and importance of digital engagement

Findings show that many older people are frequent users of a range of digital devices, including computers/laptops, mobile phones, tablets and eBook readers. A large proportion of respondents report using a computer every day or several times a week; survey findings show that 60% of respondents were digitally engaged, regularly using four or more digital technologies. Three quarters of respondents (75%) had been using a computer for more than two years and over four fifths (85%) of computer users reported using a computer every day/several times a week (Damodaran et al, 2013). Survey results also show that although small numbers of participants use a tablet or a mobile phone to access the internet, a very high percentage of those that do use their device every day or several times a week to access the internet.

The data found that older people value very highly the benefits and independence that computer use gives them, and they are often exceptionally tenacious in trying to remain digitally connected – persisting in the face of many obstacles and often without awareness or use of existing aids to accessibility. Findings also show that the potential loss of the ability to remain connected, for example, through disability, elicited strong negative responses in respondents (Olphert and Damodaran, 2013).

Digital disengagement

Eliciting data about digital disengagement poses significant methodological difficulties (for example, lack of clear external indicators and reluctance to acknowledge 'giving up' (Olphert and Damodaran, 2013). Statistical evidence suggests that between 5% and 10% of computer users do not sustain usage (Young et al, 2012). Few respondents were willing to acknowledge they had given up using a computer, but many reported challenges and frustrations in usage, including physical and cognitive limitations, memory, support, and/ or technology problems/changes (Olphert and Damodaran, 2013). Findings also suggest that lower cognitive capabilities appear to be associated with use of fewer computer functions Damodaran et al, 2013). When disengagement occurs, it is often a gradual process, rather than a single event, and usually results from a combination of factors – particularly changes in physical ability, memory, support, and/ or technology problems/changes (Olphert and Damodaran, 2013).

Help and support issues

The availability of help and support is of paramount importance to sustaining connection. More than a quarter of respondents said that support from other people was the most important thing helping them to use computers effectively (25%).

Respondents reported heavy reliance on support from family members or friends both to learn and to solve problems. Around a quarter of respondents said that human support and encouragement was the most important thing to help them use technology successfully. 'Coupledom' plays an important role, with consequential negative impacts when this is lost, for example, through bereavement (Damodaran et al, 2012a).

The study by Ramondt and colleagues (2013), cited earlier, of ICT training and learning opportunities for older people conducted in a sample of seven UK towns and cities, showed that provision is very patchy and inadequate for most users. Older research participants often expressed a preference for learning and support opportunities to be embedded in social processes in the pursuit of personal passions and purposeful social interaction in ICT-enabled activities rather than in training for qualifications/skills per se (for example, Smith, 2012).

The evidence also showed that information about support options, including aids to accessibility, typically does not reach those who need it (Sandhu et al, 2013).

Technology issues

Findings show that older people want elder-friendly, adaptable, 'customisable' hardware and software (Atkinson et al, 2010a) and that the usefulness and acceptance of adaptive software is likely to be influenced by user awareness of the concept of adaptation (Atkinson et al, 2008, 2010b, 2010c; Sloan et al, 2010), ease of use, including the level of control over suggested adaptations, and confidence that use will not adversely affect task performance (Sloan et al, 2010; Fröhlich et al, 2011).

In summary, two key determinants of user experience emerge from the findings: characteristics and features of the technology itself, and the quality and availability of ICT learning and support. These two factors are, of course, closely interrelated: technology which is intuitive, easy to use, accessible and reliable can reduce the need for learning and support. Conversely, the development of appropriate skills, knowledge, competence and confidence can reduce the perception of problems and/or provide users with the means to resolve them. The findings from this research contribute to the growing body of knowledge about the specific needs and capabilities of older people as ICT users (for example, Fröhlich et al, 2011), which can help technology designers, service providers and policymakers to achieve these objectives and thereby help to promote and sustain the digital engagement of older people.

Implications for design, policy and practice: towards better 'fit for purpose'

Through a range of dissemination events and collaborative co-design activities, the research outcomes and their implications have gained the attention of a wide range of stakeholders in business, in government, in the third sector and in older people's groups such as 50+ forums. In relation to design, there has been some limited collaboration with designers and developers to achieve a better fit between design and the needs and characteristics of older people. This kind of collaboration needs to occur as part of a wide-ranging strategic plan in which partnerships are nurtured. On policy, there are examples of successful implementation of digital inclusion policies and strategies where local government working in partnership with other stakeholders has taken on board the issues of community engagement and of sustainment of long-term active digital engagement. Regarding practice, with some notable exceptions, much of the available learning and support provision for older ICT learners is still modelled on the needs of the employment market, with an emphasis on centralised and standardised forms of delivery and content centred on basic skills training. This model of provision has high costs of delivery associated with it in order to cover significant infrastructure costs of marketing, recruitment, training, outcomes evaluation and so on. The evidence on user needs suggests these activities are inappropriate, unnecessary and, in the case of outcome evaluations, potentially a barrier to uptake by older people. Awareness of the preferences and of the particular and diverse needs of older ICT users has yet to be recognised and reflected in the design provision of ICT learning support.

Designing ICTs for an ageing society

To achieve design that is 'fit for purpose' in design, the project addressed the following two challenges.

How can ICT innovators and developers be encouraged to take into account the circumstances and needs of older people in their designs?

To be willing and motivated to design for older people, ICT innovators and developers need to develop greater awareness of the potential market of older people, better understanding of the needs and characteristics of older users, clear specifications of requirements (elicited from older users) and knowledge of the hopes and aspirations regarding the products older people would like to use.

To promote such awareness and to facilitate 'elder friendly' design, the project developed the following outputs:

- a DVD entitled Relatively Disengaged (Goodall, 2012), which uses dramatised scenarios based on project findings to convey needs and characteristics of older people;
- a design catalogue of 40 innovative product concepts developed to stimulate new ideas for products that are based on older peoples' interests and preferences (Fröhlich et at, 2012);
- a toolkit (Damodaran et al, 2012b) – see the section on practice.

How can the impact of capability change be reduced for older users of ICTs?

As reported earlier, the findings highlighted the widespread lack of awareness of the existence of accessibility aids among those who could benefit from using them. To overcome this deficiency, a software 'adaptivity framework' has been developed as a means of connecting accessibility solutions to the people who need them, at the time they need them. This makes semi-automatic adaptations to a user's device: it monitors and profiles users' moment-by-moment interaction with a computer or other device. It uses this feedback to identify short- or long-term problems and suggests (or even applies) an appropriate adaptation based on those that are inbuilt in the host device.

The software has been trialled and evaluated by a cohort of older people for usability, utility and acceptability. Feedback from the trial suggests that it helps users to become aware of accessibility features within their computers and the possibilities for adapting the interaction to meet their individual needs and preferences. As one participant commented: "It certainly opened my eyes to what can be done and what options there are" (Elaine, aged 83).

Another design idea mooted for providing a commonly needed source of help was to put users in touch with remote electronic 'mentors' (such as pre-recorded tutorials or voice or text conferencing links) at particular moments in an interaction when users find their progress stalls, due, for example, to uncertainty about the next step to take in a transaction.

Building on this research, a portable profile of individual accessibility needs is expected to become available in due course that will facilitate easier access to a wide range of technology-based services, and not just to the ICT in an individual's familiar environment. For instance, for someone experiencing a problem with readability of text, devices that incorporate an adaptivity framework that automatically resizes the text without the individual having to master the process of finding and changing settings across multiple devices and with potentially different methods of accessing and utilising such settings.

Policy

The findings of the Sus-IT research have identified the multifaceted nature of the issues associated with getting people online – and then the ongoing and far greater challenge of keeping them there – which was, of course, the rationale for the project. These issues bring into sharp focus the need for joined-up policy and strategy of all stakeholders, including government, business, the third sector and above all older people themselves, to address effectively the real challenges of digital inclusion. For example, government procurement policy and procedures have the potential to be powerful drivers of digital inclusion and participation. By requiring most, if not all, ICT products, systems and services paid for by government to include design features that are appropriate for older people and have been shown to be valued and helpful to them, change could be swift. Incentivising technology providers, ICT developers and designers to comply with such user requirements would deliver significant and widespread benefits for all users. Such policies would promote recognition of the diversity of older people, their needs and capabilities. This awareness is an important prerequisite and compelling stimulus for appropriate ICT design, which in combination with widely available and accessible community-based ICT support offers the potential for wide-ranging social and economic opportunities for all. The latter will allow integration of on- and offline support in existing venues and include outreach services to the housebound – promoting integration of health and social care. Such policies will need to underline the importance of sustained long-term provision – and at a consistent level across the country.

Practice

Delivery of community-based ICT learning and support

The following ICT learning and support requirements were articulated clearly through participative research and extensive collaboration with older people (KT Equal, 2012):

- readily available, trusted and sustained;
- delivered in familiar, welcoming and local venues;
- embedded in social activities/personal interests;
- free of time pressure and assessments;
- inclusive of problem solving/troubleshooting;
- offering impartial advice and 'try before you buy'.

These user requirements provide the underpinning for the well-developed proposition for socially embedded support in the community (Damodaran and Olphert, 2013). Success in meeting such needs are exemplified by established examples of good ICT learning support practice in the community such as the facilities offered by a 50+ Older Peoples' Forum in Derbyshire (Damodaran and Sandhu, 2016). They provide a model of ICT learning support for older people that is 'fit for purpose'.

The proposition is based on a strong evidence base, and extensive validation and development has taken place with relevant stakeholders, including older people. The proposition has been published under a creative commons licence (Damodaran and Olphert, 2013).

The proposition offers a highly flexible model for community-based ICT support venues variously termed clubs, hubs, centres and so on. Typically these use existing community venues, are locally run, address local issues and use local assets. They are often based on peer support as well as intergenerational exchange, all within a relaxed, social context and with access to professional expertise. This model has evolved to offer flexible and adaptable learning approaches to match older people's diverse needs, interests, learning speeds and styles. Reflecting local needs and assets, such community provision also has enormous potential to offer free, independent, trusted advice in clinic, helpline or pop-up shop formats, offering advice on choosing products and software, and supporting learning at all levels. Widespread availability of such support can be confidently expected to increase uptake of all forms of ICT – including health-care and telecare products – through empowering older people to try out and select devices matched to their needs and aspirations.

Informal and welcoming, these forums would offer users opportunities to learn and consolidate skills, experience a wide range of services and engage in social activities of their choice in a familiar setting. Locally run, with participation of the end users, each venue would provide services to meet generic requirements such as installation of spam filters, virus checkers and so on, as well as meeting the needs of the local community and capitalising on local assets. Help with internet banking, online safety and security, shopping online and on the high street, renewing vehicle licences, paying bills and so on would also be on offer. New skills acquired in this context would be purposeful and immediately useful. The research findings (Ramondt et al, 2013) also suggest that there would be significant benefit from sharing effective practice in, for example, engaging participants successfully in the use of digital technologies and what helps older people to learn transferable troubleshooting skills.

Figure 9.1: Proposition of ICT learning support in the community

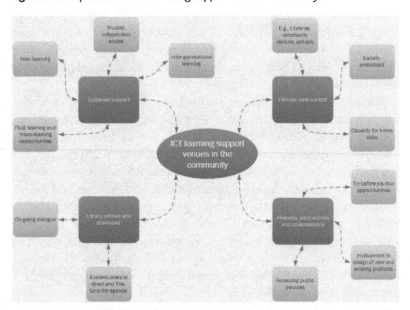

There are several benefits of community-based ICT support for collaborators and partners from beyond the community too. These include:

- opportunities for hardware, software and web accessibility designers to evaluate older users' needs and preferences;
- opportunities to trial and test prototypes and products leading to better targeting and improved design of products and services that appeal to the older market and meet the real needs of older people.

The wide-ranging benefits of applying the community support proposition are enjoyed and valued in pockets of good practice. Its application can be expected to reduce digital inequalities for its older citizens while meeting the objective of local councils to increase uptake of online services by these groups and to promote self-care. The role of ICT support in the community in empowering citizens to participate in the digital world offers such extensive benefits that it merits consideration as a strategic priority, encouraging the implementation of the proposition on a wider scale, reducing digital inequalities and moving towards the vision of widespread digital inclusion.

Developing the capacity and capability of older people to engage in research and design

To engage and empower older people, a number of existing tools and methods have been tailored to the characteristics and interests of older people and used to engage successfully and effectively with them as research participants. Some of these tools and methods are particularly relevant to technologists/researchers from computer science and engineering backgrounds seeking to involve older people in their research, design and development activities as a way of improving the match to the functionality and usability that older people want. For example, through participating in imaginative co-design workshops or 'sandpits' with older people, designers and technology providers find they are better able to understand users' needs and hear their ideas. Prompted by widespread interest in these methods, and encouraged by members of the project advisory group and by a business consultant to the NDA programme, the authors compiled a toolkit to facilitate appropriate and ethical engagement of older people in research, design and decision making (Damodaran et al 2012b). It comprises ethical and practical guidance on working collaboratively and participatively with older people.

Key findings
- Older people greatly value the benefits and independence that ICTs give them. Benefits of digital technologies and the internet include independence, personal health, self-efficacy, skills and capabilities, social interaction, economic and life chances and civic engagement and participation.
- Physical, psychological, cognitive and social changes can become barriers that affect the ability and motivation of older people to sustain their use of ICTs, and in some cases lead to them giving up.
- Many older people feel they lack sufficient digital competencies/skills and confidence to deal with technology challenges. They are motivated to learn and

improve their skills when they see the relevance of acquiring digital capabilities in facilitating or enabling the pursuit of their passions and interests.

- 'One size does not fit all', and many older people do not see the learning of standardised digital skill sets as a relevant or an appropriate goal.
- Support from other people is a key factor in helping older people to sustain their use of ICTs and to overcome problems and obstacles that typically arise in ongoing use.
- The emphasis of existing learning and training provision is on getting people online rather than helping them to sustain their digital participation.
- There is a void in ICT learning support available at home and in the community that is filled to varying degrees by family and friends on an informal and ad hoc basis.
- Learning is a social process and therefore the shrinking nature of social networks in older age is a priority need to facilitate sharing of knowledge of ever-changing digital capabilities.
- A well-developed proposition for delivering ICT learning support in the community has been developed from the Sus-IT research and is available under a creative commons licence for implementation and use.

The recommendations presented here are a small sample or sub-set of the wide range of potential actions/guidance that arise from the extensive evidence collected on the Sus-IT project. They are selected as important 'game-changers' in the current approach to digital inclusion and their implementation would be a major step towards realising the vision of sustained digital participation of older people.

Recommendations for a future research agenda

Development of indicators of disengagement

Robust and reliable evidence of the nature and scale of digital disengagement requires a systematic and widespread approach to collecting data. However a fundamental prerequisite for this is to develop appropriate and sensitive indicators of disengagement and these are lacking at present.

Longitudinal studies

Evidence is also lacking about whether people who have been identified as 'non-sustainers' do re-engage at some future point. It has been suggested that older people are less likely than younger non-sustainers to re-engage after a period of disengagement or disuse, perhaps because the factors that cause them to disengage are less likely to improve or disappear over time. Longitudinal studies are needed to explore this hypothesis.

Modelling disengagement

The authors' analysis of the disengagement process has identified that multiple and interacting factors (physical, psychological, social and technological) are involved. Each of these aspects merits further research to gain knowledge and understanding of the triggers, onset and progression of contributory factors to disengagement and in particular the way in which the factors act cumulatively or in combination to reduce and potentially to bring to an end the digital engagement of individuals.

Recommendations for setting up a local, user-led/user driven, community-based digital participation strategy

The findings and conclusions of the Sus–IT research project regarding an effective approach and strategy for promoting digital participation can be distilled into the following key recommendations:

1. *Encourage and support grassroots solutions to meet local ICT learning support needs.*

2. *Support and facilitate user-led 'buy-in' of the target users through a participative approach to eliciting their requirements and fulfilling them.*

   How:
   - Empower users through participation in discussions and co-design sandpits/workshops.
   - Elicit and facilitate specification of users' ICT learning and support needs and priorities.
   - Co-design the approach and solutions to delivering ICT learning opportunities and support.
   - Embed ICT learning in users' interests and activities.
   - Promote opportunities in the community to facilitate all relevant stakeholder groups (including older and disabled people) in working together.
   - Facilitate sharing of established good practice in relation to the preferences and needs of older people in a learning environment

and promote widespread awareness of the needs and characteristics of older ICT users.

3. *Enable low-cost/free access to ensure ICT help and learning support is readily available in the community and in the home through outreach provision.*

How:

- Provide readily available, accessible and ICT learning support and trouble-shooting assistance.
- Utilise existing available venues and facilities (for example, in schools, libraries, cafes, hospital waiting rooms, village halls) to provide continuity and sustainability of ICT learning support.
- Promote sustainability through flexible and adaptive funding models such as the social enterprise model.

4. *Design applications to serve all stakeholder groups, not just a sub-set of them.*

How:

- Design ICTs for all users:
  - Promote recognition of the significant 'grey market'.
  - Engage technology providers and developers in reducing the barriers and frustrations experienced by older ICT users.
  - Create awareness that many older people seek stability of the user interface and assistance in coping with uninvited and unwanted 'upgrades'. Older people's verbatim comments make clear that 'upgrades' are in reality often experienced as retrograde in the 'de-skilling' effect they have in making the hard-won skills learned (often at great personal cost) redundant.
  - Explore design options that would allow more stability of user experience.
- Reduce the impact of capability change:
  - Design software and hardware to better match the characteristics (including impaired capabilities), requirements and preferences of older ICT users to significantly enhance the quality of their user experience and satisfaction.
  - Reduce the demands of digital engagement, especially on cognitive load, by designs that meet diverse user requirements to be 'user-friendly', accessible and intuitive.

- Improve the adaptivity of software and hardware by the appropriate application of the adaptivity framework discussed earlier.

5. *Adopt an individually tailored, user-centric evaluation approach where the most important criterion of success is whether end users have been enabled to accomplish their goal through the ICT learning support provided. (Other essential aspects of support will, of course, include knowing how to stay safe in the online world.)*

How:

- Find out what ICT-enabled task/goal the user wishes to achieve (for example, learning to use Skype; making a payment online; locating friends and relatives; conducting a search for health information).
- Arrange for appropriate help/guidance/learning support from the wide range of formal and informal sources available in the community.
- Check that the user's goal has been achieved.
- Encourage pursuit of related goals.
- Invite the user to evaluate provision and to advise on improvements for others.

Conclusion

The evidence presented in this chapter shows that while many older people enjoy the benefits of information and communications technologies, their experience as users is characterised by many challenges. Appropriate design of the technology as well as good support can mitigate the negative impact and promote successful and continued digital engagement of older people. Without support in dealing with these challenges, individuals may become overwhelmed by these problems. This is especially the case for those who are coping alone or with limited or unreliable sources of assistance – which characterises the situation for many older people who are no longer in the workplace. In such circumstances, ICT usage tends to reduce over time and may cease entirely.

The realities of digital engagement of older people and the difficulties they have in sustaining ICT use may undermine – or at best slow down – progress on digital inclusion agendas and the implementation of digital strategies, including those of the UK government. As the implementation of the 'digital by default' strategy extends, government services in the UK are increasingly only available online. This suggests that the challenges posed for older people that have been identified by this research need to be acknowledged and addressed by policymakers and providers of services as a matter of urgency. To address the issues requires coordinated policies, strategies and practices that extend from central government across local government, the third sector and the business sector – and crucially engages older peoples' groups such as the 50+ forums in England. The know-how to achieve successful and rewarding digital participation of older people is already available from the outputs and outcomes of major publically funded research such as the NDA programme in the UK and comparable studies in other countries. Exploiting this expertise to make major changes that are appropriate and relevant – and sought by many older ICT users – has the potential to deliver inclusive connected communities. For any community or nation that realises this potential through explicitly meeting user-defined needs, the ultimate reward will be the widespread active and enthusiastic participation of the older population in the digital world and the many benefits that will follow. The evidence from this collaborative research with over 1,000 older ICT users and more than 100 research users would suggest that there is no better way to 'future proof' our ageing society.

Notes

[1] The term is believed to have been first used in the US during the Clinton administration.

[2] http://kt-equal.org.uk/uploads/monographs/digital_engagement_monograph.pdf; http://kt-equal.org.uk/uploads/monograph%20taming%20the%20dragon%20 final.pdf

References

Atkinson, M., Li, Y., Machin, C. and Sloan, D. (2010a) 'The socio-technological issues of adaptive interfaces and user profiling for accessibility', Workshop hosted at Human Computer Interaction Symposium 2010, University of Abertay, Dundee, 6 September. Available on request from the authors.

Atkinson, M., Bell, M., Li, Y., Machin, C. and Sloan, D. (2010b) 'The benefits and potential pitfalls of user monitoring', Paper presented at the Association for the Advancement of Assistive Technologies in Europe (AAATE) Workshop, Sheffield, October. Available at http:// kt-equal.org.uk/uploads/aaateoct/aaatepreceedings.pdf.

Atkinson, M., Machin, C., Li, K.Y. and Sloan, D. (2010c) 'Towards accessible interactions with pervasive interfaces, based on human capabilities', Proceedings of the International Conference on Computers Helping People (ICCHP 2010), Vienna, 14-16 July. Available at https://dspace.lboro.ac.uk/dspace-jspui/bitstream/2134/6519/1/taibhc%5b1%5d.pdf.

BBVA Research (2016) *Digital economy outlook, January 2016*, Madrid: BBVA Research. Available at www.bbvaresearch.com/wp-content/uploads/2016/01/DEO_Jan16_Cap3.pdf.

Bradshaw, H.M. (2011) *Digital inclusion: Economic and social benefits for individuals and wider society*, Social Research Report No. 26/2011, Cardiff: Welsh Government. Available at http://wales.gov.uk/topics/housingandcommunity/research/community/econsocial/?lang=en.

Cabinet Office (2004) *Enabling a digitally United Kingdom*. Available at http://webarchive.nationalarchives.gov.uk/+/http://www.cabinetoffice.gov.uk/media/cabinetoffice/corp/assets/publications/reports/digital/digitalframe.pdf.

Cabinet Office (2012) *Government Digital Strategy 2012*. Available at .

Damodaran, L. and Olphert, C. W. (2013) 'The proposition – community hubs: meeting older people's technology support needs, developing social communities and reducing isolation'. Available at http://sus-it.lboro.ac.uk/SusIT_KT_HubsOct13.pdf.

Damodaran, L., Olphert, C.W. and Sandhu, J. (2012a) 'Case studies of digital disengagement, March 2012'. Available at http://sus-it.lboro.ac.uk/publications.html.

Damodaran, L., Olphert, C.W., and Sandhu, J. (2012b) 'A toolkit for engaging older people in research, design and development of ICT based products and services, December 2012'. Available at http://sus-it.lboro.ac.uk/publications.html.

Damodaran, L., Olphert, C. W. and Sandhu, J. (2014) 'Falling off the Bandwagon? Exploring the challenges to sustained digital engagement for older people,' *Gerontology*, vol 60, no 2, pp 163-73.

DCMS (Department for Culture, Media and Sport) (2017) 'Digital skills and inclusion – giving everyone access to the digital skills they need'. Available at www.gov.uk/government/publications/uk-digital-strategy/2-digital-skills-and-inclusion-giving-everyone-access-to-the-digital-skills-they-need.

Fröhlich, D., Lim, S. and Ahmed, A. (2011) 'Supporting memory and identity in older people: findings from a 'sandpit' process', Paper presented at the Include Conference 2011, Royal College of Art, London. Available at www.academia.edu/1455912/Supporting_memory_and_identity_in_older_people_Findings_from_a_Sandpitprocess.

Fröhlich, D., Lim, C., Wood, S. and Ahmed, A. (2012) 'What older people want: a catalogue of co-designed ICT concepts'. Available at http://sus-it.lboro.ac.uk/SusIT_DWRC.pdf.

Gatto, S.L. and Tak, S.H. (2008) 'Computer, internet and email use among older adults: benefits and barriers', *Educational Gerontology*, vol 34, no 9, pp 800-11.

Goodall, D. (2012) Relatively Disengaged (DVD). Available at www.youtube.com/watch?v=zyx6p-vqQAA.

Keith, S. (2010) 'Diversity in age: the challenges of reaching the "hard to reach"', in *International Conference on Universal Technology: Proceedings*, Trondheim: Tapir Academic Publishers.

Norris, P. (2001) *Digital divide, Civic engagement, information poverty, and the Internet worldwide*, Cambridge: Cambridge University Press.

Olphert, C.W. and Damodaran, L. (2013) 'Older people and digital disengagement – a fourth digital divide?', *Gerontology*, vol 59, no 6, pp 564-70.

Olphert, C.W., Damodaran, L. and May A. (2005) 'Towards digital inclusion – engaging older people in the digital world', Proceedings of the Accessible Design in the Digital World Conference 2005. Available at www.bcs.org/upload/pdf/ewic_ad05_s7paper1.pdf.

ONS (Office for National Statistics) (2016) 'Statistical Bulletin: Internet access – individuals and households.' https://www.ons.gov.uk/peoplepopulationandcommunity/householdcharacteristics/homeinternetandsocialmediausage/bulletins/internetaccesshouseholdsandindividuals/2016 [25-10-17]

ONS (2017) 'Internet users in the UK: 2017'. Available atwww.ons.gov.uk/businessindustryandtrade/itandinternetindustry/bulletins/internetusers/2017#recent-internet-use-for-those-aged-65-and-over-is-catching-up-with-younger-age-groups.

Pew Research Centre (2016) *Smartphone Ownership and Internet Usage Continues to Climb in Emerging Economies*, http://www.pewglobal.org/2016/02/22/smartphone-ownership-and-internet-usage-continues-to-climb-in-emerging-economies/ [25-10-17]

Ramondt, L., Sandhu, J. and Damodaran, L. (2013) 'Staying digitally connected: a study of learning and support provision for older people in seven cities in England and the implications for policy and practice', *International Journal for Education and Ageing*, vol 3, no 2, pp 95–114.

Sandhu, J., Damodaran, L. and Ramondt, L. (2013) 'ICT skills acquisition by older people: motivations for learning and barriers to progression', *International Journal for Education and Ageing*, vol 3, no 1, pp 25-42.

Selwyn, N. (2004) 'The information aged: a qualitative study of older adults' use of information and communications technology', *Journal of Ageing Studies*, vol 18, no 4, pp 369-84.

Sloan D., Atkinson, M.T., Machin, C.H.C. and Li, K. (2010) 'The potential of adaptive interfaces as an accessibility aid for older web users', Proceedings of the 2010 International Cross-Disciplinary Conference on Web Accessibility (W4A), Raleigh, US, 26 -27 April. Available at https://dspace.lboro.ac.uk/dspace-jspui/bitstream/2134/6262/3/sloan-atkinson-machin-li-final%5b1%5d.pdf.

Smith, M. (2012) 'A sense of adventure: a report on older people engaging with information and communication technologies in Saltburn'. Available at http://sus-it.lboro.ac.uk/publications.html.

Statista (2017) 'Distribution of internet users in China 2016, by age'. Available at www.statista.com/statistics/265150/internet-users-in-china-by-age. Turner, K. (2012) 'Telehealth and telecare for older people', *Scottish Policy Now*, Issue 2, March 2012. Available at www.scottishpolicynow.co.uk/article/telehealth-and-telecare-for-older-people.

UN (United Nations) (2006) *World population aging 1950-2050*, New York, NY: United Nations, Department of Economic and Social Affairs.

Wangberg, S.C., Andreassen, H.K., Prokosch, H.U., Vagos Santana, S.M., Sørensen, T. and Chronaki, C.E. (2007) 'Relations between Internet use, socio-economic status (SES), social support and subjective health', *Health Promotion International*, vol 23, no 1, pp 70-7.

Young, W., Klima, G., Gadag, V., Gien, L. and Hardill, I. (2012) 'Sustaining information and communication technology use among Canadians with at least one activity limitation', *International Journal of Technology, Knowledge and Society*, vol 7, no 1, pp 1-12.

TEN

Design for ageing well

Jane McCann and Tracey Williamson

Introduction

Stereotypes of older adults as being typically impoverished and unconcerned with appearance are being challenged. Older people no longer dress distinctively and are considered to be less constrained about choice of dress than in the past (Twigg, 2013). Clothing is a major contributor to how people define and perceive themselves and is a necessary part of our everyday lives. Twigg (2013) refers to Lurie's 1992 commentry that in a distinctive resort American elders have adopted a wardrobe marked by bright colours and soft loose shapes that clearly contrasts with the traditional associations of age with sobriety and self-effacement. Twigg suggests that it is important to view these trends in context whereby casual dress, beyond white-collar office wear, is the dress of choice for most people (Twigg, 2013). This chapter looks at how the comfort attributes of more sophisticated performance sportswear may be tailored to the needs of the active ageing community.

Transient fashion ranges are normally driven by last season's sales and trend, with 'business as usual' disregarding potential consumer groups who are unable to find suitable clothing. There is no record of the 'lost' sales to active agers, dissatisfied with what is available, and there is virtually no positive fashion trend information to guide designers with regard to the requirements of the active ageing consumer. Stylish fashion is seldom geared to the physiological demands of the changing older body, resulting in uncomfortable clothing that may be difficult to take off and put on, and to fasten. During the period of the research discussed here, international high-street 'fast fashion' has continued to be youth-oriented, with the predominant colour being black. What has been lacking is the design development of stylish and comfortable functional clothing for active members of older age groups who do not perceive themselves as old and ill. Factors such as age-appropriate fit, styling, proportion and comfort all contribute to the psychological 'feel-good factor' that may be enhanced through creating ease of movement and cutting for predominant postures, as well as thermal regulation, moisture management and protection (McCann, 1999).

With regard to exercise, older people are the segment of the general population with most to gain especially where underlying disease impairment exists (Metz and Underwood, 2005). Physical exercise can also improve aspects of intellectual performance. In order to reduce the level of illness and death as well as the financial burden associated with obesity and heart disease, governments recognise the link between sport and fitness and the health of the nation. For example, the UK Outdoor Industries Association launched its Britain on Foot campaign at Westminster in October 2012 to encourage the public to get involved in outdoor activities to increase the amount of exercise taken (www.britainonfoot.co.uk), while Walking for Health represents England's largest network of health walk schemes, run by walking charity Ramblers and Macmillan Cancer Support, to help people to lead a more active lifestyle (www.walkingforhealth.org.uk).

The performance sportswear sector has always been an early adopter of textile and technology innovation (McCann, 2005). Smart outdoor clothing has the potential to make health monitoring more accessible and positive for those who wish to keep fit or for those who become unwell. The adoption of wearable technologies for the monitoring of body signs such as heart rate, temperature, respiration, activity levels and location may subsequently, over time, provide sufficient data to detect behavioural changes. Feedback may provide significant new understanding and alert the user to affirmative action, giving individuals the potential to ensure their own continued wellbeing. However, early examples of smart garment design, merging wearable electronics with technical textiles and information and communication technology (ICT), have been targeted primarily at athletes and the youth market in areas such as snow sports, mountain biking and running. Little has been done to address physical and cognitive limitations when developing wearable products and related services to ensure that they are appropriate to the real-world needs of older people (University of Wales, Newport, 2009).

Today's older people have become competent users of high-technology ICT products where they perceive that those products deliver something of value to them (Metz and Underwood, 2005). Older people are said to be capable in the use of technology but may be slower than their younger counterparts. There is the potential, therefore, for older people to address key cultural, social and behavioural limitations of their everyday lives through the use of a multifunctional, technology-enabled, garment layering system. This concept demands age-appropriate clothing, enhanced by unobtrusive assistive technology, with technology interfaces that are intuitive to use, for active seniors who will willingly wear and enjoy it. The global market for biophysical monitoring wearable systems grew from $192 million in 2005 to $265 million in 2007 in three distinct areas: health/fitness, medical and government/military (Venture Development Corporation, 2007). Smart performance textiles and novel garment manufacturing techniques may be adopted to address the long-term clothing demands of active older people who shun ugly design and uncomfortable assistive devices, perceived to be for the ill.

However, as the ability to integrate innovative technologies into older people's lives becomes more prevalent, there is a danger that developments will become both problem focused and technology led. The alternative is for innovations in design and technology to be led by the aspirations, desires and everyday needs of the end user. Set in the demographic context that in 2010, 10 million people in the UK were over 65 years old, with projections for five-and-a-half million more elderly people by 2030, and the number to nearly double to around 19 million by 2050, the development of core garment products for active ageing provides brand leaders with opportunities for future market share. In 2010, one in six people in the UK was aged 65, and by 2050 the proportion will be one in four (www.parliament.uk). This chapter reports on the collaborative research project Design for Ageing Well, part of the New Dynamics of Ageing programme. This project brought together stakeholders from academia and industry to engage with active ageing participants in the co-design of smart functional clothing, with wearable electronics, to encourage healthy exercise, social engagement and enhanced wellbeing for active ageing.

Aims and methods of the research

The Design for Ageing Well: Improving the Quality of Life for the Ageing Population using a Technology Enabled Garment System project was both cross-disciplinary and collaborative. Its aim was to adopt a design-led approach to the development of 'smart' clothing, in terms of modern functional textiles with assistive wearable technologies, to enhance autonomy and wellbeing within the everyday lives of the market-neglected, rapidly growing 'active ageing' community (60-75 years).

The prime objective was to develop a functional clothing 'layering system' for participation in walking, comprising close-fitting, **body-layer** garments, with vital signs and activity monitoring; moisture-management **base-layer** styles; **mid-layer** insulating garments with warming devices; and **outer-layer** protection, providing multi-modal user interfaces. The practical design development was to be achieved through three-dimensional body scanning of selected older users, men and women, representative of the age group. Capturing the changing size and shape of the older body would inform garment cut and fit, and the application and positioning of innovative smart textiles, with embedded technologies, within the garment layers.

This research was undertaken with a view to identifying and addressing key cultural, social and behavioural limitations in the use of technology-enabled garments, during older users' everyday lives, thereby maximising potential and choice. The technology to be developed for incorporation into a garment system would enable the acquisition, processing, storage, interpretation and feedback of information from and to the user, in their environment. The impact of the technology-enabled clothing would then be evaluated in terms of user understanding and acceptance, with prototypes in use in both the studio and the outdoors. It was hoped that the research would identify a new dynamic in potential strategies for the introduction and eventual launch of the clothing system to the intended audience.

Research methods

Collaborative design

Co-design methodology, new to clothing design, was adopted to help explain complex terminologies and practices between both academic and industry stakeholders, including technologists in electronics, clothing/textiles and gerontology. This involved the integration of academic and industry stakeholders throughout the design-led process, and engagement with active ageing research participants. Design requirements had to be assessed in terms of older users' expectations of the intelligent functioning of the whole 'clothing system'. This co-design approach would involve consultation with older research participants at every stage of the iterative process, from requirements capture, to understanding and specifying the context of use, to technical design specification and prototype development, and to the evaluation of the clothing system.

Work packages (WPs) were established and led by the partner universities, to represent the key disciplines and their related areas of responsibility: **WP1: Behaviour** (University of Westminster and University of Salford); **WP2: Clothing** (the lead institution, formerly the University of Wales, Newport, now merged to become the University of South Wales); and **WP3: Technology** (University of Ulster). Funding from Research Councils UK supported a research associate as well as a PhD student in each of the three WPs. Co-investigators, with new researchers, contributed to the development of shared 'plain' language to enable the transfer of knowledge between researchers, industry practitioners and older users. Industry experts demonstrated the attributes of functional clothing and emerging textile-based wearable technologies and componentry, to elicit feedback from end users, prior to selection for prototype clothing development.

Walking as the focus for user engagement and prototype development

Walking was found to be the predominant activity identified in surveys of older people reported on by Metz and Underwood (2005). Such activity can range from extreme hill walking to more moderate exercise. Increasing numbers of older people have been joining health clubs and gyms, with the result that the industry claims that pensioners are the fastest-growing membership group, encouraged by discount rates and specific off-peak programmes tailored to their needs (Metz and Underwood, 2005). The project team considered walking to be the most appropriate 'sport' for the focus of the research, offering the potential to include a wide target group of active ageing participants.

Recruitment of older research participants

A user reference group (URG) of male and female research participants was recruited from within a 30-mile radius of the lead university. Participants were selected for potential body scanning, identified in relation to age and body mass index (BMI) classifications, and because of their participation in walking. Processes of user engagement, uncommon within clothing design, demanded ethical approvals prior to participants engaging in activities such as digital body scanning, attending a series of co-design workshops, and eventual involvement in the co-design development and evaluation of prototypes. In addition, the University of Salford recruited a user advisory group (UAG) of 12 men and women within the designated age range (60-75 years). The members of this group were study advisers rather than participants, informing some aspects of study design and dissemination but mostly supporting the specific study of one PhD student in WP1.

Developing a shared language

The merging of electronics and textiles in functional clothing demanded the crossing of academic boundaries. Initial preparatory training was necessary for researchers unfamiliar with the language, terminology and working methods and cultures of the disparate disciplines. A cross-disciplinary mix of competencies was required across the WPs, as shown in Figure 10.1. Each of the WP teams from the partner universities provided an introduction to their area of research in the workplace: Ulster on the smart home and environment (autumn 2009); Salford on best practice in user engagement (winter 2010); and Newport on the application of smart textiles within the functional clothing layering system (spring 2010). By the final of three preparatory workshops, the URG had been recruited and so some older users joined the team for presentations from representatives of the outdoor clothing industry, setting the scene for ongoing collaboration between all stakeholders.

WP1: Behaviour

The University of Westminster, with expertise in the psychology of behaviour, used quantitative methods to gain initial insights into active ageing for healthy exercise and walking. Questionnaires were designed, with topics chosen in consultation with the wider academic team, and sent to walking groups such as that of the University of the Third Age.

Figure 10.1: Work package competencies: WPI: Behaviour, WP2: Clothing, WP3: Technology

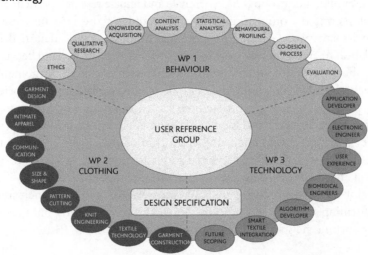

Initial findings from a pilot study, shared with partner co-investigators and researchers, provided early guidance to the technology team (WP3) with respect to the required functionality of wearable technology by older users. An early indication, later confirmed by the URG, was that the active ageing do not perceive themselves as ill, being more interested in location, communication and safety than in health monitoring.

The University of Salford, with expertise in socio-gerontology, provided experience in public involvement in research, including best practice in conducting user advisory groups (Williamson et al, 2014). This WP1 team introduced processes of engagement and use of ethnographic research methods (participant observation and interviews). An initial focus group, staged with the URG at the lead university, introduced the project and, at the same time, familiarised the research team with the protocols of user engagement. This session involved a 'show and tell' exercise, where users were asked to bring in and explain likes and dislikes in relation to their current garments worn while walking. This process enabled the researchers to gauge the level of knowledge, with respect to functional clothing attributes, within the user group. This video-recorded event also gave researchers valuable information on the range of walking types and typical levels of participation. The Salford partners provided guidance on the analysis of data gathered during the subsequent co-design workshops.

The UAG of 12 men and women (based at Salford) was established to provide independent comparative comment on older consumer design requirements, a commercial product review, and project prototype development. The PhD researcher, attached to WP1 and appointed on account of her study background in functional clothing design, helped to familiarise the UAG with the outdoor clothing sector. The UAG visited the showroom of a well-known regional company to have clothing products and related terminology explained. The UAG also carried out a comparative review of certain outdoor clothing ranges in the retail environment. This overview of outdoor clothing products enabled the UAG members to become better informed when commenting on the outputs of the co-design development process. In addition, a member of the New Dynamics of Ageing programme Older Peoples' Reference Group visited an international sports trade fair, ISPO Munich, as well as retail outlets in Munich and London, accompanied and observed by PhD researchers.

WP2: Clothing

A gap in the market

In 2008, ISPO presented findings from a market study entitled Best Ager that identified real potential for the development of sportswear for the active ageing. Findings indicated that this group is motivated to participate in sport in order to achieve a healthy lifestyle, with individual or group exercise seen as a means of preventing ill health, but that there was little suitable clothing available, as the design of sports and fitness clothing is often unsympathetic to the changing figure types of older wearers. Gradual or dramatic changes in older figure types that affect clothing design include less erect posture and the onset of conditions such as osteoporosis. Aspects of physical performance that decline with age include mobility, dexterity and the ability to reach and stretch (Metz and Underwood, 2005). The particular needs of older women suffering from arthritis demand functional clothing with enhanced ease of movement for dressing and undressing, while arthritic joints may also affect dexterity in the use of fastenings. Moreover, as Jenkins Jones (2005) has observed:

> People feel some insecurity about revealing their physical imperfections, especially as they grow older; clothing disguises and conceals our defects, whether real or imagined. Modesty is socially defined and varies among individuals, groups and societies, as well as over time. (p 24)

Performance textiles innovation

In recent decades, fibre and textile innovation innovation has escalated to encompass stretch properties (for fit, ease of movement and shape retention), lightweight insulation, knitted fleece constructions and waterproof and 'breathable' protection. More recently, smart textiles and wearable electronics have been adopted in youth-oriented clothing for fitness activities and extreme sport. Novel manufacturing techniques are now prevalent in the performance sport sector, which has always been an early adopter of textile innovation. Heat bonding may be applied for joining materials with a high percentage of synthetic fibres, with functional design details, such as zip openings, garment edges and perforations for ventilation, being laser cut to provide a clean, non-fraying finish. Waterproof zips, sleeve tabs and hood reinforcements may be bonded without stitching, offering clean design lines.

Seam-free knit techniques are seen in the structuring and shaping of intimate apparel and base-layer garments. These novel techniques may be adopted for the permanent embedding of miniaturised, textile-based, wearable electronics. For example, sports bras and men's base-layer garments, in seamlessly engineered knit constructions, incorporate sensor networks with biomedical devices linked to communication systems and display devices to monitor vital signs (Adidas). Conductive metallic fibres and polymers are used in textile assemblies such as heating panels, and for soft key boards and electronic switches that control wearable devices (Fibretronic). Heat-bonding techniques (Bemis/Sew Systems/Ardmel) are used to encapsulate wearable technology components with specific enclosures for removable devices.

The sports layering system

The tried-and-tested military-type 'layering system' is commonly adopted in the performance sport sector. This typically comprises a moisture management 'base layer', an insulating 'mid-layer' and a protective 'outer layer', sometimes referred to as an 'outer shell'. The base layer is normally of knitted construction, with seam-free garments becoming prevalent. Varied knit structures, often with elastomeric content, may be placed ('body mapped') around the body to aid moisture wicking and to offer increased support and protection. Mid-layers incorporate lofty fabrics, such as knit-structure fleeces, and woven fibre or down-filled garments to provide insulation by means of trapping still air. The outer layer, or 'shell garment', provides protection for the clothing system microclimate from ambient conditions through tightly woven and/or knitted lightweight textile assemblies incorporating waterproof/breathable membranes. A more recent innovation, the 'soft shell', provides a hybrid mix of outer protection and mid-insulation, in one textile assembly, as a softer, less noisy, multifunctional alternative for protection in moderate conditions (McCann, 2009).

Size and shape

Capturing body size and shape of the chosen age group was key to generating appropriate clothing pattern blocks and identifying optimal positioning of wearable electronics components, as the basis for technical garment design development. This was achieved in partnership with Sizemic Ltd, the liaison company to the 2001 SizeUK survey. SizeUK was the first national sizing survey of the UK population since the 1950s and the first time that the changing shape and size of the population was captured and analysed by means of 3D scanning technology (www.size.org/).

In the Design for Ageing Well project, male and female participants representative of the average height and BMI classifications of the national age group were selected for body scanning (Bougourd, 2014). Automatically generated pattern blocks, customised from the scans, were then modified to accommodate cutting for predominant postures and ergonomic movement associated with the demands of walking. The practical development of the patterns ran concurrently with the series of co-design clothing and technology workshops with the wider group of users, to inform the design development of body-layer, base-layer, mid-layet and outer-layer garments.

WP3: Technology

A lack of age-appropriate design

An initial extensive assessment of the literature was carried out to identify state-of-the-art wearable technologies and applications, and to scope and adopt appropriate assistive devices and evaluate their usability for active ageing. The findings indicated that while wearable electronics may be utilised to promote health and wellbeing they have not been readily accepted by older users due to badly designed user interfaces with small controls or displays that prevent those with a minor impairment from using them effectively. In terms of design, medical devices have generally been developed for 'ill people' with little aesthetic appeal and with data feedback that may be difficult for the wearer to read and understand. However, with appropriate design, successful deployment of this technology has the potential to revolutionise individual's care by allowing for more clinical information to be recorded in an unobtrusive manner without restricting normal daily activities, movements and location. A major benefit of such technology is that it can play a preventive role in healthcare, giving users a greater understanding of their health needs and allowing them to monitor their lifestyle and wellbeing.

Self-monitoring and communication

A collaborative design approach was adopted with users to develop a technological platform for an 'intelligent' garment layering system to support a range of functionality. The adoption of self-monitoring fitness technologies that communicate vital signs information, such as heartbeat and temperature, and assess behavioural changes in relation to posture, speed, distance, duration and repetition of movements, has important implications for both the wearer and others such as peers, family and subsequently, carers. In relation to outdoor pursuits, potential technological features encompassed information and communication, route finding and security and safety, including the ability to summon help. Other features included data mapping relevant to the identification and location of environments in which the activity takes place, and information relating to transport and infotainment.

Development of the technology and the user interface

Co-design methodology was adopted to develop a suite of wearable technology components integrated within the garment system. The assessment of the literature in the area of technology-enabled garments supported the initial development of an innovative close-fitting garment. This 'body layer' involved the customised design engineering of sports bras and close fitting vests (for men) to accommodate textile-based electrodes (sensors). Algorithms were developed to monitor vital signs and provide feedback to the wearer, including long-term monitoring of data to assess changes in behaviour.

A number of key challenges were addressed in collaboration with older users, namely the optimal places to embed the technology within the garment layering system, and the best means of providing user feedback in a positive manner through a user-friendly interface. Another challenge lay in developing product hardware, software and information content that could be customised in relation to users' needs by modifying characteristics such as font size of visual displays.

Members of the URG were engaged in a series of iterative design and evaluation exercises to assess current prototypes of the complete garment layering system, with feedback from users incorporated into the design adaptation of the ensuing prototypes. In addition, longitudinal field testing of the clothing system and the usability of the technology interface was carried out with eight users over a two-year period. Parallel laboratory-based experiments were conducted on a control cohort (from the UAG) to ensure the stability and accuracy of the placement of the technology within the garment.

Merging the disciplines: the iterative co-design process

The co-design methodology promoted user involvement throughout the iterative design process to inform garment and technology development. An overview of the stages involved is provided in Table 10.1.

Development of shared language

An initial 'show and tell' focus group revealed older people's degree of understanding of the design, textile application and functionality of available commercial products, which helped to inform the content of the subsequent series of co-design training workshops. For example, it was noted that older users' perception was that natural fibres are 'good' and synthetic 'bad', with little awareness of modern textile production. The initial session also provided an early indication of a range of types of walking activity, and levels of participation, with further detail to be elaborated during the iterative co-design process.

Concurrently, questionnaires were sent to a wider group of older walkers (including representatives of the University of the Third Age walking groups), with the results providing valuable feedback on older users' attitudes towards the use of wearable electronics. The results were ranked as a table of findings that guided the technology team and industry collaborators in the types of products required, and their functionality, to be demonstrated within the technology workshops. Further questionnaires investigated issues relating to user needs in terms of clothing functionality and design detail.

Identification of user design needs

A series of co-design investigatory workshops was conducted over a 12-month period (September 2010 to July 2011) to inform the design specification of the garment layering system for both men and women. These events comprised researchers, expert advisers, industry representatives, and URG members. User evaluations were made of comparative garments, from a selection of different clothing brands, in relation to fabric content and handle, garment fit and design detail, such as neck lines and sleeve cut. The workshops were recorded, and the resulting videos, together with extensive still photography, provided a wealth of material, allowing designers to capture both verbal comments and unspoken visual evidence of user preferences in relation to garment cut, fit and appropriateness of design detail. Analysis of the video recordings and still photography, which benefited from design researchers' tacit understandings, informed the subsequent prototype development.

Table 10.1: Overview of the iterative co-design process

Focus/activity	Tasks	
'Show and tell'	Focus group to gain overview of users' knowledge of the area	
Shared language	Training workshops in new language; clothing and electronics	
Layering system	Introduction of layering system with input from all stakeholders	
Industry liaison	Liaison with trade in studio, exhibition and retail environments	
Body scanning	Capturing size and shape of user-group representative size models	
Basic blocks	Generation of pattern blocks from body scans (four women/ three men)	
Pattern fitting	Pattern block fitting, customised to selected size models	
Block adaptation	Pattern adaptation regarding ergonomics of movement (for exercise)	
Workshops	Co-design workshops to identify and prioritise user needs	
Identification of user design requirements for clothing and wearable electronics (both functional and aesthetic)	Body layer (bras/vests)	*Comparative review of garments and wearable electronics supplied by industry with some company representatives joining co-design workshops*
	Base layer	
	Mid layer	
	Outer layer	
	Leg wear	
	Wearable electronics	
Materials/Trims	Selection appropriate to identified demands of walking	
Wearable technology	Selecting wearable electronics for monitoring, feedback and so on	
Colour workshop	Including explanation of textile/clothing global production chain	
Garment styling	Practical style development through cutting 'in the round'	
Pattern making	Pattern development to accommodate cutting for movement	
Fabric selection	Refining fabric selection throughout the garment layers	
Wearable electronics placement	Assessment of the optimal placement of wearable electronics	
Technological integration	Integration of wearable electronics within the layering system construction	
User interface	Design and positioning of the user interface technology	
Prototyping	Industry collaboration in the production of working prototypes	
Colour palette	Colour specification to contribute to potential commercial uptake	
Evaluation	Testing clothing system in the studio and outdoor environments	
	Testing functioning and usability of the wearable electronics	
Specification	Final design specification: layering system 'technology platform'	

Co-design development of prototypes

The co-design process then moved into the prototyping phase where the selected representative size models from the user group (four women and three men) became involved in fittings and design critiques on a regular basis, while the researchers, in liaison with industry collaborators, systematically developed body-, base-, mid- and outer-layer garments. The garments were cut 'in the round' to accommodate sufficient movement, such as arm lift and knee articulation. The wider URG contributed to workshops to refine the fabric and trim selection throughout the garment layers, and to define the optimal placement and testing of the wearable technology componentry, including the positioning of the user interfaces. This iterative co-design process enabled the development and evaluation of the technology-enabled garment 'layering system' as a textile-based 'platform' for wearable electronics (Figure 10.2).

Specification of clothing 'layering system' as a technology platform

Experts in product design and architecture used their skills to inform hybrid design specification methods to bridge the technical gap between the cultures of clothing, technical textiles and electronics. New methods for the integration of wearable electronics within

Figure 10.2: Garment specification with technology integration

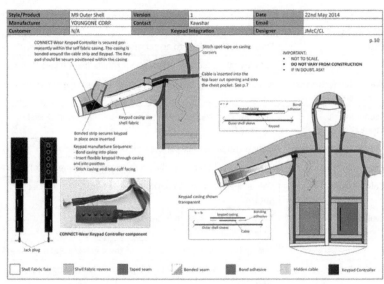

clothing construction and for the positioning of the technology user interface were tested and verified in collaboration with industry in the production of working prototypes.

Findings

Co-design process

The co-design model (new to fashion design) enabled cross-disciplinary academic and industry stakeholders to engage with older research participants in order to understand their clothing and wearable technology design requirements, and guide the design and development of technology-enabled functional clothing, with potential to facilitate outdoor healthy exercise, social engagement and enhanced wellbeing. The model promoted a shared language and understanding between stakeholders during the iterative stages as working prototypes were produced, both in the studio and in the trade environment. This approach has contributed to empirical knowledge about the sartorial wants and needs of the 'active ageing' and to an understanding that older users of technologically enabled garment systems require functionality as well as simplicity of interface and use.

The collaborative research highlighted the importance of the role of designers within the cross-disciplinary team, to act as interpreters, connectors, facilitators and visualisers. For example, the designers enabled older participants to gain confidence in communicating design needs, aspirations (and limitations) with respect to the functionality of the wearable electronics and the usability of the technology interface. A particular benefit came from placing a design graduate, as the PhD candidate, within the behaviour work package, to accompany and observe older participants walking outdoors. URG representatives were also accompanied by designers to retail outlets and to a leading international trade fair to promote shared understanding of older user needs among design, sales and marketing teams.

The merging of graphic design communication skills with product design and architecture resulted in the development of improved methods to guide the practical integration of electronic architecture and components into the clothing layering system. The techniques developed are transferrable to wider wearable electronic clothing applications.

Behaviour: the development of personas

Persona profiles were synthesised from the data collected from the co-design workshops, through video transcripts, still photography and the observations of users. Persona descriptors related to user situations and design needs designated in terms of life stage, living situation, family/peer group, fitness level and interests with direct relevance to clothing design. Four male and four female personas were created, in the 60 to 75-year age range, to correspond to the different walking types identified that, in turn, linked to the different levels of functionality demanded by the clothing layering system and the integrated technology.

Clothing: the development of the layering system

A range of 12 styles for men and 12 for women offered variations on the functional garment layering system, in age-appropriate durable styling, suited to different levels of participation in walking. Pattern blocks, generated through body scanning, provided the basis for the development of articulated blocks, to address a range of movement and postures relevant to walking and coordinated throughout the garment layers. Smart materials were selected to optimise homeostasis and to provide outer protection for the clothing microclimate. In order to function effectively, the garments constituting the layering system were coordinated in terms of style, fit, silhouette, movement and closures, with optimal positioning of the wearable electronic componentry. Colour preferences, to guide subsequent commercial uptake, were selected to be sympathetic to changing older complexions and hair colour. The proof-of-concept layering system, designed in collaboration with users, was made up of garments as follows:

- **Body layer:** sports bras and men's vests in fabrics with light compression, engineered for comfort and with bonded seaming contributing to the integration of knitted electrodes for vital signs data collection and processing.
- **Base layer:** short and long-sleeved t-shirts in close-fitting styles in moisture-management textiles, with design lines to enable movement to coordinate with other layers. User textile preferences included wool and lyocell (a man-made cellulosic fibre with cotton-type handle) in moisture-wicking blends with synthetic fibres. Prototype garment assembly included cut-and-sew and seam-free knit techniques.

- **Mid-insulation:** jackets and gilets with varied levels of thermal regulation. Garments were designed with cut and proportion, sleeve pitch and the degree of articulation, to coordinate with other layers within the system. Textile constructions included fleece, synthetic down, and quilted phase-change materials. Electronic warming panels, and the relevant componentry, were integrated into a female gilet design.
- **Soft-shell hybrid protection:** jackets, gilets and trousers in fabric constructions that merged fleece with windproof and water-repellency attributes to provide breathability and stretch for comfort, as opposed to potentially stiff and noisy waterproof protection. Relatively stable fabrics, with a smooth surface, can be more tailored than fleece with, for example, bonded zip detail, in styles that are versatile for everyday activities.
- **Outer protection:** waterproof/windproof coats, jackets and trousers in both two-layer (sandwich construction with laminated membrane) and three-layer assemblies (outer shell with separated lining). Jackets, with articulated hoods, designed to accommodate integrated electronic architecture to support the smartphone with connections to an external soft-switch user interface.

Technology: identification of user requirements

User requirements, elicited from the questionnaires, were ranked by their popularity and mapped on to possible technological solutions. During this mapping process, the limitations of the wearable nature of the systems, and cost and usability for older users, were taken into consideration. Some of the requirements could not be addressed using 'off-the-shelf' technologies, although solutions were available. Requirements such as 'Cool me' and 'Protect me if I should fall' could be addressed using advanced textile-based solutions such as breathable fabrics for cooling and dilatant materials for impact protection (for example, D3O). Requirements that could be addressed through available wearable technology applications are shown in Table 10.2, as well as those selected for use in the final prototypes.

As part of the technology-mapping process, requirements were broken down into four categories: health-related, social, safety and functional. The Shimmer platform was selected to address **health-related** requirements, as it provided three-lead electrocardiogram (ECG) recording coupled with a tri-axial accelerometer and Bluetooth module. For **social** engagement, the smartphone option was chosen as it reduced the amount of hardware to be carried. By harnessing the

Table 10.2: Technology mapping results

Requirement	Technologies available	Technology used
Keep me in contact with a group	Telephone, walkie-talkies, social networks	Smartphone
Tell me where my group members are	GPS, Google Latitude	Smartphone
Keep me warm	HeatWear (Fibretronic) EX02	HeatWear/EX02
Cool me	Fabric solutions	–
Help me navigate	GPS, Eelectronic maps	Smartphone
Call for help if I should fall	Accelerometer, smartphone, GPS	Smartphone
Protect me if I should fall	Material (for example, D30)	–
Tell me if I over-exercise	Accelerometer, heart rate monitor	Accelerometer, ECG sensor
Tell me the distance covered already	GPS	Smartphone
Tell me where to find the nearest bus stop	Maps, GPS	–
Tell me where to find the nearest facilities	Maps, GPS	–
Monitor my health for medical reasons	Heart rate monitor, temperature	ECG sensor
Interact with my mobile phone	Touchscreen textile switches	Textile switches
Interact with my portable music device	Touchscreen textile switches	Textile switches

in-built smartphone sensors, specifically the global positioning system (GPS), it was possible to send and receive information relating to the locations of group members. The high-ranking **safety** requirement was addressed through using the accelerometer located in the Shimmer sensor coupled with the processing power and communication capabilities of the smartphone. By detecting a fall via the sensor, the smartphone could automatically initiate a call to a pre-defined emergency contact. For the **functional** requirement, the use of both Fibretronic textile switches and Sony Ericsson's LiveView micro display enabled user interaction with the functionality of the smartphone. The adoption of textile switches enabled the controls of the system to be integrated within the garment system. The smartphone application was developed for the Android OS, as it provided a mature development platform as well as allowing access to a number of application programming interfaces, such as location, Bluetooth and telephony.

The smartphone acted primarily as a processing computer and secondly as a telephone. The integrated Shimmer sensor enabled the collection and processing of ECG and accelerometer data. This information was then recorded and presented to the user in real time as a heart-rate and step-count value respectively. An Apache web server was set up with a MySQL database to allow the smartphone application to send the user's current location and receive the last known locations of their friends/group members. All data recorded by the system was stored on the smartphone's secure digital memory card in an XML file. In order to provide a user-friendly way of reviewing walking data, a desktop application was developed allowing users to plug their smartphone into their home computer and review their previous walks.

In collaboration with the clothing team, the wearable electronics were positioned within the garment layering system to provide functionality for monitoring vital signs, for geographic positioning and route finding, for tracking performance, and for communicating with peers and family. A mid-layer women's gilet also incorporated a warming panel. A three-stage iterative evaluation was undertaken to obtain user feedback and develop a solution as appropriate. The first two evaluation phases were used to evaluate the system in order to produce a robust solution for evaluation in a longitudinal third evaluation. Each evaluation followed the same protocol, with a few modifications where significant changes to the prototype were required. Users were asked to evaluate the system during a walking exercise and this was followed by the completion of questionnaires by each participant. The results, user feedback and researcher observations were used to modify and develop the technology solution for the next evaluation phase.

Implications in terms of practice and product development

Practice

Co-design process

New co-design methodology, involving stakeholders from academia and industry engaging with active ageing end users, informs the development of functional clothing with wearable technologies, to facilitate healthy exercise, social engagement, autonomy and wellbeing. This approach promotes shared language and understanding for cross-disciplinary collaboration (embracing design, technology, gerontology) in identifying and addressing real, everyday design requirements of end users. Co-design development and testing of prototypes enables users to express their clothing and technology needs directly to industry stakeholders while becoming familiar with the benefits of wearable technologies previously inaccessible to them. Co-design introduces more responsible and sustainable processes for developing durable age-appropriate styling in contrast to the waste generated by fast-fashion turnover. This process has been disseminated widely at conferences and trade events as well as in project newsletters, and is the subject of a project-specific publication (McCann & Bryson 2015).

Design direction

Findings from the Design for Ageing Well project have informed interventions to 'business as usual', encouraging industry designers and product developers to address the current gap in the market for the active consumer. The research outputs provide clear, non-transient, design direction, with proof-of-concept prototypes, embracing age-appropriate shape and fit, style and proportion, fabrication, colour and technology integration. Key findings are as follows:

- **Age-appropriate size, shape and fit**:
  Current sizing is inconsistent even within the same brand. Users require garments cut to fit changing postures.
- **Less transient styling:**
  Users wish for fewer, more durable, simple, flattering styles but in a wider size range and a choice of lengths, and in multi-functional clothing layers, adaptable to a range of exercise habits and walking types.
- **Colour and texture:**
  Users prefer cheerful, age-appropriate colours and textures suitable for changing complexions and hair colour. They do not understand the current predominance of black. They have a preference for the comfort attributes of moisture-management fibres but in fabrics with a natural handle.
- **Branding (no logos):**
  Users are loyal to brands that fit self-image, but branding is perceived as advertising.
- **Price:**
  Users imply that they will purchase higher-priced garments if there are clear reasons for them being superior in use.

Technology uptake

The technology team identified a number of key points that should be taken into consideration in similar future projects:

- **Male versus female acceptance of technology**
  It was noted that, despite the problems identified during the various phases of evaluation, male participants were more accepting of the prototype than female participants. During the longitudinal evaluations, it was the male participants who maintained contact with researchers, asking questions and raising issues such as connecting the smartphone to the Desktop Viewer (personal computer).
- **Hardware usability**
  Despite the co-design approach to the developed application UI and UX, there is little that can be done to address hardware usability issues such as turning the Shimmer sensor on or off. The transmission of data from one device to another (smartphone to Desktop Viewer) should be simplified. If possible, the data transmission should take place in the background via wireless technologies. Hardware components should be easy to turn on/off and charge. However, on some devices, such as the smartphone, the on/off button requires one press to turn on, but one long press and an on-screen selection to turn off. This is confusing to older users without experience of smartphones.
- **Cost**
  Cost is a factor for the target cohort, and some users did not realise that they were using up credit on their smartphone when operating applications other than making telephone calls, for example, when downloading maps and transmitting location data. When participants used up the money allocated to their smartphones before the final evaluations, all but one decided against adding more money. As a result, those participants who had run out of credit were unable to access the map screen. Nevertheless, they were still able to record walk data (GPS information, heart rate and step count).
- **Technology maintenance**
  It was noticed during the evaluation phases that when participants had finished using technology components they felt the need to turn them off completely. Although researchers explained that devices such as smartphones and Shimmer could be put into sleep mode during charging, participants continued to turn them off.

- **Feature fatigue**

  Despite following a user-centred design approach and eliciting user requirements from a number of potential users, careful consideration should be exercised before adding all requirements to the proposed solution. During the evaluation phase, some features, despite being included throughout the duration of the prototype development, were not required by the participants. Despite the ability to personalise products, feature fatigue occurred.

- **User involvement**

  Users will engage with wearable technology (electronic and textile-based) if the functionality is simple and clear, easy to used and highly focused on their needs. Users need to be reassured of the reliability and robustness of devices and of interoperability, with the facility to upgrade and/or replace componentry. They do not wish to spend money on a product that may fail. Overall, the technology solution developed was accepted and seen as beneficial to the participants, but personalisation should be encouraged as not all participants wanted or used the same functionality.

Product development

Co-design to raise awareness of new market opportunities

The co-design process has prompted UK and international industry stakeholders, from leading brands to small to medium-sized enterprises (SMEs), to provide significant value in kind in terms of the time and expertise of their designers and product developers, both in the academic environment and in the workplace, the provision of novel materials and processes, and the development of industry-produced prototypes. Co-design has increased the outdoor industry's awareness of the decision making and buying power of the 60+ consumer, along with related business opportunities. It has raised awareness of the role of design to translate, interpret and facilitate communication between stakeholders, including garment, fabric and wearable electronics suppliers. Industry now understands the value of co-design product development with end users to increase awareness of user needs and preferences and the specific design requirements that must be addressed in order to attract them.

Early industry uptake of findings

Sizemic Ltd is progressing the research and development of mannequins for older figure types. As a result of co-design engagement in the collaborative research described here, Sprayway (the UK outdoor brand), Keela (with UK and overseas production) and Brenig (the Welsh SME) have subsequently adopted aspects of age-appropriate styling in their ongoing product development. Sprayway has benefited from direction on colour and inclusive detail and Keela on design for country clothing, while Brenig, in collaboration with the UK-based fabric brand, Aclimitise, has adopted both male and female patterns and style direction for ageing consumers. The Austrian seam-free knit producer, Blum, with production in Poland, has developed base-layer garments in collaboration with Lenzing, the producers of Tencel fibre. The technology provider, Fibretronic, has expressed a willingness to collaborate in the development of user-interface controls to be adapted to ageing dexterity. Most recently, the project team has been invited to present design findings to a major garment supplier and retailer Marks and Spencer with a view to potential collaboration. Finally, Jane McCann is leading a committee of experts to collate and define smart terms (for the first time) for online publication.

Key findings

- A functional garment layering system, as the basis for wearable technology, encourages participation in healthy exercise. Such a system comprises next-to-body garments for monitoring vital signs (pulse and breathing rates, body temperature, blood pressure and so on), mid-insulation layers incorporating heated panels, and protective outer layers accommodating communication devices with textile-based controls to provide user-friendly interfaces.

- Users accepted the benefits of technologies in relation to modern fibre properties, 'smart' material attributes (that is, those designed to include changeable properties dependent on the environment), textile-based electronics and novel garment construction techniques.

- A gap in the market exists for functional clothing and wearable technologies that older users will willingly wear to enhance comfort in terms of size and shape, movement, dexterity, thermal regulation and protection from the environment.

- A more responsible, and relatively 'slower', product development process (in comparison with transient fashion) fosters the opportunity to provide enhanced comfort in garments that are fit for purpose, with the potential for greater longevity of use.

Conclusion

The Design for Ageing Well research study has introduced new co-design methodology to guide the international textile, clothing and wearable electronics industries, which are currently neglecting the opportunity to address the gap in the global market that results from demographic ageing. It challenges the youth-oriented fashion trade driven by last season's sales figures in combination with design trend, where little record of sales to older consumers exists with no trend to guide designers. It proposes interventions to 'business as usual', with clear design guidance to promote more responsible and ultimately more sustainable, value-added, 'slower' design, fit for purpose and for the ageing market.

The study findings have demonstrated the importance of stylish, age-appropriate clothing design as a means of self-expression, in enhancing overall comfort and wellbeing by encouraging enjoyment of healthy exercise and the benefits of the natural environment. It has generated a positive image for active ageing for the design of wearable electronics in functional clothing, previously designated for use in competitive sports and as medical devices for old and ill people. Findings indicate that age-appropriate functional clothing design, with easily usable technology user interfaces, encourages people to connect socially and to participate in healthy exercise. This methodology has enabled the creation of an integrated wearable technology 'platform', with design that enhances comfort and longevity of use while contributing to independence and wellbeing.

The study has also led to better practice in the development of technical textile-driven functional clothing, where western designers are typically divorced from production carried out predominantly in the east. This can cause breakdowns in communication, with scant product specification fuelling associated waste and fashion churn resulting in a high carbon footprint alongside diminishing resources. Co-design helps to address the challenge of hybrid product design specification involving the integration of electronics into clothing, through transfer of skills from product design and architecture to describe complex clothing assembly, with strategies tested in consultation with industry collaborators.

The co-design approach has trained a new breed of cross-disciplinary academic researchers in tried-and-tested co-design process (new to clothing design) with industry practitioners and end users. International academic and industry engagement has generated research findings, with proof of concept prototypes, that have already led to knowledge exchange and potential future collaborative research. However, bringing new products to this new consumer market in future will depend on reassessing all the links in the chain contributing to the product cycle through to point-of-sale. The authors believe that a co-design approach with all stakeholders involved, from sales and marketing, to setting the design brief, to buying and retail positioning, should be adopted to promote shared understanding and enable products to be brought to market for this new consumer majority – the active ageing.

References

Bougourd, J. (2014) '3D scanning for capturing changes in size and shape with age', in J. McCann and D. Bryson (eds) *Textile-led design for the active ageing population*, Cambridge: Woodhead Publishing, pp 139–66.

Jenkins Jones, S. (2005) *Fashion design* (2nd edn) London: Lawrence King Publishing.

Lurie, A. (1992) *The language of clothes*, London: Bloomsbury.

McCann, J. (1999) 'Identification of requirements for the design development of performance sportswear', Unpublished MPhil thesis, University of Derby.

McCann, J. (2005) 'Material requirements for the design of performance sportswear', in R. Shishoo (ed) *Textiles in sport*, Cambridge: Woodhead Publishing.

McCann, J. (2009) 'Smart clothing for the ageing population', in J. McCann and D. Bryson (eds) *Smart clothes and wearable technology*, Cambridge: Woodhead Publishing, pp 346-68.

McCann, J. and Bryson, D. (eds) (2015) *Textile-led design for the active ageing population*, London: Woodhead Publishing.

Metz, D. and Underwood, M. (2005) *Older richer fitter: identifying the customer needs of Britain's ageing population*, London: Age Concern Books.

Twigg, J. (2013) *Fashion and age: Dress, the body and later life*, London: Bloomsbury.

University of Wales, Newport (2009) *New Dynamics of Ageing Newsletter 1*, Newport: University of Wales, Newport.

Venture Development Corporation (2007) *Mobile and wireless practice. A White Paper On: Wearable Electronic Systems Global Market Demand Analysis*, Third Edition.

Williamson, T., Kenney, L., Barker, A., Cooper, G., Good, T., Healey, J., Heller, B., Howard, D., Matthews, M., Prenton, S., Ryan, J. and Smith, C. (2014) 'Enhancing public involvement in assistive technology design research', *Disability and Rehabilitation: Assistive Technology*, vol 10, no 3, pp 258-65.

ELEVEN

Tackling ageing continence

Eleanor van den Heuvel

Introduction

Although every human being answers the 'call of nature' several times a day, continence is still a taboo subject. As people age, they typically become less mobile (Mottram et al, 2008) and/or need more frequent 'comfort breaks' (Milsom et al, 2001) so maintaining continence becomes a challenge. While incontinence is not a direct consequence of ageing, urinary incontinence affects 55% of women over 65 and 20% of men (Holroyd–Leduc et al, 2004). The prevalence of faecal incontinence is around 1% in the general population, rising to 17% in the very old and as much as 25% in care homes. Many factors contribute to making this condition a major problem for large numbers of older adults. Several studies have shown that urinary system function declines with age (Holm et al, 1995; Pfisterer et al, 2006; Gibson and Wagg, 2017). Another factor is the increase with age of concomitant diseases (such as congestive heart failure, Parkinson's, Alzheimer's and so on) that can result in problems with continence. In addition, mobility problems are increasingly common in older people; limitation in mobility is likely to cause difficulties with continence simply because the older person finds it difficult to reach the toilet and transfer onto it (Fonda et al, 2005).

Faecal incontinence can often be successfully treated with dietary interventions, careful bowel management regimes, and review of medication, although a small minority of people will continue to suffer with faecal symptoms. Urinary incontinence can be relieved by pharmacological, physiotherapeutic or surgical treatments, but often these treatments do not provide a complete cure and may not be appropriate for some patients, resulting in large numbers of older people needing to cope with urinary continence management issues on a daily basis. Thus, finding effective methods to enable older people to manage continence needs, especially when outside the home, is essential for successful ageing and for the maintenance of a good quality of life (Temml et al, 2000).

The impact of continence difficulties is far more than just the physical effort and expense of continence management; the problem is strongly associated with reduced self-esteem, social isolation and depression (Shaw, 2001). Problems managing continence can be extremely distressing and may all but end wider social life (Cassells and Watt, 2002; Hogg and Godfrey, 2007). Moreover, one of the major reasons that people move into residential care is an inability to cope with their continence needs (Holroyd-Leduc et al, 2004).

A study commissioned by Help the Aged (Hogg and Godfrey, 2007) found that incontinence was a likely precursor to social isolation, though the link was not inevitable. This study identified a number of factors that could affect social isolation, including personal finances, availability and quality of toilets, public awareness of continence problems, professional support and access to information.

The large number of older people affected by continence difficulties, and the huge detrimental impact of these difficulties on quality of life, was the impetus for the Tackling Ageing Continence through Theory, Tools and Technology (TACT3) project.

The core TACT3 project investigated three distinct aspects ageing continence: challenging environmental barriers to continence, led by the Helen Hamlyn Centre, Royal College of Art; improving continence services, led by University of Sheffield and Dalarna Research Institute, Sweden; and developing assistive devices for people who use continence pads, led by Brunel University, University of Manchester, University of the West of England and the BioMed Centre, Bristol Urological Institute. The project also attracted two linked Canadian projects funded by Canadian Institutes of Health Research. One project, led by Jeff Jutai, University of Toronto, investigated the impact of incontinence related stigma, and the other, led by Cara Tannenbaum, University of Montreal, developed and tested continence promotion intervention for older women (Agnew et al, 2013; Tannenbaum et al, 2013).

Aims and methods of the research

The overall aim of the TACT3 project was to reduce the impact of continence difficulties for older people. To achieve this aim, the team worked together in a knowledge transfer undertaking that focused on involving stakeholders and ensuring that project findings were publicised and where appropriate commercialised or implemented.

The project comprised three research work packages. The first, which concerned challenging environmental barriers to continence, aimed to explore the environmental barriers that prevent older people with continence concerns from participating in wider social life and to produce innovative solutions for built environment interventions that respond to the needs of the growing older population. As such, this part of the project investigated the problems associated with publically available toilets to understand the issues people face in finding, accessing and using toilet facilities away from home.

Inclusive design methods, involving 'users' throughout the design research process, were the underpinning techniques for this part of the project. In the context of this work package, users were divided into two distinct groups, toilet users and toilet providers. Initially, the project aimed simply to focus on the needs of people aged over 50, but a consultation meeting with the New Dynamics of Ageing Older People's Reference Group found that the issue of a lack of publically accessible toilets outside the home was not just a problem for older people but rather was one that concerned people of all ages. The research team therefore incorporated a methodology that included the toileting needs of those aged 0 (newborn) to 101 by interviewing 101 participants (both male and female, parents in the case of younger ages) of differing ages. Semi-structured interviews were conducted over the telephone and in person, on a one-to-one basis as well as in groups of three to four people. Interviewees were also invited to take part in design workshops, which were held after the interviews had been completed. Seven people (two men and five women) attended the workshops in which the researchers designed a participatory design game for the attendees to 'build their own toilet facilities'. Working in two groups of two and one group of three, the participants were given pictorial references of key elements that had arisen from the interview sessions and asked to incorporate those of importance to them into their designs. The grouping of participants also added a degree of wider design consideration. One pair consisted of an older man and a younger woman, another pair of older and younger women. The group of three consisted of a woman in her middle years, whose reduced mobility required her to use a wheelchair, and an older man and woman.

To understand some of the issues providers face in maintaining provision, especially to a standard expected by users, 22 different providers and associated professionals were interviewed. These included council officers overseeing public and community toilet schemes as well as representatives from park and transport services, architects, business providers and the police.

The second work package, on improving continence interventions and services, aimed to promote more effective continence treatment and support better service use outcomes by enhancing perceptions of control and efficacy in the older person. The work package was divided into two studies: one investigating patient and family carer views on continence service, and the other studying the views of continence health professionals and service managers.

Patient and family carer views were investigated in a mixed-methods study that was used to maximise recruitment, data capture and research output. A quantitative core dataset was collected from continence service users who completed a short questionnaire in clinic and a six-month follow-up to measure continence-related quality of life and to evaluate the care that users received, followed by in-depth interviews with a subset of participants. One-hundred-and twenty-three participants aged over 50 years with a diagnosis of urinary incontinence were recruited from three different settings in South Yorkshire: a specialist clinic for older people (Barnsley District General Hospital); a community clinic (Sheffield Primary Care Trust) and a surgical setting (Urogynaecology, Sheffield Teaching Hospital).

The study of health professionals had a qualitative design, incorporating semi-structured telephone interviews, with purposive sampling of participants via a stratified sampling frame based on all former English Strategic Health Authorities. The study focused on NHS Trusts in England providing a continence service for community-dwelling people aged 50 years and above and recruited 16 continence service leads.

The aim of the third research work package was to design, develop and evaluate two assistive devices that were requested by continence pad users themselves. The two devices developed were a colour-change odour detector that responds to sub-olfactory levels of ammonia (produced by stale urine) and smart underwear that detects pad leakage. Both these devices aim to mitigate some of the 'treatment effects' of managing continence needs with absorbent products. Both products were designed to warn the continence pad wearer of a problem, either odour or leakage, before the problem became evident to anyone else, thereby increasing the wearer's confidence and self-esteem.

This work package used a particularly wide range of multidisciplinary methods to develop and test the prototype products. User-focused design workshops and interviews were used to produce design specifications for both the devices.

The urine odour detector was developed using microbiological and chemical analysis to understand the odour-producing potential of different urine samples. Trained olfactory assessors were also used to grade urine odour and assess the effectiveness of the colour-change substrate.

The smart underwear was developed by integrating electro-conductive yarn sensors into the underwear by sewing two parallel conductive pathways in the location where spillage from the pad is most likely to occur. The sensor is attached to a signalling unit, which vibrates when leakage from the pad into the underwear is detected by the sensor. The signalling unit consists of a single, round, printed circuit board with a microcontroller, a vibration unit, a coin cell and associated drivers. The device is normally on and in a mode that uses minimal power (deep sleep mode). When urine wets the underwear and bridges the gap between the conductive pathways, they effectively act as a switch, turning on the signalling unit microcontroller and energising the vibration unit, alerting the wearer to the leakage event. The current flowing in the conductive pathways during active mode is 10-A. The signalling unit can be configured to provide a single or repeated warnings, as necessary. It then returns to deep sleep mode (Fernandes et al, 2011). The finished prototype complied with the Electromagnetic Compatibility Directive and the 2000 Radio and Telecommunications Terminal Equipment Regulations.

The smart underwear was clinically evaluated by women who had experienced pad leakage, in two test rounds. An initial pilot test recruited six participants who were asked to use the underwear for two weeks, completing a diary of leakage events and a final evaluation questionnaire. No major changes to the smart underwear were identified from the pilot study. The full clinical study was completed by 56 participants who were asked to complete two of the International Consultation on Incontinence Modular Questionnaires (ICIQ) – the ICIQ-Urinary Incontinence Short Form module and the ICIQ-Lower Urinary Tract Symptoms Quality of Life (ICIQ-LUTSqol) module (Kelleher et al 1997; Avery et al, 2004; Abrams et al, 2006) – before using the underwear to provide a baseline measurement.

Participants were asked to trial the device for a period of two weeks, using the device during the day for at least five days in the week if possible, and to wash the underwear as many times as they wished. During the trial period, participants were asked to complete a diary for the first week only, recording all of their urine leakage events and the performance of the smart underwear. At the end of the trial period, participants were asked to complete an evaluation questionnaire, repeat the two ICIQ questionnaires that they completed at the start of the study and to complete the Psychosocial Impact of Assistive Devices

Scale (PIADS) (Jutai and Day, 2002) questionnaire. PIADS is a validated generic tool that measures the psychosocial impact of assistive device use in three domains: competence (reflecting perceived functional capability, independence and performance); adaptability (reflecting inclination or motivation to participate socially and take risks); and self-esteem (reflecting self-confidence, self-esteem and emotional wellbeing).

Findings

Challenging environmental barriers

Three key themes that users considered a priority emerged from the design workshop:

- **Cleanliness** – it was important that toilets are seen to be clean, to communicate wider hygiene confidence.
- **Functionality** – equipment in the facilities had to be easy to use and intuitive (for example, locks that are easy to turn and with features that make it obvious whether they are locked or unlocked).
- **Technology** – users appreciated technological innovations that improved toilet provision.

Data from the interviews and workshops was then consolidated to create four personas: Yasmin, a 26-year-old trainee teacher with Irritable Bowel Syndrome; Paul, a 38-year-old photographer with three young children; Judith, aged 60 and recently retired, who took water tablets and also cared for her mother; and, finally, Leonard, aged 82, who required a walking aid for physical mobility.

These personas were developed to communicate user needs to toilet providers who were the second group of users consulted in the project.

Interviews with toilet providers raised several key issues including how to keep the toilet facilities to the high standard expected by members of the public, and deter non-toileting behaviour such as graffiti and vandalism, illegal drug use and public sex activities.

These interviews also highlighted how fractured UK toilet provision is between a number of varied providers. Some 'standalone' facilities are offered by local authorities, while other provisions may be part of the transport infrastructure (bus and train stations) or are available in shopping centres. There are also toilets provided in cafes, bars, pubs and restaurants through Community Toilet Schemes. While there has been a decline in UK 'public' toilet provision, there are still 'publicly accessible' toilets widely available.

However, it can be difficult to find out where publically accessible toilets are in any given area, what facilities they provide (such as accessible unisex cubicles, baby change facilities) and what times they are open. It emerged that the issue was not necessary a lack of toilet provision, but rather the lack of complete, accurate information on toilets. For members of the public, especially older people and those with continence concerns, poor information often had serious consequences.

Just as the provision of publicly accessible toilets is fractured, so is the information about them. Information on existing UK toilet provision is not centrally collated and no national map or database of toilets exists. This makes it difficult to include toilet information on maps and smartphone applications. Even signposts may only point to the toilets of one provider, such as the local council. Better information would allow users to find toilets that meet their various individual needs, and be a practical, affordable initiative for providers to accomplish.

Good information on toilet provision would ensure that people knew about facilities and would probably increase usage. In turn, such an increase of usage may deter non-toileting behaviours that tend to take place when facilities are not used. As a response to this need for reliable and up-to-date information, the Great British Public Toilet Map (GBPTM) was developed, for a pilot area covering the London boroughs. The GBPTM was produced by requesting and incorporating 'open data' on public toilet provision into a public participation website to improve information about the UK's public toilets. Open data is information that is machine-readable and free to reuse, in this instance information released by local authorities on the services they provide, in response to a UK government initiative to encourage greater transparency. Where councils have published open data about their toilets, this is shown on the map so that people can find the facilities. If a council has not yet published open data relating to toilet provision, users may contact the council through the GBPTM website to explain why this information is useful, and encourage the council to contribute data to the repository. The researchers also included data from National Rail and Transport for London as examples of other providers of toilets and of toilet data. The GBPTM also shows where toilet provision is adequate and serves to highlight any gaps in provision.

The use of open data will make it easier to collate a UK toilet database that is accurate and up to date, and can be made available to anyone who wants it. The website is at http://greatbritishpublictoiletmap.rca.ac.uk.

Improving continence services

Study 1: patient perspective

All participants were fairly satisfied with the continence service they had received, and some rated their experience more highly than fairly satisfactory. More than of 80% of patients reported that the cause of their problem and treatment for it was explained to their satisfaction. All participants felt that the continence service provided a comfortable environment and most reported that there was adequate privacy.

Most participants were involved in decision making about treatment, although less than 60% reported being offered a choice of treatments. Only 9% of patients attending a surgical service were offered a choice of continence aids/products, compared with 38% and 36% of patients attending a specialist and a community service respectively.

Three themes were identified from interviews with older people:

- accessibility of continence services;
- the need for patients to establish a positive relationship with their continence service professional;
- the importance of working in partnership to enable patients to self-manage their condition by reducing the impact of urinary incontinence on everyday life.

Study 2: professional perspective

Six major themes relating to barriers and facilitators of a good quality continence services emerged from the interviews with continence service managers (Orrell et al, 2013):

- Negative attitudes towards older people and UI were identified as a major barrier to good care for older people with UI. Participants felt that patients' families, and even health professionals, had little knowledge or expectation of treatment and cure, but were simply resigned to managing the condition with absorbent products.
- Continence promotion regardless of age was a closely related theme that was seen as an essential facilitator of a good-quality continence service. Several participants reported that patients and carers only expected to receive pads from the continence service because they did not know that any other treatments were available.
- Investment in service capacity was highlighted by all the interviewees as a major challenge to providing high-quality care for older people.

Increasing demands for services, staff shortages and growing waiting lists were among the problems discussed. Some areas lack equipment and clinics, while others had problems finding specialist staff to provide an integrated continence service.

- Appropriate and rapid patient referral was felt to be an important factor in delivering good care to older people with urinary incontinence. Some primary care continence services reported that patients were referred to hospital services when it was unnecessary, while others were not referred to continence services but simply allocated pads by district nurses. Frustration was expressed that hospital patients with continence problems were referred to their GP on discharge rather than directly to the continence service.
- A full patient assessment including complete history taking, physical examination, review of medication, urinary analysis, bladder scan and vaginal and rectal examination, if appropriate, was seen by all participants as being a key feature of quality continence care for older patients, as this provided the practitioner with the necessary information to make a differential diagnosis and to formulate an individual treatment plan for each patient.
- Continence education and specialist knowledge are essential for delivering high-quality continence care. Highly trained and knowledgeable staff are vital to the continence service, and training for anyone involved in caring for people with continence needs was seen as vital if a good service were to be provided.

Another feature emerging from the data collected during the interviews with continence service leads was participants' tendency to blame other health professionals for many of the barriers to a high-quality service. When other health professionals such as GP commissioners or district nurses were not identified as the main barrier to a high-quality service, family carers and/or patients themselves were seen as part of the problem. Continence service leads felt helpless to redress the situation, which may be due to a feeling among staff that their service has a low status among health professionals.

Developing assistive technologies

The odour detector had 90% response rate in vitro, responding within two minutes of exposure to stale urine. It was difficult to test the device with users because researchers could not ask participants to self-report whether the odour detector triggered reliably because they themselves would be unaware of any smell. Potential users were therefore simply asked to report on the features of the design. In the clinical evaluation, most users said that the device was a good idea and that it was easy to use. Most thought it would give them more confidence, but could not be not sure until they were able to test a fully guaranteed device. All participants were concerned about odour and the device scored positively for all three dimensions of PIADS, indicating that participants felt that the odour detector increased their self-esteem, competence and adaptability.

The prototype odour detector is shown in Figure 11.1.

The smart underwear (SUW) was tested by 56 women aged between 38 and 98 years; the average age of participants was 66 years old. All the women used absorbent pads as part of their continence management strategy and all had experienced urine leakage from their pad. Nineteen per cent of participants reported that pad leakage was a daily occurrence, with the majority (67%) experiencing pad leaks between one and six times per week.

During the period of the study, on average participants experienced leakage from the pad on 77% of the days that they completed their diaries. On average, for 87% of the time participants were alerted to pad leakage events by the smart underwear and for 59% of the time participants were not aware of pad leakage before the alert. On average, for 85% of the time participants were alerted in time to change their pad before leakage onto clothing or furnishings. A few participants were troubled by repeated false alarms, as sweating also triggered the device. Over 90% of participants thought the SUW would or might make them feel more confident and 92% thought the overall impression was good (63%) or OK (29%). The results from the ICIQ-LUTSqol revealed that quality of life status was largely unchanged in the two-week period during which the smart underwear was used, except for the effect of ability to travel, which was improved among the women.

Figure 11.1: Odour detector before activation (left) and in the presence of ammonia

The PIADS evaluation showed that the smart underwear had a positive psychosocial impact on users who completed the study in the absence of any symptomatic changes, and that it increased levels of confidence and the ability to socialise and take risks. Here is a selection of feedback from participants:

> The smart underwear and sensor made me feel more confident as I had warning about leakage; incontinence is something that is embarrassing, this product gives you more confidence to lead a normal life. (Participant SUW2 37, aged 57 years)
>
> First time in years found comfortable product to assist with condition. (Participant SUW1 03, aged 85 years, severe incontinence)
>
> It will help people that have continence problems to feel confident when going out; it gave me warning before my clothes and wheelchair cushion got wet. (Participant SUW2 04, aged 40 years, moderate-to-severe incontinence)

Nine out of every 10 users felt that the SUW did or could make them feel more confident. The prototype smart underwear evaluated in this study was effective and acceptable to five out of every 10 users and would be acceptable to an additional three out of 10 users after modification.

Figure 11.2: Smart underwear

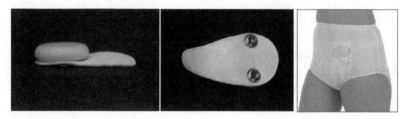

Implications

The TACT3 project has attempted to tackle continence issues for older people in three different spheres, but the one common feature that has become very clear is the huge taboo that still surrounds the topic of continence difficulties. Considering how common incontinence is, and the huge impact that the condition can have on quality of life and health, it is worrying that so little attention is paid to it.

The GBPTM website has been launched but further funding is required to populate the site nationally. The Australian National Public Toilet Map is a government-backed initiative that recognises the importance of access to toilets outside the home for creating a 'people-friendly' environment that contributes to a healthy society. Public toilets are particularly important for older people who may lack confidence to leave home when provision of toilets, and/or of information about them, is unavailable, giving rise to problems of social isolation and dependency. Lack of public toilets is a barrier to tourism and may result in street fouling, particularly at night. The implications for the UK government are clear: providing a central source of accessible, accurate information on toilets outside the home is a vital first step towards making the most efficient use of available toilet facilities. Such a resource will also indicate gaps in provision for future investment.

The taboo surrounding continence issues seems to extend to continence professionals and their patients, both in self-perceived value and in the eyes of others. Until continence services are recognised as vital to healthy ageing and patients feel empowered to demand timely and appropriate treatments, services will continue to be under-resourced and patients will continue to suffer. Since continence problems are associated with costly complications such as pressure ulcers and falls, this lack of investment is likely to prove expensive in the long term.

Developing assistive technologies to help people cope with the treatment effects of using continence pads is a means of improving outcomes for people who are dependent on these products. Again, the taboo surrounding anything to do with continence and the domination of the continence market by large manufacturers are two factors that make the commercialisation of innovative products very challenging. The perceived status of continence pad users, who may be stigmatised as old, incapable, poor and unconcerned about appearance, may be a further barrier to commercial interest in a product that must be designed for and bought by wearers themselves.

Recommendations

There are three key recommendations from the research, as follows.

- Government and local councils need to support an integrated public toilet provision information and strategy.

- Clinical commission groups need to support the provision of integrated continence services to reduce inappropriate hospital referrals, provide holistic services for the elderly in which continence is addressed as a key component and recognise the benefits of specialist services at appropriate points in the patient pathway.
- Integrated support is needed to bring continence products to the point at which the market determines their commercial success.

Key findings

- The Great British Public Toilet Map was developed to meet toilet users' requirements for clean, functional toilets accessible when and where needed and toilet providers' requirements to reduce undesirable behaviour in toilets. This online resource was designed to provide accurate essential information on public accessible toilets to allow users to locate suitable provision and to increase usage of less well-known facilities, reducing vandalism and other non-toileting behaviour.
- Older patients valued accessible continence services where they could establish a positive relationship and work in partnership with a continence professional to reduce the impact of urinary incontinence. Continence professionals agreed that it was vital for patients to have timely and appropriate access to their services. Negative attitudes towards older people and incontinence and lack of investment in services are identified as barriers to older continence patients receiving effective treatment.
- A colour-change odour detector was developed, but its efficacy was extremely difficult to test in vivo for ethical and practical reasons. Smart underwear that alerted the wearer to leakage from the continence pad before wetness spread to outer garments was developed and tested with 81 participants aged 32-98 (average age 67) (Long et al, 2015). Nine out of ten users said the smart underwear could make the feel more confident. Half the participants found the prototype effective and acceptable, and a further 30% felt it would be acceptable after modifications were made.

Conclusion

Local councils have no obligation in law to provide public toilets, and pressures on local government funding are likely to lead to more closures in an already depleted service. The GBPTM could become a valuable source of information for councils and other publically accessible toilet providers to enable them to make the best use of resources as well as being a useful tool for members of the public.

A change of attitude among commissioners and other health professionals towards older people and urinary incontinence may lead to the raising of standards in continence care for older people with this condition, whereby continence promotion regardless of age is the norm rather than pad provision. Dedicated and integrated continence services are valued by older people, with continuity of care allowing a collaborative approach to treatment of urinary incontinence and ongoing support that allows older people to feel more confident in their ability to manage their condition in daily life.

Interdisciplinary groups can make a significant contribution to the development of user-centred assistive technology designs. However, it is extremely important that appropriate support is given to successful developments to help to bridge the gap between research and commercial application. When all funding stops as soon as the research project is complete, the most difficult part of the work, the commercialisation step, is left unsupported and becomes almost impossible to realise.

References

Agnew, R. and van den Heuvel, E. (2013) 'Effectiveness of continence promotion for older women via community organisations: a cluster randomised trial', Clinical Trials, vol 10, no 1, pp 151-9.

Avery, K., Donovan, J., Peters, T., Shaw, C., Gotoh, M. and Abrahams, P. (2004) 'ICIQ: a brief and robust measure for evaluating symptoms and impact of urinary incontinence', Neurourology and Urodynamics, vol 23, no 4, pp 322-30.

Cassells, C. and Watt, E. (2002) 'The impact of incontinence in older spousal care givers', Journal of Advanced Nursing, vol 42, no 6, pp 607-16.

Fernandes, B., Gaydecki, P., Jowitt, F. and van den Heuvel, E.A. (2011) 'Urinary incontinence: a vibration alert system for detecting pad overflow', Assistive Technology, vol 23, no 4, pp 218-24.

Fonda, D., DuBeau, C., Harari, D., Ouslander, J., Palmer, M. and Roe, B. (2005) 'Incontinence in the frail elderly', in P. Abrams, L. Cardozo, S. Khoury and A. Wein (eds) Incontinence. Proceedings from the 3rd International Consultation on Incontinence, Volume 2, Paris: Health Publications Ltd, pp 1163-240.

Gibson, W. and Wagg, A. (2017) 'Incontinence in the elderly, "normal" ageing, or unaddressed pathology?', Nature Reviews: Urology, vol 14, pp 440-8.

Hogg, A. and Godfrey, H. (2007) *Incontinence and older people: Is there a link to social isolation?*, London: Help the Aged.

Holm, N.R., Horn, T. and Hald, T. (1995) 'Detrusor in ageing and obstruction', *Scandinavian Journal of Urology and Nephrology*, vol 29, no 1, pp 45-9.

Holroyd-Leduc, J.M., Jayna, M., Mehta, K.M. and Covinsky, K.E. (2004) 'Urinary incontinence and its association with death, nursing home admission, and functional decline', *Journal of the American Geriatrics Society*, vol 52, no 5, pp 712-18.

Jutai, J. and Day, H. (2002) 'Psychosocial Impact of Assistive Devices Scale (PIADS)', *Technology and Disability*, vol 14, no 3, pp 107-11.

Kelleher, C., Cardozo, L., Khullar, V. and Salvatore, S. (1997) 'A new questionnaire to assess the quality of life of urinary incontinent women', *BJOG: An International Journal of Obstetrics and Gynaecology*, vol 104, no 12, pp 1374-9.

Long, A., Edwards, J., Worthington, J., Cotterill, N. Weir I. Drake M. and van den Heuvel E. (2015) 'Clinical evaluation of a prototype underwear designed to detect urine leakage from continence pads', *Journal of Wound, Ostomy and Continence Nursing*, vol 42, no 6, pp 632-9.

Milsom, I., Abrams, P., Cardozo, L., Roberts, R.G., Thüroff, J. and Wein, A.J. (2001) 'How widespread are the symptoms of an overactive bladder and how are they managed? A population-based prevalence study', *BJU International*, vol 87, no 9, pp 760-6.

Mottram, S., Peat, G., Thomas, E., Wilkie, R. and Croft, P. (2008) 'Patterns of pain and mobility limitation in older people: cross-sectional findings from a population survey of 18,497 adults aged 50 years and over', *Quality of Life Research*, vol 17, no 4, pp 529-39.

Orrell, A., McKee, K., Dahlberg, L., Gilhooly, M. and Parker, S. (2013) 'Improving continence services for older people from the service-providers' perspective: a qualitative interview study', *BMJ Open*, 3, e002926.

Pfisterer, M., Griffiths, D., Schaefer, W. and Resnick N. (2006) 'The effect of age on lower urinary tract function: a study in women', *Journal of the American Geriatrics Society*, vol 54, no 3, pp 405-12.

Shaw, C. (2001) 'A review of the psychosocial predictors of help-seeking behaviour and impact on quality of life in people with urinary incontinence', *Journal of Clinical Nursing*, vol 10, no 1, pp 15-24.

Tannenbaum, C., Agnew, R., Benedetti, A., Thomas, D. and van den Heuvel, E. (2013) ,Effectiveness of continence promotion for older women via community organisations: a cluster randomised trial', *BMJ Open*, 3, e004135.

Temml, C., Haidinger, G., Schmidbauer, J., Schatzl G. and Madersbacher, S. (2000) 'Urinary incontinence in both sexes: prevalence rates and impact on quality of life and sexual life', *Neurourology and Urodynamics*, vol 19, pp 259-71.

TWELVE

Evaluating the visualisation of dynamic biomechanical data for healthcare and design

Alastair S. Macdonald

Introduction

The 'Envision' research described in this chapter was conducted between late 2007 and early 2009, the first of the New Dynamics of Ageing (NDA) projects to complete. The findings from the project provided the platform for further Research Councils UK funding to continue our research in this area, and so although our account is now somewhat historical, and some of the statements arising from our findings at the time relate to either the limitations of the technologies that were available to us or practices current at that point, this chapter allows us to usefully contextualise the value of this NDA Envision work with reference to what was to follow and to refer to more recently published articles where some of the themes outlined in this chapter have been discussed in more detail.

Potential value in the use of biomechanical analysis

Over four decades of research, the field of biomechanics (the study of the mechanical laws relating to the movement or structure of living organisms) has contributed knowledge about the musculoskeletal system and the way it operates dynamically in relation to muscle force and the effects of gravity. Biomechanical analysis can be used to scientifically assess the causes of the movement problems of individuals. In the healthcare context, biomechanics can be used to assess patients and to measure, for example, their progress and outcomes following treatment. In relation to the design of, for example, the built environment, furniture and transport, biomechanical analysis can be used to help provide an evaluation of the impact of design details and features on individuals' capabilities in performing a range of daily living activities, such as the impact of the variation in the height of seating or the inclusion of armrests in furniture, or the impact of the variation of worktop and stair heights in homes and buildings.

Barriers to widespread adoption

To date, biomechanical data measurement and analysis have only been used in a small number of clinical scenarios, largely in clinical gait analysis (the systematic study of locomotion in a clinical setting). These specialist sessions are expensive both in terms of the types of equipment used to collect motion data and the specialist staff required to collect and interpret the results. Due to the expense of these sessions, they are only used with those groups of patients who have the most complex movement difficulties. Interpretation of the data collected by motion analysis, particularly with clinical gait data, is considered to be problematic (Baker, 2006). 'Interpretation of biomechanical data is complex, time consuming and not readily understood by most therapists' (Coutts, 1999, p 3). The representations of biomechanical analyses as a series of 2D graphs (Loudon and Macdonald, 2009) (Figure 12.1) is of limited use when trying to communicate with those without a background in biomechanics – with other health professionals or the patient themselves (Simon, 2004). Additionally, these graphs do not provide a simultaneous view of the system of body segment movements in a dynamic context.

Background to the Envision research

In previous research, a prototype software tool had been created that visualised, for non-biomechanical specialists and lay audiences, dynamic biomechanical data captured from older adults undertaking activities of daily living (ADL) (Macdonald et al, 2007; EQUAL). From motion capture data and muscle strength measurements, a 3D animated human 'stick figure' was generated, on which the biomechanical demands of the activities were represented visually at the hip and knee joints, represented (Figure 12.2) as a percentage of an individual's maximum capability (derived from lab-based measurements (Macdonald et al, 2007), using a continuous colour gradient from green at 0%, amber at 50% through to red at 100% (Loudon and Macdonald, 2009). The potential healthcare and design applications for the visualisations were evaluated through a series of interviews and focus groups with older adults, and healthcare and design professionals, and through a specialist workshop for professionals.

Envision: the evaluation of a visualisation prototype

Figure 12.1: Two-dimensional representations of biomechanical analysis

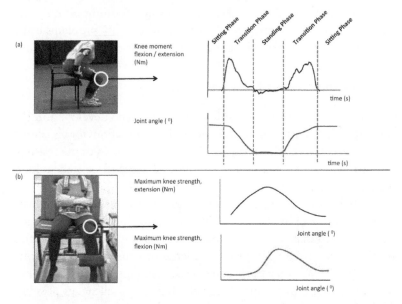

Note: This figure shows 2D plots of selected biomechanical data for the sit-stand activity for a single joint in only one rotation direction: (a) changes in the left knee joint moment in flexion/extension during the sit-stand activity; and (b) variation in maximum strength for the left knee joint compared with the angle of the joint. Two graphs are needed as different muscle groups are in use in flexion and in extension, producing different maximum values (Loudon and Macdonald, 2009).

Figure 12.2: Visualisation of biomechanical demands of activities of daily living

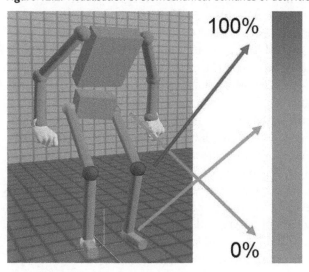

In an attempt to begin to address the issues and opportunities identified here, the Innovation in Envisioning Dynamic Biomechanical Data to Inform Healthcare and Design Guidelines and Strategy evaluated, over a 14-month period between December 2007 and January 2009, the innovative prototype described earlier as a way of communicating and understanding the complexity of older adult mobility problems using visualisations of objective dynamic movement data.

Aim and objectives of the research

The aim of Envision was to evaluate the prototype developed in the previous work and its potential for developing applications for visualising dynamic data for healthcare and design. The objectives of the research were: to gather evidence of how a range of prospective stakeholders (older adults, healthcare professionals and design practitioners) interpreted what was being represented by the visualisations; to evaluate the potential role of this tool to facilitate cross-disciplinary discourse and deepen professional practitioner understanding; and to develop insights about the mobility experience in older adults through empowering them to participate, on a more equal basis, in discussions with specialists from a range of clinical and design disciplines. At all stages possible, older adults were to be involved in the evaluation of the tool.

Research methods

The tool was evaluated through a qualitative methodology. For the purposes of evaluating the prototype, two main groups were recruited: older adults (n = 18); and healthcare and design professionals (n = 15). Older adult participants in the 60+, 70+ and 80+ age groups were recruited through the University of Strathclyde's Centre for Lifelong Learning and Age Concern Scotland. The older adults were selected to match as closely as possible the cohort of individuals (and their associated age- and health-related conditions) from whom the original data for the visualisations were obtained. The range of professions selected comprised clinical medicine, physiotherapy, occupational therapy, bioengineering, disability consultancy, engineering design and interior design. The professionals selected combined practitioners who had close experience of working directly with end users of healthcare or design. These were recruited through existing networks of The Glasgow School of Art, and the research consultancy, Journey Associates. The professionals and older people (n = 33 total) were interviewed to determine issues and themes of concern to them in regard to the effect of ageing on mobility. Two different topic guide pro forma were created for the interviews, tailored to each of the two groups, yet covering the same issues. Data analysis software was used on the recorded and transcribed interviews to identify emergent themes for discussion in the focus groups.

Three focus groups (FGs) were held to evaluate responses to the dynamic visualisations: one comprising solely older adults (FG1); the second with a range of healthcare and design professionals (FG2); and a third with a mixture of older adults and professionals (FG3). Each FG was recorded on video for later analysis, and participants asked to complete questionnaires to capture additional responses. In FG1 and FG2, the participants were shown a sequence of animations, without prior explanation. The animations were selected to show, for example, comparison of two individuals doing the same ADL task (such as lifting an object from a high shelf to a lower one, as in Figure 12.3) or the same individual doing the same task in different ways (such as rising from sitting to standing with and without using a seat's armrests, as in Figure 12.4).

In order to capture the extent of participants' initial understanding, participants were asked to write down their initial responses to a few simple questions. Following this, a semi-structured discussion was facilitated to explore in more detail the responses, understanding and interpretation of the visualisations; the insights they might provide; potential applications; and how the prototype might be improved. In FG3, the mixed group was shown short video clips of older adults' and professionals' comments from FG1 and FG2, summarising the main findings from each. Following this, the findings from FG1 and FG2 were discussed in more depth, facilitating discussion between the two groups, enabling comparison between the professionals' responses and those of the older adults.

Initial findings were presented at a national seminar promoted and supported by the Strategic Promotion of Ageing Research Capacity (SPARC) at The Glasgow School of Art in November 2008, attended by around 70 delegates, enabling further feedback to be solicited. The findings detailed in the next section, and a further analysis of the focus group videos, were also used to structure a specialist workshop with healthcare professionals and academic researchers (n = 8) to explore the potential future development and applications of the prototype; next-stage technologies; and implications for future practice, predominantly for healthcare applications. These discussions and others to identify future research and funding possibilities continued beyond the funded period of the project; research resulting from successful applications is briefly outlined in the Conclusion.

Figure 12.3: Stills from animations: comparison of different individuals lifting objects from a high to a low shelf

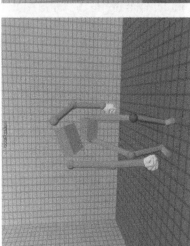

Note: From left to right: 74-year-old female with no apparent problems; 81-year-old male, osteoarthritis of knees; 67-year-old male, history of back problems and fractures.

Figure 12.4: Stills from animations: comparison of a 67-year-old male with a history of back problems and fractures performing an activity in different ways

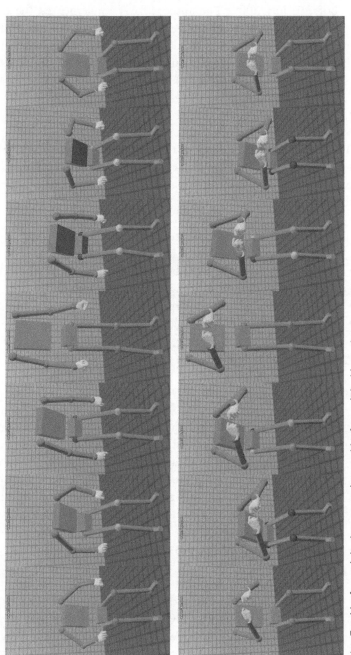

Note: Top: rising from a chair using armrests; bottom: rising from a chair without using armrests.

Findings

The findings described here were first published and made available through the New Dynamics of Ageing programme outputs and its website, in July 2009. The authors have supplemented the original findings with further illustrative material, where this exists, derived from subsequent analysis of the data acquired during Envision. Further discussion of some of this data can be found in Loudon and Macdonald (2009) and Loudon et al (2014).

Finding 1: Data accessibility

The method of visualising the dynamic biomechanical data enables people without training in biomechanics, both professional and lay older people, to access and interpret the data.

This has the following advantages:

- It enables lay people to contribute to discussions about biomechanics.
- It allows connections with experience and knowledge.
- It enables new professional insights.
- It offers understandable, objective scientific data.

Discussions about biomechanics

In the findings published in 2009, we stated:

> From both the written responses and the subsequent discussions it was clear that the 'traffic light system' [Figure 12.2] was effective as an indicator of the degree of 'pain' or 'stress' being experienced during certain activities, with green indicating 'ok' and red illustrating the 'peak' point. This intuitive understanding of the dynamic visualisations enabled the participants to effectively contribute to the discussion. This was possible without requiring a contextualised setting or introductory information. For instance, one of the older people suggested that one of the animations seemed to be 'younger', 'more flexible' and to be experiencing 'less pain' than another. Another participant could identify where problems were occurring, commenting that (with reference to the visuals) 'the hips are

more painful than the knee', and that 'his knees are sore'. (Macdonald et al, 2009), p 4)

However, this flagged up a misunderstanding from the viewer's perspective, as it was not pain that was being represented but biomechanical – or functional – demand, that is, how hard the muscles were working to support the joints as a percentage of an individual's maximum capability to do so. This illustrates not only the power of the visuals, but also the opportunity to misinterpret what is being shown.

Connections with experience and knowledge

Both groups could identify with the movements shown and relate them to either their own personal experience or professional knowledge. For example, one of the older people commented: "I see myself getting up and down from the chair." A design professional made reference to mobility issues he recognised personally, comparing animations of two different individuals conducting the same movement, reflecting age-related deterioration in mobility: "Me as a boy ... and me as I am now."

Professional insights

Healthcare professionals were able to recognise and compare levels of how hard the muscles were working and stress on joints during a full movement cycle, identifying normal and abnormal movement patterns, such as compensations made in the speed and quality of movements due to mobility problems. In another example, a clinician discussed particular movement patterns as indicative of a pre-existing condition that required the individual to make compensatory adjustments to complete a movement, causing additional strain on the hips: "They are not using their ankles to bend, and so have to compensate elsewhere."

Objective scientific data

Both clinical and design professionals indicated that such a tool might avoid the need to rely on subjective judgement, intuitive skill, and trial and error, thereby allowing more accurate diagnosis in a clinical setting on the one hand, and presenting a sound rationale for design approaches on the other.

Finding 2: Participants' empowerment

Older people are empowered to participate in the discussion of the problems and issues affecting their mobility with clinicians, healthcare practitioners and design professionals, and how these issues affect their lifestyle and quality of life.

This has the following advantages:

• It elicits expression of mobility issues.
• It improves two-way communication between older adults and health professionals.

Expression of mobility issues

Comments from participants in the older people's focus group revealed that the mode of visualisation generated empathetic responses. One person who had had two hip replacements and a knee replacement commented: "This represents my experience." Others commented: "That's my knee" and "I see myself getting up and down from the chair." They were able to relate difficulties experienced with day-to-day activities in the built environment such as ascending stairs (requiring handrail support), and difficulties entering and exiting taxis – forward descent from transport could prove problematic, and one participant tactically resorted to descending backwards down aircraft stairs while holding handrails.

Extracts from conversations contextualise these findings. The following extract from FG1 was prompted by viewing an animation of visualised data of an older adult ascending and descending stairs:

Older person 1: "I think the important thing to get across is, just like this, how valuable the handrail is ... and it gives people confidence to go upstairs. Without a handrail you say, 'Oh god, am I going to get up here?' The handrail's very important."

Older person 2: "We spoke about going upstairs holding on to both [handrails] ... but that's not possible if you're using a walking stick, you know, you've got to hold the walking stick in one hand, and just use one hand to go up."

Older person 1: "In one, it's his knee and his hip turned red, but in the other figure, there was only one, the knee turned red. Could it be … that it only affects them going upstairs instead of downstairs?"

Older person 2: "Going up stairs it's essential to have a balustrade. You could not walk upstairs … well you can but with difficulty.

Older person 3: "… you don't always get a staircase with two banisters. Coming up from the train station today, the steps were wide, so you only had the one banister."

Older person 4: "I can also get down airplane steps backwards, which is much easier, provided there's a banister. In fact it's the only way I can do it, I can't do it any other way."

The following extract from FG1 was prompted by viewing the animation of visualised data illustrated in Figure 12.4:

Older person 1: "I've got two hip replacements and a knee replacement. So I was quite familiar with their movements. Right away I say, 'That's like me.'"

Older person 2: "That's my knee … I see myself getting up and down from the chair."

Older person 3: "That is one of the exercises we do at the cardiac rehab, sit to stand, and it's just square stools you sit on. You can press on your knees like that [indicates the movement], and rock forward and up and down."

Communication between older adults and health professionals

One issue identified was the current difficulty older people had in communicating with professionals: "You can tell a doctor [your condition] but don't always feel they've quite grasped it"; "I've had problems trying to explain to doctors who won't listen." It was felt the visual and contextual nature of the animations could reduce the need for 'medi-speak', which was recognised as a barrier to communication with clients and other professionals. Older participants thought that the animations would be useful to demonstrate and explain mobility issues and to help address 'the white coat syndrome' to assist in a situation where a patient would otherwise forget or overlook an issue during a consultation. At the same time, some professionals have difficulty in providing explanations in lay terms, and it was felt that the tool "makes two-way communication very easy", that it "clearly articulates for the health professional and the older person what is going on in the joints" and that it provided an opportunity to explain and encourage normal movement patterns "to limit, mitigate or overcome pain".

Finding 3: Enhanced communication

Healthcare and design professionals can benefit from enhanced communication across disciplines, allowing a more joined-up approach to healthcare and design planning.

This has two advantages:

- It facilitates cross-disciplinary insights.
- It helps overcome problems of terminology.

Cross-disciplinary insights

The effective demonstration of sequential movements and immediacy of client feedback were features identified as facilitating the exchange of information. It was felt that viewing the animations together with professionals outside their own disciplines (for example, between an occupational therapist, a physiotherapist, a biomechanist and a designer) helped provide insights into the other professions:

> "A simple animation allowed open dialogue between a few different professionals, again the animation is objective and acted as a focus to discuss mobility. It appealed to everyone in its own particular way and wasn't a tool that in any way isolated the viewer."

The visualisations of three different individuals lifting an object from a high to a low shelf (Figure 12.3) provoked discussion about the causes of 'stress' on joints and how the problems might be alleviated. The following dialogues from FG2 when shown the animations illustrated in Figure 12.3 provide examples of detailed analyses by, and insights gained between, professionals from disparate disciplines, for example, designers and physiotherapists. This is a dialogue about real data that would not have been possible with conventional formats of presentation of biomechanical data.

Design engineer:	"One's moving a lot quicker than the other one. Me as a boy, me as I am now."
Designer:	"The person on the right looks less agile."
Design engineer:	"They're bending in a very different motion."
Physiotherapist:	"The left one's going down much further. The actual height drop is considerably more on the left, and the leg pattern's symmetrical on the left and asymmetrical on the right."
Bioengineer:	"The left figure appears to be better balanced in comparison to the right."
Physiotherapist:	"I think the person on the right has to use a lot more trunk rotation in order to achieve what they're trying to achieve."
Design engineer:	"He's having to turn in a different way. I guess the assumption is that he's got an imbalance somewhere in his joints, so he's got to do things differently if he's reaching with his left hand from the way he'd do them if he were reaching with his right hand. Which means one size doesn't fit all … one solution's not going to work for everybody. Or maybe not for the same person in two different positions."
Design consultant:	"High stress levels appear to be at the hips and the right knee."
Design engineer:	"Interestingly it's in the right knee as he stands up, as he straightens up again."
Bioengineer:	"It seems to fluctuate as well."
Physiotherapist:	"In the right figure, there's almost no movement at the ankle at all. They're totally unable to use their ankles. They're having to compensate everywhere else."
Designer:	"You get the impression they're saving their ankles and knees, but causing more pain at their hips."
Physiotherapist:	"Trunk rotation as well to be able to achieve a reach."
Designer:	"So there might be pre-existing problems in the knees and the ankles that are now causing new problems in the hip."

Overcoming problems of terminology

In particular, the tool helped to overcome barriers that result from variance in terminology used by different disciplines and the need for specialist knowledge to interpret traditional data sets. One example was the need for arms on chairs. The animations of an older adult sitting-to-standing-to-sitting immediately illustrated the differences in stress on hips and knees when comparing the use of armrests with not using armrests. A bioengineer could discuss this in terms of functional demand, a physiotherapist in terms of movement and rehabilitation strategies, a designer in terms of seat and armrest height, and an older person in terms of stiffness, pain or achievement. All of these perspectives are crucial to improve understanding and aid effective communication, and the tool facilitated the exchange of this essential information. As a result, a broad and objective understanding of issues, and facilitation of cross-disciplinary dialogue was felt likely to reduce the likelihood of conflicting approaches to patient issues.

Finding 4: Advantages of visualisation

The visualisations allow a deeper understanding of the issues within professions, both in healthcare and in design.

This has the following advantages:

- It is superior to existing techniques.
- It has educational value.
- It has ergonomic applications.
- It facilitates an understanding of differences between individuals.

Superiority over existing techniques

Clinical practitioners suggested that in their current practice it can be difficult to locate stress and strain, which can be disguised by clothing, and that they often rely on 'intuitive skill' combined with subjective comment from the patient or other third parties. The tool was considered superior to video techniques currently used during some physiotherapy approaches. The animations objectively illustrated where stresses occur, reducing dependence on intuitive interpretation and subjective judgement, which can result in misdiagnosis. Professionals also felt that data specific to an individual's needs could be interpreted with more objectivity, allowing a more detailed and accurate diagnosis.

Educational value

Some professionals commented that it had been educational to view the tool, and that they had learned that mobility issues are not restricted to isolated joints: they had not previously considered the sequencing of movements and as a result of the visualisation this was something they were now more curious about in relation to their practice.

Ergonomic applications

One proposal made by the design professionals was for the tool to be used for architectural applications and product development to objectively test the ergonomics of seating, interiors and products rather than relying on trial and error in prototypes.

Designer:	"I think it's just really evident immediately why you would ... give someone arms on chairs, without having to have some person try it, and see for themselves that this doesn't work."
Physiotherapist:	"It's a very clear indication of what's a normal movement pattern, and what's an abnormal movement pattern. And the compensations that you make when you have a problem, say a knee or a hip, and how you have to compensate, both in the speed of the movement and quality of the movement. And how you have to compensate elsewhere in the body to still achieve the same goal."
Design consultant:	"I think the figure on the left hints at the cruciality of the height of the arms of the chair."
Design engineer:	"Thinking of the person on the right trying to stand up from a bus seat ... with no arm rests by the way ... is challenging, but I can't actually do anything about that because of the legal requirements."

Understanding differences between individuals

It was suggested that the tool clearly demonstrated the variance in capacity of different individuals conducting the same task, such as rising from a chair, bending or climbing stairs, or the same individual conducting a task in different ways, reinforcing, in terms of the design of products and environments, the limitations with standardised approaches.

Implications

The findings suggest there is further potential in this visualisation method. First, there is a need to **improve the uptake and integration of biomechanical expertise and understanding into design and healthcare practice.**

The field of biomechanics is well established but it has, until now, failed to have the impact anticipated in the fields of healthcare and design. Currently, biomechanics is firmly locked into the domain of scientists and engineers whose currency is numerical data and graphs. As a field, it needs to be able to interface in a way that can 'talk' with clinicians and patients to assist in making treatment choice, and with designers in designing environments, products and services that acknowledge the mobility issues and capabilities of older people. This mode of visualising animated data has demonstrated that biomechanical data can be 'unlocked' and shared to aid understanding and inform practice.

In a design setting, a tool of this nature could be used to, for example, improve understanding in designers of the importance of ergonomics of products, and in enhancing space design and standards, particularly in relation to the ergonomic and functional attributes of products and the built environment.

For example (Figure 12.4), in rising from a seat without using the armrests the demands on the lower limb joints are close to their maximum capacity. It can also be seen that even with the use of the armrests, close to the end of rising from the chair and at the beginning of the sitting movement the demands are high at the hip joints. This indicates that any further deterioration in strength at the hip joints may cause problems for this individual, and may cause risk of falls on rising from chairs. This easy-to-see biomechanical information and understanding is of value to both the physiotherapist and the designer in determining safer mobility strategies and safer seating.

While recognised as having limited application as a standalone tool, as part of a range of healthcare assessment techniques, such a tool could provide a more holistic approach to clinical assessment, diagnosis and rehabilitation in a number of applications. As part of the designer's 'toolkit', used in discussion with physiotherapists and biomechanists, this has the potential to improve the design of the built environment.

Second, there is a need to **develop the tool, both in terms of the technologies involved and the data acquired and used.**

The focus groups, specialist workshop and subsequent discussions have led to the identification of a number of possible enhancements and potential applications of the tool, as follows (both clinical and design professionals recognised the potential of the tool within their respective practices; understandably, older people referred only to healthcare applications and not to design considerations):

- **There is a need to increase data acquisition.** Suggested improvements to the tool included extending the dataset to include full body measurements as well as including a wider range of daily tasks.
- **There is a need for more efficient data acquisitions**. To be applicable, particularly in a healthcare setting, data capture has to be quick and accurate and at minimum expense, allowing for efficient assessment and patient feedback.
- **Real-time viewing of patient movement is desirable.** A proposed ideal healthcare application of the tool would involve capturing data from a patient during a consultation and, by viewing real-time dynamic data on-screen, a two-way dialogue could be achieved between the specialist and the patient. The retention of such data could also be used to track progress in rehabilitation.
- **The tool would benefit from using new portable technology.** The generic approach and method of dynamic data visualisation has the potential to be advanced through a range of technological options, from full motion-capture laboratory set-ups, to portable wearable wireless technologies for use in the home.

Finally, there is a need to **develop – for healthcare – new or improved diagnostic, therapeutic, communication and education procedures.**

Although the tool had used data derived from relatively healthy and active older adults, during the specialist workshop it was felt that it could have a number of applications other than those that had been explored in this project. For instance, in healthcare it would allow improved aetiology, diagnosis, education, communication and therapy in a number of specific conditions, for example, in training for falls prevention, stroke, joint replacement and cerebral palsy. It was felt that this could inform surgical teams, patients, and their guardians or parents of the consequences of particular procedures, or help guide patients' recovery or rehabilitation through improved understanding of the causes and goals of certain movements. The following specific applications were identified:

- **Assessment and diagnosis.** In clinical assessment and diagnosis, it was felt that the tool would assist in communicating the exact source of pain and allow more accurate diagnosis of the cause of the problem – suggesting that it might help determine the extent of an injury as well as being used to investigate, for example, how and why deterioration has occurred. The tool offers the opportunity for cross-validation of other assessment techniques.
- **Therapy and rehabilitation.** It has the potential to be used with patients during assessment and rehabilitation to illustrate where mobility issues occur and how to overcome or avoid them; and for functional assessment, for example, in the use of prosthetics. It also allows the effectiveness of clinical interventions to be evaluated over time to establish the suitability of a particular clinical approach as well as to monitor patient progress. By increasing both patient and professional understanding of mobility issues, patient motivation could be increased.
- **Communication and education.** Within clinical practice, it was felt that this tool could be used to inform teaching and communication, for example, in occupational therapist and physiotherapist training, and to enhance patients' understanding, thereby forming a therapeutic tool to better empower patients to assist in their own recovery.
- **Prognosis and aetiology.** In the long term, with the generation of volume data sets, it may be possible to pre-empt degradation and identify signifiers of future conditions to inform healthcare strategies to limit further impairment for patients. In addition, this may provide the opportunity to explore the cause of such conditions.

Key findings

- The method of visualising dynamic biomechanical data enables those without specialist training – both professional and lay older people – to access and interpret the data.
- Older people are empowered to participate in the discussion of the problems and issues affecting their mobility with clinicians, healthcare practitioners and design professionals, and how these issues affect their lifestyle and quality of life.

- Healthcare and design professionals can benefit from enhanced communication across disciplines, allowing a more joined-up approach to healthcare and design planning.
- Visualisations of dynamic biomechanical data allow a deeper understanding of the issues within professions, both in healthcare and in design.
- There is potential to improve the uptake and integration of biomechanical expertise and understanding into design and healthcare practice.

Conclusion

'Envision' represents phase 2 of a programme of research that has extended since the start of phase 1 (EQUAL) in 2001. The findings from the evaluation of the visualisation prototype used in the Envision project (Macdonald et al, 2009) proved sufficiently encouraging to secure funding for a Medical Research Council Lifelong Health and Wellbeing grant for a phase 3 project Envisage: Promoting Physical Independence by Involving Users in Rehabilitation through Dynamic Visualisation of Biomechanical Data, which ran from 2010 to 2013 (Envisage, 2013). In Envisage, the phase 1 prototype evaluated in phase 2 Envision was further developed, in a bespoke fashion, for each of a set of three randomised controlled trials (RCTs) (Carse et al, 2014; Jones et al, 2014; Thikey et al, 2014) that were run in the context of different rehabilitation settings, namely, a rehabilitation lab, a community hospital setting and the home environment.

In the period between the acquisition (as early as 2002) of the original older adult data in phase 1, its use for phase 2 and the subsequent developments in phase 3, motion-capture and motion-sensor technologies have advanced significantly, enabling some of the ambitions discussed earlier in this chapter to be achieved, both in terms of the technologies involved (becoming less expensive and more portable for community-based use or miniaturised sufficiently for home use), and the data acquired and used (patients' own data being viewable in real time to patients and therapists) to be developed and utilised in the phase 3 Envisage research.

Our ambitions expressed here, to develop – for healthcare – new or improved diagnostic, therapeutic, communication and education procedures, are making progress through the achievements of the Envisage project, whose findings reveal the benefits of this form of visualisation being used in rehabilitation therapy settings to assist clinicians, healthcare professionals and patients themselves (Envisage, 2013).

A key aspect of the Envision research was the engagement of a range of stakeholders, whose feedback proved crucial to the understanding of the nature of the visualisations themselves: the prototype used here was an early one developed in phase 1. User engagement was developed to a much greater extent in phase 3, throughout the key stages of the project, underlining the value of participative, co-design approaches to developing new technological tools that are workable within the rehabilitation setting.

There remains the incentive for the adoption of this visualisation method to improve the uptake and integration of biomechanical expertise and understanding into design and healthcare practice; rehabilitation policy and the attitudes of the professional bodies will determine this as much as developments in the technologies, tools and interfaces for its adoption and assimilation into everyday therapeutic practice.

Our phase 3 work focused specifically on applications within a set of five rehabilitation RCTs. There are many other potential applications of the method, particularly in relation to the ageing demographic and its changing requirements, not only within healthcare delivery, but also in areas such as the design of the built environment.

Further discussion of phase 3 Envisage can be found in Macdonald et al (2010), Loudon and Macdonald (2011), Macdonald and Loudon (2011) and Loudon et al (2012, 2014). The last of these publications (Loudon et al, 2014) also provides an overview of the achievements in the three phases of this programme of research.

Acknowledgements

The Envision partnership project was conducted by The Glasgow School of Art, the University of Strathclyde's Centre for Lifelong Learning and research consultancy, Journey Associates. The support and expertise of a number of organisations also contributed to the success of the project, including the University of Strathclyde's Bioengineering Unit, Age Concern Scotland, HFE Solutions and SPARC. The dynamic digital visualisation method and tool was conceived and developed by David Loudon. The findings described and contextualised above were co-authored by David Loudon and Catherine Docherty. The research (RES-352-25-0005) was conducted with the support of the cross-council New Dynamics of Ageing programme.

References

Baker, R. (2006) 'Gait analysis methods in rehabilitation', *Journal of Neuroengineering and Rehabilitation*, vol 3, no 4, p 4.

Carse, B., Bowers, R.J., Loudon, D., Meadows, B.C. and Rowe, P.J. (2014) 'Assessing the effect of using biomechanics visualisation software for ankle-foot orthosis tuning in early stroke', *Gait and Posture*, vol 39, Suppl 1, pp S2-S3.

Coutts, F. (1999) 'Gait analysis in the therapeutic environment', *Manual Therapy*, vol. 4, no 1, pp 2-10.

Envisage (2013) *Promoting physical independence by involving users in rehabilitation through dynamic visualisation of biomechanical data*, MRC LLHW initiative, Grant Ref: GO900583.

EQUAL Integration of biomechanical and psychological parameters of functional performance of older adults into a new CAD package for inclusive design, EPSRC, Extending QUAlity of Life initiative, Grant Ref: R26856/01.

Jones, L., van Wijck, F., Grealy, M. and Rowe, P.J. (2014) 'Investigating the feasibility of using visual feedback of biomechanical movement performance in sub-acute upper limb stroke rehabilitation', *Gait and Posture*, vol 39, Suppl 1, p S48 1.

Loudon, D. and Macdonald, A.S. (2009) 'Towards a visual representation of the effects of reduced muscle strength in older adults: new insights and applications for design and healthcare', in V.G. Duffy (ed) *Proceedings of the 13th International Conference on Human-Computer Interaction, July 2009, San Diego, CA: Lecture Notes in Computer Science, Vol. 5620*, Heidelberg: Springer, pp 540-9.

Loudon, D. and Macdonald, A.S. (2011) 'Enhancing dialogues between rehabilitation patients and therapists using visualisation software', Proceedings of the 2011 5th International Conference on Pervasive Computing Technologies for Healthcare, Dublin, May, pp 394-8.

Loudon, D., Macdonald, A.S., Carse, B., Thikey, H., Jones, L., Rowe, P.J., Uzor, S., Ayoade, M. and Baillie L. (2012) 'Developing visualisation software for rehabilitation: investigating the requirements of patients, therapists and the rehabilitation process', *Health Informatics Journal*, vol 18, no 3, pp 171-80.

Loudon, D., Taylor, A. and Macdonald, A.S. (2014) 'The use of qualitative design methods in the design, development and evaluation of virtual technologies for healthcare: stroke case study', in E. Ma et al (eds) *Virtual and Augmented Reality in Healthcare 1, Vol. 68*, Heidelberg: Springer, pp 371-90.

Macdonald, A.S. and Loudon, D. (2011) 'Using qualitative people-centred co-research methods to enhance innovation within 'medical model' research', in A. Yoxall (ed) *Proceedings of the 1st European Conference on Design 4 Health 2011, July 2011, Sheffield*, pp 192-202.

Macdonald, A.S., Loudon, D. and Docherty, C. (2009) *Innovation in envisioning dynamic biomechanical data to inform healthcare and design guidelines and strategy*, NDA Research Programme, Sheffield: University of Sheffield.

Macdonald, A.S., Loudon D. and Rowe, P.J.(2010) 'Visualisation of biomechanical data to assist therapeutic rehabilitation', *Gerontechnology*, vol 9, no 2, pp 98-9.

Simon, S.R. (2004) 'Quantification of human motion: gait analysis-benefits and limitations to its application to clinical problems', *Journal of Biomechanics*, vol 37, no 12, pp 1869-80.

Thikey, H.A., van Wijck, F., Grealy, M. and Rowe, P.J. (2014) 'A virtual avatar to facilitate gait rehabilitation post-stroke', *Gait and Posture*, vol 39, Suppl 1, pp S51–S52 2.

THIRTEEN

Transitions in kitchen living: past experiences and present use

*Sheila Peace, Martin Maguire, Colette Nicolle, Russ Marshall,
John Percival, Rachel Scicluna, Ruth Sims, Leonie Kellaher
and Clare Lawton*

Introduction

In Britain today, living arrangements vary: we live on our own, as couples, in families or in non-related groups, across a range of dwelling types and experiencing different forms of domesticity and tenure. While older members of the population are likely to have experienced rented accommodation during their lives, over the past 30 years home ownership among this group has increased dramatically. The English Housing Survey for 2008-09 indicates that for people aged 65 years and over, owner-occupation has increased from less than 50% in 1981 to 75% in 2008-09, with 60% owning their home without a mortgage (DCLG, 2010). More recent data indicates the continuation of this trend, with 83% of the over-60s in England and 91% of 76- to 80-year-olds currently owner-occupiers (Ota, 2015, p 26; DCLG, 2017). The vast majority of older people live in mainstream housing in age-integrated communities; although just over half a million live in either retirement housing including sheltered and extra-care housing, and just under half a million of the most vulnerable live in care homes (Laing, 2014; Darton et al, 2012; Pannell and Blood, 2012).

For those no longer engaged in paid employment, the home environment can often form the central focus of everyday experience. So for those concerned with understanding person-environment (P-E) interaction in later life and whether design enables congruence or creates mismatch (see Lawton, 1980; Peace et al, 2006; Iwarsson, 2013), focusing attention on one domestic space within the home creates the opportunity for an in-depth analysis. In this chapter, attention centres on the domestic kitchen in mainstream and supportive housing. The kitchen has many meanings: it is a functional space, a food environment, a place of storage, an activity space and central hub. For many, it is gendered space where 'women's work' as 'housewife' was, and still is, contained and where confrontation over public/private lives has changed across the 20th century (Oakley, 1974; Silva, 2010).

Historical design, social engagement and personal need are central to literature concerning the domestic kitchen (see Eveleigh, 2004). In her book *The making of the modern kitchen* (Freeman, 2004) , June Freeman begins with two comments that have resonance for this chapter. First, 'English kitchens are commonly perceived as a combination of the "heart of the home" and "meal machine"'(p 1), and second, 'for a discussion of popular kitchen design to contribute usefully to our general understanding of the emergence of and support for particular design styles ... requires both empirical and historical data' (p 1). While her empirical research situated within design history considers design issues for households where a new kitchen has recently been installed, our concern is to understand how people in later life incorporate their life history experiences and ongoing embodiment into their interaction with kitchen space in domestic and supportive settings. So we have been looking not only at the design of the 21st century kitchen but also how that has been informed by past experience.

Aims of the research

The research was collaborative and multidisciplinary, involving The Open University's School of Health, Wellbeing and Social Care, and Loughborough University's Design School. It brings together a team of social gerontologists, ergonomists and designers. The overall aim of the study was to investigate historically and contemporarily the experience of the kitchen for people in their sixties to their nineties living in a variety of 'ordinary' and 'supportive' housing in England. The wider objectives were to:

- provide a historical understanding of the material, social and psychological environments of kitchen experience guided by life events;
- provide a contemporary understanding of the current material, social and psychological environment of the kitchen, examining role, function and design and utilising mixed methods to understand activities;
- consider P-E fit through the juxtaposition of individual health and wellbeing, kitchen living and the potential for improving the kitchen to meet needs;

- extend theoretical development in environmental gerontology through focused multidisciplinary research and triangulation of data that is historical and contemporary, individual and contextual, and qualitative and quantitative;
- develop an archivable resource of stories and experiences from older people that provides an understanding of user requirements for inclusive kitchen design or adaptation of value to practitioners.

Research methods

We developed a comprehensive mixed-methods approach to capture past and present kitchen living where each participant met with the researchers at least two, if not three, times during 2009-10 and a number of data sets were recorded.

The first interview gathered an oral history of kitchens experienced across the life course, informed by a housing history record and a life-topic event guide, for example, first remembered home; parental home when a teenager; leaving home and setting up first house as an independent person. Following this interview, the participant was asked to undertake self-completion records of routine kitchen activities and basic demographic information. At this point the participant was offered a digital camera to take pictures of the 'good' and 'bad' aspects of their kitchen, although most preferred the researcher to do this.

The second semi-structured interview, often undertaken at a follow-up visit, focused on the current kitchen, how well it met the person's abilities and needs and any coping strategies they adopted. It contained both multiple choice and open-ended questions. The interview also considered the person's health and wellbeing as well as their activities. It covered aspects such as physical abilities (mobility and dexterity), sight, hearing, whether the person cooked and what they liked to eat, followed by a discussion of activities and difficulties relating to various tasks such as cooking, washing, ironing, recycling and feeding pets.

Sketches were made of the kitchen layout; photographs taken of interesting features, problems and solutions or adaptations directed by participant(s); and measurements recorded to calculate the kitchen 'work triangle' (between the cooker, fridge and sink) and kitchen area. Measurements were also taken of the height of the lowest cupboard shelf to consider accessibility. Finally, light levels were recorded in three particular locations: at the kitchen sink, and where food was prepared and eaten, for example, at the kitchen table. These recordings were taken both with the kitchen lights on and off.

The team had several face-to-face meetings to plan the study, share skills and to conduct piloting, involving, for example, a gerontologist leading a pilot oral history interview with an ergonomist observing, and then reversing the roles for the current kitchen interview. Five pilot participants were involved at this stage. Research analysis was undertaken collectively. Full ethical approval was sought and gained from both research institutions prior to the work being undertaken.

Characteristics of the research participants

The main study involved a purposive sample of 48 people living in urban and semi-rural areas within Bristol and Loughborough. The participants were chosen to meet specific criteria based on age, housing type and gender. The age range was deliberately chosen to include people in their sixties through to their nineties to consider the impact of different age groups on design issues. Participants were recruited across three age groups (60-69, 70-79, and 80+), with 16 people in each group. There were 31 female participants and 17 males (see Table 13.1), reflecting differences in life expectancy and dates of birth ranged from 1919 to 1948.

In terms of ethnicity, 46 participants were White British and two Asian or British Asian. Of the 48 participants, five were couples, each person in the couple being interviewed separately, so the total number of homes in the sample was 43. These included 14 detached or semi-detached houses, nine bungalows, seven terraced houses or town houses and 13 apartments, seven of which were unsupported while six were in sheltered or extra-care accommodation. The floor area, measured for 32 of the kitchens, ranged from under 6 square metres (for a semi-detached bungalow built in 1985) to 24 square metres (for a detached house built in 1972) (Maguire et al, 2014).

Information was also gathered about participants' education, income and ethnic background, and who else lived in the household. The

Table 13.1: Age and gender of purposive sample

Age group	Men	Women	Total
60-69 years	10	6	16
70-79 years	4	12	16
80-91 years	3	13	16
Total	17	31	48

Note: n = 48.
Source: Peace et al (2012, p 3).

information collected demonstrated the diversity of the sample. With regard to others in the household, 27 participants lived on their own while 21 lived with a spouse or partner. Of the 41 who provided household income information, 30 had a total income of less than £20,000, while 11 had an income of £20,000 or more.

Findings

The strength of the findings from this research lies in the detailed understanding of personal competence within the kitchen that is brought to the discussion of P-E interaction by considering the past, the present and the future of kitchen living. This complexity is discussed in the concluding section but, first, we outline the results from the different data sets.

The past

As indicated earlier, participants were born between 1919 and 1948, during three decades of interwar/Second World War/postwar upheaval in terms of housing stock and living arrangements in the United Kingdom (Colquhoun, 1999). The housing histories show childhood experience of the kitchen across housing types from detached to terraced, encompassing not only different experiences of access to services, such as sources of energy – coal, gas and electricity – but also of the development of domestic equipment. For example, both gas and electricity were developed in the 19th century but not seen widely in domestic housing until the 1920s, and connection was variable across locations. In terms of domestic equipment, many of the older participants talked about the 'copper' and cooking linked to coal-fired heating, whereas the gas thermostat for cookers was created in 1923[1] and the electric cooker was more popular from the 1930s.[2] Such appliances were beyond the budget of many people.

The detailed narratives provided through the oral history interviews were analysed thematically by The Open University/Loughborough team. This was done collectively, with each team member reading and drawing out issues from two or three transcribed interviews and discussing the findings to agree themes that were common across all stories. The following themes identified were:

- space
- equipment/utilities
- tasks
- storage

- social etiquette
- meaning and identity
- changes made.

Here we can only give brief comment on this collective history focusing on childhood recollections. For the two 'Asian' participants, there were some cultural differences concerning kitchen history, for example before moving to England, but little difference noted in current kitchen use.

The kitchen as hub and allied spaces

For our participants, meanings often focused on the kitchen as a hub of the family home, a "living kitchen", where "we as a family lived" and "where everything happened". The childhood homes lived in during the interwar period predated the advent of central heating and typically the kitchen was the "cosiest place to be". One participant invoked a feeling of warmth and centeredness when she said:

> "There were also two fireside chairs in there, of course this was the era of no television so we listened to the radio in there. It was really only when we had visitors that we moved into the other room."

Of course, the kitchen was a busy place, not least on laundry day, when the copper was lit, the 'dolly' blue added, and the smells of washing and drying clothes pervaded the atmosphere (Zmroczek, 1992). Some participants enthusiastically described that sense of smell, with one recalling the "lovely smell of black lead [from the cooker] ... [and the] delicious smell of jam cooking". Others spoke of the natural light and airiness of childhood kitchens. One remarked: "I thought it was absolutely wonderful, it was a nice, light, airy kitchen."

Those recollecting childhood homes with sculleries or utility areas sometimes described this room as a 'back kitchen'. For those who had no bathroom, the scullery was also a room for strip washing (a thorough, all-over wash) or bathing. As well as enabling functional activities to take place in discrete spaces, sculleries and utility areas in childhood homes freed up the 'main' kitchen area as a 'sitting kitchen' with space for a table for eating meals and as a social area, with sufficient space to play board games, make plasticine models, do homework or make a den. In more recent times, the kitchen has even become a space to entertain visitors.

Equipment and interior design

Participants regularly told us that, compared with homes with fitted kitchens of the present era, their childhood kitchens contained minimal appliances and furniture, sometimes "just a sink, draining board and cupboards". Standard items included the deep, ceramic, Butler or Belfast sink; the 'copper' water heater, and the free-standing cabinet. The householder often had to provide the cupboards themselves. While out in the yard, there might be a meat safe where "if you were roasting you saved the fat but there were a separate jar for beef, mutton or pork". Participants reflected on the lack of a fridge, saying that there was little need for one as food was kept cool and fresh in the air-vented pantry or larder and that less food required storing, as it was often bought seasonally and daily. Pantries were often located against an outside wall to keep them cool. "Mother didn't have a washing machine" was another fairly typical statement, as most families in the 1920s, '30s and '40s made use of the copper to heat up water for washing, and the "jolly old dolly board" and the mangle for extracting surplus water; laundry would often be hung up indoors, on rails – a 'Dutch airer' above the bath or "along the passage way". During the moves people made from childhood homes to those they occupied as young independent or newly married adults, they would often amalgamate a 'hotch potch' of items, inherited or donated, some of which they would keep and some discard as their family and income grew.

Participants were particularly pleased to replace items that were labour-intensive and out of date in appearance. Some recalled their first washing machine when their first child was born, bigger freezers that met the needs of a growing family, along with matching saucepan sets. Participants also recalled the improvements in design that influenced new purchases, such as single-tub washing machines to replace the twin tub, as this was 'the modern way' and made the kitchen more 'upmarket'.

Tasks and roles

Childhood learning on the job

Many of our participants recounted having been brought up to help in the kitchen, doing chores and errands, washing and drying up, preparing vegetables and cooking. They recalled with pleasure memories of icing the cake, but also tasks that relied more on labouring, such as turning the mangle or pumping water. Evidently, children were expected increasingly to do more as they grew older, or, as one person described it, to "shop, chop and do our bit". Girls were often expected to assume increasing kitchen responsibilities prior to marriage, but a number of our male participants consistently undertook kitchen tasks as boys, examples being one whose mother was chronically sick and another who was raised in a children's home and expected to become self-sufficient in kitchen tasks.

A woman's place

It is common to hear and read that homes in the first half of the 20th century, and particularly kitchens, were the prime responsibility and focus of women (Roberts, 1984). While it is true that the majority of domestic tasks were and continue to be carried out by women, our participants' stories indicate that men played a significant role, not least in respect of the kitchen. Various participants spoke of how their husbands or fathers had been responsible for the heavier and dirtier jobs, such as filling the water tub and cleaning the fire grate. Men were also involved in construction – making and designing fixtures and fittings, tiling the kitchen, building wall cupboards and making a kitchen table. Men who lived rurally might do the slaughtering when meat was on the menu, while participants also spoke of their contribution to cultivating food that could be stored, cooked or preserved by the women. One participant's father "put spuds in" and "anywhere he could get stuff, it would come back into the kitchen". Of course, not all men contributed to the cooking of food. Some were said to have had peripheral, occasional or specific roles, such as washing up or cooking only on a Sunday or at Christmas.

Shared responsibility

Our female participants, like their mothers and grandmothers, tended to do more cooking and take more kitchen responsibility than their husbands. However, relatively young married women participants tended to share kitchen tasks with their husbands. Additionally, male and female carers in our sample had assumed more responsibility if their partners had become disabled. Past experiences of learning kitchen tasks on the job, through active engagement as well as close observation, affected our participants' desire to pass on skills to their children and grandchildren, for example helping them learn to bake and prepare vegetables. This was an aspect of kitchen living that participants wanted to maintain and where generations could help each other.

The present: early 21st century

Discussion of the current kitchen focused on carrying out and managing everyday activities in the context of kitchen layout, design and equipment. The 48 research participants had a range of physical abilities: 17 had sight problems; 13 had hearing difficulties problems; 26 had problems with access and movement, and found it difficult to reach or bend down in the kitchen; and 19 reported dexterity problems relating to using kitchen implements. It was found that participants' health problems tended to increase with age. Nine people used mobility aids and one was a wheelchair user (female, aged 61) whose needs underlined the importance of inclusive design solutions for effective kitchen use. There were no instances of 'deserted' kitchens, where participants were unable to use their kitchen, leaving tasks to a home carer or family member.

The participants generally ate a cooked meal each day (either cooked by themselves or their partners, brought in or cooked at the local community centre). Participants seemed generally aware of the need to eat healthily, and this was necessitated for some by health conditions such as diabetes.

Participants were asked about their capabilities with respect to common kitchen tasks: food and meal preparation, washing up/dishwasher use, making hot drinks, using a microwave, and washing and drying clothes and sheets. Figure 13.1 shows the number of participants who stated that they had difficulties carrying out each type of task.

Issues and coping strategies

Common problems reported were reading small instructions on packaged food or other kitchen products and seeing the cooker controls. Bright sunlight also made oven or microwave controls hard to read. Some put on glasses to help them see, but this could be a hazard if leaning over hot oven plates. Measurement of lighting levels showed that food preparation areas were poorly lit, both naturally and artificially, with light readings falling well below recommended minimum levels. This could represent a safety risk when using sharp implements.

Figure 13.1: Number of participants experiencing problems with specific tasks

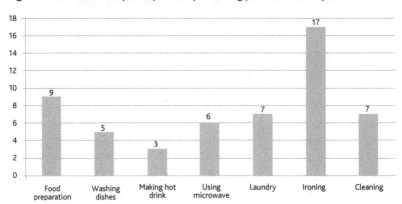

To improve kitchen lighting, different strategies were employed such as lowering a light over the kitchen table, installing lighting under cupboards, using table lamps to illuminate a work surface, and placing a mirror over the sink to reflect light from a window located behind the participant. Despite the use of hearing aids by some, several people experienced problems hearing the doorbell or the phone ring when the kettle was on, or were distracted by humming from a ceiling light. Coping strategies included simply not leaving things unsupervised for long in the kitchen or, when moving to another room, leaving the kitchen door open.

To address problems of reaching or stretching, to use appliances or cupboards, participants coped by crouching rather than bending down, using steps to get to higher shelves, and pulling themselves up using the worktop. Arguably steps could pose a danger for some older people, although participants who used them tried to minimise the risks by careful usage. Some participants had carousel shelving installed to avoid having to reach into a cupboard or to make access easier by locating several items together such as jam or marmalade jars, and herb and spice bottles. One participant had new wall cupboards put up at a lower level than standard.

Many participants owned special gadgets for opening jars, cans and milk cartons to overcome limitations of dexterity, movement and strength caused by painful arthritis. Less support was apparent for tasks such as lifting a heavy pan or dish, or turning a difficult knob or tap. Some had installed lever taps, with others wishing they had done so. Although several participants received help from others with shopping, many did it themselves, sometimes using mobility aids such as a stick or scooter. No one stated that they shopped online. Physical disability was the main barrier to preparing food, for example, pain and lack of strength when peeling and chopping, or backache when standing for baking and cooking. Sitting for food preparation (requiring a lower work surface) and taking rest breaks were useful strategies. Space for a kitchen table was not always available, so eating, especially when living alone, would take place in a living or dining room, sometimes on a tray and often with a TV or radio turned on for entertainment and company.

A number of coping strategies for washing up were put forward such as installing a slimline or counter-top dishwasher and using it frequently, loading utensils into the dishwasher as they were used, and hand washing items if not very dirty. Lifting a full kettle could be difficult or unsafe for those with reduced strength, so some participants used a small, lightweight kettle or heated water in microwave. Adequate light and colour contrast for crockery, work surfaces and surface edges was necessary for those with impaired vision.

Forty-five people owned a microwave, making it an important kitchen appliance. Problems of use included the microwave being located at the wrong height or the door being on the wrong side, a tendency to overcook food, and difficulty transporting food from the microwave, when hot, to the table or work surface. An oven/microwave combination was often found to be useful and convenient.

When washing and drying clothes, opening the appliance door was sometimes problematic if space was restricted. General strategies for managing the household washing and drying included using radiators or a clotheshorse for drying in a warm area such as a conservatory, washing small amounts at a time, and doing washing in the afternoon and drying it with heaters overnight. Some people in sheltered accommodation had a shared laundry facility, while one couple used a commercial laundry. Ironing was the task that caused most problems, with ironing boards being heavy to carry and hard to fold and unfold. Strategies adopted to make ironing easier were using the ironing board for large items only, buying clothes that did not need much ironing, leaving the board set up (often in a room other than the kitchen), and not ironing underwear or sheets.

Kitchen cleaning problems included difficulties moving an appliance so as to get behind it, bending to clean the oven and fridge, stretching down from a wheelchair, reaching to clean the windows and vacuuming the kitchen carpet. One person placed vinyl off-cuts on top of wall units so they could be removed and cleaned. Everyone did recycling. Most had a waste bin in the kitchen and many had a designated space or containers for items to recycle. Problems included bending to empty the pedal bin and knowing which bags or bins to put different items of waste or recycling in and manoeuvring the 'wheelie bin' or separate containers to the pavement or roadside.

The future

A survey was conducted with a further group of older people to obtain their reactions to ideas and concepts behind the smart or 'techno kitchen'. There were 45 respondents, comprising 30 females and 15 males, aged from 60 to over 90 years. Participants were given a list of possible technological enhancements or innovations that might help someone in the kitchen, and were asked to state whether they themselves would like to have these features in their own kitchen.

A selection of the innovations, shown in order of increasing popularity, together with the percentage of people wanting them, is shown in Table 13.2.

The results show that there is enthusiasm for certain types of technological support. Greater interest was expressed in technology that increased safety in the kitchen, such as innovations that automatically turned off appliances and provided warnings and alerts, or addressed immediate problems. There was interest in a kitchen facility to read out small print on food packaging or cleaning materials. There was also positive support for adjustable wall cupboards that could move up and down for easy access. One person who was 4 foot 11 inches (1.5 me) in height felt that this would be very helpful and would suit households with people of different heights and reach capability. Another said that this would bring the cupboard down to their eye line and reach. There was also interest in a worktop that could be lowered temporarily for use while seated, although this would be at the expense of cupboard space underneath. This could maintain people's interest in cooking and independence later in life. However, reduced cupboard space in the kitchen would have to be taken into account.

Advanced technological support seems to have potential for making kitchens easier to use, but more needs to be done to make consumers aware of how they work or of the fact that they are currently available. The growth in smart homes and ability of the householder to interact with them remotely will increase this awareness. An understanding of older people's views remains critical to ensure that these developments are useful and acceptable to kitchen users in the future.

Participants were also asked to suggest their own innovations. There was a requirement from two people for more help to use energy and water more efficiently in the kitchen, for example, a plug to cut down on energy use by avoiding standby or a better mixer tap so that hot water was delivered quickly rather than running it until it warmed up. Two people wanted a facility (perhaps integrated into the fridge) to automatically check the sell- or use-by dates on products such as eggs or cheese to inform the user whether they are still safe to eat. Some people light-heartedly asked to be able to hand over whole tasks to technology – a device or robot to do the ironing, cook, clean, serve food, do the shopping and the washing and drying up.

Table 13.2: Level of support for kitchen innovations in survey

Kitchen innovation	Percentage of participants in favour
Automatic turn off of electrical appliances such as iron, toaster or oven when the person leaves the house.	91%
Possible flood alert warning.	81%
Quick-cooling oven hob.	73%
Task light that comes on automatically when needed.	69%
Remote control of windows and blinds.	69%
Ability to raise or lower worktop or sink height for easier standing or seated use.	58%
Ability to raise or lower cupboard height for easier access.	56%
A device to scan and read out small text on packaging.	50%
Auditory or visual read-out of fridge contents to save opening the door and wasting energy.	36%

Source: Maguire et al (2014).

Recommendations

The following are important recommendations concerning changes to the current kitchen that arose from the study. The first section is directed at older people, their families and social networks to help make kitchens easier to use and to support independent living in later life. The second section is aimed at kitchen designers, suppliers, retailers and fitters, who, when giving professional advice, should think about the wellbeing of the older person using the space.

Recommendations for users

The following are suggestions for small adaptations and larger changes to make the kitchen easier to use.

Easier access

- Put the most commonly used or heavier objects (for example, breakfast items and saucepans) on the lower shelves of a wall cupboard or the higher shelves of a base unit.
- If wall cupboards are too high, consider having them repositioned at a lower, more convenient, height. Consider glass-fronted cupboards to aid a poor memory.
- Replace floor-standing cooker with a mid-level oven or dishwasher with a countertop version.
- Install cupboard units with drawers, pull-out shelving or a larder unit. Some units contain racks that allow plates and bowls to be placed upright so they can be lifted out more easily.
- If window handles are hard to reach over a sink or work surface, attach an extension to the handle or cord so that it can be pulled back and closed more easily.
- Use lightweight pet beds and raised feeding bowls that require less bending for both the pet and owner.

Work surfaces and use of space

- In a new kitchen, locate the oven close to the work surface so there is space to put down pan(s) or set up plates. Place the hob close enough to the sink so that saucepans can be easily transported and drained.
- Identify a specific corner for storing recyclable items so that fewer visits are needed to recycling bins outside.
- Use any wall space for extra shelves, hooks for utensils, or a strip from which to hang utensils.
- Use a lightweight iron and find a place where the ironing board can stay set up for ease of use.
- 'Install a small kitchen table or pull-out table as an extra work surface, for example, for food preparation.
- If there is space for an ironing board choose one that is lightweight and easy to fold. Irons are also heavy, so smaller travel irons can be a lightweight alternative that may make the task easier. If space is limited, a table can be used for ironing by placing a folded towel under the garment to protect the surface.
- A washing machine and tumble drier can be stacked to save space but recognise issues of height and reach in relation to safety. Similarly, consider a ceiling rack for drying clothes.
- Consider using a trolley for moving food or utensils to and from the kitchen to the room or area where food is eaten.

Lighting and flooring

- If lighting is poor, use fluorescent strips for even distribution of light, spotlights for directional illumination, and LED lighting for a bright natural effect.
- Use under-shelf lights or table lamps to give extra light for food preparation and reading small text on packaging. Some LED table lamps have a built-in magnifier that can be useful for reading instructions on food packaging.
- If visual impairment is an issue, select colours for work surface and utensils that contrast well.
- Choose light-coloured flooring for easier cleaning and cushioned material for a more comfortable feel underfoot.

Recommendations for professionals

Professionals may wish to consider the following when giving advice to an older person (or their family/ friends/carers) when updating or installing a new kitchen.

Heights

- Offer rise-and-fall worktop systems, adjustable cabinet brackets, pull-down shelves and pull-out accessories to make the kitchen a more user-friendly space. When in-store, use an adjustable table to determine the ideal worktop height for the customer.
- Although more costly, offer electrically powered cabinets that lower and raise the cabinet height at a touch of a button and provide greater accessibility to users. (Bear in mind that the work surface below has to be kept clear.)
- Place electrical outlets at a more convenient height than standard, but no lower than 38 cm) from the floor.
- Raise the dishwasher off the floor by 15-20 cm), and make it accessible from either side, to increase access.

Flexibility

- Install a base cabinet on wheels with a brake system to transport hot dishes from worktop to table, or create a moveable worktop area based on the needs of the activity.
- Locate pull-out shelves just below the worktop to create an accessible working space to prepare food.

- If there is insufficient room to set up an ironing board, a table top protected with a heatproof cover can be used as an ironing surface.
- Install a drawer or shelf unit alongside the sink for easier access to cleaning products or frequently used utensils.
- Use cabinet accessories that make the cabinets more accessible, such as adjustable shelves, drawer dividers, Lazy Susan turntables and glass-fronted panels for easy viewing.
- Build space for a table and chair into the kitchen design so that users who like to cook are able to sit while preparing food.

Lighting

- Install glare-free general lighting and task lighting to increase visability and create a safe domestic environment. The addition of under shelf lighting may be useful.

Safety

- Use single-lever taps that require less strength to operate, or touch-control taps that can be turned on and off with one touch.
- Provide cupboard door handles that are easy to grasp and pull without awkward hand movements for those with limited dexterity.
- Install cooktops or hobs with controls on the front to eliminate the need to reach across hot burners. Some models have staggered burners for extra safety.
- Also consider an oven with a door that slides under the base or the side, to provide great accessibility.
- Offer cupboards and drawers with features such as pull-out drawers and shelves; hinges that open more widely than standards (for example, to 170 degrees)
- Provide colour contrast to assist people with vision impairment.

Key findings
- Oral histories of the kitchen from the 1920s, '30s and '40s show that space, storage, equipment, tasks, meanings, social etiquette and adaptation were central concerns that continue to affect everyday living.
- The contemporary kitchen is a place of both instrumental and social activity for older women and men. Certain activities, skills and routines imbue meaning and support identity.

- Research participants discussed problems with reaching, bending, hearing, seeing and dexterity in the kitchen; poor lighting was common. All these factors are important considerations for improved ergonomic design.
- Person-environment fit is often maintained through ongoing adaptation in the kitchen, yet people sometimes lack information or the capacity to make small changes or to cope with new equipment, installation or building work.
- Problems can often be addressed with small, low-cost adaptations, but greater benefits may be obtained from a redesigned, inclusive kitchen. Ageism in design needs to be challenged.

Conclusion

The multidisciplinary approach of this research has enabled a greater understanding of environmental complexity within person-environment fit for people at different points in their lives. Participants' oral histories of kitchen living have shown how they have engaged functionally, creatively, socially and psychologically within varied kitchens. Research into the contemporary kitchen shows that as a functional space it becomes more embodied as people age (Huppert, 2003) and that the interface between person and environment needs to be discussed and recognised by designers, architects, manufacturers, retailers of kitchen equipment as well as occupational therapists, older people and their families. The study has identified a number of ergonomic problems as well as innovative adaptations and new kitchen features that can overcome them. Through discussion with participants, such adaptations have formed the basis for a concise kitchen design guide for dissemination to consumers, designers and manufacturers to help make kitchens easier to use and promote independent living (The Open University and Loughborough University, 2012).

In light of the problems observed during the study, currently available technological solutions were identified, such as motorised cupboards, work surfaces that could be raised and lowered, and the ability for appliances to automatically shut down if left on by mistake when the occupier leaves the house. Yet it was also noted that people may lack confidence in, and knowledge of, new technology in the home. The design of new technical solutions to assist people in the kitchen clearly needs to be useful, feasible, simple and marketed to all if they are to be accepted.

A further challenge for kitchen designers, manufacturers, retailers and installers is to recognise the importance of the kitchen as an environment enabling people in later life to stay within their own home and as their physical and cognitive health changes (see Dementia Services Development Centre, 2013) . Obviously, changes within kitchens can be constrained by the basic design within specific architectural space, and fully fitted kitchens are likely to be harder to modify than the more modular kitchens from the past. There is a continuing need for kitchen design that takes on board the concerns and considerations of a wide range of people. Kitchens need to be more flexible and able to be adapted to meet people's changing needs as they grow older. Future planning through inclusive design is therefore essential.

Notes
[1] www.homeappliancecare.co.uk/blog/consumer-advice/history-of-domestic-gas-supply
[2] www.bbc.co.uk/ahistoryoftheworld/objects/C-dCHv9UQ0WATlInMqradA

References
Colquhoun, I. (1999) RIBA (Royal Institute of British Architecture) *Book of 20th century British housing*, Oxford: Architectural Press, Butterworth Heinemann.

Darton,R., Baumker,T., Callaghan,L., Holder, J., Netten, A. and Towers, A. (2012) 'The characteristics of residents in extra-care housing and care homes in England', *Health and Social Care in the Community*, vol 20, no 1, pp 87-96.

DCLG (Department of Communities and Local Government), (2010) English Housing Survey stock report 2008, London: DCLG.

DCLG (Department for Communities and Local Government) (2017) *English Housing Survey: Headline report, 2015-16*, London: DCLG.

Dementia Services Development Centre (2013) Improving the design of housing to assist people with dementia: Dementia Design Series, University of Stirling: Scotland, http://www.cih.org/resources/PDF/Scotland%20general/Improving%20the%20design%20of%20housing%20to%20assist%20people%20with%20dementia%20-%20FINAL.pdf

Eveleigh, D.J. (2007) *A history of the kitchen*. The Sutton Life Series, Stroud: Sutton Publishing.

Iwarsson, S. (2013) 'Implementation of research-based strategies to foster person-environment fit in housing environments: challenges and experiences during 20 years', in R.J Scheidt and B. Schwarz (eds) *Environmental gerontology: What now?*, London and New York, NY: Routledge, pp 69-78.

Freeman, J. (2004) *The making of the modern kitchen*, Oxford, New York: Berg.

Huppert, F.A. (2003) Designing for older users, in J. Clarkson, R. Coleman, S. Keates and C. Lebbon (eds) *Inclusive design: Design for the whole population*, London: Springer-Verlag.

Maguire, M., Peace, S., Nicolle, C., Marshall, R., Sims, R., Percival, J. and Lawton, C. (2014) 'Kitchen living in later life: exploring ergonomic problems, coping strategies and design solutions', *International Journal of Design*, vol 8, no 1, pp 73-91.

Oakley, A. (1974) *Housewife*, London: Penguin Books.

Ota, S. (2015) *Housing an ageing population (England)*, Briefing Paper No.07423, London: House of Commons Library.

Pannell, J. and Blood, I. (2012) *Supported housing for older people in the UK: An evidence review*, York: Joseph Rowntree Foundation. Available at www.jrf.org.uk/sites/files/jrf/sheltered-retirement-housing-full.pdf.

Peace, S., Holland, C. and Kellaher, L. (2006) *Environment & identity in late life: a cross-setting study*, Maidenhead,Open University Press.

Peace, S., Percival, J., Maguire, M., Nicolle, C., Marshall, R., Sims, R. and Lawton, C. (2012) Transitions in kitchen living, NDA Findings 13, Sheffield: Univeristy of Sheffield. Available at www.newdynamics.group.shef.ac.uk/assets/files/NDA%20Findings_13.pdf.

Silva, E. (2010) *Culture, technology, family: Influences on home life*, Basingstoke: Palgrave.

Roberts, E. (1984) *A woman's place: An oral history of working class women 1890-1940*, Oxford: Blackwell.

The Open University and Loughborough University (2012) *The easier kitchen: Making it happen*, Published through The Open University, See www.lifelongkitchens.org

Zmroczek, C. (1992) 'Dirty linen: women, class, and washing machines, 1920s-1960s', *Women's Studies International Forum*, vol 15, no 2, pp 173-85.

FOURTEEN

Biomechanical constraints to stair negotiation

Constantinos Maganaris, Vasilios Baltzopoulos, David Jones,
Irene Di Giulio, Neil Reeves, James Gavin, Alistair Ewen,
Stephanie King and Mike Roys

Introduction

The majority of falls in old age occur during stair descent (Svanstrom, 1974; Tinetti et al, 1988; Startzell et al, 2000; Hamel and Cavanagh, 2004). The physical injuries arising from such falls are of obvious concern, but of equal importance is the fear of falling, and loss of confidence and mobility. Therefore, it is imperative to establish effective measures to reduce the risk of stair falls and accidents, in order to maintain independence and quality of life in old age.

Stair ascent is challenging, and becomes increasingly difficult as people get older. However, paradoxically, it is during stair descent where problems are more common. This is because stepping down is a very complex task, for which the downward movement of the body has to be controlled and balance maintained each time the foot contacts the step (McFadyen and Winter, 1988; Riener et al, 2002). Our ability to do this depends on many factors, including muscle strength, joint mobility, proprioception, vision and balance ability, all of which deteriorate with age (for example, Evans and Campbell, 1993; Grimston et al, 1993; Maki and McIlroy, 1996; Reeves et al, 2006).

Two critical design characteristics in a staircase that are related to these functional parameters are the step-rise, which is the height of each step, and the step-going, the depth of the step. It is possible that older individuals may be less able to generate the muscle forces required to support the body on the upper step or to control the motion when landing on the lower step. In fact, we have already documented that older people use more of their available muscle strength in their knee extensors and ankle plantarflexors to ascend and descend a staircase than younger people (Reeves et al, 2008, 2009). Previously, we examined stair negotiation of standard step dimensions (going: 280 mm, rise: 170 mm) with older adults. However, it is likely that age-related differences are amplified, with greater strength reserves required for more demanding stair-negotiating tasks (particularly higher step-rise) for the old. On the other hand, if the step-going is small (as is often the case in older homes), the ball of the foot of the lead leg will be placed towards the front edge of the step during descent, risking a slip. Motor control and balance deterioration with old age could amplify the problem and a systematic study of stepping errors and how they vary in younger and older participants as the step-rise and step-going are manipulated is required.

Another approach for minimising the fall risk and improving the safety of older people on stairs is to improve their competence and confidence so that they can cope better with the demands of the built environment. Muscle strength and joint flexibility can be significantly improved by specific exercise training, as can balance and motor skills (see, for example, Reeves et al, 2006; Cristopoliski et al, 2009; Granacher et al, 2013). However, wide-scale training programmes may not translate into improvements in tasks such as stair descent. Therefore, a more effective approach would be to design individual and task-specific training programmes.

Aims of the research

The aim of our work is to find ways of improving the confidence and competence of older people when descending steps and stairs. We explored two means of doing this. One was to examine the design of stairs, and specifically the step-rise and step-going, since older people may lack the strength to cope with high steps and have difficulty landing safely on narrow steps. The second approach was to determine whether muscular strength and joint mobility training could ameliorate the age-related deterioration of function. The first approach has policy implications since it may lead to revisions of the current building regulations relating to stair design, while the second will result in clear guidelines concerning the efficacy (and ultimately, the cost effectiveness) of training interventions. The data on the efficacy of exercise training is being currently analysed. The information presented here is based on the first experimental approach, the manipulation of step dimensions and their effect on the biomechanics of stair negotiation in younger and older individuals.

Research methods

Participants

Twenty young (12 men, eight women; mean ± SD; age, 29 ± 5 years; height, 1.76 ± 0.13 m; mass, 78.2 ± 21.9 kg) and 19 older participants (10 men, nine women; age, 74 ± 3 years; height, 1.67 ± 0.11 m; mass, 75.1 ± 19.6 kg) provided written informed consent to participate in the study.

Data from seven young (three men, four women; mean ± SD; age, 30 ± 6 years; height, 1.72 ± 0.13 m; mass, 76.8 ± 29.5 kg) and seven older adults (two men, five women; age, 74 ± 4 years; height, 1.65 ± 0.09 m; mass, 64.8 ± 9.1 kg) were analysed for centre of mass–centre of pressure (COM-COP) separation during negotiation of a standard stair configuration. These participants were selected based on quality of marker visibility of kinematic data.

Data of selected individuals was also analysed during the ascent (six participants: four young [three men, one woman]; age, 31 ± 6 years, height, 1.67 ± 0.11 m, mass, 65.3 ± 7.3 kg; two older [one man, one woman]; age, 77 ± 6 years, height, 1.64 ± 0.02 m, mass, 63.8 ± 6.2 kg) and the descent (nine participants: five young [three men, two women]; age, 31 ± 5 years, height, 1.68 ± 0.12 m, mass, 86.8 ± 36.6 kg; four older [three women, one man]; age, 73 ± 3 years, height, 1.59 ± 0.08 m, mass, 62.3 ± 4.6 kg) of two more demanding stair configurations: high rise and short going (see Table 14.1). Participant selection was based on gender match and quality of marker visibility for specific configurations.

Muscle strength

Maximal strength tests were performed on a dynamometer (Cybex NORM, New York) for both legs, during shortening and lengthening contractions (see Figure 14.1). Participants performed maximal effort knee extension and ankle plantarflexion contractions at four different joint-angular velocities. From the moment-angular velocity curve reconstructed for each joint, the joint moments corresponding to velocities similar to those during stair negotiation were identified. For each participant, the maximum muscle strength measured by dynamometry was compared against the corresponding joint moment produced during stair negotiation. This allowed the calculation of the percentage of the maximum muscle strength reserves used by the knee extensor and plantarflexor groups during stair negotiation.

Figure 14.1: Strength measurement for the knee extensors on an isokinetic dynamometer

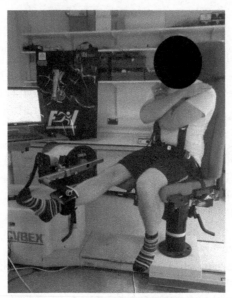

Postural balance

Balance ability was determined with a single-leg balance test with the participants standing on a self-selected leg on an AMTI OR 6-7 force platform (Advanced Mechanical Technology, Inc., Watertown, MA, US), with the other leg raised. Trials began once a single-leg stance was attained; thereafter, individuals attempted to balance in upright stance for a period of 30 seconds. Eyes were open throughout, and foot movement was allowed to maintain balance; however, the use of external support was not allowed. A trial was deemed as **completion** when balance was maintained for 30 seconds, or as **fail** when balance was held for less than 30 seconds due to the participant using external support or making ground contact with the non-dominant leg.

Ground reaction force data was continuously sampled (1000 Hz) during the trial, from which the maximum and minimum COP excursions in both the medial-lateral and anterior-posterior directions were extracted. The COP area was determined from medial-lateral and anterior-posterior COP excursions, respectively, by subtracting minimum and maximum values, before multiplying the differences to give a rectangular area (mm^2). For fails, the trial was deemed to have ended one second prior to the investigator signalling a failed trial. This eliminated severe imbalance just prior to failure.

Due to numerous fails for the older group, a balance index was established for each individual to allow comparison between data for the younger and older participants. The index was based on balance time and COP area. Completions, achieving 30-second balance, were assigned a time index of 1; fails, unable to hold 30-second balance, received an index of < 1 (determined as percentage of maximum, 30-second balance time attained). A COP index was then calculated for each participant as the product of the time index and COP area. The completion participant with the lowest COP area had, therefore, the highest balance index score, against which the rest of the cohort was measured. Comparative measures were made by dividing the highest balance index score (1) by the COP index for each participant, thus establishing individual balance index score (< 1 relative to highest).

Stair negotiation

Participants performed the stair negotiation trial on an instrumented seven-step staircase (step one = bottom step; step seven = top step) with force platforms on steps two to five (Figure 14.2).

Figure 14.2: Instrumented staircase used for stair negotiation

Both the step-going (depth) and the rise (height) could be adjusted. Six going/rise configurations were used during the trials (Table 14.1). Trial order for step configurations was randomly allocated per participant. Handrails were provided on both sides of the staircase and a harness system suspended from a trolley and girder on the ceiling of the laboratory was used to support the participant in the case of a fall during the tests (see Figure 14.3). The staircase was situated in a movement analysis laboratory containing a 10-camera Vicon Nexus optoelectronic movement analysis system (Vicon Motion Systems, Oxford, UK). The 10 cameras were positioned to track the movements of retro-reflective markers that were attached to participants while they performed the stair negotiation task. Kinematic data was collected at 100 Hz.

Table 14.1: Six stair configurations showing step-going and step-rise dimensions

Configuration	Going (mm)	Rise (mm)
One	325	305
Two	325	225
Three	325	175
Four	275	175
Five	225	175
Six	175	175

Figure 14.3: An older adult ascending (left) and descending (right) the instrumented staircase with the aid of handrails

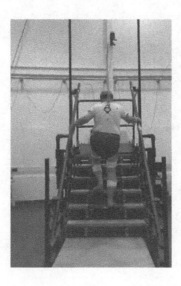

Kinetic and kinematic data

Forty-three markers were attached with double-sided tape to the participant using a modified, full-body Plug-in Gait marker (Vicon Motion Systems, Oxford, UK) set prior to testing. Following this, a static trial was performed that was used to allow the software to define biomechanical parameters prior to analysis of the dynamic trials. For the dynamic trials, participants were required to perform three stair ascent and three stair descent trials for each of the six configurations. One ascent and one descent trial for each configuration was selected for further analysis. For the ascent trials, the participants were asked to stand stationary at the bottom of the staircase in front of step one prior to ascending it and to stop with their feet together on reaching the top of the staircase. During the descent trials, they were asked to stand stationary at the edge of step seven prior to descending the staircase and to stop with their feet together after stepping off step one. Participants were asked to perform the tasks in a normal manner at a self-selected pace. All testing was performed barefoot to eliminate the effects of different footware.

During the tests, data was collected from the four force platforms (kinetic) and from the 10 cameras (kinematic). This data was synchronised within Nexus software (Vicon Motion Systems, Oxford, UK) for further processing. Trials for analysis had the markers labelled according to the markers set used. Gait-cycle events (foot contact and foot off) were defined and any gaps in marker trajectory of less than 10 samples were filled. Trials with trajectory gaps within the region of interest of greater than 10 samples were eliminated from consideration for analysis. Unlabelled markers were removed, the kinematic and kinetic data was filtered, and then individual trials were saved.

Saved trials were processed further in Visual 3D (C-Motion, Inc., Germantown, MA, US). A suitable biomechanical model that defined the body segments, their relationship to each other and the body measurement to be used in the model was created in Visual 3D and saved as a template. For each participant, the trials to be analysed and the static trial were imported into Visual 3D. The model template was attached to the trials and the measurements for the particular participant were entered into the model. The model was applied to the static model initially to calculate the parameters that would be used in the dynamic trials. Each dynamic trial was processed and the model outputs were exported.

From the stair negotiation trials, it was possible to determine the foot clearances and joint moments. The foot clearances were defined as the distances between the heel and the edge of the step during stair descent and between the toe and the edge of the step during stair ascent. In both cases, vertical and horizontal (in the direction of travel) clearances were extracted for both the leading and trailing foot. The joint moments for the left and right knee and ankle joints were determined using inverse dynamics from the data collected. These represented the joint moments generated during the stair negotiation tasks and were taken as a measure of the muscle strength used during the task. The ratio between the maximum muscle strength measured during the stair negotiation trials and the maximum muscle strength measured on the dynamometer at a similar angular velocity is referred to as 'strength reserve' and is an indication of how much of the maximum muscle strength available was used during stair negotiation.

Centre of pressure and centre of mass

The centre of pressure (COP) of the ground reaction force was measured from force platforms embedded in steps two to five. Each platform sampled data in x, y and z directions at 100 Hz. The centre of mass (COM) was calculated by the Visual 3D software from kinetic and kinematic data collected using the Vicon motion-capture system. The COM-COP separation in the sagittal plane was calculated as the difference in the distance between the occurrences of respective centres (mass and pressure). Minimum and maximum values of COM-COP separation were used to represent anterior (forward) and posterior (backward) deviation during stair ascent and descent. To examine the effect of limb difference, we analysed COM-COP separation for right-foot lead and left-foot lead stair negotiation.

Of the sub-group COM-COP separation for high-rise configuration, only descent data was analysed due to the poor anterior pelvis marker visibility as a result of the increased hip flexion in ascent.

Statistical analysis

Normal distribution of data was verified by the Shapiro-Wilk test. Where data violated normality, the Mann-Whitney test was used to compare differences for variables between young and older participants. Otherwise, independent samples t-tests were used to compare differences. Two-way ANOVAs (age x stair configuration; two x six) were performed, with Tukey post-hoc tests, to identify effects and differences in strength reserves for both muscle groups. Relationships between balance and step clearance indices were examined for stair ascent and descent using Spearman's Rank Correlation Coefficient. Level of significance was accepted as p < 0.05. Data was analysed using IBM SPSS Statistics Version 21 (IBM Corp, Armonk, NY).

Statistical analyses were not conducted for sub-group data, due to limited participant numbers; subsequent interpretation of COM-COP separation data were based on observations. For interpretation, the position of the COM is relative to the COP (that is, in front, COM in front of COP; behind, COM behind COP), and referred to throughout.

Results

Strength reserves during ascent

For all staircase configurations, the older participants worked at a higher proportion of maximal knee extensor capacities during ascent compared with the younger participants (Figure 14.4). Younger individuals used greater strength reserve when ascending stair configuration two (rise, 225 mm; depth, 325 mm) than configuration four (rise, 175 mm; depth, 275 mm) and six (rise, 175 mm; depth, 175 mm; p < 0.05). Older individuals used similar strength reserve for all configurations.

For all staircase configurations, there was a non-significant trend for the older plantarflexors working at a higher proportion of strength reserves during ascent compared with the young (Figure 14.5).

Figure 14.4: Knee extensor strength reserves used in the ascent of six different staircase configurations

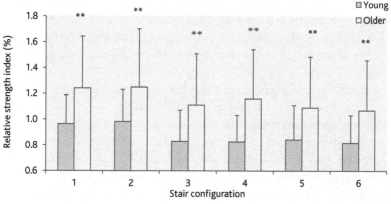

Notes: Values are means ± SD; significant difference ** p < 0.01.

Younger individuals used greater plantarflexor strength reserve when ascending stair configuration one (rise, 305 mm; depth, 325 mm) than configurations three (rise, 175 mm; depth, 325 mm) to six (rise, 175 mm; depth, 175 mm; $p < 0.05$). Older individuals required greater plantarflexor strength reserves to ascend stair configuration one than configurations four to six.

Figure 14.5: Plantarflexor strength reserves used in the ascent of six different staircase configurations

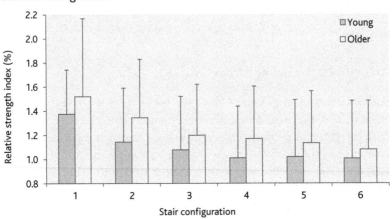

Strength reserves during descent

Aside from staircase configuration one, when ascending all other configurations older adults operated at a higher proportion of knee extensor strength reserve than the young (Figure 14.6). The use of knee extensor strength reserve increased with increasing step-rise, from configurations three to one ($p < 0.01$). No difference was shown for older adults. With reducing step-going (configurations three to six), there was a non-significant trend towards both groups using greater strength reserves.

For staircase configurations three (rise, 175 mm; going, 325 mm) and five (rise, 175 mm; going, 225 mm), older adults worked at a higher proportion of maximal plantarflexor capacities during descent than the young (Figure 14.7). The use of plantarflexor strength reserve increased with increasing step-rise, from configurations three to one ($p < 0.01$). No difference was shown for older adults. By reducing step-going (configurations three to six), both groups operated at lower plantarflexor maximal strength capacities. Older adults decreased plantarflexor strength between configurations three and six, and four and six, whereas the younger adults decreased plantarflexor strength between five and six.

Figure 14.6: Knee extensor strength reserves used in the descent of six different staircase configurations

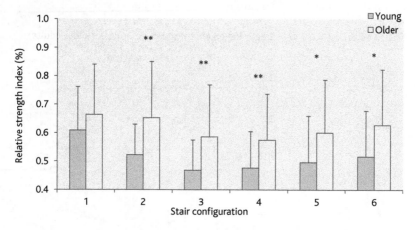

Notes: Values are means ± SD; significant difference * P < 0.05; ** P < 0.01

Figure 14.7: Plantarflexor strength reserves used in the descent of six different staircase configurations

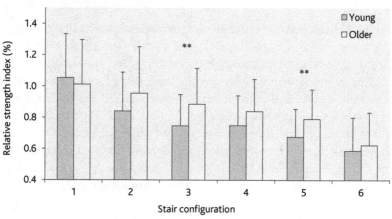

Notes: significant difference ** P < 0.01

Balance test

All the younger participants (n = 20) completed the 30-second balance test, while only seven older participants maintained single-leg balance for 30 seconds. Figure 14.8 shows the distribution of the single-leg endurance times for older adults.

Figure 14.8: Distribution of single-leg balance endurance times for older adults

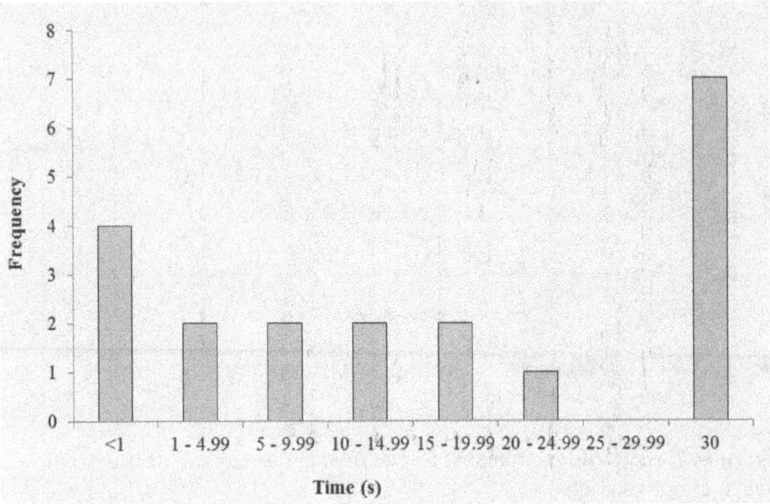

Table 14.2 presents the relationship between balance ability and step clearance for (a) the leading foot, and (b) the trailing foot, during ascent. The trailing foot step clearance was more closely related to balance in young than the older, while the leading foot step clearance was more weakly linked with balance compared to the trailing foot step clearance in the vertical direction for both leading and trailing feet in the young; no relationship was seen for older adults. Stair descent showed correlation between balance ability and lead foot clearance in the young and old (Table 14.3a). No relationship was shown for balance ability and trail foot step clearance in the young and old.

Step clearance during ascent

Anterior-posterior clearances of the lead foot were similar between the two groups for all seven steps. Vertical clearances of the lead foot were similar, except for the final step, which was significantly lower in older adults (16.3 ± 3.2 mm; young: 18.3 ± 2.7 mm; p = 0.03). Anterior-posterior clearances of the trail foot were significantly lower in older adults for steps one (older: 16.4 ± 2.4 mm; young: 19.1 ± 3.2 mm; p = 0.001) and five (older: 16.9 ± 2.7 mm; young: 19.8 ± 3.0 mm; p = 0.001). Vertical clearances of the trail foot were not significantly different between groups. When averaged across all seven steps, anterior-posterior clearance was similar for the lead, but significantly lower for the trail foot in older adults (older: 17.8 ± 3.7 mm; young: 19.7 ± 4.0 mm; p = 0.03; Figure 14.9). As a seven-step average, vertical clearance was similar for both lead and trail feet between groups.

Table 14.2a: Relationship (ρ) between balance ability and step clearance of the leading foot during stair ascent in the young and older groups

Anterior-posterior clearance	Young		Older		Vertical clearance	Young		Older	
	ρ	Sig	ρ	Sig		ρ	Sig	ρ	Sig
Step 1	-0.23	0.3	0.14	0.6	Step 1	-0.33	0.1	0.28	0.3
Step 2	0.39	0.09	0.18	0.5	Step 2	-0.28	0.2	0.05	0.8
Step 3	0.33	0.2	0.32	0.2	Step 3	-0.43	0.06	0.10	0.6
Step 4	0.04	0.9	0.16	0.5	Step 4	0.04	0.8	0.13	0.5
Step 5	0.01	0.9	0.41	0.08	Step 5	-0.57	0.008*	0.11	0.6
Step 6	0.32	0.2	0.28	0.2	Step 6	-0.44	0.05*	-0.10	0.6
Step 7	-0.31	0.2	0.14	0.6	Step 7	-0.51	0.02*	-0.12	0.6

Notes: significant correlation; *p < 0.05.

Table 14.2b: Relationship (ρ) between balance ability and step clearance of the trailing foot during stair ascent in the young and older groups

Anterior-posterior clearance	Young		Older		Vertical clearance	Young		Older	
	ρ	Sig	ρ	Sig		ρ	Sig	ρ	Sig
Step 1	-0.45	0.05 *	-0.07	0.8	Step 1	0.35	0.1	0.03	0.9
Step 2	-0.50	0.03 *	0.27	0.3	Step 2	0.57	0.009*	0.43	0.06
Step 3	-0.31	0.2	-0.13	0.6	Step 3	-0.15	0.5	-0.10	0.6
Step 4	-0.48	0.03 *	0.13	0.6	Step 4	0.44	0.05*	0.34	0.1
Step 5	-0.02	0.9	0.23	0.4	Step 5	0.65	0.002*	0.01	0.9
Step 6	0.11	0.6	-0.07	0.8	Step 6	0.16	0.5	0.22	0.3
Step 7	0.14	0.5	0.06	0.8	Step 7	-0.09	0.7	0.23	0.3

Notes: significant correlation *p < 0.05.

Table 14.3a: Relationship (ρ) between balance ability and step clearance of the leading foot during stair descent in the young and older groups

Anterior-posterior clearance	Young		Older		Vertical clearance	Young		Older	
	ρ	Sig	ρ	Sig		ρ	Sig	ρ	Sig
Step 1	-0.42	0.07	0.35	0.1	Step 1	0.28	0.2	-0.02	0.9
Step 2	0.03	0.9	-0.10	0.6	Step 2	-0.17	0.4	0.00	0.9
Step 3	-0.37	0.1	-0.11	0.6	Step 3	-0.33	0.1	-0.44	0.06
Step 4	-0.41	0.08	0.28	0.2	Step 4	-0.08	0.7	-0.22	0.3
Step 5	-0.19	0.4	0.15	0.5	Step 5	-0.13	0.5	-0.10	0.6
Step 6	-0.16	0.5	-0.47	0.05*	Step 6	-0.11	0.6	0.14	0.5
Step 7	-0.45	0.05*	-0.15	0.5	Step 7	-0.21	0.3	-0.39	0.1

Notes: significant correlation *p < 0.05

Table 14.3b: Relationship (ρ) between balance ability and step clearance of the trailing foot during stair descent in the young and older groups

Anterior-posterior clearance	Young		Older		Vertical clearance	Young		Older	
	ρ	Sig	ρ	Sig		ρ	Sig	ρ	Sig
Step 1	-0.14	0.5	0.05	0.8	Step 1	0.27	0.2	0.02	0.9
Step 2	-0.25	0.2	-0.08	0.7	Step 2	-0.14	0.5	0.13	0.5
Step 3	0.12	0.6	-0.02	0.9	Step 3	0.19	0.4	0.03	0.9
Step 4	0.17	0.4	0.07	0.7	Step 4	-0.13	0.5	-0.05	0.8
Step 5	0.22	0.3	-0.05	0.8	Step 5	-0.02	0.9	0.38	0.1
Step 6	0.13	0.5	-0.11	0.6	Step 6	-0.17	0.4	0.45	0.05
Step 7	0.19	0.4	-0.08	0.7	Step 7	0.37	0.1	0.12	0.6

Step clearance during descent

Anterior-posterior clearance of the lead foot was not significantly different between groups for all steps in descent. Vertical clearance of the lead foot was significantly lower for older adults at step three (older: 15.0 ± 1.1 mm; young: 16.5 ± 2.1 mm; p = 0.02), but similar elsewhere. Anterior-posterior clearances of the trail foot were significantly lower in older adults for steps two (older: 15.5 ± 1.6 mm; young: 17.2 ± 2.5 mm; p = 0.02) and six (older: 15.5 ± 1.4 mm; young: 17.2 ± 2.5 mm; p = 0.001). Vertical clearances of the trail foot were similar in descent between groups. For mean clearance of all seven steps, anterior-posterior clearance was similar for the lead foot, but the trail foot was lower in older adults (older: 16.9 ± 2.4 mm; young: 16.0 ± 1.8 mm; p = 0.03; Figure 14.10). As a seven–step average, vertical clearance was similar for both lead and trail feet between groups.

Figure 14.9: Mean anterior-posterior clearance for all seven steps in lead and trail feet for young and older adults during stair ascent

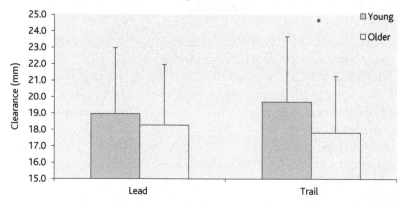

Notes: Values are means ± SD; significantly different * P < 0.05

Figure 14.10: Mean anterior-posterior clearance for all seven steps in lead and trail feet for young and older adults during stair descent

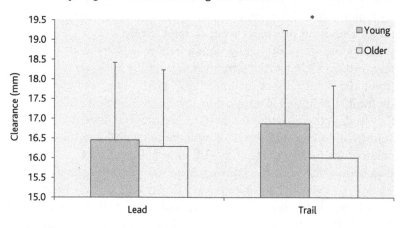

Notes: Values are means ± SD; significantly different * P < 0.05

Balance and clearance (seven-step average)

Balance index was significantly related to vertical clearance of the lead foot in the younger ($\rho = 0.69$; $p = 0.001$), but not the older participants. Balance index was negatively related to vertical clearance of the trail foot in the younger ($\rho = -0.6$; $p = 0.006$), but not the older adults.

Sagittal-plane COM-COP separation

During ascent, the COM-COP separation appeared similar between groups with the right foot leading (in front: young, 167.1 ± 27.5 mm; older, 138.1 ± 11.3 mm; behind: young, 139.1 ± 25.0 mm; older, 158.9 ± 32.2 mm; in the sagittal plane. With the left foot leading, COM-COP separation was greater for the younger than the older in front of the body (young, 155.4 ± 22.0 mm; older, 135.9 ± 14.6 mm), but similar behind (young, 160.4 ± 30.7 mm; older, 154.5 ± 16.1 mm). In descent, the COM-COP separation was no different between groups with the right foot leading (in front: young, 192.3 ± 24.6 mm; older, 190.5 ± 19.9 mm; behind: young, 138.9 ± 16.1 mm; older, 135.4 ± 23.7 mm; in the sagittal plane. With the left foot leading, COM-COP separation appeared greater for older adults in front (older, 212.6 ± 29.6 mm; young, 190.5 ± 42.8 mm), and greater for the young behind (young, 138.6 ± 19.7 mm; older, 114.5 ± 23.9 mm).

Ascending the high-rise configuration staircase with the right foot leading, COM-COP separation was 179.9 ± 69.3 (in front) and 223.2 ± 84.0 mm (behind) for four younger participants, and 367.3 (in front) and 253.0 mm (behind) for one older woman. With the left foot leading, separations were 150.2 ± 26.8 (in front) and 199.7 ± 33.1 mm (behind) for younger adults, and 139.3 (in front) and 251.3 mm (behind) for one older woman, respectively.

Ascending the short-going configuration staircase with the right foot leading, COM-COP separation was similar between younger (in front, 103.4 ± 19.8 mm; behind, 107.7 ± 34.5 mm) and older adults (in front, 109.5 ± 11.2 mm; behind, 118.3 ± 23.8 mm. With the left foot leading there was no COM-COP separation difference between younger (in front, 117.4 ± 28.7 mm; behind, 92.4 ± 13.5 mm) and older adults (in front, 115.0 ± 33.9 mm; behind, 106.6 ± 1.3 mm). Descending the high rise configuration staircase with the right foot leading, COM-COP separation was 219.8 ± 44.3 (in front) and 159.3 ± 24.1 mm (behind) for five younger, and 192.4 ± 40.8 (in front) and 180.9 ± 40.3 mm (behind) for four older adults. With the left foot leading, separations were 195.3 ± 56.8 (in front) and 162.8 ± 43.9 mm (behind), and 188.9 ± 25.3 (in front) and 169.0 ± 10.1 mm (behind), for the younger and older adults, respectively.

Descending the short-going configuration with the right foot leading, COM-COP separation was 142.0 ± 36.1 (in front) and 102.4 ± 24.4 mm (behind) for five younger, and 135.9 ± 7.8 (in front) and 71.3 ± 10.5 mm (behind) for four older adults. The COM-COP separations for left-foot leading were 134.1 ± 38.2 (in front) and 102.4 ± 24.4 mm (behind), and 139.4 ± 40.4 (in front) and 78.9 ± 9.5 mm (behind), for younger and older adults, respectively.

The total COM-COP excursion (in front and behind) in the sagittal plane during stair negotiation is displayed in Table 14.4 for both age groups. The largest excursion was shown for right-foot lead, descent in older adults (345.3 ± 39.0 mm), and the smallest for left-foot lead, ascent in older adults (332.5 ± 20.3 mm). During ascent, total excursion was greater for young adults; during descent, total excursion was similar between groups.

Table 14.4: Sagittal-plane total excursion between the centre of mass and the centre of pressure during stair negotiation in the young and older adults

		Sagittal-plane total excursion (mm)	
		Young (n = 7)	Older (n = 7)
Ascent	Right-foot lead	306.2 ± 31.2	297.0 ± 39.5
	Left-foot lead	315.8 ± 29.5	290.4 ± 26.6
Descent	Right-foot lead	331.3 ± 19.2	325.9 ± 30.3
	Left-foot lead	329.1 ± 33.4	326.9 ± 37.6

Note: Values are means ± SD.

Frontal-plane COM-COP separation

During ascent, the frontal plane COM-COP separation appeared greater for older adults with the right foot leading (older, 73.0 ± 16.8 mm; young, 67.3 ± 18.7 mm), yet greater for younger adults with the left-foot leading (young, 108.8 ± 18.3 mm; older, 86.4 ± 16.1 mm). Ascending the short-going configuration with the right foot leading, COM-COP separation was greater in the younger (116.4 ± 14.0 mm) than the older adults (98.9 ± 29.5 mm). Separation was similar between older (100.9 ± 10.9 mm) and younger adults (97.3 ± 8.1 mm) with the left foot leading. Ascending the high-rise configuration with the right foot leading, the COM-COP separation was greater for the younger adults (143.8 ± 11.9 mm) than the older adults (129.4 mm). With the left foot leading, greater separation was shown for the younger adults (140.9 ± 13.7 mm) than for one older adult (93.6 mm).

During descent, the COM-COP separation appeared greater for young adults with the right foot leading (young, 143.5 ± 22.4 mm; older, 109.6 ± 18.7 mm) and similar between groups with the left foot leading (young, 114.2 ± 44.3 mm; old, 107.6 ± 31.7 mm). Descending the high-rise configuration with the right foot leading, COM-COP separation was greater in the younger (171.6 ± 24.4 mm) than the older adults (138.1 ± 45.5 mm). With the left foot leading, COM-COP separation was greater for the younger (166.2 ± 40.2 mm) than the older adults (104.1 ± 27.4 mm).

Descending the short-going configuration with the right foot leading, COM-COP separation was greater for the younger (166.1 ± 38.7 mm) than the older adults (151.6 ± 61.9 mm). With the left foot leading, separation was smaller for the younger (129.0 ± 50.1 mm) than the older adults (142.3 ± 31.8 mm).

Combined sagittal- and frontal-plane COM-COP separation

Combined across sagittal and frontal planes, COM-COP separations were similar for right-foot leading between younger (medio-lateral 45.5 mm, anterior-posterior 167.1 mm) and older adults in ascent (medio-lateral 36.1 mm, anterior-posterior 131.7 mm). Greater COM-COP separation was shown for the younger adults with left-foot leading (medio-lateral 113.1 mm, anterior-posterior 155.4 mm) than the older adults (medio-lateral 92.0 mm, anterior-posterior 130.5 mm). Combined COM-COP separation was greater descending with the right foot leading for younger (medio-lateral 154.6 mm, anterior-posterior 194.2 mm) than for older adults (medio-lateral 137.8 mm, anterior-posterior 209.2 mm. Little difference in COM-COP separation was shown between groups descending with the left foot in lead (young, medio-lateral 37.9 mm, anterior-posterior 199.9 mm; older, medio-lateral 29.7 mm, anterior-posterior 225.7 mm).

Handrail use

Older adults (n = 2) used one handrail during descent of the high-rise configuration, and tended to rotate their body towards the supporting handrail. Conversely, younger adults (n = 2) maintained body orientation in the direction of travel, although one also used the handrail. Older adults (*n* = 2) used one handrail when descending the staircase in the short-going configuration, and appeared to rotate their body towards the supporting handrail. However, body rotation seemed more pronounced for the short-going than the high-rise configuration. During stair ascent, the older participants did not alter their stair negotiation strategy with the short-going configuration.

Summary points

Lower-body strength

Older adults used higher strength reserves for the knee extensors and the plantarflexors during stair ascent and descent, compared with the younger group. This was apparent on most stair configurations and may suggest that older adults operated closer to their strength limits than the younger group. As a consequence, older individuals would be expected to have less strength reserve to overcome unanticipated increases in demand, therefore potentially increasing the fall risk. During stair ascent, regardless of age, step-rise was the most influential factor. Less strength was required to negotiate stairs with low rises (175 mm) than higher rises. When rise was increased, individuals worked at a higher strength capacity during descent, in order to meet the increased demands of lowering the body mass by a greater distance. Therefore a low step-rise would require less strength during ascent and descent for both the younger and older participants, and may therefore limit fall risk by allowing the individual to operate within their strength limits. The lower maximal force reserves used in the plantarflexors when the step-going was reduced was most apparent during descent. This may, in part, result from altered foot placement strategy, as available tread becomes less than the length of the foot.

Balance ability

During the balance trial, 65% of older adults could not complete the 30-second trial and 20% could not maintain balance for longer than one second. These results show an inability by older adults to maintain a safe, single-leg balance for at least 30 seconds. Biomechanical and physiological deteriorations during ageing are implicated as factors in the poor balance performance in older adults (Maki and McIlroy, 1996). It is well reported that loss of muscle mass and strength are associated with ageing, in addition to a declining proprioceptive ability (Hurley et al, 1998). With a reduced sense of body movement and external forces acting on the body, older individuals would be less aware of being out of balance, and, with reduced muscle strength, more unlikely to be able to prevent a fall. This could lead to an inability by older adults to support their own mass during single-leg standing for more than a short period of time.

Stair negotiation in ascent

During stair ascent, older adults displayed lower vertical clearance for the final step with the lead foot, lower anterior-posterior clearance for first and fifth steps with the trail foot, and lower anterior-posterior clearance as a seven-step average with the trail foot.

The foot clearance results presented for stair ascent could be further evidence of the muscle atrophy and consequent reduction in muscle strength expected with old age (Evans and Campbell, 1993). It could be argued that the older adults would exhibit greater step clearance since they are more at risk from trips and would try to avoid them by overcompensation. However, the results presented here suggest that older adults clear the edge of the step by a smaller margin than younger adults. There are two related mechanisms that could account for the results presented. The first is reduced muscle strength. There is the possibility that the muscle strength of the older adults was insufficient to raise the foot high enough above the step edge. This, however, may not be the main mechanism and it is more likely that older adults are unable to support their mass on a single limb for the duration of the single-limb support period, which causes their body to move vertically downwards. The other potential mechanism is reduced proprioception. If the older adults had reduced proprioception, they might not be as aware as younger adults of the position in space of their feet. To some extent, proprioception is aided by visual cues. However, it is important to note that in the majority of cases where reduced clearance was reported visual cues would be limited. Cases involving the toe of the trailing foot would occur behind the body and unless older adults made a conscious effort, they would be unable to see the position of the toe of the trailing foot as it cleared the edge of the step.

Stair negotiation in descent

During stair descent, older adults displayed lower vertical clearance for the third step with the lead foot, lower vertical clearance for second and sixth steps with the trail foot, and lower anterior-posterior clearance as a seven-step average with the trail foot. On average, older adults exhibited lower clearance during stair descent with the trailing foot. They also showed some reduced clearance for the leading foot. This may be a similar mechanism to that operating during stair descent. During stair descent, muscle weakness may be such that older adults are unable to support their body mass sufficiently to produce a controlled descent from one step to the next. However, there is also the possibility that reduced proprioception could be involved. During stair descent, the trailing foot would be hidden from view. Similarly, the heel of the trailing foot would be hidden from view unless the older person moved their upper body far beyond their supporting foot.

Stair negotiation: relationship between balance ability and stair clearance

During stair ascent, those with greater balance ability displayed higher anterior-posterior clearance with the trail foot, higher vertical clearance with the trail foot, and lower vertical clearance with the lead foot. Participants who had greater balance ability were generally the younger adults and they exhibited greater clearance with their trailing foot during stair ascent than the older adults. This may explain why younger adults do not trip as often on stairs as older adults do. Young adults with greater muscular strength would be more capable of producing a controlled ascent from step to step. Although the toe of the trailing foot would be equally hidden to the young adults, their greater proprioception would give them a better knowledge of the position of their foot relative to the edge of the step and they would be able to ensure that the toe cleared the step. This group also exhibited a reduced clearance with the lead foot during ascent compared with the older adults. Given that the toe of the leading foot is more visible during stair ascent, the additional visual cue could give the young adults greater confidence in their ability to clear the step without tripping.

During stair ascent for young adults, greater balance index was associated with higher average lead-foot clearance and lower average trail-foot clearance. In general, the younger adults exhibited a greater balance index than the older adults. These results suggest that those participants with better balance index also had a greater clearance between the toe and the step edge during stair ascent for the lead foot and reduced clearance during stair ascent for the trailing foot. Those with better balance abilities would be more stable while supported on one limb than those with reduced balance abilities and would be more controlled in their ascent of the staircase. With this stable platform, they would be able to control their foot clearance. This seems to be the case for the trailing foot, which has a reduced clearance compared with that for participants with lower balance abilities. However, it could be expected that they would also exhibit a reduced clearance with the leading foot, but this was not the case. Given that the leading foot is visible during stair ascent, this result appears to be opposite of what would be expected.

The young also appear to ascend and descend both standard and short-going staircases more quickly (standard ascent, 114 steps per minute; short ascent, 102 steps/min; standard descent, 122 steps/min; short descent, 122 steps/min), than the older adults (standard ascent, 99 steps/min; short ascent, 87 steps/min; standard descent, 111 steps/min; 100 steps/min). In addition, the younger adults had a greater mean mass than the older adults. Together, these findings would suggest that the young have a greater forward momentum than the older adults. This would not only be momentum of the body as a whole, but more importantly that of the swinging limb. Greater forward momentum of the swinging limb could lead to over-swinging and possibly account for the greater foot clearance for the younger compared with the older adults.

In older adults, there was no association between balance ability and stair clearance. This is contrary to what would be expected. However, it should be noted that only 35% of the older participants were capable of completing the balance task and 20% failed to maintain a single-leg balance for more than one second. The balance ability of an older participant who performed the task for less than one second could appear to be similar to another participant who lasted for 30 seconds, but had more movement of their centre of pressure during that time. Although measures were taken to counteract this possibility with the balance index, it may not have been entirely eliminated as a source of error.

COM-COP separation

During the stair negotiation of a standard configuration staircase, similar COM-COP separation was shown between the young and older adults, irrespective of which foot was used to lead. When imposing greater task demand by increasing step-rise (from 175 to 305 mm), older adults displayed greater COM-COP separation in the rearward direction than younger individuals. This may suggest a more conservative strategy, whereby the COM is positioned behind the COP to prevent forward falling. However, this was observed only when the right foot was leading. With increased step-rise, both younger and older elected to use the right handrail when descending.

When imposing greater task demand by shortening the step-going (from 275 to 175 mm), both the younger and the older adults altered their strategy. During descent, handrail use was adopted and foot contact patterns were altered to manage the reduced step area. This configuration also appeared to be lead-foot specific. When leading with the left foot, the young had a larger excursion of the COM, relative to the COP, than the older adults. This was evident for both the forward (in front) and backwards (behind) separation. Conversely, with the right foot leading the situation was reversed. Older adults exhibited greater forwards and backwards separation than the young. Limb dominance was not recorded; therefore it was not possible to attribute lead-foot differences to footedness.

Combining forward (in front) and backwards (behind) separation, total COM-COP excursion showed that the young deviated more than the old during stair ascent. Consistent for both feet, this may indicate that older adults restrict their movement degrees of freedom in ascent. However, older adults had greater total COM-COP excursion during stair descent. This may relate to muscle strength and proprioceptive control. Our results have shown that older adults operate closer to maximal strength when compared with the young in stair negotiation. With less strength in reserve, the older adults may have less control of their body mass against gravity than the young and this could manifest itself in greater excursion of the COM.

Examining the left to right excursion of the COM (medio-lateral), three of the four configurations showed that the COM moved away from the supporting limb. This was not evident during stair ascent using the standard stair configuration. When leading with one foot, the COM separates from the COP in the direction of the supporting limb. This was similar between age groups. During standard configuration descent, the COM separated from the COP in the direction of the leading limb. This was also the case with the increased rise and the shorter going, and the right handrails were used during all these trials to aid balance.

When overall COM-COP data (anterior-posterior, medial-lateral) are combined, the data shows similar magnitude and direction of separation in the younger and older adults. For most configurations, these results show that the COM moves relative to the COP in the direction of the leading limb, not the supporting limb.

Handrail use

Observations suggest that the standard stair configuration was not demanding enough to elicit significant differences in stair negotiation strategy between younger and older adults. It should be noted, however, that a number of trials on the standard configuration staircase for the older adults were not suitable for analysis due to the use of the handrails. This would suggest that older adults are more likely than younger adults to alter their stair negotiation strategy, even for the standard configuration, if required. This finding was reinforced with the trials on more demanding configurations where the older adults who were able to negotiate the standard configuration staircase without the use of the handrails now made use of the handrails; however, this was not restricted to the older adults, as one of the younger adults also used one handrail during a high-rise configuration descent.

The older adults appeared to find both the high-rise and short-going configurations more demanding than the younger adults. They altered their strategy more than the younger adults by making use of the handrails, but also by rotating their body in the direction of the handrail being used to give them more security. Rotation of the body allows the task to be performed while maintaining the COM closer to the COP, whereas with the body in the direction of travel, more extremes of body movement are required, which are likely to move the COM beyond the COP.

The short-going configuration also posed more difficulties for the older adults than the younger ones. The older adults rotated their bodies in the direction of the handrail being used. They also rotated their feet in the direction of the handrail used. The body was more rotated than it was during the high-rise configuration and rotation of the feet would be almost inevitable for comfort. However, it would also be a strategy alteration to enable the front of the foot to make more contact with the step. Younger adults descended the short-going staircase with some foot rotation, while maintaining the body in a forward orientation.

Stair ascent with the short going was not particularly demanding for young and older adults. Although step-going was reduced, the step space was large enough to accommodate the front of the foot, which is the foot part typically making contact with the step during ascent. Although stair negotiation is a difficult task, older adults are capable of performing the task by altering their strategy. This could be by using handrails for support and security or by moving their body in a different manner than the young.

Implications

The study gave rise to the following implications:

- Considering that older adults use greater strength reserves at the ankle and knee joints during stair negotiation, future resistance training interventions should focus on maintaining strength in the relevant musculature.
- In terms of stair design, step-rise imposes the highest demand to older individuals. A focus on optimising step-rise and step-going may reduce lower-limb muscle strength demands, and potentially lower fall risk.
- In older adults, balance ability is not related to stair clearance during ascent or descent.
- COM-COP separation differences between younger and older adults for high step-rise and short step-going configurations suggest staircases that increase the task demand challenge the maintenance of stability, particularly in older adults.
- Older adults are capable of negotiating standard stair configurations, although they adopt different strategies to do so. However, these strategies become more common and exaggerated as the staircase configuration becomes more demanding. Many older residences throughout Europe have staircases that would no longer be permitted in modern residential buildings, and it is for these staircases that altered negotiated strategies would be found.

Key findings
- Older adults descend stairs by relying more on their knee and ankle joint muscles than younger adults.
- Stair descent strategies reliant on placing both feet on the same step result in a slower gait, with reduced lower-limb joint ranges of motion. The 'pause' that is created by this tandem double support means that the muscles surrounding the ankle and knee do not need to control the lowering of the entire body mass on to the next step; instead the leg is lowered to the next step.
- Placing two feet on each step during descent can be achieved by walking facing forwards or sideways. Both strategies can reduce the demands on the lower limb; however, the control over the centre of mass differs. Walking sideways results in an increased movement of the centre of mass into/towards the staircase during single-limb stance, which is followed by a rapid acceleration down the staircase in the transition between stance and swing. Alternatively,

walking forwards results in less centre of mass movement and a more constant, but lower, acceleration down the staircase.

- Older adults almost always make negotiation strategy changes when descending a short-going staircase, while younger adults are less likely to do so. When descending a staircase with a shorter going, older adults stand on a single leg for longer than younger adults. Their centre of mass also moves slower than in younger adults.

- Resistance and stretching exercise training in older adults improves knee and ankle muscle strength, as well as ankle flexibility, but has little influence on lower-limb joint motions during stair descent. Exercise training resulted in greater joint moment production at the ankle and hip, and less at the knee. By increasing step-rise, the opposite occurred, as greater knee-joint moment was produced. It seems that training improvements in lower-limb maximum strength have allowed older adults to meet the demands of stair descent by redistributing moments across joints.

Conclusion

In summary, our findings show that during stair negotiation, older adults use greater strength reserves than younger adults at the ankle and knee joints. Furthermore, step-rise appears to be the most crucial factor influencing the strength demands for both younger and older adults. Where older adults had poorer balance ability and, often, lower stair clearance, these quantities were not related. The COM-COP separation findings suggest that negotiating a standard stair configuration does not pose a challenge for either older or younger adults. However, greater horizontal COM-COP separation for the young may relate to confidence and use of potential ranges of motion when ascending a standard stair configuration. By increasing step-rise, older adults' COM-COP separation also increased posteriorly in descent. This may reflect a compensatory strategy to aid balance maintenance and prevent instability. Furthermore, stability differences between the younger and older adults were lead foot-dependent, which may relate to individual limb preference. These results are pertinent to stair design and training methodologies for older individuals, in particular, identifying the task demands imposed by altered step-rise and step-going. From the current project, additional kinetic and kinematic data is under analysis, which will improve our understanding of the perceptual, biomechanical and physiological demands of stair negotiation in older adults.

Acknowledgements

We thank the anonymous participants for taking part to this experiment. We also thank Emily Kingdon for support with the data collection and Alexander Ireland for his technical support.

References

Cristopoliski, F., Barela, J.A., Leite, N., Fowler, N.E. and Rodacki, A.L. (2009) Stretching exercise program improves gait in the elderly', *Gerontology*, vol 55, no 6, pp 614-20.

Evans, W.J. and Campbell, W.W. (1993) 'Sarcopenia and age-related changes in body composition and functional capacity', *Journal of Nutrition*, vol 123, (2 suppl) pp 465-8.

Granacher, U., Gollhofer, A., Hortobágyi, T., Kressig, R.W. and Muehlbauer, T. (2013) ,The importance of trunk muscle strength for balance, functional performance and fall prevention in seniors: a systematic review', *Sports Medicine*, vol 43, no 3, pp 627-41.

Grimston, S.K., Nigg, B.M., Hanley, D.A. and Engsberg, J.R. (1993) 'Differences in ankle joint complex range of motion as a function of age', *Foot and Ankle International*, vol 14, no 4, pp 215-22.

Hamel, K.A. and Cavanagh, P.R. (2004) 'Stair performance in people aged 75 and older', *Journal of the American Geriatrics Society*, vol 52, no 4, pp 563-7.

Hurley, M.V., Rees, J. and Newham, D.J. (1998) 'Quadriceps function, proprioceptive acuity and functional performance in healthy young, middle-aged and elderly subjects', *Age and Ageing*, vol 27, no 1, pp 55-62.

Maki, B.E. and McIlroy, W.E. (1996) 'Postural control in the older adult', *Clinics in Geriatrics Medicine*, vol 12, no 4, pp 635-58.

McFadyen, B.J. and Winter, D.A. (1988) 'An integrated biomechanical analysis of normal stair ascent and descent', *Journal of Biomechanics*, vol 21, no 9, pp 733-44.

Reeves, N.D., Narici, M.V. and Maganaris, C.N. (2006) 'Myotendinous plasticity to ageing and resistance exercise in humans', *Experimental Physiology*, vol 91, no 3, pp 483-98.

Reeves, N.D., Spanjaard, M., Mohagheghi, A.A., Baltzopoulos, V. and Maganaris, C.N. (2008) 'The demands of stair descent relative to maximum capacities in elderly and young adults', *Journal of Electromyography and Kinesiology*, vol 18, no 2, pp 218-27.

Reeves, N.D., Spanjaard, M., Mohagheghi, A.A., Baltzopoulos, V. and Maganaris, C.N. (2009) 'Older adults employ alternative strategies to operate within their maximum capabilities when ascending stairs', *Journal of Electromyography and Kinesiology*, vol 19, no 2, e57-e68.

Riener, R., Rabuffetti, M. and Frigo, C. (2002) 'Stair ascent and descent at different inclinations', *Gait & Posture*, vol 15, no 1, pp 32–44.

Startzell, J.K., Owens, D.A., Mulfinger, L.M. and Cavanagh, P.R, (2000) 'Stair negotiation in older people: a review', *Journal of the American Geriatrics Society*, vol 48, no 5, pp 567–80.

Tinetti, M.E., Speechley, M. and Ginter, S.F. (1988) 'Risk factors for falls among elderly persons living in the community', *New England Journal of Medicine*, vol 319, no 26, pp 1701–7.

Part Three
Global ageing

FIFTEEN

Ageing, wellbeing and development: Brazil and South Africa

*Armando Barrientos, Valerie Møller, João Saboia,
Peter Lloyd-Sherlock and Julia Mase*

Introduction

There is considerable diversity of population trends across low- and middle-income countries and not all have reached the final stage of demographic transition. Despite this, population ageing is accelerating in almost all countries, particularly in middle-income emerging economies. The speed of demographic change poses significant policy challenges for these countries, and they have limited time to set in place the necessary institutions (Lloyd-Sherlock, 2010).[1] Building a knowledge base capable of supporting effective policies addressing rapid population ageing in such contexts is urgent. This chapter reports on the design and main findings of the research project Ageing, Well-Being and Development: A Comparative Study of Brazil and South Africa.

The research focuses on the wellbeing of older people and their households. For all countries, successfully meeting the challenges of population ageing involves ensuring that older populations enjoy adequate levels of wellbeing. For countries like Brazil and South Africa, the main challenge is to ensure that older people, and public policy that targets them, are fully integrated into economic and social development. A key hypothesis guiding the research project was that ageing, wellbeing and development are closely interlinked.

- The research aimed to provide answers to the following questions:
- What are the main effects of individual ageing on the dynamics of household income and livelihoods in Brazil and South Africa?
- What are the effects of individual ageing on household dynamics?
- With the benefit of cross-country comparisons, which are the institutions and social structures that could best support 'active ageing' in developing countries?

- What is the impact of pension entitlements and other anti-poverty programmes on the wellbeing of older people and their households?

This research examined the impact of individual ageing on the wellbeing of older people and their households in low-income areas Brazil and South Africa, with a view to informing appropriate policies to address the challenges of accelerated population ageing in developing countries. The main source of information for this study was a longitudinal and comparative survey of older persons and their households in South Africa and Brazil constructed as part of the project. Building on an earlier study in the two countries undertaken in 2001-03, we collected a second round of survey data by visiting the same households in 2008/09. A panel dataset of older people and their households enabled the analysis of changes over time in their wellbeing and livelihoods, and comparisons across the two countries (Lloyd-Sherlock et al, 2012a). This was complemented by a substantial qualitative dataset of in-depth interviews with case study households.

Brazil and South Africa had been selected for the 2001-03 study because, at that time, both countries had relatively embracing pension schemes for older people. In the case of Brazil, this had been achieved through a multi-pillar approach combining substantial contributory and non-contributory schemes. In South Africa, the non-contributory scheme accounted for the large majority of pensions, particularly for poorer households. At the time of the first study, the value of the basic benefit paid out by these schemes was roughly similar (US$300 per month). There were other important similarities in the countries' economic and social development, including progressively upgraded welfare systems driven by a return to democratic governance. Between 2002 and 2008, the experiences of Brazil and South Africa diverged to some extent, with Brazil enjoying particularly high rates of economic growth, leading to a fall in unemployment and an increase in welfare spending. One of the interests of this study was to assess how these diverging national contexts affected the wellbeing of older people and their households in each country.

Research on the relationship between ageing and wellbeing has often noted an apparent divergence in the evolution of subjective and objective wellbeing indicators in later life (Diener and Suh, 1997). A majority of studies finds that self-reported life satisfaction is stable for older groups, just as their conditions of daily living appear to deteriorate (Kunzmann et al, 2000; Pinquart and Sorensen, 2000). In cross-section studies, this paradox can be attributed to the confounding effect of cohort differences (Schilling, 2006). Less is known about the relationship between ageing and wellbeing in developing countries (Deaton, 2007). Using panel data collected from older people in Brazil and South Africa covering objective and subjective indicators, the analysis in this chapter throws light on the relationship existing between individual ageing, wellbeing, and deprivation. The analysis finds that, on average, measured deprivation falls for a sample of older people between 2002 and 2008. However, social stratification in South Africa leads to significant differentials in observed improvements in wellbeing over time for older people (Møller, 2011).

The study of changes in wellbeing among older people and their households was supplemented with an analysis of social policies and institutions in the two countries with relevance to older groups. In Brazil and South Africa, governments have taken the lead in their regions in expanding the reach and scope of social policy (Barrientos et al, 2013). Innovative policies and programmes introduced since the mid-1990s have extended the reach of non-contributory pensions and other anti-poverty transfer programmes (Lloyd-Sherlock, 2006; Barrientos, 2008). The research examined the contribution of social policy to wellbeing outcomes among older people and their households (Barrientos and Mase, 2012).

A comparison of older people's wellbeing levels in 2002 and 2008 found improvement over time. This is true for a range of wellbeing indicators: per capita household income and expenditure; multidimensional measures; and life satisfaction measures. For low-income households, pension income, especially non-contributory pension income, is essential to their wellbeing, livelihoods and social inclusion.

The rest of the chapter is divided into three main sections. The next section describes the research objectives, methodology and data. The section after that presents the main findings. A further section summarises the main implications of this research for researchers and policymakers. A final section concludes the chapter.

Research objectives, methodology and data

The overall aim of the research project was to examine the dynamic effects of individual ageing on the wellbeing of older people and their households in Brazil and South Africa, with a view to informing appropriate policies to address the challenges of accelerated population ageing in developing countries. As noted, the potential linkages existing between ageing, wellbeing and development were a particular focus of the project.

The research had four main objectives. The first was to examine the effects of individual ageing on older households' income and livelihoods in Brazil and South Africa. It involved tracing the changes in wellbeing and livelihoods over time for a sample of low-income households in the two countries, and the factors that influence them. This is essential to understanding the impacts of rapid population ageing in the two countries concerned.

The second objective was to examine the effects of individual ageing on household dynamics, and especially intergenerational relations and care. Older people live, and age, in households. The composition and social relations within the household are key dimensions determining the wellbeing of older people (Mase, 2013).

The third objective was to identify the impact of pension entitlements and other anti-poverty programmes on the wellbeing of older people and their households. Pension benefits are the main social policy instrument addressing population ageing. The issue is the extent to which, in a developing country context, pensions support greater economic and social inclusion of older people.

The fourth objective was to examine, using cross-country comparisons, the institutions and social structures capable of supporting 'active ageing' and enabling households with older people to contribute to, and participate in, social and economic development. This dimension of the research developed out of a body of research providing evidence on the broader developmental impact of transfers to older people in developing countries (Møller and Sotshongaye, 1996; Saboia, 2005; Ferreira, 2006).

The study collected information at three levels: a household survey of around 1,000 households each in Brazil and South Africa, providing detailed information on their demographic and socioeconomic status, and including a supplement on all persons aged 55 and over; over 30 in-depth interviews of selected survey respondents in each country; and social and ageing policy and institutional environment in each of the countries.

A second wave of the 2002/03 household surveys in Brazil and South Africa, which sampled just over 1,000 households each in the Western and Eastern Cape region of South Africa, and Rio and Ilheus in Brazil, was collected in 2008/09.[2] The sample frame in both countries was provided by census areas; the sample was proportionate to size, and stratified by urban and rural areas in Brazil and South Africa, and additionally by race in the case of South Africa. The survey instruments comprised a household questionnaire with a section collecting information on all household members, and a supplement collected on all household members aged 55 and over, with questions on their entitlements, relations to other household members, health status, goals, social networks and community participation, and income decisions. The instruments were similar in all respects across the two countries. In South Africa, the questionnaires were translated into Xhosa and Afrikaans.

The original sampling design targeted households containing at least one person aged 55 years and older in 2002. Respondents were interviewed by enumerators who administered the questionnaires in the preferred language of the respondents. The survey consisted of a main household questionnaire that included a number of sections that asked for information regarding living conditions, household composition, economic activity, income and assets, expenditure, health and quality of life. The respondent for the household survey was identified (by the household members) as being the most knowledgeable about household finances acted as the respondent on behalf of the household. In addition to the household questionnaire, an older person supplement was included and administered to up to three individuals living in the household who were aged 55 years or older at the time of interview. In the older person supplement, questions were asked about social grants, income handling, economic activity, health, life satisfaction and wellbeing.

Table 15.1 shows the household sample panel and attrition. Significant attrition was to be expected given the age group and low-income location focus of the survey. In the event, the second round of data successfully located a high number of households.[3]

The household survey data enabled the construction of a longitudinal dataset (combining data collected in 2002) with standard variables across time and countries. The multidisciplinary composition of the research team fostered the application of diverse methods of analysis appropriate to the specific research questions addressed (Lloyd-Sherlock et al, 2012a).

Table 15.1: Household survey sample and attrition

	Brazil	South Africa
2002 households sample, of which:	1,006	1,107
Matched (2002 and 2008) households	615	719
Attrited (2002 only) households	391	388
Replacements (2008 only) households	391	254

Main findings

The main aim of this section is to present the main findings from the research, including the findings from the design and application of the project methods as well as the findings relating to the research questions identified above.

Capturing wellbeing among older people in developing countries requires a multidimensional perspective and a focus on households.

In Brazil and South Africa, and especially in low-income households, older people's wellbeing and livelihoods are interlinked with those of their extended families, whether or not they co-reside. This makes it harder to assess older people's wellbeing separately from that of their families. Resources are largely shared within extended households, including the resources contributed by older persons.

In the context of Brazil and South Africa, older people have access to relatively large income transfers, thus making a large financial contribution to their households and communities (Møller and Sotshongaye, 1996; Lloyd-Sherlock et al, 2012b; Møller and Radloff, 2013). This is particularly the case among older people living in extended households, a majority of households in low-income areas in South Africa and Brazil. Furthermore, households are not fixed, but can constitute and reconstitute in response to changes in household livelihoods (Mase, 2013). It is in this context that older people can make a contribution to the wellbeing of others within the household and community. In developing countries at least, understanding the effects of individual ageing necessitate information on the households within which older people live.

On average, comparisons of older people's wellbeing levels in 2002 and 2008 show improvement.

This is true for a range of wellbeing indicators: per capita household income and expenditure; multidimensional measures; and life satisfaction measures (Barrientos and Lasso de la Vega, 2016). We measured wellbeing outcomes for older people on a range of subjective and objective indicators in 2002 and 2008. The indicators included self-reported health status; self-reported life satisfaction; personal safety; social participation; financial control; debt; durables; source of drinking water; and per capita household expenditure. For each dimension of wellbeing, a deprivation threshold was set. For example, on financial control deprivation is associated with having no control over one's own income, and on expenditure respondents are deprived if they find themselves on the bottom two quintiles of expenditure. We adopted a counting approach focusing on the number of deprivations observed per individual. The distribution of deprivations for 2002 and 2008 for the panel sample of older people in South Africa is shown in Figures 15.1.

Figure 15.1: Multidimensional deprivation in the South Africa panel, 2002-08

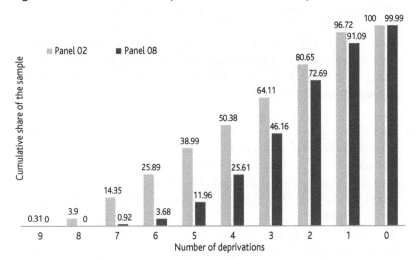

As can be seen from Figure 15.1, the share of the sample with a given number of deprivations or more is lower in 2008 than in 2002. The improvement in multidimensional deprivation is less pronounced in Brazil than in South Africa, but the same conclusion applies. On average the wellbeing of older people and their households in the two countries improved from 2002 to 2008 (Barrientos and Lasso de la Vega, 2016).

Individual ageing is not necessarily associated with an inevitable decline in wellbeing in developing countries.

The finding that wellbeing improved for among the sample of older people is very significant. This is especially the case taking into account that our research was focused on older populations in areas with high levels of poverty and deprivation. The significance of this finding is better appreciated when locating this finding in a wider setting. In both countries, analysis of the panel sample, that is individuals and households observed both in 2002 and 2008, indicates that on average ageing by six years does not correlate with a decline in wellbeing. On the contrary, and for the samples of older people in the two countries, wellbeing indicators suggest wellbeing improves with ageing.

It is, of course, important to identify the main factors responsible for this improvement in wellbeing, especially the possible roles of demographic change and policy changes. Changes in the size and composition of households could lead to improvement/decline in wellbeing with household income remaining constant. Changes in the value of transfers could be responsible for changes in wellbeing in the absence of changes in household composition.

The overall improvement in older people's wellbeing nets out significant change in wellbeing at the household level over time.

Analysis of changes in household poverty status for both countries between 2002 and 2008 shows a high incidence of transitions. It shows transitions out of and into poverty for households with older people. Tables 15.2 and 15.3 show poverty status transitions for both samples.

South Africa and Brazil lack official poverty lines. The analysis uses a poverty line set at R515 (2008 Rand) or US$PPP 96 per person per month in South Africa. For Brazil, the poverty line will be set at R207 (2008 Reais) or US$PPP125 (Barrientos and Mase, 2012). Focusing on the South Africa sample to begin with, just over one fifth of all households managed to exit poverty by 2008; however, just over 7% of all households were not poor in 2002 but fell into poverty by 2008.

Table 15.2: Poverty status transitions in the South Africa panel using per capita household expenditure

2002		2008		
		% not poor	% poor	
	% not poor	16.71	7.43	24.14
	% poor	22.00	53.86	75.85
		38.71	61.29	100

Table 15.3: Poverty status transitions in the Brazil panel using per capita household expenditure

		2008		
		% not poor	% poor	
2002	% not poor	47.32	15.28	62.60
	% poor	14.31	23.09	37.40
		61.63	38.37	100

Over one half of all households remained in poverty. For the Brazil sample, close to one sixth of all households exited poverty by 2008, but around the same share of households who were not poor in 2002 fell into poverty in 2008. Around a quarter of all households in Brazil sample remained poor in both years.

The tables show an overall rise in poverty incidence for South Africa and an overall fall in poverty incidence for Brazil. Estimates based on per capita household income actually reverse this finding and indicate a fall in poverty incidence for Brazil and a rise in poverty incidence for South Africa. The tables show the necessity of looking beyond the mean improvements in wellbeing for the two samples of older people. As the poverty transition figures show, it is possible to find significant change in poverty status over time, in both directions, at the household level.

Why were transitions into poverty more prevalent for the South African households than their Brazilian counterparts? One simple explanation is that the real-terms value of the Brazilian pension increased by more (46%) than the South African one (12%) between 2002 and 2008 (Lloyd-Sherlock et al, 2012a). At the same time, the wider economic and social context in Brazil was more conducive to poverty reduction than South Africa's. For example, open unemployment in South Africa in 2008 was three times that for Brazil, reducing livelihood opportunities for older people and their families.

Overall, a majority of older people in Brazil and South Africa are satisfied with their lives.
Whether they are asked about their current lives, or their lives taken as a whole, a majority of older people reported feeling satisfied or very satisfied with their lives. A higher proportion of Brazilian older people reported being with their lives compared with their South African counterparts. A majority of older people in each of the two countries reported being satisfied with their intra-family relationships and with the respect they receive from others. Figures 15.2 and 15.3 provide information on these findings.

Figure 15.2 shows high levels of life satisfaction can be observed among older people in both Brazil and South Africa. Elders reporting dissatisfaction represent a relatively small proportion of all respondents; around 7% in Brazil and 22% in South Africa. However, there is a marked difference between the two country samples. In Brazil, levels of satisfaction are significantly higher than in South Africa. This mirrors the findings for transitions into and out of poverty. As well as the income-related explanations given earlier, a higher prevalence of infectious disease in South Africa may have played a significant role in reducing life satisfaction scores there. Relatively high rates of crime and violence in South Africa may also have been a factor: 43% of respondents there referred to significant problems of crime and violence in their communities. The survey also asked respondents to assess their lives taken as a whole. As shown in Figure 15.2, the differences across the two samples are carried over, but they become less pronounced when their lives are taken a whole.

Figure 15.2: Life satisfaction among respondents aged 60 and over in Brazil and South Africa

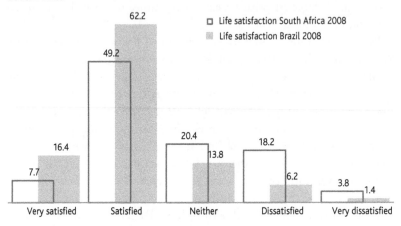

Figure 15.3: Self-reported satisfaction with life achievements among respondents aged 60 and over in Brazil and South Africa

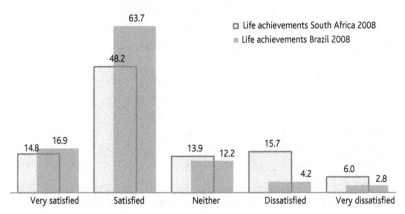

For low-income households, pension income, especially non-contributory pension income, is essential to wellbeing, livelihoods and social inclusion.

In the absence of pension income, households with older people are likely to be significantly poorer, less resilient, and less well integrated economically. In both countries, non-contributory pensions act more as an income transfer to poorer households than individual retirement income.

Other dimensions of social policy are important to the wellbeing of older people too.

An increased proportion of survey households in both countries reported receiving child and disability benefits, reflecting the expansion of income transfer programmes directed at children in poor households in the two countries. A third of Brazilian households surveyed in 2008 had joined a new national scheme providing low-interest loans for pensioners.

It is to be expected that the range of quality of appropriate health services would influence the wellbeing of older people in Brazil and South Africa. Our institutional analysis revealed that health services for older people were generally more available in Brazil than in South Africa (Cohn, 2009; Coovadia et al, 2009). As well as programmes screening for common non-communicable diseases and promoting home visits by health workers, the Brazilian government had established a scheme to reduce the cost of generic medication for older Brazilians (Lloyd-Sherlock et al, 2012b). Despite this, the proportion of older people reporting that their health was good or very good was broadly similar in each country (37% Brazil; 30% South Africa). More surprisingly, a quarter of Brazilian households reported not having access to necessary medication, compared with less than 3% of households in South Africa. In fact, rather than an indication of superior health service delivery in South Africa, this difference is more likely to reflect lower levels of health awareness among older people, due to limited screening for hypertension, diabetes and other conditions (Lloyd-Sherlock et al, 2012c). This shows the dangers of interpreting self-report health data at face value.

Recommendations

- Several recommendations arise from the research, as follows:
- It is useful to combine indicators based on per capita income with other approaches to wellbeing, including reported satisfaction and

multidimensional indices. Together, they have the potential to provide robust and comprehensive insights into temporal and spatial variations in wellbeing. Particular care must be taken in interpreting older people's self-reported health status.

- Brazil and South Africa represent different models of social policy addressing ageing. In the case of South Africa, pensions were primarily financed a non-contributory social assistance basis. In Brazil, contributory social insurance pensions were more prominent, even among relatively poor households. Their success in promoting the wellbeing of older people in disadvantaged settings shows that there is no single 'best practice' approach (Barrientos et al, 2013).

- Comparing Brazil and South Africa in the context of changes in those countries between 2002 and 2008 reveals that older people's wellbeing is strongly influenced by the nature of pension provision, but is also affected by other aspects of social policy, as well as economic performance and labour market conditions.

- Other developing countries need to pay attention to income security in old age. Large-scale pensions are essential to the wellbeing, livelihoods, and social inclusion of older people, but need to be complemented with policy interventions addressing other dimensions of wellbeing.

Key findings

- The underlying conceptual framework of the study combined theoretical approaches to wellbeing stressing the primacy of functionings and capability. Wellbeing was evaluated from a multidimensional perspective that captured basic functionings, income and consumption, and older people's perceptions of life satisfaction and social and economic integration. It finds that a focus on the contribution of older people to the development of their households and communities is justified by the developing country context.

- Capturing wellbeing among older people in developing countries requires a multidimensional perspective and a focus on households. In Brazil and South Africa, and especially in low-income households, older people's wellbeing and livelihoods are interlinked with those of their extended families, whether or not they co-reside. This makes it harder to assess older people's wellbeing separately from that of their families. In the context of Brazil and South Africa, older people have access to relatively large income transfers, thus making a large financial contribution to their households and communities.

- Individual ageing is not necessarily associated with an inevitable decline in wellbeing in developing countries. In both Brazil and South Africa, analysis of the panel sample (that is, individuals and households observed both in 2002 and 2008) indicates that on average ageing by six years does not correlate with a decline in wellbeing. On the contrary, wellbeing indicators suggest wellbeing improves with ageing. However, further research will attempt to identify the extent to which improvements in wellbeing among older people and their households are explained by demographic and policy changes. Changes in the size and composition of households could lead to improvement/decline in wellbeing with household income remaining constant. Changes in the value of transfers could be responsible for changes in wellbeing in the absence of changes in household composition.

- Overall, a majority of older people in Brazil and South Africa were satisfied with their lives. Whether they were asked about their current lives, or their lives taken as a whole, a majority of older people felt satisfied or very satisfied with their lives. A higher proportion of Brazilian older people reported being satisfied with their lives compared with their South African counterparts. A majority of older people in each of the two countries reported being satisfied with their intra-family relationships and with the respect they receive from others.

- For low-income households, pension income, especially non-contributory pension income, is essential to wellbeing, livelihoods and social inclusion. In the absence of pension income, households with older people are likely to be significantly poorer, less resilient, and less integrated economically. In both countries, non-contributory pensions act more as an income transfer to poorer households than individual retirement income.

Conclusion

The research project Ageing, Well-Being and Development: A Comparative Study of Brazil and South Africa had four main research objectives. It is helpful to return to these objectives and assess what, if any, progress was made.

The first objective was to examine the effects of individual ageing on older households' income and livelihoods. The longitudinal and comparative dimensions of the data collected enabled the study of our respondents' wellbeing six years after the initial observation. The findings indicate that on average the wellbeing of older people and their households improved over time. The expectation is that individual ageing results in a declining wellbeing and livelihoods, and that this is perhaps more marked in low-income locations in developing countries. Our findings should encourage further research and thinking on this issue. To a significant extent, wellbeing is produced by a range of individual factors, policies and institutions. Our analysis shows that individual ageing need not be associated with a decline in wellbeing and livelihoods as people age, providing that institutions are in place to support the contribution of older people to their families, communities and society. In particular, the income security afforded by pension schemes in both countries, and the fact that a majority of older people live in extended households, have an important influence on maintaining levels of wellbeing in old age.

It is important to underline that even where wellbeing levels improve as individuals age *on average*, this is not true of all older people and their households. Significant numbers of older people remained in poverty through the period, while other households fell into poverty or escaped poverty. The situation of older households that remained in poverty throughout the period should be a matter of great concern. As regards livelihoods, our data shows rapid withdrawal of older people from paid employment following pension receipt. However, and particularly for female pensioners, the labour contribution of older people to their households in terms of care increased in line with their withdrawal from market employment.

The second research objective was to examine the effects of individual ageing on household dynamics, and especially intergenerational relations and care. Older people live, and age, in households. The main findings were that the composition and social relations within the household remained fairly stable. However, pension receipt is associated with marginal changes in household composition in South Africa, a fact that is well established in the literature. Gender differences in intra-household relations, and therefore in the impact of pension receipt and other changes in the income sources of the household, can be largely explained by the care provision by older household members. Our study was able to confirm some of the findings from the literature examining older households' living arrangements in South Africa, but much more work is needed to construct a reliable picture of household dynamics associated with individual ageing in low-income settings.

The third objective was to identify the impact of pension entitlements and other anti-poverty programmes on the wellbeing of older people and their households. South Africa and Brazil have longstanding and relatively generous non-contributory pension provision. Our findings confirm earlier research suggesting that, in a developing country context, non-contributory pensions can support greater economic and social inclusion of older people. In this round of research, we were particularly interested in examining the impact of extension of social assistance provision to poor families with children in both countries.

The introduction of the Child Support Grant in South Africa and Bolsa Escola/Bolsa Família in Brazil raised a number of issues related to the interaction of these programmes with non-contributory pensions. We found that there was very little overlap between these interventions for our respondent households. Child and family transfers did not seem to undermine the effectiveness of non-contributory pension programmes in improving the wellbeing of recipient households. On the contrary, the absence of significant overlap in transfer receipt indicates that child and family transfers reach a different group of households in poverty. Moreover, there was strong indication that the perceived effectiveness of transfers to older people was key to enabling the extension of transfers to other groups. Looking ahead, it will be important to consider the articulation of social assistance to different groups in poverty, and proposals for further integration.

Finally, the fourth research objective was to examine, using cross-country comparisons, the institutions and social structures capable of supporting 'active ageing' and enabling households with older people to contribute to, and participate in, social and economic development. Our findings provide strong indications that a majority of older people in the two countries take an active part in the life of their households and communities. We have highlighted the contribution of social transfers in this context. However, we feel that more research is needed to develop a conceptual framework to enable a systematic and comprehensive understanding and study of the contribution of older people to developmental processes. This is work in progress in a developing country context.

Notes

[1] A doubling of the share of a country's population aged 65 and over, from 7% to 14%, took 115 years in France, 69 years in the US and 45 years in the UK, but it will take 19 years in Singapore, 21 years in Brazil, and 26 years in China (Kinsella and He, 2009).

[2] The survey data collected as part of this study has been archived with the UK Data Archive (http://data-archive.ac.uk) and the South African Data First Archive at the University of Cape Town. For a report of the main findings see Barrientos et al (2003).

[3] The figures for poverty incidence for Brazil are higher than the estimates for the population as a whole. This is explained by the fact that we collected data from poorer locations in Brazil and South Africa, and also by the fact that our estimates rely on expenditure data as opposed to income.

References

Barrientos, A. (2008) 'Cash transfers for older people reduce poverty and inequality', in A.J. Bebbington, A.A. Dani, A. De and M. Walton (eds) *Institutional pathways to equity. Addressing inequality traps*, Washington, DC: World Bank, pp 169–92.

Barrientos, A. and Lasso de la Vega, C. (2016) 'Ageing, wellbeing and deprivation in later life: a multidimensional counting approach', *Journal of Poverty Alleviation and International Development*, vol 7, no 2, pp 1-35.

Barrientos, A. and Mase, J. (2012) 'Poverty transitions among older households in South Africa and Brazil', *European Journal of Development Research*, vol 24, no 4, pp 570-88.

Barrientos, A., Lloyd-Sherlock, P., Ferreira, M., Gorman, M., Legido-Quigley, H., Møller, V., Saboia, J. and Wernick Vianna, M.L.T. (2003) *Non-contributory pensions and poverty prevention. A comparative study of Brazil and South Africa*, Manchester: IDPM and HelpAge International.

Barrientos, A., Møller, V., Saboia, J., Lloyd-Sherlock, P. and Mase, J. (2013) '"Growing" social protection in developing countries: lessons from Brazil and South Africa', *Development Southern Africa*, 30, no 1, pp 54-68.

Cohn, A. (2009) 'A reforma sanitaria brasiliera após 20 anos do SUS: reflexões' ['The Brazilian Health Reform 20 years after the SUS: Reflexions'], *Cadernos de Saúde Pública*, vol 25, no 7, pp 1614-19.

Coovadia, H., Jewkes, R., Barron, P., Sanders, D. and McIntyre, D. (2009) 'The health and health system of South Africa: historical roots of current public health challenges', *The Lancet*, vol 374, no 9692, pp 817-34.

Deaton, A. (2007) *Income, aging, health and wellbeing around the world. Evidence from the Gallup World Poll*, Cambridge, MA: NBER.

Diener, E. and Suh, E. (1997) 'Subjective well-being and age: an international analysis', *Annual Review of Gerontology and Geriatrics*, in K.W. Schaie and M.P Lawton (eds) *Annual Review of Gerontology and Geriatrics. Volume 17: Focus on Emotion and Adult Development*, New York, NY: Springer, pp 304-24.

Ferreira, M. (2006) 'The differential impact of social-pension income on household poverty alleviation in three South African ethnic groups', *Ageing & Society*, vol 26, no 3, pp 337-54.

Kinsella, K. and He, W. (2009) *An Aging World: 2008. International Population Reports*, Washington, DC: US Census Bureau.

Kunzmann, U., Little, T.D. and Smith, J. (2000) 'Is age-related stability of subjective well-being a paradox? Cross-sectional and longitudinal evidence from the Berlin Aging Study', *Psychology and Aging*, vol 15, no 3, pp 511-26.

Lloyd-Sherlock, P. (2006) 'Simple transfers, complex outcomes. The impacts of pensions on poor households in Brazil', *Development and Change*, vol 37, no 5, pp 969-95.

Lloyd-Sherlock, P. (2010) *Population ageing and international development*, Bristol: Policy Press.

Lloyd-Sherlock, P., Barrientos, A., Møller, V. and Saboia, J. (2012a) 'Pensions, poverty and wellbeing in later life: comparative research from South Africa and Brazil', *Journal of Aging Studies*, vol 26, no 3, pp 243-52.

Lloyd-Sherlock, P., Minicuci, N., Beard, J. and Chatterji, S. (2012c) 'Social protection and the health of older people in developing countries: establishing the health effects of pensions and health insurance', *International Social Security Review*, vol 65, no 4, pp 51-68.

Lloyd-Sherlock, P., Saboia, J. and Ramírez-Rodríguez, B. (2012b) 'Cash transfers and the well-being of older people in Brazil', *Development and Change*, vol 43, no 5, pp 1049-72.

Mase, J. (2013) 'Do households recompose around the South African social pension?', Unpublished PhD thesis, University of Manchester.

Møller, V. (2011) *Perceptions of fortune and misfortune in older South African households: Social pensions and the 'good life'*, Grahamstown: Rhodes University.

Møller, V. and Radloff, S. (2013) 'Perceptions of fortune and misfortune in older South African households: social assistance and the "good life"', *Social Indicators Research*, 111, pp 633-64.

Møller, V. and Sotshongaye, A. (1996) '"My family eats this money too": pension sharing and self-respect among Zulu grandmothers', *Southern African Journal of Gerontology*, vol 5, no 2, pp 9-19.

Pinquart, M. and Sorensen, S. (2000) 'Influences of socio-economic status, social network, and competence on subjective well-being in later life: a meta-analysis', *Psychology and Aging*, vol 15, no 2, pp 187-224.

Saboia, J. (2005) 'Non-contributory pensions and poverty prevention among the elderly in Brazil', in A.A. Camarano (ed) *Sixty plus: The elderly Brazilians and their new social roles*, Rio de Janeiro: IPEA.

Schilling, O. (2006) 'Development of life satisfaction in old age: another view of the "paradox"', *Social Indicators Research*, 75, pp 241-71.

SIXTEEN

Ageing, poverty and neoliberalism in urban south India

Penny Vera-Sanso
Project team: Suresh Veeraraghavan, Marlia Hussain, Joe
Henry, Arul George and Barbara Harriss-White

Introduction

Chennai, a highly dense and growing city of 4.7 million people, is a particularly apt context for studying three global processes that are having greater impacts on developing countries than on developed countries. The first process, population ageing, is growing fastest in developing countries, which are already home to two thirds of the world's people aged 60 and over, and after China and the United States, India has the largest global population of people aged 80 and above (over 11 million) (UN DESA, 2015, pp 9, 17). Second, the rate of urbanisation in developing countries is much faster than in developed countries. Ninety per cent of the world's urban population growth will happen in Asia and Africa, such that by 2050 52% of the urban population will be located in Asia. India currently has the world's second largest urban population at 410 million people (UN DESA, 2014, pp 11-12). Third, developing countries are increasingly drawn into the global economy where pre–existing inequalities are deepening (UN DESA, 2005, 2013; Ortiz and Cummins, 2011).[1]

Chennai provides an example of where developing cities might be headed. It is located within the Chennai Metropolitan Area, comprising 8.9 million people living in Chennai city and its suburbs, and is located within the state of Tamil Nadu, which is the most highly urbanised state in India.[2] It is not only India's fourth largest metropolitan agglomeration, but also one of the fastest growing metropolitan economies.[3] A by-product of Chennai's prodigious growth is that nearly 30% of its population lives in slums (Chandramouli, undated). In a city with a literacy rate of 90% (Census of India, undated a), these slum dwellers demonstrate that education is now widely accepted; consequently, the child labour rate has seen a rapid decline since the

1980s, though the absolute number of child labourers remains large (Kak and Pati, 2012).[4] Alongside high levels of urbanisation, Tamil Nadu's fertility rate has fallen below replacement level (Government of India, 2011a), resulting in a rapidly growing age band of over-60s (10.4% of the state population, that is, over 7.5 million people) and an even faster growing 80+ age band (1.03%, about 750,000 people) (Census of India, undated b). By comparison India's over 60 population represents only 8.6% of the total population. As of 2011, life expectancy in Tamil Nadu is 69 years for men and 72 years for women (Census of India, undated c).

Alongside demographic changes have come significant economic transformations. Pre-liberalisation, Chennai combined diversified formal sector manufacturing and a prolific film industry with informal sector services and retail. Since liberalisation in 1991, Chennai has successfully orientated itself towards the global economy: it is one of India's most important centres for information technology (IT) and business process outsourcing, and its manufacturing sector is rapidly expanding, especially for the international automotive, electronic and textile markets. Yet trade liberalisation has by no means benefited everyone; rather it has led to the deepening immiseration of the growing number of informal sector workers (NCEUS, 2009; Naidu, 2016) through declining regular work, increasing casual work and downward pressure on informal sector wages (Kaur et al, 2007; Singh and Sapra, 2007). In a country where 92% of working people work in the informal economy or have informal employment within the formal economy (NCEUS, 2009, p 13), where 45% of children under age 3 are stunted, denoting a long-term lack of adequate nutrition as well as recurrent and chronic illness (IIPS, 2009, p 13) and where 55% of women and 24% of men are anaemic (IIPS, 2009, p 49), it must come as no surprise that older people need to contribute to provisioning and family care work.

Yet until recently the contribution of older people to their families, communities and the economy through their paid and unpaid work has not been recognised. At the root of the failure to recognise older people's role in the economy are the erroneous assumptions that older people are frail and cannot contribute and that their needs are limited and easily met by family members (Vera-Sanso, 2004, 2007). The effects of these assumptions can be seen in a pension policy where coverage is limited and pension value is meagre and eroded by inflation (Vera-Sanso, 2010), and in official data collection policies that exclude older people, either at the data collection stage or at analysis. For example, the National Family Health Survey does not collect data on the health of women over the age of 49 nor men over the age of 54, and the National Sample Survey (NSS), set up in 1950, undertook its first survey of older people in 1986-87, its second in 1995-96 and its most recent one in 2004.[5] With the exception of one recent report (Government of India, 2011b), the Government of India, when analysing census data, chooses to use concepts such as 'working generation' (15-59 years) and 'old-age dependency ratio' that do not take into account that nearly 40% of people aged 60+ are working (Government of India, 2011b, p 15).[6] By contrast to the assumption that older people's most basic needs are being met, the little evidence available suggests that even in better-off households the nutritional status of older people is 'considerably worse' than that of younger people (Gillespie and McNeill, 1992, p 98) and that among the poor anaemia rates may be high and body mass index low, even reaching to starvation status for 15% of older people, especially among women (Public Health Resource Network, 2014).

The failure to recognise older people's paid and unpaid work is not only rooted in the nation's self-perception that 'India supports its aged' but is also the outcome of the System of National Accounts (SNA). By externalising the labour inputs critical to ensuring the reproduction of the labour force, on a day-to-day and generational basis, and creating a context in which that unpaid work and worker is devalued, the SNA encourages the depletion of capacities and resources for social reproduction (Picchio, 1992; Ironmonger, 1996; Hoskyns and Rai, 2007). Similarly, the persistence in using stylised economic indicators that do not reflect reality, such as dependency ratios that assume everyone between the ages of 15 and 59 works and everyone aged 60 and above is dependent, not only plays an important role in the failure to recognise older people's economic roles but also justifies the defining and stigmatising of the older generation as a looming policy issue. By misrepresenting the scale of old-age dependency and by diverting the planning gaze from age-based labour market segmentation, these indicators not only misconstrue the structure of the labour force, but play a role in licensing age discrimination (Vera-Sanso, 2013, 2014).

In contrast to the large body of research that posits population ageing as a looming economic and social problem (World Bank, 1994; Rajan et al, 1999; UNFPA, 2002; Holzmann and Hinz, 2005), there is now an emerging body of work that recognises older people's paid and unpaid contributions to the *whole* economy, including social reproduction, though by no means does all of that focus positively on the contribution that older people make to wider society (Carr, 2005; Johnson and Mutchler, 2014). Research on work, productive and active ageing in later life in high-income countries (Taylor and Walker, 1994; Chiu et al, 2001; Walker, 2006), and on older women's contribution to the care economy (Burnette, 1997; Arber and Ginn, 1990; Smith, 2002) and on volunteering (Wheeler et al, 1998; Martinson and Minkler, 2006), is more established than research on older people's work in low- and middle-income countries.

Research on all aspects of later life remains sparse in low- and middle-income countries, despite the absolute numbers of people involved. In terms of older people's work, the literature is particularly recent despite older people's paid and unpaid work making a significant contribution to wider society. In contexts where intervening generations are lost, often through HIV/AIDS, older people, particularly grandmothers, raise orphaned children and do so with little, if any, institutional support (Bachman de Silva et al, 2008; Nyanzi, 2009). Grandparents also play a critical role in raising a nation's gross domestic product and increasing foreign exchange reserves: they do so by making it possible for women to join the workforce, including the international workforce. For example, Bolivian grandmothers anchor an international care chain that sees them caring for grandchildren while their daughters care for more privileged children in Spain (Bastia, 2009). Similar care chains ground rural–urban work migration in China (Luo, undated; Judd, 2009). Nor is older people's support for younger people limited to childcare; their downward transfers play an important role in supporting younger family members (Schroder-Butterfill, 2004). More recently, older people's paid work and income generation have come to light (for example, Vera-Sanso, 2007, 2013, 2014; Alam and Barrientos, 2010; Government of India, 2011b; Selvaraj et al, 2011; Alam and Mitra, 2012) and older people's role in buttressing the national and global economy (Vera-Sanso, 2012) and their vulnerability as workers to shocks in the global economy (Harriss-White et al, 2013) are among the findings of the research project described in this chapter.

The research project

The research[7] that is the subject of this chapter was stimulated by the work Vera-Sanso undertook in Chennai's slums between 1990-92, prior to India's liberalisation measures beginning to take effect, as well as work she had undertaken in 2000 in two villages in western Tamil Nadu on older people from the most socially stigmatised and economically deprived caste, Chakkliyars, at a time when local industries and agriculture were in crisis (Vera-Sanso, 2007). This earlier research made it clear that the widespread presumption that in India (or other 'traditional cultures') older people can retire from work and rely on family support is untenable in impoverished communities, especially for those reliant on insecure, irregular and low-paid informal work.

Aims of the research

The project's objective was to uncover the impact of neoliberal policies on older people in developing countries and to do so by tracing the backward and forward linkages of what older people do. Initially, the project's main aim was to understand the impact of neoliberal growth on the capacity of the older urban poor to be self-supporting or to access support from their families, and to do so by studying older people's location within the wider context of urban poverty. Seeking to move away from a predetermined approach of what to study in relation to older people, the project cast its net wide to examine the interplay of factors in the social, cultural, economic, political, legal and planning environments that impinge on older people's capacity to work, retain control of their incomes and gain access to family and state resources. As the research progressed, however, it became clear that while there were many pressures that severely constrained older people's capacity to make a living, retain control of their earnings or to access support from the state and or family, older people also gained much satisfaction from earning money and supporting their families and benefited from the sociality of working – though there were clearly variations depending on the work. Collaborating with a local research centre, the Centre for Law, Policy and Human Rights Studies, Chennai, to undertake the research and get the results into the public arena, the study's second aim was to stimulate a national debate on older people and their rights as adults, workers and citizens.

Methods

The study applied a mixed-method, exploratory approach. In 2007, it started with an 800-household survey in five of Chennai's slum settlements, which included every fifth or eighth household in each slum, depending on its size. By tracing networks of relatives and their relative proximity, the survey identified the 'intergenerational load' people across the slums carried. (No assumptions were made regarding direction of labour and resource transfers between generations.) This was followed by a focus on older people through free-flowing discussions with 179 older people who took the lead, usually relating their migration and work histories, their experience of intergenerational relations, access to public goods, their housing concerns and their aspirations and concerns about their family's wellbeing, their health and so on. In order to capture the potential impacts of the international economic crisis of 2008 and global spikes in commodity prices, three rounds of an economic survey were undertaken comparing economic circumstances with the period 12 months prior to the first economic survey. This provided data on income, assets, savings and debts as well as eliciting informants' judgements of whether and in what direction their circumstances had changed and the criteria they used to determine this. In moving around Chennai, it became apparent that our study of five settlements across the city, while uncovering 40 occupations for people aged 60+, did not remotely cover the variety of occupations that could be seen in Chennai's public spaces. A convenience photographic survey was undertaken between 2007 and 2013, reflecting the paths taken by six researchers as they lived and worked in Chennai, in order to document at least some of this range. It soon became apparent that street vending, particularly street markets, are mainly 'staffed' by older people, despite a widespread discourse of older people 'not working' and pavement stalls frequently being described as 'my daughter's'. To capture how central older people are to street markets as well as the vicissitudes of street marketing, one large street market was monitored for four years, vendors were interviewed, and the early morning city's flower and vegetable wholesale markets were monitored for five days between 3am and 8am.

For the follow-on study (2012-13), 40 pensioners from the original study were asked what difference the state's doubling of the social pension (from Rs400 to Rs1,000 per month by early 2011) had made to them. The main objective of the follow-on study was to build on the 2007-10 project's impact on social pensions in Tamil Nadu by stimulating a national debate on the circumstances and contributions of older people. This required not only identifying powerful new ways of disseminating research, but also finding ways of generalising the main research findings, in order that they would not become pigeon-holed in the 'that's Chennai, Chennai's always different' box. Two strategies were employed. First, the project undertook the production of two documentaries, *We're Still Working* and *The Forgotten Generation*, using informants taken from Chennai, rural Rajasthan and tribal Maharashtra.[8] Local non-governmental organisations (NGOs) The Association of Strong Women Alone and Kashtakari Sanghatna anchored the filming in Rajasthan and Maharashtra, providing informants and local expert advice. Second, in order to extend the scope further, The Hindu National Photo Competition on the Working Elderly was launched in collaboration with *The*

Hindu, one of India's most widely read newspapers. The competition asked contestants to submit photos taken in the past year that depicted older workers in a positive light, demonstrating their endurance and contribution. The competition produced nearly 3,000 photos, many with commentary, demonstrating that older people work across India in a hugely diverse range of work and environmental contexts.[9] The online gallery of photographs (http://bit.ly/19Y6jqp) represents a globally unique collection of work that older people do. Despite the range depicted, this collection is by no means exhaustive, as contestants photographed only what they came across; it does not record work that older people do in the middle of the night, nor their work in offices, factories, hospitals, hotels, restaurants and so on to which the public does not have access.

The 800-household survey revealed that the presumption that the working generation is aged 15-59 is erroneous; instead, work generally starts at a later age and its pattern of curtailment in later life is considerably more contingent and gender-nuanced. In 2007/08, 2% of 10- to 14-year-olds were working and only 24% of 15- to 19-year-olds were working, a figure close to the percentage of 70- to 74-year-olds classed by informants as working. In other words, Chennai's slum dwellers, including older slum dwellers, have accepted that children's education is a family priority, with the result that there were twice as many women in the slum workforce aged 60 and above than girls/women aged 15-19 and slightly more men aged 60 and above than boys/men aged 15-19, many of whom were in apprenticeship and would be better described as 'more learning than earning'. Slum families find themselves caught in a pincer movement between a local labour market, swelled by a large youth bulge, in which employers use credentialism to select the most compliant employees, and a competitive global economy that demands an increasingly educated, low-paid workforce.

The survey demonstrated that the youth bulge is also contributing to age discrimination against men in some sections of the labour market, beginning when they reach their early forties. In addition to age discrimination, older men are facing a reorganisation of the labour market that marginalises middle-aged and older workers, increasingly relegating them to the most irregular, poorly paid work available, that of casual and piece-rate work. In the slums there is a long tail of men working into their nineties. Women's work pattern is typically one where they enter the workforce in mid-life, often to compensate for men's declining real incomes. Sixty-two per cent of women classed as working are aged over 40; 37% are aged 45-49 and 20% are aged 65-

69. In other words, the standardised institutional discourse that defines the 'working generation' as 15-59 years and the old-age dependency ratio fails to capture the reality that in the slums work is more closely aligned with what is commonly thought of as post-retirement age than with early working life, and that for women the association of work with later life is stronger than it is for men (Vera-Sanso, 2012).

Qualitative data drawn from the 179 interviews demonstrated that being classed as 'working' is as much about gender–age identity as it is about whether a person works. Women are less likely to be classed as working; instead, they are classed as 'helpers' in another person's micro-business, usually a daughter's, or as 'passing time' no matter whether that business was started by them or they are the primary or only worker. Older men, by contrast, spend much time searching (or more accurately waiting) for casual work and are classed as working up to the point that they have given up their search for work. The resulting overall pattern is that men's economic contribution to the household is largest at the beginning of the marriage and declines over the life course and women's economic contribution starts with no paid work and no 'helper' role and then rises over the life course to compensate for men's declining contributions to the household and continues into deep old age (Vera-Sanso, 2012). While this reverses the usual claims that women are dependent in old age, it supports quantitative research on mortality risk for older men and women in rural Bangladesh, which found that risk is raised for spouseless older men, but not for older women; their risk is raised where they do not have two surviving sons, demonstrating that reduced fertility may have greater long-term negative effects on women than men (Rahman, 1991).[10]

The need for older people, particularly older women, to work into late life arises from the way Chennai is incorporated into the global economy. Aside from the pressure for better and longer education and training, the city's rapid expansion and density places housing at a premium. In 2007/08, 97% of rents in the slums studied were more than Rs300 a month, at a time when the social pension was Rs400 per month. Consequently, even the few people who *did* receive a pension had to work both to supplement it to meet their basic living costs and to pay their rents.[11]

Further, the economic surveys revealed that the majority of slum households, not just slum households in which older people lived, were affected by the global economic crisis, global price hikes in food and fuel and the impact of climate shocks (flooding, rising temperatures and humidity) (Harriss-White et al, 2013). While the urban poor are trapped in seasonal cycles of extreme events and environmental insults that lower incomes and assets and raise costs and debts, it was the price rises and insufficient work (due to the contraction of the economy) that most people identified as the cause of their declining economic circumstances. This led to their deteriorating debt status and reduced food consumption (cutting protein, vegetables and meals) and compromised capacity to replace broken and worn-out household items. The economic surveys demonstrated that events initiated by speculation in the financial fortresses of London and New York *do* quickly find their way to the doors of slum dwellers; they found that men and women above the age of 60, and households headed by people over the age of 60, suffered the most from the predations of global markets, especially if they undertook waged work in the service sector (Harriss-White et al, 2013).[12]

In this context of reduced consumption, when populations are already confronting stunting and anaemia, family networks must make choices about how resources are utilised. In these circumstances, older people reduced their consumption further, delayed seeking healthcare, provided cash to younger relatives and, in the case of older women, increased their labour inputs into paid work, 'helping out' or taking on unpaid work in order to allow younger woman to join the workforce. These transfers of resources and labour did not just happen between relatives living in the same household but among people in family networks, including networks that spread across the urban–rural divide (Vera-Sanso, 2012). In impoverished households, older people are not the ones with the strongest claims to family resources. When poverty deepens, older people absorb a greater share of deprivation, both as a matter of expectation and out of their desire to reduce their children's and grandchildren's suffering.

By combining an analysis of what older people do and theorising their backward and forward linkages, it soon becomes clear that older people, far from being a drain on family or national resources, are in fact buttressing the global economy. We have already seen that their paid and unpaid work is important for keeping family budgets positive (see also Durr-e-Nayab, 2010 on Pakistan), both by working directly themselves or releasing younger women into the workforce and in helping to ameliorate and even absorb downturns in the global economy. The importance of older women's role as unpaid labour in family businesses is demonstrated by vending businesses collapsing when these 'helpers' and 'time passers' become terminally ill and die. As vendors and as porters in wholesale markets and as auto rickshaw and cycle rickshaw transporters of vendors and their wares from the market, older people are an important linchpin linking the urban and rural economies.

(Fifty per cent of Indians work in agriculture and agriculture-related industries, a good proportion of whom are themselves over 60.) The incomes and homes of older slum dwellers, or the incomes of the younger women that they have released into the workforce, are used to further younger people's education, including the education of grandchildren who come to Chennai from rural areas for IT and other training. Older women's take-up of heavy domestic work (including queuing for water lorries, carrying pots of water, clearing sewage-laden storm water and so on) and care work (covering shortfalls in education and health provision), substitutes for the state's failure to provide adequate social and physical infrastructure, allowing the state to invest in policies that favour foreign direct investment. If we trace the links forwards from older people's paid and unpaid work, we can see that, by taking on the work that younger people no longer do, older people contribute to Chennai's place in the global economy by providing low-cost services to Chennai's current and future workforce and by providing low-cost inputs to industry. In taking on social reproductive work, older people are not only patching over the impacts of the state's neoliberal policies of favouring capital, particularly foreign capital, they are also releasing younger women into the workforce at exactly the moment when the population's age structure could potentially produce a demographic dividend (Vera-Sanso, 2013). The World Bank (2008) has identified expanding employment, increasing productivity, raising human capital and drawing women into the workforce, in order to increase per capita productivity, as critical to realising a demographic dividend, and, of course, a low-cost, skilled labour force is seen as the way forward to cornering a larger share of the global economy. It is unquestionable that older people contribute significantly to each strategy identified by the World Bank, barring, it might be thought, increased productivity. However, even here older people can be seen to contribute, as increased productivity can be achieved either by increasing output, assuming wages stay the same, or sustaining output but reducing wages, or reducing wages faster than output. Age discrimination in wages effectively increases the productivity of older people's labour. (For age-based income inequalities, see Vera-Sanso, 2007, 2013; Ghosh et al, 2010; Harriss-White et al, 2013.)

This leaves us with the question of what working does for older people. Paid work can provide social recognition, and a sense of self-worth and sociality. Those who live alone specifically point to their ability to spend their money how they wish, not needing to ask others for money nor feeling answerable to them over not pooling it with the rest of the family. That is the potential. The downside is that incomes are small and they have negligible, if any, cushion for illness. The main issue that older workers face is whether they are in trades, or can move into trades, that give them control over their work, allowing them to tailor work to their needs and capacities. Paid domestic work, for example, is arduous and leaves the employer in control, able to determine income, hours and continuity of employment. Breaking bricks is physically depleting and isolating work. Waiting, with little success, for small building repair work, produces negligible income and low self-esteem. Pulling a cycle rickshaw facilitates control over the work process, and vending similarly enables older people to control the intensity and hours of work as well as having a high degree of sociality. Unfortunately, while these two trades provide important livelihoods for older people and low-cost services for the working population, they are under attack by the authorities for not being commensurate with India's image of itself as a modernising nation. Planners, and individuals who are using public interest litigation to move the courts against street markets, are endangering vending livelihoods. Further, the government's 12th Five Year Plan has explicitly identified the refrigerated distribution of food 'from farm to fork' as an arena that the corporate sector should move into in order to reduce food waste, although the plan readily admits that there is no data on the extent of food wastage and that India has a significant energy deficit. If implemented, this measure would have a negative impact on the livelihoods of many older people who are engaged in the distribution chain that brings produce from the wholesale market to the final consumer (market porters, cycle rickshaw pullers, auto rickshaw drivers and street vendors).

While work can give older people choices, and being dependent on impoverished others does not, and while paid work can often be less onerous than the heavy social reproductive work that living in slums demands, older people need the wherewithal to enable them to refuse to take on the most physically depleting and menial work available to them and to determine how much they work. Such dimensions are multi-levelled. Older people's rights as workers need to be recognised and protected by the state, as does their right to work, particularly age-friendly work that enables older people to control the extent and intensity of their work. In some parts of rural India, the Mahatma Gandhi Rural Employment Guarantee Scheme does provide work for older people that sets age-friendly daily workload quotas. Most importantly, older people need the certainty of a meaningful pension on which they can depend. The project's 2012-13 follow-up study of the impact of the 125% increase in old-age pensions from Rs400 to

Rs1,000 between late 2010 and early 2011 demonstrated that pensions, at this rate, do not relieve older people of the need to work, but do give them a greater sense of security, and a feeling that they stand a better chance of bridging the monthly income:expenses gap, as all people working in the insecure and unstable informal economy must. It is unlikely that a larger pension would encourage all older people to stop working completely, as the benefit of working is not just one of having an income, but of being seen to have an income and of being able to help household and close relatives trapped in, and trying to escape, the uncertainties of the informal economy. What an adequate and reliable pension will do is to put older people in the driving seat, allowing them to decide what type of work and how much work they do, and if and when they will stop working.[13]

Impact

A central aim of the 2007-10 and 2012-13 projects was to generate a debate on older people's contribution to family and economy, their rights as workers, and rights to work and pensions. An innovative strategy of combining standard academic outputs (articles, chapters and conference papers) was combined with new methods for gaining the attention of policymakers, activists, NGOs, journalists and the general public. These included newspaper articles, policy notes presented to policymakers in Chennai and Delhi, the documentaries and photo competition mentioned earlier in the chapter and a photo exhibition/essay created out of the convenience photo survey of Chennai, undertaken by the research team and supplemented with photos taken in rural Rajasthan, that demonstrated older people's role in social reproduction and the economy.[14] Pop-up exhibitions were held at pension rallies and government offices in India and at international conferences in India and Europe. The research project spurred an initial 25% rise in pensions in late 2010 in Tamil Nadu and helped place old-age pensions on the agenda for the state elections, resulting in a further 100% rise in pensions in spring 2011 for three million pensioners. Research presentations to activists at the project's conference in March 2010 in Chennai and in August 2010 to the 4th National Convention of the Right to Food and Work Campaign (RTF), India's highly successful network of activists and NGOs spurred a unanimous resolution to campaign for a universal pension, index-linked to inflation. In August 2011, the Pension Parishad was formed by members of the RTF and others. Having set a universal pension rate at Rs2,000, half the minimum wage, by 2013, the Pension Parishad placed the universal pension on the policy agenda. It secured a public announcement from the then national government in support of universality and secured a commitment 'to strive progressively realise the objective' of 'adequate' pensions for senior citizens in the National Food Security Act 2013 (Clause 31 and Schedule III, 3(d)). By February 2014, with over 200 NGOs, academics and politicians from across all the major parties supporting the campaign, the Pension Parishad made the Rs2,000 universal pension an election issue for the 2014 national elections. While the new central government did not support either a raised pension nor the extension of the social pension to cover those without a pension, the Pension Parishad has worked successfully with a number of states and union territories to significantly supplement central government pension provision. The Pension Parishad continues to work towards making the social pension scheme inclusive, adequate and reliable across India. If the Pension Parishad is successful, it will not only have completely reversed the Government of India's strategy of primarily relying on the family to support older people, irrespective of the family's capacity to do so, but will have moved the pension from a political gift to a citizen right. The project team continues to present its research to members of the Pension Parishad and RTF and is working with HelpAge International to secure recognition of older people's roles and rights as workers and to work.

Recommendations

The research has identified the following needs:

- to circumvent the distortions inherent in concepts that do not reflect the situation on the ground, specifically the concept of working age as 15–59 (or 64) and the old-age dependency ratio, by using actual census data on who is working/not working;
- to prevent discrimination against older people in the gathering and analysis of national-level data, as occurs with the National Family Health Survey and census;
- to recognise older people's belonging to and participation in family-based networks, rather than assuming they are rigidly fixed to only one household;
- to recognise older people's paid and unpaid work and their rights to work and as workers, providing them with the worker protections afforded to other age groups.

- to provide an adequate, universal pension sufficient to allow older people to choose if, when and how much they work and to enable them to refuse demeaning and physically depleting work.

Key findings

- Chennai's population structure is ageing rapidly, with the result that old-age poverty is now a significant and rising, though largely overlooked, problem. In the five slum areas studied, 12% of people were aged 60 and over and 5% were aged over 70 years, demonstrating comparatively long life expectancies for those surviving into old age.
- Older people's economic activity is often under-recognised, even by older people themselves. Twenty-eight per cent of people surveyed over age 60 considered themselves to be working, as did 20% of people aged 70-79.
- Research, as well as observations of a street market from 2007-10, uncovered a significant number of older people playing extensive, unpaid, 'helper' roles in a son's or daughter's petty business. A further tranche of older people, largely older women, undertook unpaid childcare, housework, fetching water and other supporting roles for family members in order to release younger family women into the workforce. The importance of older people's unpaid labour is evident from the collapse of businesses and the withdrawal of younger women from the workforce when older people's unpaid labour is no longer available due to accident, illness or death.
- Social welfare policies demonstrate insufficient understanding of either the dynamics of intergenerational relations in the context of severe poverty or the specificities of old-age poverty as well as the lower priority placed on old-age welfare. The main plank for old-age welfare – the public resource-capped, poverty-targeted, non-contributory pension – is not available to a large proportion of the qualifying older urban poor.
- Having uncovered the mismatch between conceptualisations of old-age dependence and non-participation in the economy and older people's actual contribution, the research provides evidence for mainstreaming age into all policy, planning and practice. It demonstrates that relegating the older urban poor solely to the remit of social welfare departments fails to recognise their rights, needs and contribution to the economy and places them at the mercy of declining welfare budgets.

Conclusion

The study challenged the perception of older people as dependants who are, or should be, looked after by their families. It demonstrated that older people make a significant contribution to family, society and economy, playing a substantial role both in bridging the shortfalls in state provision for people living in low-income settlements and reliant on public services (education, health, infrastructure) and in providing a skilled yet comparatively low-paid workforce for the global economy. It demonstrated that older people, far from being a demographic problem, are the ones who, under current state provision, will facilitate the realisation of India's potential for a demographic dividend. Older people, along with others, physically absorb the impacts of global financial crises. The state policy and planning trends look as though they will undermine the potentials of age-friendly occupations for older people. This study revealed the extent to which public and private discourses represent older people – that is, *older adults* – as frail, dependent, non-workers, with limited needs. From demographic concepts, through policy measures, to the labour market and intergenerational relations, older adults are too often recognised not for what they do but for an erroneous, essentialist, infantilising, conceptualisation of what they are – as no longer equals of the unmarked category of 'adult'. In placing the research before the public, NGOs, activists, academics, planners and politicians, the study has helped to bring attention to the needs, contribution and rights of a population of *adults* who have been assiduously ignored and misrepresented.

Notes

[1]   See Chant (2013) for a comprehensive overview of how gender and class inequalities are manifested in cities of the global south.

[2]   Forty-three per cent of the state's population live in urban areas (National Health Mission Tamil Nadu? undated).

[3]   A London-Chennai comparison is illuminating. Both are vibrant economic centres of in-migration. In 2001, Chennai's population growth rate was 13%; by 2011 the rate had slowed to that of London (7%) albeit Chennai's population density is over five times that of London (27,000 people per square km as against London's 5,000 people per square km) (Census of India, undated d; ONS, 2012, p 23).

[4]   In India, 'slum' is a technical and legal term with deep political salience arising from the burden placed on the state by the 1956 Slum Area (Improvement and Clearance) Act to provide minimum housing standards and rehouse slum dwellers in non-slum conditions on the same site. The Corporation of Chennai has failed to notify any slums since 1985, which is one of the foci of slum-dweller associations' current campaigns. State and local governments are coming under increasing pressure from

central government and national institutions to reduce the minimum number of households required for slum notification from 60 households to 20. The Census of India categorises all congested and insanitary areas of 20 households or more as 'slums'.

5   In 2014, the NSS included older people in an all-age, 27-page health survey report to the extent of including a table on morbidity over the prior 15 days and a table on the number of people hospitalised in the previous year.

6   As older women are more likely to be defined as 'helping out' or 'passing time', the number of older workers may well be higher than 40%.

7   Funding was received from the University of London and from five UK research councils (Economic and Social Research Council [ESRC], Arts and Humanities Research Council, Medical Research Council, Biotechnology and Biological Sciences Research Council, Engineering and Physical Sciences Research Council) through the New Dynamics of Ageing programme. The 2007-10 project was conducted in collaboration with the Centre for Law, Policy and Human Rights Studies, Chennai, with a team comprising Suresh Veeraraghavan, Marlia Hussain, Joe Henry, Arul George and Barbara Harriss-White (grant number RES-352-25-0027). The ESRC provided follow-on-funding for impact and updating work, 2012-13, conducted with Suresh Veeraraghavan, Marlia Hussain, Swathi Priya and Jacqueline Longina (ES/J020788/1).

8   We're Still Working is available for streaming in English at http://vimeo.com/78510012, and in Hindi at http://vimeo.com/81929055.

9   The competition and public awareness of older workers was foregrounded by five weeks of articles in *The Hindu* and a social media campaign that produced 34,000 votes from the public for pictures they liked.

10   Two sons were found to compensate for the uncertainties of a son's capacity to support a parent in the precarious livelihood contexts found in Bangladesh. Having more than two sons did not have an impact – supporting research that older people are deemed by sons to have limited needs (Vera-Sanso, 2004).

11   In 2004/05, the Planning Commission declared that Rs538 per month was the sum needed to meet the urban calorific norm of 2,100 calories per day.

12   The quantum of waged work, such as domestic work, was set by the employer; by contrast, self-employed people, such as street vendors, were initially more able to extend their work hours. However, as time passed, markets contracted and extended work hours did not insulate the self-employed.

13   Pension amounts and reliability of delivery are widely variable in India (Chopra and Pudussery, 2014; Vera-Sanso, 2015).

14   The photo essay 'We work, we contribute, we don't retire!' is available at www.koodam.org/photo_essay.

References

Alam, M. and Barrientos, A. (eds) (2010) *Demographics, employment and old age security: Emerging trends and challenges in South Asia*, Delhi: Macmillan.

Alam, M. and Mitra, A. (2012) 'Labour market vulnerabilities and health outcomes: older workers in India', *Population Ageing*, vol 5, no 4, pp 241-56.

Arber, S. and Ginn, J. (1990) 'The meaning of informal care: gender and the contribution of elderly people', *Ageing & Society*, vol 10, no 4, pp 429-54.

Bachman de Silva, M., Beard, J., Cakwe, M., Nkosi, N., Parikh, A., Quinlan, T., Skalick, A., Tshabangu-Soko, S., Zhuwau, T. and Simon, J. (2008) 'Vulnerability of orphan caregivers vs. non-orphan caregivers in KwaZulu-Natal', *Vulnerable Children and Youth Studies: An International Interdisciplinary Journal for Research, Policy and Care*, vol 3, no 2, pp 102-11.

Bastia, T. (2009) 'Women's migration and the crisis of care: grandmothers caring for grandchildren in urban Bolivia', *Gender and Development*, vol 17, no 3, pp 389-401.

Burnette, D. (1997) 'Grandparents raising grandchildren in the inner city', *Families in Society: The Journal of Contemporary Social Services*, vol 78, no 5, pp 489-501.

Carr, D. (2005) 'Changing the culture of ageing: a social capital framework for gerontology', *International Journal of Ageing*, vol 7, no 2, pp 81-93.

Census of India (undated a) 'Provisional population total Tamil Nadu'. Available at www.census.tn.nic.in/state_ppt_rural_urban.php.

Census of India (undated b) 'C-14 Five year age group data by residence and sex'. Available at www.censusindia.gov.in/2011census/C-series/C-14.html.

Census of India (undated c) 'SRS Based Life Table 2010-14', Available at http://www.censusindia.gov.in/Vital_Statistics/SRS_Life_Table/Srs_life_Table.html.

Census of India (undated d) 'Chennai District: Census 2011 data'. Available at www.census2011.co.in/census/district/21-chennai.html

Chandramouli, C. (undated) Housing stock, amenities and assets in slums - census 2011', Registrar General & Census Commissioner, India. Available at www.censusindia.gov.in/2011-Documents/On_Slums-2011Final.ppt.

Chant, S. (2013) 'Cities through a "gender lens": a golden "urban age" for women in the global South?', *Environment and Urbanisation*, vol 25, no 1, pp 9-29.

Chiu, W.C.K., Chan, A.W., Snape, E. and Redman, T. (2001) 'Age stereotypes and discriminatory attitudes towards older workers: an East-West comparison', *Human Relations*, vol 54, no 5, pp 629-61.

Chopra, S. and Pudussery, J. (2014) Social Security Pensions in India: An assessment, *Economic and Political Weekly*, XLIX, 19, pp 68-74.

Durr-e-Nayab (2010) 'Demographic transition in Pakistan: implications for old age employment and economic security', in M. Alam and A. Barrientos (eds) *Demographics, employment and old age security: Emerging trends and challenges in South Asia*, Delhi: Macmillan, pp 37-55.

Gillespie, S. and McNeill, G. (1992) *Food, health and survival in India and developing countries*, Delhi: Oxford University Press.

Ghosh, N., Goldar, B.N. and Mitra, A. (2010) 'Population ageing and its implications on the labour market: the South Asian experience', in M. Alam and A. Barrientos (eds) *Demographics, employment and old age security: Emerging trends and challenges in South Asia*, Delhi: Macmillan, pp 198–233.

Government of India (2011a) *India human development report 2011: Towards social inclusion*, Delhi: Oxford University Press.

Government of India (2011b) *Situation analysis of the elderly in India*, New Delhi: Ministry of Statistics and Programme Implementation.

Harriss-White, B., Olsen, W., Vera-Sanso, P. and Suresh, V. (2013) 'The impact of shocks on workers in urban slums in south India', *Economy and Society*, vol 43, no 3, pp 398-429.

Holzmann, R. and Hinz, R. (2005) *Old-age income support in the 21st century: An international perspective on pension systems and reform*, Washington, DC: World Bank.

Hoskyns, C. and Rai, S. (2007) 'Recasting the global political economy: counting women's unpaid work', *New Political Economy*, vol 12, no 3, pp 297-317.

Ironmonger, D. (1996) 'Counting outputs, capital inputs and caring labour: estimating gross household product', *Feminist Economics*, vol 2, no 3, pp 37-64.

Johnson, K. and Mutchler, J. (2014) 'The emergence of a positive gerontology: from disengagement to social involvement', *Gerontologist*, vol 54, no 1, pp 93-100.

Judd, E. (2009) 'Starting again in rural west China: stories of rural women across generations', *Gender and Development*, vol 17, no 3, pp 441-51.

Kak, S. and Pati, B. (eds) (2012) *Enslaved innocence: Child labour in South Asia*, Delhi: Primus Books.

Kaur, R., Ghosh, P.K. and Sudarshan, R.M. (2007) 'Trade liberalization and informality in the rice processing industry', in B. Harriss-White and A. Sinha (eds) *Trade liberalization and India's informal economy*, New Delhi: Oxford University Press, pp 123–32.

Luo G (undated) *China's family support system: Challenges and solutions under the circumstances of rural-urban female labour migration*, Geneva: UNRISD.

Martinson, M. and Minkler, M. (2006) 'Civic engagement and older adults: a critical perspective', *The Geronotologist*, vol 46, no 3, pp 318-24.

Naidu, S.C. (2016) 'Domestic labour and female labour force participation: adding a piece to the puzzle', *Economic and Political Weekly*, 5 November, pp 101-8.

National Health Mission Tamil Nadu (undated) 'State at a glance'. Available at www.nrhmtn.gov.in/statglance.html.

NCEUS (National Commission for Enterprises in the Unorganised Sector) (2009) *The challenge of employment in India: An informal economy perspective*, Delhi: NCEUS.

Nutrition in India (2009) *National Family Health Survey, 2005-6*, Mumbai: IIPS

Nyanzi, S. (2009) 'Widowed mama-grannies buffering HIV/AIDS-affected households in a city slum of Kampala, Uganda', *Gender and Development*, vol 17, no 3, pp 467-79.

ONS (Office for National Statistics) (2012) '2011 Census – population and household rstimates for England and Wales, March 2011', Statistical Bulletin. Available at www.ons.gov.uk/ons/dcp171778_270487.pdf.

Ortiz, I. and Cummins, M. (2011) *Global inequality: Beyond the bottom billion. A rapid review of income distribution in 141 countries*, UNICEF Social and Economic Policy Working Paper, New York, NY: UNICEF.

Picchio, A. (1992) *Social reproduction: The political economy of the labour market*, Cambridge: Cambridge University Press.

Public Health Resource Network (2014) *A snapshot of the health and nutrition of the ageing/elderly poor: Survey of 102 participants of pension*, New Delhi: Parishad Dharna. Available at http://bit.ly/1hFmqlO.

Rahman, O. (1991) 'Family matters: the impct of kin on the mortality of the elderly in rural Bangladesh', *Population Studies*, vol 53, no 2, pp 227-35.

Rajan, S.I., Mishra, U.S. and Sarma, P.S. (1999) *India's elderly: Burden or challenge?*, New Delhi: Sage Publications.

Schroder-Butterfill, E. (2004) 'Inter-generational family support provided by older people in Indonesia', *Ageing & Society*, vol 24, no 4, pp 497-530.

Selvaraj, S., Karan, A. and Madheswaran, S. (2011) *Elderly workforce participation, wage differentials and contribution to household income*, Building Knowledge Base on Population Ageing in India, Working Paper 4, New Delhi: UNFPA.

Singh, N. and Sapra, M.K. (2007) 'Liberalization in trade and finance: India's garment sector', in B. Harriss-White and A. Sinha (eds) *Trade liberalization and India's informal economy*, New Delhi: Oxford University Press, pp 42–123.

Smith, K. (2002) Whose minding the kids? Child care arrangements: Spring 1997, Current Population Reports, P70-86. U.S. Census Bureau, Washington, DC,

Taylor, P. and Walker, A. (1994) 'The ageing workforce: employers' attitudes towards older people', *Work, Employment and Society*, vol 8, no 4, pp 569-91.

UN DESA (United Nations Department of Economic and Social Affairs, Population Division) (2005) *The inequality predicament: Report on the world social situation 2005*, New York, NY: United Nations.

UN DESA (2013) *Inequality matters: Report on the world social situation 2013*, New York, NY: United Nations

UN DESA (2014) *World urbanization prospects, 2014 revision: Highlights*, New York, NY: United Nations

UN DESA (2015) *World population ageing*, New York, NY: United Nations.

UNFPA (United Nations Population Fund) (2002) *Situation and voices: The older poor and excluded in South Africa and India*, Population and Development Strategies Series No. 2, New York, NY: UNFPA.

Vera-Sanso, P. (2004) '"They don't need it, and I can't give it": filial support in south India', in P. Kreager and E. Schröder-Butterfill (eds) *Ageing without children: European and Asian perspectives*, Oxford: Berghahn, pp 77-105.

Vera-Sanso, P. (2007) 'Increasing consumption, decreasing support: a multi-generational study of family relations among south Indian Chakkliyars', *Contributions to Indian Sociology*, vol 41, no 2, pp 225-48.

Vera-Sanso, P. (2010) 'Gender, urban poverty and ageing in India: conceptual and policy issues', in S. Chant (ed) *Elgar international handbook on gender and poverty*, Cheltenham: Edward Elgar, pp 220-6.

Vera-Sanso, P. (2012) 'Gender, poverty and old age in urban south India in an era of globalisation', *Oxford Development Studies*, vol 40, no 3, pp 324-40.

Vera-Sanso, P. (2013) 'Ageing, work and the demographic dividend in South Asia', in J. Field, R. Burke and C. Cooper (eds) *Sage handbook on aging, work and society*, London: Sage Publications, pp 170-85.

Vera-Sanso, P. (2014) 'Reconceiving the impact of population change: a class and gender based analysis of ageing in poverty in urban south India', in N. Gooptu and J. Parry (eds) *The persistence of poverty in India*, New Delhi: Social Science Press, pp 99-126.

Vera-Sanso, P. (2015) 'What is preventing India from developing an inclusive national framework for older people?', *Population Horizons*, vol 12, no 2, pp 77-87.

Walker, A. (2006) 'Active ageing in employment: its meaning and potential', *Asia-Pacific Review*, vol 13, no 1, pp 78-93.

Wheeler, J., Gorey, K. and Greenblatt, B. (1998) 'The beneficial effects of volunteering for older volunteers and the people they serve: a meta-analysis', *International Journal of Aging and Human Development*, vol 47, no 1, pp 69-79.

World Bank (1994) *Averting the old-age crisis: Policies to protect the old and promote growth*, Washington, DC: World Bank.

World Bank (2008) *Sri Lanka: Addressing the needs of an aging population*, Washington, DC: World Bank.

SEVENTEEN

Conclusion

Alan Walker

The 15 substantive chapters in this volume represent roughly half of the projects in the New Dynamics of Ageing (NDA) programme, while its twin volume contains the other half (Walker, 2018: forthcoming). Both were preceded by a pathbreaking collection that engaged all of the programme's projects in multi-disciplinary analyses of six themes that are central to any informed discussion of the future of ageing (Walker, 2014). That seminal collection was tagged as the 'new science of ageing' because the NDA programme represented a major investment in the new era of multidisciplinary research on ageing. The 57 co-authors of that book provide an excellent example of that multidisciplinarity at work. They applied it to the understanding of ageing; the roles of arts and design in transforming the experience of ageing; healthy ageing; food and nutrition; and participation and social connectivity. In doing so, they recognised that ageing and old age cannot be comprehensively understood from any one disciplinary perspective. This does not mean that only multidisciplinary research matters – far from it, as each discipline has unique contributions to make – but these must be combined in order to gain maximum insights into the meaning of ageing and the challenges if presents.

This volume and its twin are different from the first book. Here we have separated the various NDA projects into individual chapters so that the specific contributions of each of them can be highlighted. A majority of the projects were themselves multidisciplinary, so that approach runs consistently through each volume. As pointed out in Chapter One, the parcelling of the chapters into sub-themes was purely a function of the complexion of the final programme. Although the NDA was set up with key research topics highlighted, because of the peer review process there was no guarantee that all of them would be part of the final programme. As it happens, there is rough correspondence between the original programme specification and the final group of projects that were funded. Broad groups of projects are represented thematically, in this volume covering active and healthy ageing, designing for an older population and global ageing, while the twin volume covers autonomy and independence, biological perspectives, nutrition and representations of old age. Rather than repeat the syntheses in the first book in this series, this chapter extracts the key findings from each chapter. In each case, for space reasons, these are limited to only the most impportant ones. Fuller details are in the chapters and on the NDA website (www.newdynamics.group. shef.ac.uk).

Key findings

Chapter Two: Modelling ageing populations to 2030

- Demand for informal care by older people with disabilities and their adult children is projected to rise faster than supply over the next 20 years. Demand for informal care from adult children is projected to rise by over 50% by 2032.
- Demographic changes will affect family relationships and availability of kin, and lead to patterns of more complex relationships involving step-children, half siblings and former partners.
- The numbers of disabled older people will increase sharply. Although most of the extra year-of-life expectancy will be years free from disability, years with disability will also increase.
- Reducing the proportion of life with disability at the oldest ages seems attainable, but only through a 10% reduction in the prevalence of major diseases, which would require substantial advances in preventive and treatment strategies underpinned by basic and applied research.

Chapter Three: Working Late

- An age-diverse workforce maintains knowledge, skills and experience within organisations. Promoting an age-positive culture is key and examples of best practice can help organisations manage age diversity.
- Flexible working practices such as flexitime, part-time working and working from home can prove beneficial in helping employees continue working into later life.
- Older workers have concerns about being fit for work and their ability to do their job in the future. Workers can provide useful input to design when thinking about reducing physical stress on the body. The research outlined in the chapter captured more than 200 design ideas from workers relating to healthy working and reducing

physical and mental stress on the body. Over half were deemed as low-/no-cost ideas.

Chapter Four: Healthy ageing across the life course

- Objective measures of physical capability are useful markers of healthy ageing; older community-dwelling adults who have stronger grip strength, faster walking speed, or better performance on chair rising and standing balance tests live longer, have fewer health problems and have higher levels of positive mental wellbeing than people who perform less well in these tests.
- There is robust evidence that those in better socioeconomic circumstances in childhood as well as adulthood have better capability at older ages. Not only an individual's own socioeconomic circumstances but also those of the area in which they live matter; living in a wealthier neighbourhood in childhood or adulthood is linked with better capability later in life.
- Childhood cognitive ability and other aspects of early experience are associated with adult cognitive capability and wellbeing.
- Despite high estimates of heritability, the evidence of genetic effects on physical and cognitive capability is limited. Associations between change in telomere length and physical capability are also weak and inconsistent.

Chapter Five: Measuring the quality of later life

- Ethnic minority elders have poorer health status than their White British counterparts, despite being younger on average: 18% rate their health as 'poor' compared with 4-5% of the average. They are also more likely to live in large households: only 5% reported that they live alone, compared with 48-49% of the general population of older people. They have twice as many relatives to help them, but fewer friends.
- Ethnic minority elders are less likely than the general older population to consider themselves as ageing 'very' or 'fairly' actively.

Chapter Six: Engagement in musical activities

- Measures of wellbeing were consistently higher among the music participants in the study described (n = 398) than among the comparison group (n=102).

- There was some positive change over time on quality of life measures for those involved in musical activities.
- Participants reported social, cognitive, emotional and health benefits of participation in music.

Chapter Seven: Combating social exclusion through community arts

- Older people, especially those who live in disadvantaged areas, can experience multiple forms of exclusion, including social isolation. Such social exclusion can contribute to detriments in health and quality of life. There is a need to explore ways of promoting greater opportunities for social engagement by older people.
- A range of different community activities – including arts, gardening and physical exercise – were developed for the study. Interviews and questionnaires were used to assess the views of older residents and relevant community stakeholders. In addition, the researchers documented the processes involved in developing the activities. Participants reported evidence of social isolation and were enthusiastic about the activities. While they emphasised the benefits of participation, they also articulated some concerns about continuing financial and human support for the activities.

Chapter Eight: Connectivity of older people in rural civic society

- The most important aspect of attachment to community for older rural residents is feeling that one's community is safe and secure. The characteristics of their communities that survey respondents rated as 'very important' to their sense of belonging mainly related to the place (for example, 'being surrounded by beautiful physical landscape') rather than to the people (for example, 'having people in my community recognise me and talk to me').
- Later life was described by respondents as a period of continuing or renewed interests in leisure pursuits that involved adaptations to individuals' circumstances and abilities in older age – including living in a rural place. Survey results showed an overall decline with age in leisure participation, particularly in more physically demanding activities, and activity patterns became increasingly centred on the home. Despite this reduction in levels of leisure participation, many individuals, including those in advanced old age, reported taking up new hobbies and leisure pastimes.
- The majority of older people surveyed did not regard transport as a barrier to participation in local community activities. However,

important minorities found transport to be a severe limitation (5%) or in fact to prevent involvement (7%). Nearly half of those respondents aged 80 and over reported some degree of difficulty participating in activities because of a lack of transport and 15% said they were prevented from being involved for this reason.

- Some people are enmeshed within the rural landscape, through lives spent working and living in it, and hence are not accustomed to seeing or discussing it as a separate 'thing out there'. Remembering and sharing deep knowledge of the landscape, gained, for example, through having worked in it, can generate emotions in the present and enrich a person's sense of place.
- Many of the households in the survey experienced significant financial difficulties and material hardships: seven out of 10 older people did not receive any interest from their savings, half were unable to make regular savings of £10 per week and more than one third were unable to afford an annual holiday away from home.
- There was a 'normalisation' of poverty with persons in state pension only households reluctant to mention problems with their standards of living. Older old and more established residents were the least inclined to mention financial difficulties. For example, 16% of the older poor who had lived in the local area for more than 30 years reported financial difficulties compared with 30% of those who had moved to their place of residence in the previous five years.

Chapter Nine: Fit for purpose

- Older people greatly value the benefits and independence that computer use gives them. Benefits include independence, personal health, self-efficacy, skills and capabilities, social interaction, economic and life chances and civic engagement and participation.
- Physical, psychological, cognitive and social changes can become barriers that affect the ability and motivation of older people to sustain use of computers, and in some cases lead to them giving up.
- Many older people feel they lack sufficient digital competencies/ skills and confidence to deal with technology challenges. They are motivated to learn and improve their skills when these are enabling the pursuit of their passions and interests.
- Support from other people is a key factor in helping older people to sustain their use of computers and to overcome problems and obstacles that they are likely to face.

- The emphasis of existing learning and training provision is primarily on getting people online rather than helping them to develop the skills and confidence necessary to sustain their digital participation.

Chapter Ten: Design for ageing well

- A functional garment layering system, as the basis for wearable technology, encourages participation in healthy exercise. Such a system comprises next-to-body garments for monitoring vital signs (pulse and breathing rates, body temperature, blood pressure and so on), mid-insulation layers incorporating heated panels, and protective outer layers accommodating communication devices with textile-based controls to provide user-friendly interfaces.
- Users accepted the benefits of technologies in relation to modern fibre properties, 'smart' material attributes (that is, those designed to include changeable properties dependent on the environment), textile-based electronics and novel garment construction techniques.
- A gap in the market exists for functional clothing and wearable technologies that older users will willingly wear to enhance comfort in terms of size and shape, movement, dexterity, thermal regulation and protection from the environment.
- A more responsible, and relatively 'slower' product development process (in comparison with transient fashion) fosters the opportunity to provide enhanced comfort in garments that are fit for purpose, with the potential for greater longevity of use.

Chapter Eleven: Tackling ageing continence

- Older people identified three themes as the most important in providing a quality continence service:
  - accessibility of continence services;
  - establishing a positive relationship with the continence service professional;
  - reducing the impact of urinary incontinence on everyday life.
- Professionals identified three key features of continence services:
  - providing patient education about continence;
  - creating a friendly and welcoming environment for patients;
  - involving patients and carers in decisions about the choice of treatments.
- With regard to public toilets, users identified three priorities:
  - cleanliness – it was important that toilets are seen to be clean, to communicate wider hygiene confidence;

- functionality – equipment in the facilities had to be seen to work;
- technology – users appreciated technological innovations to improve toilet provision.
• Toilet providers identified two main priorities:
  - How to maintain toilet facilities to the high standard expected by members of the public.
  - How to deter non-toileting behaviour such as graffiti and vandalism, illegal drug use and public sex activities.

A major output from this project, The Great British Toilet Map, was developed to help to fulfil the needs of both users and providers.

Chapter Twelve: Dynamic biomechanical visualisations

• Visualising dynamic biomechanical data enables those without specialist training – both professional and lay older people – to access and interpret the data.
• Such visualisations empower older people to participate in discussions about the problems and issues affecting their mobility with clinicians, healthcare practitioners, and design professionals, and about how these issues affect their lifestyle and quality of life.
• Healthcare and design professionals can benefit from enhanced communication across disciplines, allowing a more joined-up approach to healthcare and design planning.
• The visualisations allow a deeper understanding of the issues within professions, both in healthcare and in design.
• There is potential to improve the uptake and integration of biomechanical expertise and understanding into design and healthcare practice.

Chapter Thirteen: Transitions in kitchen living

• Oral histories of the kitchen from the 1920s, ' 30s and ' 40s show that space, storage, equipment, tasks, meanings, social etiquette and adaptation were central concerns that continue to affect everyday living.
• The contemporary kitchen is a place of both instrumental and social activity for older women and men. Certain activities, skills and routines imbue meaning and support identity.
• Survey participants discussed problems with reaching, bending, hearing, seeing and dexterity in the kitchen; poor lighting was

common. All these factors are important considerations for improved ergonomic design.

- Person-environment fit is often maintained through ongoing adaptation in the kitchen, yet people sometimes lack information or the capacity to make small changes or to cope with new equipment, installation or building work.
- Problems can often be addressed with small, low-cost adaptations, but greater benefits may be obtained from a redesigned, inclusive kitchen. Ageism in design needs to be challenged.

Chapter Fourteen: Biomechanical constraints to stair negotiation

- Older adults descend stairs by relying more on their knee and ankle joint muscles than younger adults.
- Stair descent strategies reliant on placing both feet on the same step result in a slower gait, with reduced lower-limb joint ranges of motion. The 'pause' that is created by this tandem double support means that the muscles surrounding the ankle and knee do not need to control the lowering of the entire body mass on to the next step; instead the leg is lowered to the next step.
- Placing two feet on each step during descent can be achieved by walking facing forwards or sideways. Both strategies can reduce the demands on the lower limb; however, the control over the centre of mass differs. Walking sideways results in an increased movement of the centre of mass into/towards the staircase during single-limb stance, which is followed by a rapid acceleration down the staircase in the transition between stance and swing. Alternatively, walking forwards results in less centre of mass movement and a more constant, but lower acceleration down the staircase.
- Older adults almost always make negotiation strategy changes when descending a short-going staircase, while younger adults are less likely to do so. When descending a staircase with a shorter going, older adults stand on a single leg for longer than younger adults. Their centre of mass also moves slower than in younger adults.
- Resistance and stretching exercise training in older adults improves knee and ankle muscle strength, as well as ankle flexibility, but has little influence on lower-limb joint motions during stair descent. Exercise training resulted in greater joint moment production at the ankle and hip, and less at the knee. By increasing step-rise, the opposite occurred, as greater knee-joint moment was produced. It seems that training improvements in lower-limb maximum strength

have allowed older adults to meet the demands of stair descent by redistributing moments across joints.

Chapter Fifteen: Ageing, wellbeing and development

- Capturing wellbeing among older people in developing countries requires a multidimensional perspective and a focus on households. In Brazil and South Africa, and especially in low-income households, older people's wellbeing and livelihoods are interlinked with those of their extended families, whether or not they co-reside. This makes it harder to assess older people's wellbeing separately from that of their families. In the context of Brazil and South Africa, older people have access to relatively large income transfers, thus making a large financial contribution to their households and communities. Individual ageing is not necessarily associated with an inevitable decline in wellbeing in developing countries. In both Brazil and South Africa, analysis of the panel sample (that is, individuals and households observed both in 2002 and 2008) indicates that on average ageing by six years does not correlate with a decline in wellbeing. On the contrary, wellbeing indicators suggest well-being improves with ageing. However, further research will attempt to identify the extent to which improvements in wellbeing among older people and their households are explained by demographic and policy changes. Changes in the size and composition of households could lead to improvement/decline in wellbeing with household income remaining constant. Changes in the value of transfers could be responsible for changes in well-being in the absence of changes in household composition.

- Overall, a majority of older people surveyed in Brazil and South Africa were satisfied with their lives. Whether they were asked about their current lives, or their lives taken as a whole, a majority of older people feel satisfied or very satisfied with their lives. A higher share of Brazilian older people were satisfied with their lives compared with their South African counterparts. A majority of older people in each of the two countries reported being satisfied with their intra-family relationships and with the respect they receive from others.

- For low-income households, pension income, especially non-contributory pension income, is essential to wellbeing, livelihoods, and social inclusion. In the absence of pension income, households with older people are likely to be significantly poorer, less resilient, and less integrated economically. In both countries, non-contributory pensions act more as an income transfer to poorer households than individual retirement income.

Chapter 16: Ageing, poverty and neoliberalism

- Chennai's population structure is ageing rapidly, with the result that old-age poverty is now a significant and rising, though largely overlooked, problem. In the five slum areas studied, 12% of people were aged 60 and over and 5% were aged over 70 years, demonstrating comparatively long life expectancies for those surviving into old age.
- Older people's economic activity is often under-recognised, even by older people themselves. Twenty-eight percent of people surveyed over age 60 considered themselves to be working, as did 20% of people aged 70-79.
- Research as well as observations of a street market from 2007-10 uncovered a significant number of older people playing extensive, unpaid, 'helper' roles in a son's or daughter's petty business. A further tranche of older people, largely older women, undertook unpaid childcare, housework, fetching water and other supporting roles for family members in order to release younger family women into the workforce. The importance of older people's unpaid labour is evident from the collapse of businesses and the withdrawal of younger women from the workforce when older people's unpaid labour is no longer available due to accident, illness or death.
- Social welfare policies and the national old-age policy demonstrate insufficient understanding of either the dynamics of intergenerational relations in the context of severe policy or the specificities of old-age poverty as well as the lower priority placed on old-age welfare. The main plank for old-age welfare – the public resource-capped, poverty-targeted, non-contributory pension – is not available to a large proportion of the qualifying older urban poor.
- Having uncovered the mismatch between conceptualisations of old-age dependence and non-participation in the economy and older people's actual contribution, the research provides evidence for mainstreaming age into all policy, planning and practice. It demonstrates that relegating the older urban poor solely to the remit of social welfare departments fails to recognise their rights, needs and contribution to the economy and places them at the mercy of declining welfare budgets.

Thematic connections

As is evident from the chapters in this volume and the key findings extracted above, the projects contained in the NDA programme were rich and varied. Apart from being part of the NDA programme, what connects the projects and their chapters? There are at least five thematic connections. First, of course, is their umbilical link to the core programme theme of the changing dynamics of ageing. Each of the chapters illustrates different, sometimes overlapping, aspects of this dynamic change – from community-based examples of change in terms of social engagement (Chapter Seven) to global issues such as ageing and development (Chapters Fifteen and Sixteen). Second, there is their widespread concern with wellbeing and the quality of later life. Sometimes this is explicit, as in Chapters Four and Five, and sometimes it is implicit, as in Chapters Ten and Eleven. Third, there is an open policy and practice orientation throughout the chapters, which is evident in the key findings summarised above. With regard to design practice, this book embraces IT, textiles, secnar technology, computer visualisation, ergonomics and biomechanical architecture. Fourth, the rich variety of methods employed by the NDA researchers provides a unique array of insights into the effective application of the methods to very different ageing issues. These insights will be of particular use to early career researchers. Finally, this book provides proof of the case made in the first publication in this series (Walker, 2014), that the scientific communities in the ageing field are committed to multidisciplinary research. I hope the UK research councils will continue to support that commitment.

References

Walker, A. (2014) (ed) *The new science of ageing*, Bristol: Policy Press.

Walker, A. (2018: forthcoming) (ed) *The new dynamics of ageing, Volume 2*, Bristol: Policy Press.

Index

Page numbers in *italics* refer to figures or tables.

cognitive benefits, Music for Life project
112–14
cognitive capability, HALCyon project
childhood and adult 66, 71
and relationship with physical capability
63
underlying biology and 68, 69
Commission on Funding of Care and
Support (CFCS), Dilnot 20, 22, 24,
27, *27*, 28, *29*, *30*, 31
community arts
to challenge social exclusion 132–3
see also Call-Me study
community-based workers 141–2, 142–3
community health interventions, success
in 132–3
community map 140
connectivity of older people in rural areas
see Grey and Pleasant Land project
continence, tackling ageing *see* Tackling
Ageing Continence through Theory,
Tools and Technology (TACT3)
project
critical human ecology approach to social
connectivity 159–60, *159*

D

data harmonisation 62
Deci, E. 105, 106
dementia, social activity inversely related
to 130
demographic change
developing countries 307, 325, 326
Japan 15
UK 15, 195
worldwide 15, 169
Design for Ageing Well: Improving
the Quality of Life for the Ageing
Population using a Technology
Enabled Garment System project 7,
193–218
age-appropriate functional clothing
design 193, 195, 202, 212
aims 195–6
background 193–5
co-design process 196–7, 203–7, *205*,
211, 214, 216–17
findings 207–11, 215
behaviour, persona development 208
clothing, development of layering
system 208–9
co-design process 207
technology, identification of user
requirements 209–11, *210*
gaps in clothing market for active older
consumers 7, 200, 212, 215
implications of research
co-design process 211–12

design direction 212
practice 211–14
product development 214–15
technology uptake 213–14
layering system 195–6, 201, 206, *206*,
208–9, 211, 215
methods 196–207
co-design process 196–7, 203–7, *205*
developing a shared language 198,
198, 204
recruitment of participants 197
walking as focus for prototype
development 197
Work Package 1: Behaviour 196,
198–9, *198*
Work Package 2: Clothing 196–7,
198, *198*, 200–2
Work Package 3: Technology 197,
198, *198*, 202–3
diet and influence on healthy ageing 66
digital divide 169–70, 170–1
digital engagement and disengagement *see*
Sus-IT project
digital policy, UK government 171–2,
180, 187–8
Dilnot Commission 20, 22, 24, 27, *27*,
28, *29*, *30*, 31
disabled older people projections 18, 34

E

education
level and link to adult cognitive
wellbeing 66
priority in Chennai 330–1, 334
emotional benefits, Music for Life project
116–19
English Housing Survey 257
Envisage: Promoting Physical
Independence by Involving Users
in Rehabilitation through Dynamic
Visualisation of Biomechanical Data
253–4
Envision project evaluating visualisation
of dynamic biomechanical data 8,
235–56
aims and objectives 238
background to research 236–8, *237*
barriers to widespread adoption 236,
237
findings 242–50, 252–3
advantages of visualisation 248–50,
253
data accessibility 242–3, *242*, 252
enhanced cross-disciplinary
communication *240*, 246–8, 253
participant empowerment 244–6, 252
implications *241*, 250–2
healthcare applications 251–2

memories
  changing neighbourhoods 134–5, 140
  community map project 140
  connectivity through rural 155, 158
  of kitchens past 261–5
Mendes de Leon, C.F. 130
Menec, V, 156, 158
mental health and music participation
  116–19
Modelling Ageing Populations to 2030
  (MAP2030) 3, 15–35, 348
  aged over 85 projections 18
  background to analysis 21–2
  childless cohort projections 18
  demographic trends 15–16
  disabled older people projections 18,
  348
  factors influencing social care costs
  17–18
  financing schemes analysis 22–4
  government planned reforms and Dilnot
  Commission recommendations 20, 22,
  24, 27, *27*, 28, *29*, *30*, 31
  health status of older population
  projections 18
  informal care under pressure 19, 20, 348
  key findings 348
  methods and assumptions 24–5
  models used in long-term care
  projections 19–20, 24–5
  mortality rates 18
  projections 31–2
  recommendations 20
  resources to meet increased social care
  costs 15–17
  results 26–30
    distributional effects of funding
    reforms 28–30
    projections of public expenditure on
    long-term care 26–8
  self and state funding of social care 19
mortality rates 18, 62, 65, 103, 130.
  in Bangladesh 332
multidisciplinary research 1–2, 10–11, 347
muscle strength in stair negotiation 277–8
  strength reserves during ascent 285–6,
  285, 286, 295
  strength reserves during descent 286–7,
  287, 295
  tests 279, *280*
  training to improve 278, 301, 302
Music for Life project 5, 103–28
  aims 104
  engagement with music, benefits
  attributed to 103, 109–20
    cognitive benefits 112–14
    creativity and expression 119

    emotional benefits and mental health
    116–19
    intergenerational activities 120, 124–5
    musical identity 119
    performance 120
    physical health benefits 114–16
    social benefits 110–12
  facilitators 120, 121–2, 123
  findings 105–23, 124
  follow-on project 123
  group participation benefits 109
  implications for policy and practice 123
  intergenerational activities 104, 111,
  120, 124–5
  methods 104–5
  overcoming barriers to participation
  122–3
  participants 105–6
  quality of life measures 105, 106, *107,*
  108, 124
  wellbeing, participation and 106–9, 124

N

National Child Development Study
  (NCDS) 61
National Family Health Survey, India
  326–7
National Sample Survey (NSS), India 327
National Survey of Health and
  Development (NSHD) 61, 62, 63, 64,
  65, 66, 67
neighbourhoods, disadvantaged
  Call-Me study participants and
  perceptions of 134–8
    anger and frustration over social
    exclusion 136–8
    narratives of decline 134–5
    rejection of outsider negative
    representations of 135–6, 139–40
  community-based workers in 142–3
  need to find ways of promoting social
  inclusion in 131–2
  paradox of neighbourhood participation
  131
  residents' strong attachment to 130–1
  social exclusion in 129–30, 131–2, 141
  social support networks in 142
neoliberalism, poverty and ageing in India
  study *see* poverty, neoliberalism and
  ageing in India study
New Dynamics of Ageing (NDA)
  programme 1–3, 347–8
  Canadian 2, 12–14
  objectives 2
  projects 2–3, 10–12
  themes 2
Nexus software 283

measures of wellbeing and deprivation thresholds 312–13, *313*

pension income in low-income households 317, 319

poverty status transitions 314–15, *314*, 320

social policies and wellbeing 317

wellbeing linked with that of extended family 312, 318

methodology 308, 310–11

paradox in studies of ageing and wellbeing 308

pensions 308, 310, 317, 319, 320–1

recommendations 317–19

sample panel and attrition 311, *311*

selection of countries 308

social policies and 309, 317, 318

working age

assumptions in India 327, 331, 332, 337

increasing in UK 39

working in India, poverty and

advantages and disadvantages of work for older people 334–5

care work of older people 328

erroneous assumptions of working age 327, 331, 332, 337

impact of attending school on work patterns 331

men's work patterns 331, 332

older people's paid and unpaid work and contribution to global economy 326–7, 327–8, 330, 333–4, 338

releasing of younger women into workforce 333, 334

women's work patterns 331–2, 335

Working Late project 4, 39–58

age discrimination 40, 47, 53, 54

age of workforce, increasing 39

aims and methods 41–7

dynamics of later life working 42–3

journey to work 43

occupational health provision 43–4

Organiser for Working Late (OWL) 45–7

Walking Works Wonders intervention 44–5

barriers to later life working 39–40

distribution of research outputs 42, 54

findings 47–52, 55

dynamics of later life working 47–8, 52–3

journey to work 48–9, 53

occupational health provision 49–50, 53

Organiser for Working Late (OWL) 52, 53–4

Walking Works Wonders intervention 50–2, 55

flexible working 47–8, 49, 52–3, 55

implications of research 52–4

lack of research on older workers 40–1

legislation in response to ageing work population 42

recommendations 54–5

video case studies 48, 52, 53

work–life balance 48

workplace design 40–1, 42, 45–7, 52, 53–4, 55

workplace design 40–1, 55

Organiser for Working Late (OWL) 45–7, 52, 53–4

World Bank 327, 334

World Health Organization 69, 158

Quality of Life (WHOQOL) 82, 85

Quality of Life (WHOQOL)-OLD 86, 92, 94